The Cambridge Companion to Jewish American Literature

For more than two hundred years, Jews have played important roles in the development of American literature. *The Cambridge Companion to Jewish American Literature* addresses a wide array of themes and approaches to this distinct yet multifaceted body of writing, among them literary history, immigration and acculturation, Yiddish and Hebrew literature, popular culture, women writers, literary theory and poetics, multilingualism, the Holocaust, and contemporary fiction. This collection of specially commissioned essays by leading figures discusses Jewish American literature in relation to ethnicity, religion, politics, race, gender, ideology, history, and ethics, and places it in the contexts of both Jewish and American writing. With its chronology and guides to further reading, this volume will prove valuable to scholars and students alike.

D0401646

THE CAMBRIDGE
COMPANION TO
JEWISH AMERICAN
LITERATURE

EDITED BY
HANA WIRTH-NESHER
MICHAEL P. KRAMER

CAMBRIDGE
UNIVERSITY PRESS

PUBLISHED BY THE PRESS SYNDICATE OF THE UNIVERSITY OF CAMBRIDGE
The Pitt Building, Trumpington Street, Cambridge CB2 1RP, United Kingdom

CAMBRIDGE UNIVERSITY PRESS
The Edinburgh Building, Cambridge, CB2 2RU, UK
40 West 20th Street, New York, NY 10011–4211, USA
477 Williamstown Road, Port Melbourne, VIC 3207, Australia
Ruiz de Alarcón 13, 28014 Madrid, Spain
Dock House, The Waterfront, Cape Town 8001, South Africa

http://www.cambridge.org

First published 2003

Printed in the United Kingdom at the University Press, Cambridge

Typeface Sabon 10/13 pt.   *System* LATEX 2$_\varepsilon$ [TB]

A catalogue record for this book is available from the British Library

ISBN 0 521 79293 2 hardback
ISBN 0 521 79699 7 paperback

CONTENTS

CONTRIBUTORS

EMILY MILLER BUDICK teaches American literature at The Hebrew University of Jerusalem and holds the Ann and Joseph Edelman Chair in American Studies. She has published many essays and several books on the American romance tradition, including *Fiction and Historical Consciousness*, *Engendering Romance*, and *Nineteenth-Century American Romance*, as well as *Emily Dickinson and the Life of Language* and *Blacks and Jews in Literary Conversation* (Cambridge University Press). She recently edited *Ideology and Jewish Identity in Israeli and American Literature*. Her current project concerns Holocaust fiction in Israeli and American literature.

TRESA GRAUER is Lecturer in the Department of Foreign Literatures and Linguistics at Ben-Gurion University of the Negev. Her recent publications include " 'The Changing Same': Narratives of Contemporary Jewish American Identity," in *Mapping Jewish Identities*, ed. Larry Silberstein and " 'A Drastically Bifurcated Legacy': Homeland and Jewish Identity in Contemporary Jewish American Literature," in *Divergent Jewish Cultures: Israel and America*, eds. Deborah Dash Moore and S. Ilan Troen.

SUSAN GUBAR is Distinguished Professor of English at Indiana University. She has co-authored and co-edited a number of books with Sandra M. Gilbert including *The Madwoman in the Attic*, its three-volume sequel, *No Man's Land*, and the *Norton Anthology of Literature by Women*. Her most recent publication is *Poetry After Auschwitz: Remembering What One Never Knew*.

SUSANNAH HESCHEL is the Eli Black Associate Professor of Jewish Studies at Dartmouth College, New Hampshire, in the Department of Religion, and serves as Chair of the Jewish Studies Program. She is the author of numerous studies of modern Jewish thought, including *Abraham Geiger and the Jewish Jesus*, which won a National Jewish Book Award, and is co-editor of *Insider/Outsider: Multiculturalism and American Jews*. Since 1999, she has served on the Academic Advisory Committee of the US Holocaust Memorial Museum.

MICHAEL P. KRAMER chairs the English Department and directs the Anne Shachter Smith Memorial Project in Literature at Bar-Ilan University. He has published *Imagining Language in America* and *New Essays on Bellow's Seize the Day*, as well numerous essays on American and Jewish literary and intellectual history. His current projects include a study of Jewish American thought and writing called "The Art of Assimilation" and, with Menahem Blondheim, "The Orthodox Jewish Sermon in America."

ALAN MINTZ is the Chana Kekst Professor of Hebrew Literature at the Jewish Theological Seminary, New York. He has been the co-editor of *Prooftexts: A Journal of Jewish Literary History* since its founding in 1981. He is the author most recently of *Popular Culture and the Shaping of Holocaust Memory in America* and *Translating Israel: Contemporary Hebrew Literature and its Reception in America.*

DAVID G. ROSKIES is Professor of Jewish Literature at the Jewish Theological Seminary, New York. He is the author of *Against the Apocalypse*, *A Bridge of Longing*, *The Jewish Search for a Usable Past*, and other studies in Jewish cultural history. He is co-founder and co-editor of *Prooftexts* and is Editor-in-Chief of the New Yiddish Library.

MAEERA Y. SHREIBER is Assistant Professor of English at the University of Utah. She is the author of numerous articles in scholarly journals (including *PMLA* and *Genre*) and in essay collections; she is the co-editor of both *Dwelling in Possibility: Women Poets and Critics on Poetry* and *Mina Loy: Woman and Poet*. She is currently completing a book on Jewish American poetry and poetics.

ALAN WALD is Director of the Program in American Culture and Professor of English at the University of Michigan. He is the author of five scholarly books on the US literary Left and editor of "The Radical Novel Reconsidered" series at the University of Illinois Press.

PRISCILLA WALD is Associate Professor of English and an Affiliate in the Center for the Study of Medical Ethics and Humanities and in the Women's Studies Program at Duke University, North Carolina. She is author of *Constituting Americans: Cultural Anxiety and Narrative Form* and Associate Editor of *American Literature*. She is currently at work on a book about contagion, genetics, and culture.

DONALD WEBER is Professor of English and American Studies at Mount Holyoke College, Massachusetts. He has published widely on Jewish American literature and popular culture, and has recently completed a study entitled "Haunted in the New World: Mapping Modern Jewish American Culture."

HANA WIRTH-NESHER is Associate Professor of English and American literature at Tel Aviv University and coordinator of the Samuel L. and Perry Haber Chair on the Study of the Jewish Experience in the United States. She is the author of *City Codes: Reading the Modern Urban Novel*, editor of *What is Jewish Literature?* and *New Essays on Call It Sleep* (Cambridge University Press), and has written numerous essays on English, American, and Jewish literature. She is currently completing a book to be entitled *Call It English: The Languages of Jewish American Writing*

RUTH R. WISSE is Martin Peretz Professor of Yiddish Literature and Professor of Comparative Literature at Harvard University. She is the author of *The Modern Jewish Canon, I. L. Peretz and the Making of Modern Jewish Culture, A Little Love in Big Manhattan: Two Yiddish Poets,* and *The Schlemiel as Modern Hero*. She has edited and co-edited several volumes of Yiddish literature in translation. She has also written widely about Jewish politics, including *If I Am Not For Myself: The Liberal Betrayal of the Jews*.

SHIRA WOLOSKY is Professor of English and American Literature at the Hebrew University in Jerusalem. Her publications include *Emily Dickinson: A Voice of War, Language Mysticism, The Art of Poetry,* and *Poetry and Public Discourse*, volume IV of *The Cambridge History of American Literature*, as well as numerous articles on poetics, literary theory, and feminism. She was a Guggenheim fellow in 2000.

CHRONOLOGY

1492 Expulsion of Jews from Spain.
      Columbus' first voyage. Crypto-Jews said to be among his crew.

1654 Twenty-three indigent Sephardi Jews arrive in New Amsterdam from Brazil. *Shearith Israel* congregation founded in 1656.

1658 Newport, Rhode Island becomes home to Jews.

1722 Public conversion of Judah Monis at Harvard College.

1740 Parliament passes law allowing Jews to become citizens in British colonies.

1775 Battle of Lexington and Concord. American Revolution begins.

1776 Declaration of Independence. Francis Salvador, Jewish patriot, killed in battle.

1790 Moses Seixas and Newport Congregation welcome President Washington to Newport.
      Approximately 1,500 Jews in the United States.

1820 Jewish population doubles to 3,000.

1825 Cornerstone ceremony for Ararat, Mordecai M. Noah's planned Jewish colony near Buffalo, New York.

1826 Law passed in Maryland allowing Jews to hold public office.

1836 Jewish population stands at 6,000.
      Immigration of German Jews begins from Bavaria.

1843 Isaac Leeser founds *The Occident* in Philadelphia.
      B'nai Brith, a Jewish lodge, founded.

1854 Isaac Mayer Wise, *History of the Israelitish Nation*. Founds *The Israelite* in Cincinatti.
      Lévi-Strauss sells canvas pants to miners in California.

1860 Jewish population rises to 150,000.
      Wise publishes *First of the Maccabees*.
      Abraham Lincoln elected President. Civil War begins the following year.

1862   Judah Benjamin, former US Senator, becomes Attorney General and, later, Secretary of State of the Confederacy.

1881   A quarter million Jews in the United States.
        Pogroms in Russia. Mass immigration of East European Jews begins.

1882   Emma Lazarus, *Songs of a Semite*.

1883   Fundraising event for pedestal to Statue of Liberty. Emma Lazarus contributes "The New Colossus."

1885   Pittsburgh Platform, renouncing Jewish nationality, adopted by Reform rabbis.

1888   Famed Orthodox preacher Rabbi Jacob Joseph of Vilna becomes Chief Rabbi of New York.
        Jewish Publication Society of America founded in Philadelphia.

1892   American Jewish Historical Society founded.

1896   Abraham Cahan, *Yekl: A Tale of the New York Ghetto*.

1897   Founding of the Yiddish *Daily Forward* in New York.

1898   Morris Rosenfeld, *Songs from the Ghetto*.

1900   Jacob Gordin, *God, Man, and the Devil*.
        Over 1,000,000 Jews in the United States.

1901   *Jewish Encyclopedia* begins publication.

1904   The Jewish Museum founded in New York City.

1909   Gertrude Stein, *Three Lives*.

1912   Mary Antin, *The Promised Land*.
        Henrietta Szold founds Hadassah women's organization to aid Jews in Palestine.

1913   Lynching of Leo Frank.

1914   World War I begins.

1915   Horace Kallen, "Democracy *Versus* the Melting Pot."
        Founding of the *Menorah Journal*.

1916   Funeral of Sholem Aleichem in Manhattan.
        Louis Brandeis, first Jewish Supreme Court Justice, appointed.

1917   Abraham Cahan, *The Rise of David Levinsky*.
        Communist Revolution in Russia.

1918   Sholem Asch, *Uncle Moses*.
        Mani Leyb, *Lider* (Poems).
        Rose Cohen, *Out of the Shadow: A Russian Jewish Girlhood on the Lower East Side*.

1919   Moyshe-Leyb Halpern, *In nyu york* (In New York).

1920   Anzia Yezierska, *Hungry Hearts*.
        Nearly 3.5 million Jews in the United States.

1921   Joseph Opatoshu, *In Polish Woods*.
       Judah Leib Lazerow, *Mateh Yehuda* (The Staff of Judah).
1922   Ludwig Lewisohn, *Up Stream: An American Chronicle*.
       Hebrew newspaper *HaDoar* begins publication.
1923   Marcus Loew and Louis B. Mayer establish the Metro-Goldwyn-
       Mayer Corporation (MGM).
1924   Johnson Act restricts immigration.
1925   Anzia Yezierska, *Bread Givers*.
1926   Edna Ferber, *Show Boat*.
1927   Al Jolson stars in *The Jazz Singer*.
1929   Anna Margolin, *Lider* (Poems).
       The Goldbergs begins on radio.
       Stock market crashes. Great Depression begins.
1930   Michael Gold, *Jews Without Money*.
1931   The Marx Brothers star in S. J. Perelman, *Monkey Business*.
       Lamed Shapiro, *New Yorkish*.
       Charles Reznikoff, *By the Waters of Manhattan*.
1932   Fannie Hurst, *Imitation of Life*.
       H. Leivick, *Lider* (Poems).
1933   Israel Efros, *Vigvamim Shotkim* (Silent Wigwams).
       Charles Reznikoff, *Testimony*.
       Albert Einstein flees Nazi Germany, arrives in the United States.
1934   Henry Roth, *Call It Sleep*.
       Mordecai Kaplan, *Judaism as a Civilization*.
       Tess Slesinger, *The Unpossessed*.
       Daniel Fuchs, *Summer in Williamsburg*.
       Founding of *Partisan Review*.
       Baseball star Hank Greenberg decides not to play for Detroit Tigers
       on Yom Kippur.
1935   Clifford Odets, *Waiting for Lefty*.
1937   Meyer Levin, *The Old Bunch*.
       Delmore Schwartz, *In Dreams Begin Responsibilities*.
       Ephraim Lisitzky, *Medurot do'akhot* (Dying Campfires).
       Kadya Molodowsky, *In the Country of My Bones*.
       Jacob Glatstein, *Yidishtaytshn*.
1938   Muriel Rukeyser, *Book of the Dead*.
       Irving Berlin, "God Bless America." The song is sung at both the
       Democratic and Republican conventions the following year.
1939   Nathanael West, *The Day of the Locust*.
       World War II begins. First reports of Holocaust reach the United
       States.

Jewish population nears 4,000,000.

1943 Jacob Glatstein, *Gedenklider* (Memory Poems).

1945 Isaac Bashevis Singer, *The Family Moskat*.
Founding of *Commentary* magazine.

1946 Isaac Rosenfeld, *Passage from Home*.
Jo Sinclair, *Wasteland*.
Sholem Asch, *East River*.

1947 Laura Hobson, *Gentleman's Agreement*.
Arthur Miller, *All My Sons*.
5,000,000 Jews in the United States.

1948 Irwin Shaw, *The Young Lions*.
Norman Mailer, *The Naked and the Dead*.
Israel declares independence. War with neighboring Arab states.

1949 Arthur Miller, *Death of a Salesman*.
Ephraim Lisitsky, *Eleh toledot adam (In the Grip of Cross-Currents)*.

1950 Lionel Trilling, *The Liberal Imagination*.
Your Show of Shows premieres on NBC.

1951 Alfred Kazin, *A Walker in the City*.
Julius and Ethel Rosenberg convicted of espionage for the Soviet Union. Sentenced to death by Judge Irving Kaufman. Executed in 1953.

1952 Leslie Fiedler, *An End to Innocence*.

1953 Isaac Bashevis Singer, "Gimpel the Fool."
Saul Bellow, *The Adventures of Augie March*. First National Book Award to Jewish writer.

1955 Herman Wouk, *Marjorie Morningstar*.

1956 Saul Bellow, *Seize the Day*.
Abraham Joshua Heschel, *God in Search of Man*.
Allen Ginsberg, *Howl and Other Poems*.
The Diary of a Young Girl (Anne Frank) opens on Broadway.

1957 Bernard Malamud, *The Assistant*.

1958 Bernard Malamud, *The Magic Barrel*.
Karl Shapiro, *Poems of a Jew*.
John Hollander, *A Crackling of Thorns*.
Leon Uris, *Exodus*.

1959 Grace Paley, *Little Disturbances of Man*.
Philip Roth, *Goodbye, Columbus*.
First appearance of satirical comic strip "Feiffer" by Jules Feiffer.

1960 Eli Wiesel, *Night*.

1961 Tillie Olsen, *Tell Me a Riddle*.
Allen Ginsberg, *Kaddish and Other Poems*.
Joseph Heller, *Catch-22*.

Edward Wallant, *The Pawnbroker*.

Eichmann trial in Jerusalem.

1963 Betty Friedan, *The Feminine Mystique*. Three years later co-founds the National Organization for Women (NOW).

1964 Saul Bellow, *Herzog*.

Civil Rights workers Michael Schwerner, Andrew Goodman, and James Cheney murdered in Mississippi.

Fiddler on the Roof opens on Broadway.

1965 Lionel Trilling, *Beyond Culture*.

Norman Mailer, *An American Dream*.

Bob Dylan, "Like a Rolling Stone."

Neil Simon, *The Odd Couple*.

Joseph B. Soloveitchik, "The Lonely Man of Faith."

Vatican Council repudiates Jewish collective guilt for execution of Jesus.

Sandy Koufax refuses to pitch in the World Series on Yom Kippur.

1966 Eli Wiesel, *The Jews of Silence*.

Louis Zukofsky, *All the Collected Short Poems*.

Susan Sontag, *Against Interpretation*.

1967 Chaim Potok, *The Chosen*.

The Six-Day War in Israel.

1968 Barbra Streisand stars in *Funny Girl*.

1969 Philip Roth, *Portnoy's Complaint*.

1970 Saul Bellow, *Mr. Sammler's Planet*.

1971 Adrienne Rich, *When We Dead Awaken*.

E. L. Doctorow, *The Book of Daniel*.

Cynthia Ozick, *The Pagan Rabbi*.

1972 Isaac Bashevis Singer, *Enemies, A Love Story*.

Lionel Trilling, *Sincerity and Authenticity*.

Leslie Fiedler, *To the Gentiles*.

First woman ordained as Reform rabbi.

1973 Adrienne Rich, *Diving into the Wreck*.

Maxine Kumin, *Up Country*.

Erica Jong, *Fear of Flying*.

Harold Bloom, *The Anxiety of Influence*.

The Jewish Catalog: A Do It Yourself Kit.

Henry Kissinger is first Jew to be appointed Secretary of State.

Yom Kippur War in Israel.

1974 Grace Paley, *Enormous Changes at the Last Minute*.

1975 E. L. Doctorow, *Ragtime*.

David Mamet, *American Buffalo*.

Sacvan Bercovitch, *The Puritan Origins of the American Self*.

1976 Irving Howe, *World of Our Fathers*.

Marge Piercy, *Woman on the Edge of Time*.

Nobel Prize for Literature awarded to Saul Bellow.

1977 Irving Howe, ed. *Jewish American Stories*.

Woody Allen, *Annie Hall*.

1978 Nobel Prize for Literature awarded to Isaac Bashevis Singer.

1979 Philip Roth, *The Ghost Writer*.

1980 Cynthia Ozick, *The Shawl*.

Geoffrey Hartman, *Criticism in the Wilderness*.

Jewish population close to 6,000,000.

1982 Kate Simon, *Bronx Primitive*.

Adrienne Rich, "Split at the Root, An Essay on Jewish Identity."

1984 Robert Pinsky, *The History of My Heart*.

1985 Lore Segal, *Her First American*.

1986 Art Spiegelman, *MAUS, a Survivor's Tale*.

Benjamin and Barbara Harshav, eds. *American Yiddish Poetry*.

Sanford Budick and Geoffrey Hartman, eds., *Midrash and Literature*.

Founding of *Tikkun* magazine.

1987 Philip Roth, *The Counterlife*.

Jorie Graham, *The End of Beauty*.

Jonathan Pollard convicted of spying for Israel.

1988 Wendy Wasserstein, *The Heidi Chronicles*.

1989 Howard Nemerov first Jew appointed Poet Laureate of the United States.

First *Seinfeld* episode.

1990 Irena Klepfisz, *A Few Words in the Mother Tongue*.

Joyce Antler, ed. *America and I: Short Stories by American Jewish Women Writers*.

1993 Rebecca Goldstein, *Strange Attractors*.

Opening of Holocaust Museum in Washington.

1994 Henry Roth, *Mercy of a Rude Stream*.

Tony Kushner, *Angels in America*.

Steven Spielberg's *Schindler's List* wins Academy Award.

1995 Melvin Bukiet, *While the Messiah Tarries*.

Victor Perera, *The Cross and the Pear Tree, A Sephardic Journey*.

1996 Thane Rosenbaum, *Elijah Visible*.

"Too Jewish?: Challenging Traditional Identities" opens at The Jewish Museum, New York.

President Bill Clinton attends funeral of slain Israeli Prime Minister Yitzhak Rabin.

1997   Cynthia Ozick, *The Puttermesser Papers*.
        Philip Roth, *American Pastoral*.
        Allegra Goodman, *Kaaterskill Falls*.
        Aryeh Lev Stollman, *The Far Euphrates*.
        Diane Matza, ed. *Sephardic–American Voices*.

1999   Jaqueline Osherow, *Dead Man's Praise*.
        Marge Piercy, *The Art of Blessing the Day*.
        Joseph Lieberman is Democratic Vice-Presidential candidate.

2000   Philip Roth, *The Human Stain*.
        Saul Bellow, *Ravelstein*.

2001   Bob Dylan, *Love and Theft*.
        Publication of *Jewish American Literature: A Norton Anthology*.

HANA WIRTH-NESHER AND MICHAEL P. KRAMER

Introduction: Jewish American literatures in the making

"Try not to love such a country!" exclaims Mottel the cantor's son, the orphaned Russian Jewish immigrant child in Sholem Aleichem's only New World novel, when he discovers that in America "it's not allowed to hit somebody smaller than yourself" (*Adventures of Mottel the Cantor's Son*, 260). Mottel's bittersweet Yiddish praise echoes – if unintentionally and somewhat ironically – a declaration made more than a hundred years earlier by the Sephardi banker Moses Seixas, warden of the Hebrew Congregation in Newport, Rhode Island, in an address to George Washington, newly elected President of the United States:

> Deprived as we hitherto have been of the invaluable rights of free citizens, we now ... behold a government erected by the majesty of the people, a government which to bigotry gives no sanction, to persecution no assistance, but generously affording to all liberty of conscience and immunities of citizenship, deeming every one of whatever nation, tongue or language, equal parts of the great governmental machine.
>
> (Schappes, *A Documentary History of the Jews*, 79)

These two passages help chart an important theme in the history of Jewish life in America. For millennia, Jews had lived under the rule of many other peoples, both in the Land of Israel and in exile in Europe, Africa, Asia, and South America. They sometimes enjoyed periods of tolerance, prosperity, and quasi-autonomy; often they suffered oppression, poverty, and violence. Throughout their history, in good times and bad, the Jews were considered to be different – religiously, ethnically, racially, and hence politically – a distinction, by the way, they did not always contest. When they came to America, however, they discovered – whether with unambiguous relief, or cautious optimism, or seasoned skepticism – that *America* was different. For many scholars, this theme gives coherence and distinctness to Jewish American history in general – and to Jewish American literary history in particular. "Without the opportunities, freedom, and openness found in this land," writes the editor of the recent multi-volume history, *The Jewish People in America*, "American Jewry would not have been able to realize its energies and talents and become what it is today" (Feingold, *The Jewish People in America*, I, xi).

Those energies and talents are remarkably evident in the fields of literature and culture. Indeed, it would be hard to conceive of these areas in the twentieth century *without* Jewish artists and writers. Of the seven American Nobel Laureates in literature since the end of the Second World War, two have been Jews – Saul Bellow and Isaac Bashevis Singer – and countless other awards (Pulitzer Prizes, National Book Awards, P.E.N./Faulkner Awards) have been garnered by Jewish American authors over the last century. Landmarks of modern and contemporary American culture are products of Jewish American experience (to name only a few): in drama, Arthur Miller's *Death of a Salesman*, Lillian Hellman's *The Children's Hour*, David Mamet's *American Buffalo*; in film, Woody Allen's *Annie Hall* and Steven Spielberg's *E.T.*; in American musical theater, *Porgy and Bess* (George and Ira Gershwin), *My Fair Lady* (Lerner and Lowe), *West Side Story* (Bernstein, Sondheim, Laurents, and Robbins); in American song, Irving Berlin's "God Bless America" and Bob Dylan's "Blowin' in the Wind"; in poetry, Allen Ginsberg's *Howl* and Adrienne Rich's "Diving into the Wreck"; and in fiction, Gertrude Stein's *Three Lives*, Bellow's *Herzog*, Philip Roth's *Goodbye Columbus*, Nathanael West's *Miss Lonely Hearts*, the stories of Cynthia Ozick and Grace Paley, and Paul Auster's *New York Trilogy*. And any bibliography of the most significant works of American literary and cultural criticism would encompass the writings of Daniel Aaron, Sacvan Bercovitch, Harold Bloom, Leslie Fiedler, Susan Gubar, Geoffrey Hartman, Myra Jehlen, Alfred Kazin, Leo Marx, Walter Benn Michaels, Susan Sontag, Alan Trachtenberg, Lionel Trilling, among many others.

It is certainly tempting to tell the story of Jewish American literary history in this celebratory, appreciative tone – as a movement from trouble to triumph, darkness to light, slavery to redemption, cultural deprivation to cultural flowering. And it is difficult to deny that many Jews, among them many Jewish writers and scholars, have thought of the American experience in just this way. But the story conceals as much as it reveals. To begin with, Jewish creativity did not begin in America, nor has it ever been restricted to periods free from persecution and turmoil. The Jews did not need America in order to flourish creatively. But they did flourish differently there, and that story needs to be told.

Or, better yet, *those stories*. Much more than a century separates Moses Seixas from Sholem Aleichem's Mottel – differences in class, culture, and language; in genre, tone, and audience – substantive differences that should not be obscured by their common American theme and their shared religio-ethnic designation. The history of the Jews in America is not linear. It unfolds as successive, largely discrete waves of immigration – roughly speaking, Spanish–Portuguese (1654–1830), German (1830–1880), East European (1880–1924), and post-Holocaust (1940 to the present) – and different tales of accommodation and resistance. Each wave of immigrants brought along, besides a common but abstract sense of peoplehood, its own cultural baggage – e.g. its own language (Ladino, German, Yiddish), its own religious and cultural traditions (Sephardi, Reform, Hassidic, and Misnagdic), its own particular collective memories (expulsion, emancipation, pogroms) – and each produced a literature reflecting both its distinct heritage and its peculiar experience of acculturation.

Seixas was a well-to-do descendant of Spanish and Portuguese Jews; Mottel, the fictional representation of the poor, East European masses. And while these groups of Jews assumed a common bond, their differences were so deep that they often looked at each other with suspicion – if not with outright hostility. For example, when Abraham Cahan, future editor of the Yiddish *Daily Forward*, arrived at Ward's Island (a forerunner of the more famous Ellis Island) from Lithuania in 1882, he observed there, contemptuously, "one wealthy young [Portuguese] Jewish lady who belonged to the cream of monied aristocracy," whose visits to the immigrants ' never undermined her status as an aristocrat" (Cahan, *The Education of Abraham Cahan*, 354). The following year, that same young woman, a poet named Emma Lazarus, would write a sonnet about the Statue of Liberty in which she referred to Cahan and his immigrant cohorts, sympathetically yet condescendingly, as the "wretched refuse" of Europe's "teeming shores" (Chametzky et al. *Jewish American Literature*, 106). Each wrote what might be called "Jewish American literature." But it is problematic to say that they belonged to a common literary tradition. Although they (more or less) shared knowledge of sacred Hebrew writings, the poetry of Emma Lazarus looks back upon the works of the medieval Spanish Jewish poet and philosopher Judah Ha-levi, the German Romantic Heinrich Heine, and the American philosopher Ralph Waldo Emerson, whereas the writings of Abraham Cahan reflect, for instance, the satires of modern Yiddish literature, the sermons of itinerant East European *maggidim* (preachers), the socialism of Karl Marx, and the realisms of Leo Tolstoy and William Dean Howells.

This makes the task of the literary historian difficult indeed. Ruth Wisse has argued that "modern Jewish literature is the repository of modern Jewish experience" and, as such, "the most complete way of knowing the inner life of the Jews" (Wisse, *The Modern Jewish Canon*, 4). Yet the phrase "modern Jewish experience" is hardly self-evident, and knowing "the inner life of the

Jews" no simple matter, particularly in America. Not only were the experiences of Jews from various places and backgrounds different *before* coming to America, but Jews had widely different experiences *in* America as well. It is one thing to live in a small but closely-knit, well-to-do community of Sephardi Jews in Newport in 1790; another for a German Jewish immigrant in the mid-nineteenth century to become a peddler on the American frontier where few if any Jews lived; another yet to join a poor but established community of East European *landsleit* (compatriots) in the densely populated Lower East Side of New York in the first decade of the twentieth century; and still another to have endured the Holocaust and been transformed from a displaced person into a "survivor" in Queens or Short Hills, New Jersey.

If the American difference gives coherence to Jewish American literary history, it is a very incoherent coherence indeed. In fact, it may make more sense to talk about many Jewish American literatures – which is, in effect, what the contributors to this volume do. In America, Jews from different places, times, and backgrounds were confronted with a range of opportunities and challenges, and their literary responses were manifold. Not all Jews loved "such a country," not unequivocally at least, and not as they found it. While many thought America so hospitable they deemed it a new promised land (as Susannah Heschel explains), others, like the Orthodox preacher Judah Leib Lazerow, judged such thinking short-sighted and self-deceptive, warning his audience, "If someone should whisper to you that . . . here, in the land of liberty, it is as if we were in our own land, the land of Israel . . . do not think thus!" (Lazerow, "The Staff of Judah," 497). A great many remained ambivalent, as Priscilla Wald argues in her chapter on the East European immigrants, wavering between the rousing sentiments of Irving Berlin's "God Bless America!" and the popular ghetto adage, "a curse upon Columbus!" Some were happy to reconfigure Judaism in the American grain, as Michael Kramer explains, while others struggled to maintain their Judaism as their ancestors had practiced it, refusing to change their language, their names, or their dress. Some were disappointed to find that, sadly, America was all too often a place where it was allowed to hit those "smaller than yourself," Jews and others, joining the left-wing circles that Alan Wald documents, or forging alliances with African Americans in the face of American racial politics, as Susan Gubar describes. Others, like some of the postwar intellectuals Ruth Wisse discusses, expressed their commitment to American democracy by veering to the right. Some embraced America passionately, assimilating as quickly and completely as they could. Others, like David Roskies' Yiddishists, rendered the American difference in a language retained from a European past, reshaped on American soil, and accessible only to Jewish readers; or like Alan Mintz's Hebraists, in a rehabilitated ancient language being readied for a Zionist future; or, like Hana Wirth-Nesher's multilingual writers, in polyglot traces and echoes that could serve as collective memory.

Nor were the worlds of the immigrants the same as those of their children, and certainly not of their grandchildren. What one generation feels keenly, another barely notices. What one appreciates (or dreads) another takes for granted. What is for one a lived past becomes for another a nuisance, a tale too-often told; for another, a matter of indifference; and for still another, legend, nostalgia, something to be mined in an effort to create a usable past.

Or, more precisely, usable *pasts*. Consider the case of Sholem Aleichem. On May 13, 1916, 150,000 Jewish Americans lined the streets of Manhattan to pay their respects to the writer whose voice they identified as their own, or rather, as their authentic *original* voice, the one that was already somewhat foreign to their children's ears. Sholem Aleichem's funeral cortege has often been cited as a defining moment in Jewish American cultural life as masses of Jewish immigrants mourned not only for the man who had enriched their lives in the sweatshops in which they worked and in the tenements in which they lived, but more significantly mourned for the world that he represented, the world that they had left behind in Europe.

In 1943, as Jews in Europe were being herded into concentration camps, Maurice Samuel published *The World of Sholem Aleichem* in New York. During those traumatic times, when the sons and daughters of immigrants feared for their European brethren as well as for their own social acceptance in America, Samuel took on the task of translating into American terms a Jewish culture that was being annihilated, to preserve it for non-Yiddish speaking second-generation Americans. Mourning the inevitable loss entailed in translation (he called one translation a linguistic pogrom), he nevertheless saw himself as a transparent medium for conveying a homogeneous Old World that needed to be cherished. He observed that American Jews required an "old country" and that Sholem Aleichem's characters, such as Tevye the Dairyman, served well as a "forefather" because he was simple and "primitive," because he was both Job *and* Charlie Chaplin, and because he represented the spirit of a language and the spirit of a people. Identifying Sholem Aleichem as closely linked with his characters and his world, Maurice Samuel labeled him an authentic folk voice, a usable past for American Jewry (Samuel, *The World of Sholem Aleichem*, 184).

Reviewing Samuel's book that same year, the writer Isaac Rosenfeld heard a different voice in Sholem Aleichem, one that he argued was far more characteristic of Jewish writing, namely that of alienation. Bringing the New York intellectuals' blend of Freud and Marx to the Yiddish author's fictional world, Rosenfeld described a Sholem Aleichem whose characters suffer from alienation "even from the class struggle, the alienation, when all else is restored, of being homeless on the earth" ("The Humor of Sholem Aleichem," 113). Suggesting that Samuel "might have devoted more attention to the individual stature of the man and the techniques of his craft" (111), Rosenfeld reclaimed Sholem Aleichem for Art, refashioned the Yiddish writer in the image of his coterie of second-generation New York Jewish writers and intellectuals who came of age in the 1930s and 1940s. Author of *Passage from Home*, the *Bildungsroman* of these self-consciously modernist writers, Rosenfeld enlisted Sholem Aleichem on the side of alienation: "his was the humor which loves the world from which it seeks to be delivered" ("The Humor of Sholem Aleichem," 112). By the 1960s, the enormously popular American stage and screen version *Fiddler on the Roof* portrayed a warm-hearted liberal Tevye whose devotion to tradition could coexist with tolerance for intermarriage and individualism. And Cynthia Ozick's 1989 excoriation of *Fiddler* echoes Rosenfeld: "That the sophisticated chronicler of a society in transition should be misconstrued as a genial rustic is something worse than a literary embarrassment" (*Metaphor & Memory*, 183). Samuel offered a folk voice in an elegiac spirit with his eye turned toward Europe, Rosenfeld constructed a Sholem Aleichem who could serve as a precursor for a young generation of American Jewish intellectuals for whom alienation was a transhistorical and cosmopolitan badge of honor, the Broadway musical combined nostalgia with American integrationism, and Ozick aimed to restore Sholem Aleichem's particular historical texture and artistic achievement for a generation even further removed from Yiddish culture, "university-educated, perhaps, but tone-deaf to history" (*Metaphor & Memory*, 184). And in yet another twist, Ruth Wisse has read Sholem Aleichem as a proto-Zionist, his work containing "the first genuinely autonomous Jewish territory to appear in modern Jewish literature" (*The Modern Jewish Canon*, 42).

Each generation – each group within each generation – invokes the Sholem Aleichem that it needs. In other words, just as different experiences or constructions of "Jewish" generate different kinds of literature, so they generate different stories *about* Jewish American literature, in which diverse authors play leading roles and the same author may be portrayed in various ways. The same may be said for notions of "American," the other conceptual component of Jewish American literature. The past few decades in particular have been, to borrow Sacvan Bercovitch's coinage, "a time of dissensus" (Bercovitch, *The Rites of Assent*, 353) for American literary and cultural study. Mottel the cantor's son's heady exclamation – "Try not to love such a country!" – is no longer (if it ever were) the unambiguous rallying cry of Americanist literary scholars. (For some, it seems, it has even become a moral imperative of sorts.) "What is American literature?" has become a more difficult question to answer. Traditional notions of canon have been challenged, thereby breaking down oppositions such as "mainstream" and "marginal" literature or "popular" and "high" culture. New voices have begun to be heard, in particular of women and ethnic writers. The question of American exceptionalism has been reopened. Transnational and multi-lingual approaches to the culture of the United States turn away from an insistence upon the uniqueness and distinctiveness of the American experience to suggest that American culture has always and necessarily been interactive with other cultures, emphasizing the modification of shared features in an American setting. Such rethinking has resulted in more than a reopening of the canon to accommodate a greater diversity of voices than in the past; it has also exposed, as Werner Sollors has argued, that the very distinction between "ethnic" and "American" is flawed – that many traits and values ascribed to an ethnic American's descent culture are actually not culture-specific at all but take on ethnic resonance only when contrasted with values to which one has consented in becoming an American. In his terms, we should move "beyond ethnicity" and recognize that such constructions are themselves expressions of American culture. And Sacvan Bercovitch has argued compellingly that the dissensus itself, for all its contestations and reformulations, is not so much a sign of the breakdown of the American ideology but a function of it, a way America has of transforming opposition into a mode of revitalizing itself.

Jewish American literary study has gained from these reformulations – and has much to offer. In this intellectual climate, more scholars than ever – indeed, more readers in general – are willing to listen to the accented voices of immigrant writers, both men and women, and ready to consider seriously and sensitively the cultures and languages the Jews brought with them and culti-vated in America. We have grown more sensitive to the web of transnational filiations that pervade Jewish American texts and have learned to question parochial formulations of a literature that has itself always been the fruit of a culture of exile, diaspora, homecoming; of a literary world in which Jewish authors from one country read and interact with Jewish authors from other countries; of a community in which Jews from America are intimately con-cerned with the European Holocaust and with the fate of the State of Israel. And for these very reasons, some scholars have become increasingly skep-tical of the specific reconfigurations of America's multicultural map around what David Hollinger has called "the ethno-racial pentagon" of European, Asian, African, Hispanic, and indigenous peoples: whereas once Jews were part of the triple melting pot of Protestant–Catholic–Jew, the demise of religion as a central feature of differentiation in America and the foreground-ing of race relegate Jews to a dehistoricized and culturally vacant category of "whiteness" (Hollinger, *Postethnic America*, 30). Between the dominant position of the white majority and the marginal position of peoples of color (having been perceived as such for most of America's history), American Jews have no clearly designated place on America's multicultural map which acknowledges their difference. For instance, Jews have an entirely different notion of country of origin from European Americans. After all, not all Jews (including Jewish Americans) trace their ancestry to Europe, and even when they do, immigrants fleeing pogroms from the Pale of Settlement to which they were restricted did not consider themselves to be Russians, and to conflate German Jews with non-Jewish Germans is to invoke a historical irony too tragic to accept silently. Besides, Jews have for millennia understood their ancestral homeland to be not in Europe but in the Middle East – a fact of which Europeans were more than willing to remind them. Moreover, Jewish identity is itself constituted of both descent and consent models, of genealogy and of performance, of ethnicity and religion. The fascinating and variegated forms of Jewish identity in modern America may even be undermining conventional oppositions, as that inscribed in the title of sociologist Steven Cohen's 1988 study, *American Assimilation or Jewish Revival?*. Some are even willing to argue that assimilation itself be reconstrued as a form of ethnic art. Given that the Jewish American experience cannot easily be assimilated into existing models of multiculturalism, it poses a challenge to them – a challenge that has not as yet been satisfactorily answered.

We hope this volume will contribute to a more nuanced understanding of Jewish American literature and of American literature in general. The questions and counter-questions inherent in any discussion of this field have made editing this volume daunting. Decisions about what to exclude proved far more difficult than what to include. Perhaps our most significant decision was to incorporate discussion of major authors in broad conceptual chapters rather than in the traditional format of devoting whole chapters to individual writers. This organizing principle has meant that the same writer may be discussed in several different contexts, for example Mary Antin as immigrant writer, as woman writer, and as multilingual writer, and it has also enabled our contributors to introduce new or neglected authors and works. As a result, the chapters in this volume provide both a general history of Jewish American writing and an introduction to its current and developing modes of study. And yet, in a longer volume, we would have included areas that we were regrettably not able to address here, such as full chapters on drama and theater, on representations of Israel, on autobiography, on translation, on Rabbinic literature, and on mixed media (such as cartoons). Although we begin before the massive waves of East European immigration and their Yiddish culture, our chapters primarily focus on Ashkenazi culture because it constitutes the bulk of Jewish American writing. In recent years, however, Sephardic American voices have begun to be heard, and they deserve critical attention (see Tresa Grauer's chapter), as well as Canadian Jewish literature, which falls outside the parameters of our collection.

We believe that this volume can serve two complementary purposes. First, it addresses those genres, topics, and authors that are widely read and taught and have become (or are rapidly becoming) the "standard" areas of Jewish American literary study; for instance, the East European immigrant experience (Roskies, Priscilla Wald), the "renaissance" of Jewish writing in the 1950s, including the fiction of Bellow, Malamud, Roth, and Singer (Wisse, Gubar); the ethics and aesthetics of representation of the Holocaust (Budick, Gubar); Jewish writing and gender (Gubar, Shreiber, Grauer); poetry and popular culture (Weber, Wolosky, Roskies, Mintz). Second, and just as important, we have mapped out subjects that are of significance to Jewish American culture but are only beginning to receive the literary-critical attention they deserve: the writings of Sephardi and German Jews which predate the mass immigration from Eastern Europe (Kramer); the vast and fascinating body of Yiddish and Hebrew writing produced in America (Roskies, Mintz); theological and literary-critical writings considered as imaginative literature (Heschel, Wolosky); literature that addresses the race question in America (Gubar); multilingualism and transnationalism in Jewish writing and reading (Wirth-Nesher).

It was also clear to us at the outset that we should not aim to be encyclopedic, but rather provide the groundwork for further study of a rich and growing field by casting a wide net – historically, thematically, linguistically, and generically. The field of Jewish American literature is not restricted to one relatively short, well-defined period: it extends over two centuries and is open-ended, continuing to develop in interesting and important ways. In recent years scholars in the field have employed a variety of critical approaches in their readings, such as ethnic studies, feminism, and post-structuralism, all represented in this volume. We have been guided by the principle of diversity, in period, genre, theme, style, and approach. But no net is ever wide enough. Tresa Grauer, in her chapter on contemporary literature that closes this volume, reminds us that twenty-five years ago Irving Howe predicted that Jewish American writing found "its voice and its passion" at exactly the moment that it approached disintegration. "The flourishing of Jewish American writing in the quarter century since Howe's publication," argues Grauer, "attests to the limitations of any single definition of Jewish American literature" (see p. 269 below). To underscore this point and to emphasize the debates around the very concept of Jewish American writing, we have entitled this introduction, "Jewish American literatures in the making."

Michael Kramer's research for this volume was supported by the Israel Science Foundation (Grant no. 859/00–2). Hana Wirth-Nesher would also like to thank the Israel Science Foundation and to acknowledge the help of the Samuel L. and Perry Haber Chair on the Study of the Jewish Experience in the United States at Tel-Aviv University. Special thanks to our able research assistants: Aden Bar-Tura, Yael Kliers, and Sonia Weiner.

REFERENCES AND SUGGESTED FURTHER READINGS

Bercovitch, Sacvan. *The Rites of Assent: Transformations in the Symbolic Construction of America*. New York and London: Routledge, 1993.

Biale, David, Michael Galchinsky, and Susannah Heschel, eds. *Insider/Outsider: American Jews and Multiculturalism*. Berkeley: University of California Press, 1998.

Cahan, Abraham. *The Education of Abraham Cahan*. Trans. Leon Stein, Abraham P. Conan, and Lynn Davison. Intro. Leon Stein. Philadelphia: Jewish Publication Society of America, 1969.

Chametzky, Jules et al., eds. *Jewish American Literature: A Norton Anthology*. New York and London: W.W. Norton & Company, 2001.

Cohen, Steven M. *American Assimilation or Jewish Revival?* Bloomington: Indiana University Press, 1988.

Feingold, Henry, series ed. *The Jewish People in America*. 5 vols. Baltimore and London: Johns Hopkins University Press, 1992.

Gurock, Jeffrey S., ed. *American Jewish History*. 8 vols. New York and London: Routledge, 1998.

Hollinger, David. *Postethnic America*. New York: Basic Books, 1995.

Howe, Irving, ed. *Jewish American Stories*. New York: New American Library, 1977.

Kramer, Michael P. "Race, Literary History, and the 'Jewish' Question." *Prooftexts: A Journal of Jewish Literary History* 21 (2001): 231–293.

Lazerow, Judah Leib. "The Staff of Judah." Eds. and trans. Menahem Blondheim and Michael P. Kramer. In *The Multilingual Anthology of American Literature*. Eds. Marc Shell and Werner Sollors. New York: New York University Press, 2000.

Malin, Irving and Irwin Stark, eds. *Breakthrough: A Treasury of Contemporary American-Jewish Literature*. New York: McGraw Hill, 1964.

Ozick, Cynthia. *Metaphor & Memory*. New York: Vintage, 1989.

Rosenfeld, Isaac. "The Humor of Sholem Aleichem." In *Preserving the Hunger: An Isaac Rosenfeld Reader*. Ed. Mark Shechner. Detroit: Wayne State University Press, 1988.

Roskies, David G. *The Jewish Search for a Usable Past*. Bloomington: Indiana University Press, 1999.

Samuel, Maurice. *The World of Sholem Aleichem*. New York: Knopf, 1943.

Schappes, Morris U., ed. *A Documentary History of Jews in the United States, 1645–1875*. New York: The Citadel Press, 1952.

Sholem Aleichem. *Adventures of Mottel the Cantor's Son*. Trans. Tamara Kahana. New York: Collier Books, 1961.

Sollors, Werner. *Beyond Ethnicity: Consent and Descent in American Culture.* New York and Oxford: Oxford University Press, 1986.

Solotaroff, Ted and Nessa Rapoport, eds. *Writing Our Way Home: Contemporary Stories by American Jewish Authors.* New York: Schocken Books, 1992.

Wirth-Nesher, Hana, ed. *What Is Jewish Literature?* Philadelphia: Jewish Publication Society, 1994.

Wisse, Ruth R. *The Modern Jewish Canon: A Journey Through Language and Culture.* New York: The Free Press, 2000.

I

MICHAEL P. KRAMER

Beginnings and ends: the origins of Jewish American literary history

> In the beginning God created the heaven and the earth.
> (Genesis 1:1)

> Rabbi Isaac said: He did not have to begin the Torah but with, "This month shall be unto you the beginning of months" [Exodus 12:2], which is the first commandment that Israel was commanded. So why did He open with, "In the beginning"? Because of this: "He hath declared to His people the power of His works, to give them the heritage of the nations" [Psalms 111:6]. So if the nations of the world would say to Israel, "You are thieves, since you have conquered the lands of the seven nations," they could say to them: "The entire earth belongs to the Holy One, Blessed be He. He created it and gave it to whom He saw fit. According to His will, he gave it to them; and according to His will, He took it from them and gave it to us."
> (Rashi on Genesis 1:1)

It may seem self-evident that the Bible should begin "in the beginning." But Rashi, the quintessential medieval Jewish exegete, did not think so. He plainly understood a thousand years ago what we post-moderns think only we have discovered, that every narrative has a purpose, that every beginning is a means to an end.

The Bible begins at the beginning, Rashi tells us, because, in narrative terms, it will eventually take the Children of Israel not only to the foot of Mount Sinai but also to the banks of the Jordan – because, in terms of genre, it is not only a book of laws but also a national chronicle, a historical defense of sovereignty. Cosmogony legitimates conquest.

Why does Rashi begin his commentary with this particular gloss? Here, too, the answer is not self-evident. Plainly, his meditation on biblical beginnings had no practical political purpose: a millennium had passed since Jewish sovereignty ceased in Judea; another millennium would go by before the idea of return to a Jewish national homeland would become a serious political option. Surely religious law was more immediately relevant to medieval, diasporic Jews. Rashi could have begun in other ways – with a grammatical analysis of the prepositional phrase, "In the beginning," say, or with homiletical readings of key words such as "beginning" and "God." (Both, in fact, follow his initial gloss.) Moreover, none of the earlier midrashic compilations in which Rabbi Isaac's gloss appears, and upon which Rashi drew, position the gloss so prominently. So why does Rashi begin with the question of sovereignty?

Writing in France at the end of the eleventh century, the Crusades looming or already begun, Rashi may very well have chosen this beginning because sovereignty never seemed so far away (Sicherman and Gevaryahu, "Rashi and the First Crusade"). He may have felt he needed to reiterate at that moment of crisis what was, after all, a central tenet of Jewish faith, that the children of Israel – despite being politically powerless, dispersed among the nations, caught between cross and crescent – were still God's chosen people and the true heirs of Canaan. In this light, the gloss may be seen as a calmly defiant call to peer past the competing claims of Christians and Moslems, to look beyond the centuries of exile and alterity, to rise above the violence and victimization, to climb the *Pisgah* heights of textual intention and see the promised land. "He took it from *them*," Rashi writes, "and gave it to *us*." Not only to our ancestors, he implies, but even to *us*. Even in exile. Even though we can do nothing about it. In the beginning God created the heaven and the earth, and in the end He would restore the Jews to Zion. Contemporary history has little relevance, Rashi seems to suggest, when God's overarching plot is taken into account, when the ends are authorized in the beginning.

Why begin a discussion of the origins of Jewish American literary history with Rashi? Certainly there are other options. A recent textbook anthology of Jewish American literature (Chametzky et al., *Jewish American Literature*), for instance, begins reasonably with a petition penned by the early Jewish settlers in New Amsterdam to grant them civil rights – fitting prelude to a sanguine, forward-looking narrative of Jewish achievement in America. Earlier studies begin with non-Jewish perceptions of the Jew in early American literature (Mersand, *Traditions in American Literature*, Harap, *The Image of the Jew*), as if Jewish American creativity were born in ethnic self-consciousness and Jewish American literary history were a story of the gradual rise of self-confidence and self-expression. Beginning with Rashi anticipates a different kind of Jewish American story, one that necessarily begins *in medias res*. To be sure, not all works of Jewish American literature derive immediately from the cultural tradition represented by Rashi's commentary. Some do, among them works I discuss in this chapter. But the vast majority of literature discussed throughout this volume does not. Nor is such a beginning meant to suggest that only those works that somehow preserve or engage pre-American Jewish tradition (Rashi's or some other) deserve inclusion in Jewish American literary history: such privileging not only would greatly limit but would also distort the range and variety of the literature produced by Jews in America. To take the long view is neither to make a moral judgment nor to chart an exclusivist cultural tradition but to suggest an historiographical approach: to take the measure of Jewish literary creativity by using the tape of the past, even when that creativity amounts to cultural discontinuity or abandonment.

As such, beginning with Rashi serves a twofold purpose. First, Rashi offers us an instance of medieval Jewish thinking about Jewish history and destiny against which later instances of Jewish thought can be compared and contrasted. Second, he also presents us with a way of thinking about Jewish *literary* history. Indeed, the imaginative force of Rashi's beginning, his view of Jewish history and destiny, is sustained by and conditioned upon the implicit history of Jewish literature embedded in his text. He explains why the Bible begins at the beginning by tracing his commentary back to *its* interpretative origins. His geneaological claim ("He gave it to *us*") is reinforced by an exegetical chain: he glosses Rabbi Isaac's earlier midrash, which glosses Psalms 111 as a gloss on Genesis 1. Rashi begins, in other words, by situating himself within a continuous and ongoing literary tradition. His commentary seems to suggest that Jewish literary history – or, as he no doubt understood it, *mesorah*, the transmission of tradition – looks toward the future by throwing the Jews back upon their covenantal origins and keeping land, lineage, and law linked imaginatively together. His meditation on beginnings draws its imaginative force from its own belatedness, its reliance on earlier texts, its *un*originality: the unbroken textual tradition effectually substitutes for, and thus defies the vicissitudes of, the political history of the Jews.

Centuries later, when Jewish scholars in Germany (and later in England and America) laid the groundwork for modern Jewish literary historiography, something like Rashi's notion of the compensatory value of literary history resurfaces. The literary traditions of other peoples were defined by shared territory and common language, it was widely held, but Jewish literature flourished despite the absence of these elements. For these early scholars of Jewish studies (known as *Wissenschaft des Judentuums*), the expanded Jewish literary tradition was the "portable fatherland" (Waxman, *A History of Jewish Literature*, I, xv) of the Jews, the sign and guarantor of their national survival during exile. To begin the story of modern Jewish literature in the pre-modern Jewish past is not to state the obvious but, with Rashi, to defy the evident differences between past and present. But while the rift that Rashi's commentary sought to bridge was temporal, spatial, political, and lamented, the rupture that modern Jewish literary history tried to repair was also cultural – and, ironically, much desired. It is by now a common-place that modern Jewish history is marked by a break with the past – often deliberate, even radical – and these scholars supported the modernization of Jewish religion, culture, and society. Their task was to see the changes in Judaism as continuity – an act of insight or imagination often bolder than Rashi's. It is one thing for Rashi to identify himself with Rabbi Isaac, another to see the spirit of Moses Maimonides in Benedict Spinoza, or that of Isaiah in Karl Marx. To call modern Jewish literature Jewish is more often than not to speak metonymically, to substitute a discerned (or imagined) Jewish part for the complex cultural whole. To locate modern Jewish writing within the same history as, say, Rashi and Rabbi Isaac is to make a political assertion as much as a cultural observation, one that may obscure as much as it clarifies (Kramer, "Race").

To imagine Jewish *American* literature in terms of continuity is even more of an intellectual feat. Much of early Jewish American history is also marked by a break with the past, a break exacerbated by America's distance from established Jewish communities, by the lack of a central religious and com-munal authority, and, after the Revolution, by American ideology. European nationalism threw Europeans back upon their past and generated a parallel response from their Jews; American ideology trumpeted a break with the past. If early Jewish literary historiography is haunted by the question of continuity, the American quest for literary nationality is fueled by the ideo-logical imperative of autochthony. Again and again in the late eighteenth and nineteenth centuries we hear the obsessive call for American writers to throw off the chains of European influence. "We have listened too long," Emerson wrote, "to the courtly muses of Europe" ("The American Scholar," 62). As if it were possible to imagine American literature as anything but a branch of English literature. As if the Pilgrims left all their cultural baggage on board the Mayflower when they stepped on to Plymouth Rock. As if Emerson in-vented the essay, or Hawthorne the romance, or Whitman the epic. In short, the question of beginnings is answered differently in America than in Europe: if the point of Jewish literary history is to look beyond rupture to connec-tion, the point of American literary history is to look through connection to rupture. If the central question of early Jewish literary discourse has to do with cultural continuities, with belatedness and indebtedness, the central question of early American literary discourse has to do with originality and self-sufficiency – not what makes it the same but what makes it different.

In a sense, early Jewish American writers and thinkers found themselves in a conceptual bind, looking backward to Jewish origins and forward to American vistas. I offer this dilemma heuristically, as a preliminary way of thinking of the beginnings of Jewish writing in America – of the first two centuries of sermons, orations, poems, and novels that Jews of the Sephardic and German waves of immigration wrote – and of the diverse and divergent sources of the literature. For the theme of this chapter is the concept of origins as it emerges in early Jewish American writing, the various ways Jews in America tried to make sense of America's place in Jewish history and the place of the Jews in America.

Judah Monis (1683–1764), an Italian Jew probably of Portuguese descent, was the first Jewish man of letters in America, publishing a volume of religious discourses (*The Truth, The Whole Truth, and Nothing But the Truth*) in 1722 and *A Grammar of the Hebrew Tongue* in 1735. He was also the first Jewish faculty member at Harvard, placing him at the beginning of a distinguished Jewish American tradition (Klingenstein, *Jews in the American Academy*, 1–2). Moreover, Monis was probably the first serious representative of traditional Jewish learning in America: he reportedly "studied in the Jewish academies of Leghorn and Amsterdam" and was "truly read and learned in the Jewish Cabals and Rabbins, a Master and Critic in the Hebrew" (Kramer, "The Conversion of the Jews," 178). His writings evidence an ability to quote the Bible, the Talmud, and various midrashic and kabbalistic texts, along with a slew of medieval Jewish philosophical and exegetical works – including, to be sure, Rashi. In the end, however, Monis became a Christian.

Or, to be more exact, a New England Puritan. When Monis arrived in Boston in 1720 he entered a society remarkable for its passionate, multi-layered fascination with the Jews. To begin with, the Puritans, like other Christians, read the Hebrew scriptures typologically, as adumbrations of Christian experience: they understood the Israelite exodus from Egypt, their wanderings through the wilderness, and their conquest of the Promised Land of Canaan as foreshadowings of Christ, the Christian church, and each individual Christian's spiritual journey from sin to salvation. The biblical promises of restoration and renewal were construed to mean regeneration and to be transferred to Christians, the spiritual Israel, the *new* Chosen People. Moreover, as Sacvan Bercovitch explains, the Puritans read their exodus from England and their errand into the American wilderness as the historical fulfillment of the biblical type, giving the world a *new*, geographically specific Promised Land (*The American Jeremiad*, 75–80). At the same time, like other Protestant millenialists, the Puritans believed that the Jews still had a special role to play in history. Increase Mather explained the "Miraculous manner of GOD's preserving the *Jewish Nation*" at Monis' baptism: "it is an unprecedented and incomprehensible thing, that GOD should for *Two Thousand Years* preserve this People dispersed among other Nations, without being confounded with them in their Religions and Customs, as is usual among all dispersed People; this clearly Demonstrates that GOD has preserved them for some great design, which what can it be but their Conversion?" (Colman, *Discourse*, ii–iii). They looked forward to the conversion of the Jews, their redemption from obstinacy and error, as a sign that the end of times was near. Monis' apostasy was an affirmation of the Puritans' place in sacred history.

For Rashi, the beginning authorizes the end, as Israel's *future* redemption is cast as a *return* to Zion, a renewal of the Past (Lamentations 5:21). By seeking to refute the "nine principal arguments the Modern Jewish Rabbins do make to prove the Messiah is yet to come" (Friedman, "Judah Monis," 3), Monis hoped to free the Future from the Past. For Monis, as for his Puritan sponsors, the end redeems the beginning: just as the Old Testament is seen to foreshadow, and thus be fulfilled by the New, so Monis' Jewish beginnings are given meaning by his Christian end. For this reason, Monis was never asked to renounce his Jewish origins. Indeed, his place in Puritan society was inextricably bound up with his identity as a Jew. His book bears the dedication, "To my Brothers *According to the Flesh*." He kept his Sabbath on Saturday. His tombstone bears the inscription: "Here lies buried Rabbi Judah Monis, M.A." (Kramer, "The Conversion of the Jews," 178–179). But the significance of his Jewish origins was wholly determined by the Puritan society in which he lived. The Puritans assimilated Monis into their New World eschatology; Monis assimilated the Puritan vision of history, refuted Rashi (as it were), and recreated himself as an *American* Jew. His two books may thus be construed as the Jewish literary fruit of his American experience, and Jewish American literary history may be thus said to originate in the conversion of Judah Monis.

Monis knew that his "Brethren *According to the Flesh*" would not approve of his conversion. "I do expect the News of my Embracing the Christian Religion [having] come to your Ears some time ago, has been somewhat surprizing to you all," he wrote in his dedication, "and I am afraid you did not think it to be the best you ever have heard" (Colman, *Discourse*, i [v]). In America, conversion never developed into what Michael Ragussis has called a "culture of conversion" – never became what it did, say, for Heinrich Heine, perhaps the most famous literary convert to Christianity in nineteenth-century Europe. Not because Jews were more pious in America (plainly they were not) but because America was too open – because, as Heine wrote of America: "Everyone over there can find salvation his own way" (Diner, *A Time for Gathering*, 37). Antisemitism remained, missionary societies plied their trade, and some Jews did convert, but by and large American Jews, even those with tenuous attachments to Judaism, found other ways to negotiate the rhetorical terrain between themselves and America – particularly after the Revolution.

Consider the August 1790 address of Moses Seixas (1744–1809), warden of the Hebrew Congregation of Newport, to President George Washington. "Permit the children of the stock of Abraham," Seixas begins, "to join with our fellow-citizens in welcoming you to New Port" (Schappes, *Documentary History of the Jews*, 79). In some ways, the address echoes the deferential addresses of contemporaneous Jewish leaders to European monarchs, but with at least one crucial difference. Seixas identifies the Jews in a twofold manner: on one hand, as "the stock of Abraham" and, on the other hand, as "fellow-citizens." Before and elsewhere, these two terms were mutually exclusive. But Seixas offers both, with no overt attempt to mediate between the two, to convert one into the other. They were both: Jews by descent (to use Werner Sollors' terminology) and Americans by consent. It was a revolutionary (if deferential) declaration, wholly appropriate to the Revolutionary occasion. "Deprived as we have hitherto been of the invaluable rights of free citizens," he explains,

> we now, with a deep sense of gratitude to the Almighty disposer of events, behold a government, erected by the majesty of the people, a government which to bigotry gives no sanction, to persecution no assistance, but generously offering to all liberty of conscience and immunities of citizenship, deeming every one, of whatever nation, tongue, or language, equal parts of the great governmental machine. (Schappes, *Documentary History of the Jews*, 79)

Jews had a long history of petitioning for their rights in the New World, beginning as early as 1656, when a group of Jewish businessmen in New Netherlands protested Peter Stuyvesant's withholding of their privileges to the Dutch West India Company. But this was different: Seixas' address was not a petition at all. European Jewish leaders extolled their monarchs for their toleration of the Jews, their loyal subjects. But as Washington explains in his response to Seixas's address: "It is now no more that toleration is spoken of, as if it was by the indulgence of one class of people that another enjoyed the exercise of their inherent natural rights" (Schappes, *Documentary History of the Jews*, 80). When all men are created equal – when "the people" is defined politically, rather than ethnically or religiously – then the Jews are, by definition, "equal parts of the great governmental machine."

The implications of this formulation are not only political but also rhetorical. By making Judaism a matter of conscience, immune to governmental interference, America offered the Jews not only equal rights but also a new, secular narrative, with a new beginning and a new, palpable end. *Hitherto*, the Jews had been persecuted; *now* they are part of the great governmental machine. *Hitherto*, Jews had been tolerated, at best; *now* liberty is spoken of, not toleration. The history of exile and dispersion that Rashi's exegesis had looked beyond (and that Mather had rendered in providential terms) now takes on a prominence and a significance of its own, drawn from the self-evident truths of American history. Theoretically, this new story is wholly secular, a story of rights and liberties, not redemption or salvation: it does not in principle seek to replace the sacred history of the Jews. So argued, at least, the Reverend Gershom Mendes Seixas (Moses' brother and *Hazan* of the Spanish–Portuguese *Shearith Israel* synagogue in New York) in a discourse preached the previous November. Recalling the history of the Jews from God's promise to Abraham to the destruction of the Temple, he concludes:

> *From that period even until now*, our predecessors have been, and we are still at this time in captivity among the different nations of the earth; and though we are . . . made equal partners of the benefits of government by the constitution of these states . . . still we cannot but view ourselves as captives in comparison to what we were formerly, and what we expect to be hereafter, when the outcasts of Israel shall be gathered together

and "we shall be established under our own king – the Messiah the son of David" (*A Religious Discourse*, 12, my italics).

Gershom Seixas' protestations only underscore the fact that, in the early years of the republic, the Jews were faced with two competing historical narratives, difficult to keep apart and difficult to reconcile. No doubt some in the Reverend Seixas' audience found his argument dissonant: it was surely easier for Rashi to see the promised land in the shadow of the Crusades than for American Jews to see captivity in the afterglow of the Revolution. One history was secular, the other sacred: but in the heady days of the New Republic, despite the separation of church and state, the line between the sacred and secular was increasingly blurred. America's secular achievements – the spread of democracy, economic progress, territorial expansion – took on sacred overtones and a civil religion emerged. The typological vision of the New England Puritans was being transformed and extended to all America and to all Americans. Eventually, the allure of the rhetoric would prove difficult for many Jews to resist. Indeed, for all his talk of "liberty of conscience and immunities of citizenship," Moses Seixas cannot keep from addressing Washington in biblical terms. He remembers "with pleasure . . . when the God of Israel who delivered David from the peril of the sword shielded your head in the day of battle," and he prays that "the angel who conducted our forefathers through the wilderness into the promised land may graciously conduct you through all the dangers and difficulties of this mortal life" (Schappes, *Documentary History of the Jews*, 79). But while such language establishes common rhetorical ground between American Jewry and the American President, while it confers religious legitimacy upon current events, it does not challenge the validity of his brother's vision of history. In 1790, for the most part, the two narratives remained separate.

Much of the literature of American Jews may be said to have originated in the duality of Seixas' address to Washington. On one hand, it allowed Jews to be Jews, to express their ethnic difference, to retain (like Gershom Seixas) the moral imperative of "in the beginning"; on the other hand, it freed Jews to be Americans, to put aside their ethnic difference without having to renounce it, to tell the tale of hitherto/now with impunity. The separation of sacred and secular set the stage for Mordecai Manuel Noah (1785–1851), diplomat, editor, politician, and one of the first two Jewish dramatists in America. (The other was Isaac Harby.) Noah was, in Seixas' terms, both a devoted child of the stock of Abraham and a patriotic citizen of the United States, the most prominent Jew in antebellum America, as well as the most flamboyant – and the most maligned. Frequently the target of antisemitic slurs, he was the self-appointed champion of Jewish causes. At the same time, Noah's "early hankering for the national drama" (Schuldiner and Kleinfeld, *Selected Writings*, 65) led to his joining the quest for American literary nationality. He wrote four full-length plays in that quest: *She Would Be a Soldier* (1819), *The Siege of Tripoli* (1820), *Marion, the Hero of Lake George* (1822), and *The Grecian Captive* (1822). None of these plays, nor much of his other writing (say, the journalism collected in *Essays of Howard*, 1820) have anything to do with Judaism. They belong to Jewish American literary history, not because their content is in any way recognizably Jewish, but simply by virtue of Seixas' twofold definition of the American Jew.

As one historian puts it succinctly, "Noah was a curious mix" (Hertzberg, *The Jews in America*, 93). Nowhere is the literary quality of that mix more evident (or more curious) than in his notorious Ararat address. In 1820, just as his career as an American dramatist was taking off, Noah petitioned the New York State assembly for permission to buy Grand Island in the Niagara River, near Buffalo, to build a colony for immigrant Jews – a preparatory stage to their restoration to Palestine. With a self-promoting nod to the biblical Noah, he called it Ararat. The plan was very much of its time and place: America had been trying to attract immigrants since colonial times, and there were other plans to attract Jews at that time, by Jews and non-Jews alike (Schappes, *Documentary History of the Jews*, 141–147). When Rebecca Gratz mentions these schemes (Noah's in particular) in a letter to a friend, she questions "whether they have taken the wisest plans," but does not doubt the immigrants "would be happier under such a government" (Schappes,

Documentary History of the Jews, 149). Noah's idea of restoration had fewer precedents, but in an era of proliferating religious revivals, millenialist sects, and social reform movements, the notion could hardly be called unusual. What is remarkable, however, is the peculiar interplay of narrative elements in his address.

On Thursday, September 15, 1825, Noah organized an elaborate, theatrical procession of musicians, soldiers, politicians, clergymen, masons, and Noah himself, dressed as the "Judge of Israel" in "robes of crimson silk, trimmed with ermine and a richly embossed golden medal suspended from the neck" (Schuldiner and Kleinfeld, *Selected Writings*, 106). The band played a march from Handel's *Judas Maccabeus* as the procession entered a church near Grand Island. After a prayer service, Noah delivered his address, to which, the *Buffalo Patriot* reported, "a crowded auditory listened with profound attention" (Schuldiner and Kleinfeld, *Selected Writings*, 107). What they heard was a melange of distinct, even opposed, but mutually sustaining rhetorics, of the rising glory of America and "Renew our days as of old." Like Gershom Seixas, Noah's account of Jewish history was essentially that of Rashi – a vision that looks to the future by gazing longingly backwards. The Jews "have long been captives in a land of strangers," he asserted, but they "never should and never will relinquish the just hope of regaining possession of their ancient heritage" (114, 112). "Two thousand years have nearly elapsed since the dissolution of the Jewish government" and they are "scattered over the face of the globe," but they "have been destined by Providence to remain a distinct people," to "retain their homogenousness of character – the peculiarity of their tenets, the identity of their faith" (112). Indeed, Noah declares, "no part of our religion... should be altered, nothing should be taken from the law" (123). And indeed, Jews have "carefully preserved the oracles of God assigned to their safe keeping." *Remain, retain,* and ultimately *regain*. For Jews, the American asylum is "temporary and provisionary" (112). To them, America may be the "happy land" but it is not the "promised land" (124), and they look forward to the fulfillment of the biblical prophecies.

One thing that distinguishes Noah's vision from that of Seixas is that, for Noah, America has a decided role to play in the providential history of the Jews. Noah's sense that America was not just another place of exile emerges most fancifully in speculations that the American Indians – who are "a brave and eloquent people, with an Asiatic complexion, and Jewish features," who "are divided into tribes," and whose "language and dialect are evidently of Hebrew origin" – are descendants of the ten lost tribes of Israel (122). "If the tribes could be brought together, could be made sensible of their *origins*, could be civilized. And restored to their long lost brethren," he exclaims, "how clearly have the prophecies been fulfilled...how providential our deliverance" (123, my italics). Noah was so taken with the idea that two years after the spectacle at Grand Island, he published an extended *Discourse on the Evidences of the American Indians Being the Descendants of the Lost Tribes of Israel*. But Noah has another story to tell as well, a secular tale of progress and enlightenment, and this story sets him apart from Reverend Seixas even more. Noah calls his address a "declaration of independence," and his opening paragraph clearly and deliberately echoes Jeffersonian rhetoric. America's role in the restoration of the Jews to their former glory has precisely to do with its role in secular history, in the rise and spread of liberalism. While the Jews still patiently endure, "the march of learning and science has been rapid and successful," Noah notes, "and mankind are better qualified to estimate the blessings of toleration and liberal views...than at any former time" (112). Because America is the place where these blessings are most perfectly enjoyed, because it has itself effected these changes, he argues, the Jews ought to come to America. For all their constancy, bravery, and endurance, it seems, the Jews are still in need of regeneration – exile and oppression have taken their toll – and America is the only place for that regeneration to take place. For the Jews successfully to return whence they came, America had gloriously to rise.

Noah's Ararat address originates in the interplay of two disparate historical discourses, one liberal and progressive, the other sacred and retrospective. The two discourses are divergent but mutually sustaining: the rising glory of America prepares the way for the restoration of the Jews; and the restoration of the Jews justifies the rising glory of America. Significantly, the balance gives way at certain points in the address, where liberalism seems to dictate the character of Jewish tradition. While Seixas looks forward to the restoration of the Davidic monarchy, Noah "deem[s] it expedient to reorganize the nation under the direction of the judges," as the office "was not hereditary, conforms in some respect to that of chief Magistrate, and is in accordance with the genius and disposition of the people of this country" (113). By and large, however, each discourse retains its narrative and ideological integrity, each its own beginning and end. And while Ararat was a political failure – no Jew ever immigrated to Noah's "city of refuge" (111), and its cornerstone, now in a museum in Buffalo, is all that remains of one of the most unusual incidents in Jewish American history – Noah's rhetorical symbiosis nevertheless constitutes a notable Jewish American literary achievement.

Noah would return to the theme of Restoration later in his career: in 1845 he published a *Discourse on the Restoration of the Jews*, and in 1849, an *Address...to Aid in the Erection of the Temple at Jerusalem*. By then, however, the German wave of immigration had begun to make its mark on Jewish society and culture in America. The writers of that wave, particularly those associated with the movement for religious Reform, would significantly alter the way Jews in America understood the relationship between the two discourses. What was expedient for Noah – the attempt to make potentially objectionable points of Jewish law compatible with American values – becomes central to their thinking and would find its full expression in the decades to come in what Jonathan Sarna has called, "The Cult of Synthesis." Susanna Heschel will explain the theological and political implications of their thought in the next chapter. My concerns here are literary.

When Isaac Mayer Wise arrived in New York from Bohemia in 1846, he was appalled by the lack of culture, particularly among Jews. He did note that "among the Portuguese Jews there was Mordecai Noah, who had achieved prominence, through his literary and political activity." Otherwise, however, "nothing worthy of note had been accomplished in this quarter." In regard to Jewish learning, the situation was even worse. "There was not one leader who could read unpunctuated Hebrew," he recalled, "or...had the least knowledge of Judaism, its history, and literature." In general, "ignorance swayed the scepter, and darkness ruled" (*Reminiscences*, 23–24). Moreover, he found German Jews not only culturally impoverished, but embarrased of their Jewishness. In a critique similar to W. E. B. Du Bois's analysis of the debilitating effects of "double-consciousness" in *The Souls of Black Folk* (1903), Wise judged that antisemitism "had demoralized the German and Polish Jew, and robbed him of his self-respect." "He parodies and imitates, because he has lost himself," he wrote, "and lacks the consciousness of manhood in himself" (*Reminiscences*, 330–331). The solution seemed clear to him. Unlike Du Bois, who called upon Blacks to acknowledge and cultivate their Africanness, Wise proposed a two-pronged approach. First, he took it upon himself to "popularize by spoken and written words as much Jewish learning as I might posses, in order to inculcate in others respect for Jewish literature" (332). But, "in order to gain the proud self-consciousness of the free-born man," he also insisted that "the Jew must become an American." By this he meant not only that the Jew must become part of the great governmental machine, as Moses Seixas suggested, but that they "become American through and through" (331).

Wise approached his self-appointed mission with passion and commitment, writing prolifically: history, theology, journalism, homily, polemic, apologetics, liturgy, fiction. (Wise published most of his fiction under the pen name of "The American Jewish Novelist," making him first in that distinguished line.) For all his concern about Jewish literacy, however, Wise did not link himself to Rashi's exegetical chain. To the contrary, like Judah

Monis, Wise utilized his learning to break the chain and, assimilating the dominant discourse of his time and place, to forge a new relationship between Jewish past and present, fashioning himself as an *American* Jew. With the *Wissenschaft* scholars he read and admired, Wise took ethnic pride in and strength from the literary accomplishments of Jews, both ancient and modern, but refused to accept their religious authority over him. Hence the editorial audacity of *Minhag America* (1857), the revised prayerbook "suitable for America" whose publication Wise spearheaded. "We had to sacrifice everything related to throne, crown, and dynasty to the land of freedom," he explained, and "everything cabbalistic and everything dealing with the sacrificial cult, the messiah, the return to Palestine...as well as the laments about persecutions, were simply eliminated and were replaced by modern concepts" ("The World of My Books," 129).

Simply eliminated. This verbal wave of the hand belies the extraordinary imaginative daring that propelled his entire literary career. That daring can be seen already in Wise's first major work, the ambitious and controversial *History of the Israelitish Nation...Derived from the Original Sources* (1854). To derive Jewish history "from the original sources" meant that he was summarily doing away with Rashi, Rabbi Isaac, and the ideology of return, treating the Bible as a source (one among many), and reading it from "the democratic point of view" ("The World of My Books," 122), thus reworking the story of Jewish national origins in the image of the American present. The Israelite exodus from Egypt, he wrote, "is the first time in history, that a nation claimed and attained its rights; the first time that a despot was chastised by an offended and oppressed people" (*History*, 66). A similar strategy emerges in his fiction. In *The First of the Maccabees* (1860), an historical romance of the Hasmonean revolt in the second century BCE, Wise has Matathia, father of Judah Maccabee, utter these sentiments: "The despotic will of Antiochus will shatter into atoms on the rock of Israel's fortitude. The blood of our saints impregnates the tree of liberty with new strength...I say, woe unto him who submits to the unjust mandates of a foreign despot, renounces his inalienable rights, and forgets his duties" (7, 10). To be sure, Wise meant not only to redefine Judaism but also to redefine America. Viewing the Jewish past through the eyes of the American present, he went on to claim that the American present found its origins in the Jewish past – looking forward to such works as Oscar Straus' *The Origin of Republican Form of Government* (1885). As he put it: "Moses formed one pole and the American revolution the other, of an axis around which revolved the political history of thirty-three centuries" (*History*, iv). Putting the words of the American founding fathers in the mouths of Jewish historical figures, Wise breaks down the barrier that separated Jewish from American narratives in the writings of the Seixases and Mordecai Noah. American history and Jewish history coalesce, and the history of the Jews becomes "a useful and welcome contribution to *American* literature" (ix, my italics).

Wise's mission to create and disseminate Jewish American literature centered much of the time on *The Israelite*, the newspaper he founded in Cincinnati in 1854. He had little problem acquiring news, sermons, and history – even if he had to write much himself. But he promised his readers poems and stories, and these (he later protested) he was more reluctant to write himself. Still, he did produce anonymously at least a dozen fictions in English and German that were published serially in the paper and its German supplement, *Die Deborah*, along with many unsigned poems. He felt he had little choice. Eventually H. H. Moos and Nathan Mayer "relieved" him of the task of novel-writing. But the only Jewish poet in America he seems to have thought of was Penina Moise (1797–1880), and, Wise writes, she was "already very much on the decline" ("The World of My Books," 126–127). There were a few others: Rebecca Hyneman (1812–1875) and Octavia Harby Moses (1823–1904). The not-yet-controversial Adah Isaacs Menken (1835–1868) contributed regularly between 1857 and 1859. But plainly, the tradition of Jewish American poetry that Maeera Shreiber describes in chapter 9 was still in its swaddling clothes.

Emma Lazarus (1849–1887) was only five years old when *The Israelite* began appearing. Of Sephardic–German descent, her family had been in America since colonial times. Her maternal great-grandfather actively supported the Revolution, and her cousin, Benjamin Cardozo, became a justice of the Supreme Court. Her father, a wealthy sugar merchant, brought his children up in the upper-class, cultured circles in New York and Newport. She was taught French, German, and Italian, and her first book of poetry, *Poems and Translations: Written Between the Age of Fourteen and Sixteen*, published privately by her father in 1866, including renderings of Hugo, Dumas, Schiller, and Heine. The volume drew a kind response from Ralph Waldo Emerson, and her second volume, *Admetus and Other Poems* (1871), was dedicated to him. Her next volume, *Alide*, a novel about Goethe, appeared in 1874 and was praised by Ivan Turgenev. Emerson read her verse drama, *The Spagnoletto* (1876), in manuscript and told her – he had become a mentor by then – that he could not put it down. She was far and away the most successful Jewish writer in America since Mordecai Noah and was personally affronted when Emerson did *not* include one of her poems in his anthology, *Parnassus*. Clearly she did not think of herself as a Jewish but as an American writer – which, indeed, she was. The closing lines of her Statue of Liberty sonnet, "The New Colossus," are among the most well-known lines of poetry ever written in America: "Give me your tired, your poor, / Your huddled masses yearning to breathe free, / The wretched refuse of your teeming shore. / Send these, the homeless, tempest-tost to me, / I lift my lamp beside the golden door!" (*The Poems of Emma Lazarus*, 1, 203). We might say that the symbolic power of the sonnet is rooted in large part in Lazarus' ability to articulate American cultural myth: America assimilated the poem, in other words, because the poem so thoroughly assimilates America.

Lazarus published poetry and prose in the most prestigious journals of the her day, in *Lippincott's*, *Scribner's*, and *Century*, and had no particular need to publish in the Jewish press. Eventually she would choose to. The turning point in her career came around 1880, when news of the East European pogroms reached America, along with the first Russian immigrants, and she took on the twin causes of the immigration (though she had very little in common culturally with the immigrants themselves) and, more controversially, the establishment of a Jewish homeland in Palestine. She began to write about Jewish subjects, unapologetically, fiercely, both in secular journals and in the Jewish press. Her *Songs of a Semite* was published in book form by *The American Hebrew* in 1882; the series of proto-Zionist essays she called *An Epistle to the Hebrews* appeared that same year. She began to think of herself as a Jewish poet though what this meant to her is not always clear. Or rather, it seems to have meant several different things. On one hand, like Wise, she valorizes and champions "a thorough interpenetration with [Judaism's] historic memories and poetic traditions" (*An Epistle to the Hebrews*, 13) and, on the other hand, insists that true Judaism is "not the teaching of the *Thora*, not the inculcation of the Talmud, not the preservation of the Hebrew tongue, not the maintenance of Synagogue worship" but a "spiritualized form of our belief" (25), which could be distilled from, but not dependent upon, those traditions. Then again, she also adopts the terms of romantic racialism and talks freely about the "Hebrew genius" and "the fire of our Oriental blood" (29, 20), as if being Jewish were fundamentally and necessarily only a matter of descent.

Lazarus' confused or eclectic sense of the origins of her Jewish art may be explained by the fact that hers was a thoroughly modern American Judaism, emphatically self-conscious, culled and constructed from a variety of sources. She did not have to break Rashi's exegetical chain because, for her, it was already broken – both as a matter of personal indifference and, later, as the Judaism she professed was, at bottom, the Reform Judaism of Wise and others. The "historic memories and poetic traditions" that she celebrates and masters became hers only after, and to the extent that, she decided to embrace them. She learned her Jewish history from both Jewish historians such as Heinrich Graetz and Christians such as British historian Henry

Hart Milman. She had a special relation to the Golden Age in medieval Spain and the Enlightenment in Germany – no doubt in part because of her Sephardic–German descent, but also because those were periods when secular, along with Jewish learning, flourished among the Jews. Her favorite modern Jewish poet was Heinrich Heine, the ambivalent apostate, whose poems she translated (her *Poems and Ballads of Heinrich Heine* appeared in 1881) and who represented, in her words, both "vanished Hellas and Hebraic pain" (*The Poems of Emma Lazarus*, I, 203). Her sense of the Jewish mission to the world draws heavily upon the rhetoric of Reform thinkers and preachers, but she utterly and vehemently refused to discard Jewish nationalism. Her Jewish nationalism was derived and authorized in large part neither from Rashi (about whom she wrote two poems) nor even from Rabbi Judah Halevi, whose poetry she translated (first from German translations, then, haltingly from a late-learned Hebrew), but from the early secular Zionist Leo Pinsker, whose *Autoemancipation* she read and admired, and, even more centrally, from Christian writers such as Laurence Oliphant and, most importantly, George Eliot: in the dedication to her verse tragedy *A Dance to Death*, Lazarus wrote that Eliot "did most among the artists of our day towards elevating and ennobling the spirit of Jewish nationality" (*The Poems of Emma Lazarus*, II, 69). And her commitment to the immigrants owes as much to the American rhetoric of asylum in Tom Paine's *Common Sense* and St. John de Crevecoeur's *Letters From an American Farmer* or even, in a more oblique sense, in Cotton Mather's *Magnalia Christi Americana* as to the prophecies of Isaiah and Jeremiah.

Lazarus' version of American origins reflects her complex and contradictory Jewish origins. Consider her sonnet, "1492":

> Thou two-faced year, Mother of Change and Fate,
> Didst weep when Spain cast forth with flaming sword,
> The children of the prophets of the Lord,
> Prince, priest, and people, spurned by zealot hate.
> Hounded from sea to sea, from state to state,
> The West refused them, and the East abhorred.
> No anchorage the known world could afford,
> Close-locked was every port, barred every gate.
> Then smiling, thou unveil'dst, O two-faced year,
> A virgin world where doors of sunset part,
> Saying, "Ho, all who weary enter here!
> There falls each ancient barrier that the art
> Of race or creed or rank devised, to rear
> Grim bulwarked hatred between heart and heart!"
> (*The Poems of Emma Lazarus*, II, 22)

Lazarus' subject is the coincidence of two historical events – the expulsion of the Jews from Spain and the discovery of America – and her strategy, the juxtaposition of two disparate historical discourses: the history of the Jews as perennial exiles and the history of America as immigrant asylum. The juxtaposition is given significance through the curious Janus-faced figure of the "two-faced year" that, through a sequence of gestures (weeping, smiling, unveiling), defines historical process as a fated movement from East to West, from old to new, from exile to redemption. On one hand, like Wise, Lazarus reconfigures American mythology as an expression of the Jewish spirit: the story of American origins begins with the Jews and ends with words that echo the prophet Isaiah, "Ho, everyone that thirsteth, come ye to the waters." "In that day shall this song be sung in Judah: We have a strong city; salvation will God appoint for walls and bulwarks." "Open ye the gates, that the righteous nation which keepeth the truth may enter in" (55:1, 25:12, 26:1–2). On the other hand, Lazarus' vision here is essentially Miltonic, as Spanish paradise lost looks forward to the "virgin [American] world" of paradise regained. Just as Milton's "flaming sword" of Genesis 3:24 and *Paradise Lost* Book XII signals Adam's learning "that suffering for Truth's sake / Is fortitude to highest victorie" (lines 569–570), so Lazarus' "flaming sword" signals, if only implicitly here, the Jews' acceptance of their fate. Or, as Lazarus wrote in 1882 of the Russian pogroms, "once more we prove / How strength of supreme suffering still is ours / For Truth and Law and Love" (*The Poems of Emma Lazarus*, II, 3) – and for America. Even the expulsion from Spain has its place in God's design; it, too, is a fortunate fall. A Christian lesson, to be sure, but that is precisely Lazarus' point. For if there is any truth to Christianity, she often argued, it is the Jews who embody it best.

Lazarus' poetry marks a clear turning point in Jewish American literature, as it gazes at the new East European immigrants – the "wretched refuse" of Europe's "teeming shores"; the "ignoble relic" (*The Poems of Emma Lazarus*, II, 14) of Israel's glorious past – through the eyes of the Sephardic–German experience of America. The new immigrants themselves gazed at America with different eyes. Many could see American myth *as* myth: from their ghetto tenements, they looked skeptically at "all the whimsical metamorphoses wrought upon the children of Israel of the great modern exodus by the vicissitudes of life in this their Promised Land of today" (Cahan, *Yekl*, 14). Immigrant preachers, linked in an unbroken chain to Rashi and Rabbi Isaac, insisted on eternal truths, truths sadly too familiar to them. Glossing Genesis 12:1 ("And the Lord said unto Abram: 'Get thee out of thy country...'"), Rabbi Judah Leib Lazerow commented that "in each and every generation and in each and every place they will teach [Abram's seed] this portion of 'Get thee out' – Get thee out, people of Israel, for this is not your place! And the portion of 'Get thee out' that began in the days of Abram has not yet ended." Still, they knew that America was not another Russia, and as they looked back, they also cautiously looked forward. "Thank God that in this country of ours, the land of freedom and liberty, the land of America, they have not *yet* begun to teach us the portion of 'Get thee out,' " Lazerow continued. "And *we hope* that they will never teach us this portion to the end of time" (*The Staff of Judah*, 493, my italics).

REFERENCES AND SUGGESTED FURTHER READINGS

Bercovitch, Sacvan. *The American Jeremiad*. Madison: University of Wisconsin Press, 1978.

Cahan, Abraham. *Yekl and the Imported Bridegroom and Other Stories of The New York Ghetto*. New York: Dover, 1970.

Chametzky, Jules et al. *Jewish American Literature: A Norton Anthology*. New York and London: W. W. Norton & Company, 2001.

Colman, Benjamin. *Discourse . . . Before the Baptism of R. Judah Monis . . . To which are added Three Discourses Written by Mr. Monis Himself*. Boston, 1722.

Diner, Hasia. *A Time for Gathering: The Second Migration, 1820–1880*. Baltimore: Johns Hopkins University Press, 1992.

Emerson, Ralph Waldo. "The American Scholar." In *Selected Writings of Emerson*. Ed. Donald M. McQuade. New York: The Modern Library, 1981.

Friedman, Lee M. "Judah Monis, First Instructor in Hebrew at Harvard University." *Publications of the American Jewish Historical Society* 22 (1914): 1–24.

Harap, Louis. *The Image of the Jew in American Literature: From the Early Republic to Mass Immigration*. Philadelphia: Jewish Publication Society, 1974.

Hertzberg, Arthur. *The Jews in America: Four Centuries of an Uneasy Encounter*. New York: Simon and Schuster, 1989.

Klingenstein, Susanne. *Jews in the American Academy, 1900–1940: The Dynamics of Intellectual Assimilation*. New Haven: Yale University Press, 1991.

Kramer, Michael P. "New English Typology and the Jewish Question." *Studies in Puritan American Spirituality* 3 (1992): 97–124.

"Emma Lazarus Discovers America in '1492.' " In *Following Columbus: America, 1492–1992*. Ed. Miriam Eliav-Feldon. [Hebrew] Jerusalem: The Zalman Shazar Center for Jewish History, 1996.

"Race, Literary History, and the 'Jewish' Question." *Prooftexts: A Journal of Jewish Literary History* 21 (2001): 231–293.

"The Conversion of the Jews and Other Narratives of Self-Definition: Notes Toward the Writing of Jewish American Literary History; or, Adventures in Hebrew School." In *Ideology and Jewish Identity in Israeli and American Literature*. Ed. Emily Miller Budick. Albany: State University of New York Press, 2001.

Lazarus, Emma. *An Epistle to the Hebrews*. Ed. Morris U. Schappes. New York: Jewish Historical Society of New York, 1987.

The Poems of Emma Lazarus. 2 vols. Boston and New York: Houghton, Mifflin, 1889.

Lazerow, Judah Leib. *The Staff of Judah*. Eds. and trans. Menahem Blondheim and Michael P. Kramer. In *The Multilingual Anthology of American Literature*.

Eds. Marc Shell and Werner Sollors. New York: New York University Press, 2000.

Lichtenstein, Diane. *Writing Their Nations: The Tradition of Nineteenth-Century American Jewish Women Writers*. Bloomington: Indiana University Press, 1992.

Mersand, Joseph. *Traditions in American Literature: A Study of Jewish Characters and Authors*. New York: Modern Chapbooks, 1939.

Ragusis, Michael. *Figures of Conversion: The "Jewish Question" and English National Identity*. Durham, NC: Duke University Press, 1995.

Rashi. *Pentateuch with Targum Onkelos, Haphtaroth, and Rashi's Commentary*. 5 vols. Trans. and eds. M. Rosenbaum and A. M. Silbermann. New York: Hebrew Publishing Company, *c.* 1935.

Sarna, Jonathan D. "The Cult of Synthesis in American Jewish Culture." *Jewish Social Studies* 5 (Fall 1998, Winter 1999): 52–79.

Schappes, Morris U., ed. *Documentary History of the Jews in the United States, 1654–1875*. Rev. edn. New York: Citadel Press, 1952.

Schuldiner, Michael and Daniel J. Kleinfeld, eds. *The Selected Writings of Mordecai Noah*. Westport, CT and London: Greenwood Press, 1999.

Seixas, Gershom Mendes. *A Religious Discourse*. New York, 1789.

Sicherman, Harvey and Gilad J. Gevaryahu. "Rashi and the First Crusade: Commentary, Liturgy, Legend." *Judaism* 48 (1999): 181–197.

Sollors, Werner. *Beyond Ethnicity: Consent and Descent in American Culture*. New York and Oxford: Oxford University Press, 1986.

Spencer, Benjamin Townley. *The Quest for Nationality: An American Literary Campaign*. Syracuse, NY: Syracuse University Press, 1957.

Waxman, Meyer. *A History of Jewish Literature*. 5 vols. New York and London: Thomas Yoseloff, 1960.

Wise, Isaac M. *History of the Israelitish Nation*. Albany, 1854.

  The First of the Maccabees. Cincinnati: Bloch & Co., 1860.

  Reminiscences. Ed. and trans. David Philipson. Cincinnati: Leo Wise and Company, 1901. 2nd edn. New York: Central Synagogue, 1945.

  "The World of My Books." Trans. Albert H. Friedlander. *American Jewish Archives* (June 1954): 107–148.

Wolosky, Shira. "An American-Jewish Typology: Emma Lazarus and the Figure of Christ." *Prooftexts* 16 (1996): 113–125.

2

SUSANNAH HESCHEL

Imagining Judaism in America

America as a site of Jewish liberation has been one of the guiding myths of the modern Jewish imagination. Above all, America meant redemption from Europe, which symbolized both Judaism's subservience to Christianity and Jews' confinement within the strictures of Judaism. In the nineteenth and early twentieth centuries, Jewish thinkers spoke of America as the great hope for the future of Judaism because its democratic principles embodied the true moral essence of Judaism. American Judaism was the real Judaism, while Europe represented a Judaism distorted by centuries of persecution and economic discrimination. Protestant thinkers, well before the colonial period, had identified the New Land with the Bible, and themselves with Israel; as Herman Melville declared in *White Jacket* (1850), "We Americans are the peculiar, chosen people – the Israel of our time; we bear the ark of the liberties of the world" (*Redburn, White Jacket, Moby Dick*, 506). For Jewish thinkers, Protestantism could not stand alone in claiming a privileged place in America; Judaism, the original Israel, had to stand beside it as the religion informing the American democratic enterprise and bearing its own manifest destiny in the world. In an 1898 resolution, leaders of Reform Judaism in America declared that "America is our Zion...The mission of Judaism is spiritual, not political...to spread the truths of religion and humanity throughout the world" (Sarna, "Converts to Zionism," 189).

Until well into the twentieth century, America was imaginatively constituted by Jewish thinkers through a set of projections drawn from Enlightenment ideals of tolerance, pluralism, and freedom of religion, all of which were identified as biblical ideals. They were to be applied theologically as well as politically to produce a regenerated Judaism. Isaac Leeser in the early nineteenth century viewed America as the nurturer of what would become a revived Jewish religious observance, and Elliot Cohen proclaimed in *Commentary* in November 1945 that American Jews "will evolve new patterns of living, new modes of thought, which will harmonize heritage and country into a true sense of at-home-ness in the modern world. Surely, we who have survived catastrophe, can survive freedom, too" ("An Act of Affirmation," 2). The American liberation would also bring about a new kind of Jew; for Kaufmann Kohler, America would restore the manliness of Jews that Europe had undermined: America was "a country that rolled off the shame and the taunt of the centuries from the shoulders of the wandering Jew, to place him, the former Pariah of the nations, alongside of the highest and the best, according to his worth and merit as a man" (*Hebrew Union College*, 198).

The political nuances of American Jewish thought become clear only when viewed in comparison to Jewish thought of the same period in Europe, primarily Germany. The initial emergence of modern Jewish thought in Germany during the late eighteenth and early nineteenth centuries came with a radical agenda. Rather than offer compliance with Christian demands for changes in Judaism, there was to be no quid pro quo for emancipation, as Moses Mendelssohn insisted. What had to change was Christianity, its claims to exclusive truth, and its contempt for Judaism. From its inception, Christianity had colonized Judaism intellectually, conquering and taking over its holy scriptures, fundamental theological ideas, its prophets and its God, all the while claiming that Judaism had lost it religious legitimacy. The work of the major nineteenth-century German Jewish theologians was a revolt of the colonized, an effort to overthrow Christian theological hegemony. Jewish thinkers sought to undermine Protestantism's legitimacy by claiming Jesus was a Jew and Christianity was a theological error, a false understanding of Jesus' Jewish faith and teachings.

While elements of the German Jewish arguments about Christianity were sometimes repeated in the United States, the context was different. Emancipation was not at stake, since political rights for Jews were assumed from the outset in America. The political framework influenced religious thought as well: in contrast to Europe, Jewish thinkers in America did not seek an overthrow of Protestantism. They sought instead a position of theological equivalence, claiming that Judaism was the authentic source of America's democracy, just as it was the source of Christianity's essential teachings. The principles of the Constitution and the Bill of Rights, like the teachings of Jesus, were simply expressing the values of the Hebrew Bible.

Yet as much as Jews viewed America as an expression of Jewish values, they transformed Judaism in accord with American principles into a religion of democracy. If European Judaism signified a backward, Orthodox religiosity, America meant freedom within Judaism to develop liberal religious expressions, and to do so by means of a democratic process. What that meant was eliminating the role of chief rabbi and strengthening the control of laity over rabbis' decisions regarding liturgy and ritual that, in Europe, had been under rabbinic authority. For Mordecai Kaplan, for example, "The ancient authorities are entitled to a vote – but not to a veto," a radical repudiation of classical Judaism's authoritarian structure (Kaplan, *Not So Random Thoughts*, 263). Even Zionism, when it attained support from liberal Jews, was viewed as an essentially American phenomenon. For Louis Brandeis, for example, Zionism was not only compatible with American Zionism, but expressed the ideals of the Pilgrims, the American Revolution, and American democracy (Sarna, "Converts to Zionism," 198).

Jewish optimism regarding America, and the desire to be liberated from the confines of European Judaism, ended with the Second World War, and Jewish thought in the last decades of the twentieth century reversed itself. America was no longer a place where Judaism could be nurtured and experience a renaissance; instead, America was enticing Jews to assimilate and intermarry at rates that would soon lead to a sharp diminution of the size of the community. In addition, many Jewish thinkers argued, post-World War II America seemed to have lost its ideals and values and required Judaism to save it from self-destruction. In a reversal of the earlier American Jewish attitude, Europe was no longer viewed as a place of confinement, but as a source of inspiration that would rescue American Judaism from what was felt to be its moribund state.

Late twentieth-century Jews were nagged by their awareness that America was a compelling enticement to abandon their religion and identity. Judaism, many feared, was no match for the American adventure, politically and culturally, a fear that had motivated a not insignificant number of Orthodox Jewish immigrants earlier in the century to return to Europe, believing their religious commitments were endangered. Others stayed, but never fully trusted the religious structures; the Kopycznitzer Rebbe, for example, would not eat meat because he did not trust the ritual slaughter in the United States. After World War II, however, the only guarantee for future Jewish survival in America, according to many, was either modern Orthodoxy or the social and religious ghettos of ultra-Orthodoxy, represented by Williamsburg, Lakewood, Monsey, and New Square, communities that fence its members from any contact with American popular culture and intellectual life (Farber and Waxman, *Jews in America*, 405). For some, even the modern Orthodoxy championed in Germany by Samson Raphael Hirsch and exemplified in the United States by Yeshiva University was too lenient in its claim that Torah and secular studies could coexist. Instead, East European ultra-Orthodoxy came to be viewed nostalgically, as the only authentic form of Jewish life, with American Jews doomed unless they followed its model or at least revived a taste of its traditions. The problem, however, was that East European Judaism became valorized at a time when it had ceased to exist. Imitating a defunct community gave rise to a sense of artificiality, as if Jewishness were being staged, rather than expressed.

Starting in the 1840s, European rabbis with liberal convictions began arriving in the United States and introduced formal programs of religious reform, together with theological justifications, to their congregations: Max Lilienthal arrived in 1845; Isaac M. Wise in 1846; David Einhorn, 1855; Samuel Adler, 1857; Bernard Felsenthal, 1858; and Samuel Hirsch, 1866. For some, such as Lilienthal, it was historical method that made belief in divine revelation of scripture untenable and that overturned the immutability of Jewish religious practice. For Wise, elevated religious sensibilities had preserved Judaism, until they were overtaken by "the multitude of thoughtless observances of rabbinical forms" (Philipson, *The Reform Movement*, 478). The "unmeaning practices" of Judaism had to be eliminated not only because they hindered "the heart and understanding," but because they stimulated public mockery. At the same time, Jews had an important role to play in the modern world: "they are still the chosen people, destined to become the Messiah of the nations of the earth," declared Felsenthal in 1858, but that goal could only be achieved by separating "the eternal and indestructible kernel of Judaism from its tattered encasings" (Philipson, *The Reform Movement*, 472, 471). After relinquishing the outdated ceremonies and beliefs of Judaism, wrote Hirsch in 1844, while still living in Germany, the Jew "may not be a mere spectator of the world of the modern age, but must give himself heart and soul to it" (Philipson, *The Reform Movement*, 487).

The goal, wrote David Einhorn in his inaugural sermon in Baltimore in 1855, was "the liberation of Judaism for ourselves and for our children, so as to prevent the estrangement from Judaism" (Philipson, *The Reform Movement*, 481). External authority and hierarchy, Einhorn insisted, ran contrary to religion, which had to be grounded in freedom of faith and personal autonomy. His views led him to condemn not only Orthodox Judaism, but moderate Reform positions, such as articulated by Wise, and also, in the name of freedom, to take a strong stance in opposition to slavery – in contrast to many of his Reform rabbinical colleagues.

The elements marking the first century of Reform Judaism in America are similar to those found in Protestant postmillenialism: the centrality of the inward and spiritual, rather than the outward and ceremonial; betterment of society; teachings of morality, rather than the miraculous or supernatural. At an 1869 conference of rabbis in Philadelphia, chaired by Einhorn, principles were adopted that articulated both a universal message of Judaism and an insistence on the centrality of inner devotion and sanctification. Unlike the Protestants, however, Reform Judaism had no fifth wheel of evangelical revivalism, in the aftermath of the Second Great Awakening, to distract its adherents. For most American Jews of the period, Jewish observance was understood primarily in terms of a rational statement of faith, principally in God and in a vaguely defined divine inspiration of the Bible, rather than the obligatory practice of an authoritative Jewish law. Few Jews practiced their religion at home in any Orthodox sense, and most were eventually willing to accept the reforms of synagogue worship that began to be introduced in mid-century. Nor was ethnicity as yet playing a role. Rather, Jewishness was expressed, primarily and often exclusively, by going to the synagogue. Isaac Mayer Wise declared, "We are Jews in the synagogue and Americans everywhere else" (Jick, *The Americanization of the Synagogue*, 173). The centerpiece of the service was the sermon, in imitation of Protestant worship, bolstered by the conviction that synagogue attendance, like church attendance, was above all an American activity, and practicing Judaism and being American were not antithetical. The sermon's topic, moreover, was generally an affirmation of American values and their centrality to Judaism.

The writings of nineteenth-century Reform rabbis energized Jewish thought in America. They failed to develop into formal theology, however, due in part to the absence of institutions of Jewish higher learning and of an educated audience of laity, as existed in Europe. In addition, the rabbis' arrival coincided with an era of Christian revival that militated against theology. American evangelicals were, by the nature of the movement, uninterested in formal theology or intellectual debate, and, as a result, created no intellectual structure for their movement – precisely at a time when German Protestants, by contrast, were reaching a pinnacle of sophisticated theological speculation. As Henry Steele Commager has commented, "during the nineteenth century and well into the twentieth, religion prospered while theology went slowly bankrupt" (Mead, *The Lively Experiment*, 55).

The absence of a sophisticated Christian theological tradition in the United States affected Jewish thought. There was no community with which Jewish thinkers could engage and hone the intellectual level of a formal Jewish theology. As a result, the publications of German Jewish thinkers in the United States were not received by a critically attuned academic audience, in contrast to Germany, where Jewish thinkers found a lively (if critical or even hostile) audience among their Christian counterparts.

It also meant that no formally articulated Christian theological anti-Judaism was being developed (apart from whatever was transmitted from abroad, or from earlier theological writings), in contrast to Germany, where Christian theological denigrations of Judaism grew sharply in the nineteenth century and contributed significantly to negative perceptions of Jews. For example, in listing the various factors that shaped negative views of Jews in America, the historian Jonathan Sarna does not even mention Christian theology among them, an absence inconceivable to a student of European Jewry. Various explanations have been offered for American religious tolerance of Judaism, ranging from Calvinist appreciation of the Old Testament (in contrast to Lutheran denigrations), to the deflection of Protestant hostility toward Catholicism, to Mead's comment that "there really was not much time in America for the traditionally antagonistic religious groups to learn to live together in peace. But there was space" (Mead, *The Lively Experiment*, 13). Or, as Perry Miller writes, more cynically, Protestants "did not [willingly] contribute to religious liberty, they stumbled into it, they were compelled into it, they accepted it at last because they had to, or because they saw its strategic value" (Mead, *The Lively Experiment*, 19).

American Christianity has been affected by the presence of Jews perhaps more deeply than by any other nationality. Indeed, the presence of a vibrant Judaism has challenged, if not forced, America to take seriously its own principles of religious tolerance and pluralism. Without Judaism, American pluralism may have been limited to Christian sectarianism, the tolerance of Catholics by Protestants, rather than genuine religious freedom. The Jews also found contradictions. Poverty coexisted with extraordinary riches, discrimination with political and legal rights and promises. While poverty and discrimination continued to plague Jews in America, they focused theologically on the promise of America. They skillfully emphasized an image of a Europe beset by intolerance and antisemitism that became crucial in bolstering their commitment to America. In dedicating a new synagogue in Charleston, South Carolina in 1841, Gustav Poznanski proclaimed, "This country is our Palestine, this city our Jerusalem, this house of God our temple" (Philipson, *The Reform Movement*, 467). The Other was not only Europe, but European Judaism, represented as oppressive, backward, and authoritarian. In fleeing Europe, the Jews in America could flee Judaism. Reform Rabbi Samuel Adler, just after arriving in New York in 1857, declared, "Behind us lies Egypt, the Middle Ages, before us the sea of Talmudic legalism ... The spirit indwelling here in the West, the spirit of freedom, is the newly-born Messiah" (Philipson, *The Reform Movement*, 483).

Religion, writes James Turner, "waxed fat and prosperous in the Gilded Age" (*Without God*, 226). The theological universalism of the era implied both a striving for Christian hegemony over the entire world, not just America, and also a belief in the "moral proprietorship over the nation" (Moorhead, *World Without End*, xvii). Such Christian claims inspired Jewish thinkers to assert competitively that not Christianity but Judaism held the rightful claim to a universal religious message. One of the most important figures in American Jewish thought, Kaufmann Kohler (1842–1926), became the spokesperson for liberal Judaism during that era, after arriving from

Germany in 1869. In defining Judaism as essentially an "eternal moral idea" rooted in subjective experience, Kohler declared, "The Bible is holy not because it is inspired, but because and insofar as it does still, inspire. It is not true because God has spoken the word, but because in the truth, the comfort, the hope, the final victory of justice which it holds out, you hear God speak to you in soul stirring strains" (Meyer, *Response to Modernity*, 273, n 25). Speaking in the voice of the liberal Protestantism of his day, Kohler's Judaism was optimistic, believing in the possibility of limitless social improvement, even while American Jews of German descent were disdainful of the massive influx of East European Jewish immigrants. The goal of the Reform movement's Pittsburgh Platform, formulated by Kohler, is "to solve, on the basis of justice and righteousness, the problems presented by the contrasts and evils of the present organization of society" (Meyer, *Response to Modernity*, 388), a formulation that encompassed the goals of the Protestant Social Gospel movement as well. Modernization, technology, and rationalism were embraced by Jews, as by Protestants, as tools of a progress toward mastery of the world that would ultimately create a kingdom of God on earth. Meanwhile, as Priscilla Wald will elaborate in the next chapter, Jewish immigrants in Hollywood began adopting blackface in an effort to distinguish themselves from African Americans in the eyes of white Christians and make certain that Jews would be classified in America as white.

For all its assertions of liberation and tackling social evils, the theology of the Reform movement was also a tactic of evading the central challenges to theology that arose during the Gilded Age. Biblical criticism, for example, questioned not only God's revelation of scripture, but the religious superiority of biblical teachings that was a tenet of Reform Judaism. Darwinism's challenge to the moral universe, through its assertion of a naturally occurring moral development, further undermined the Reformers' claim of Judaism's moral distinctiveness. Finally, the comparative study of religion demonstrated the untenability of any religion's claim to uniqueness. By placing the central elements of Judaism in a protected shell of subjectivity and inspiration that could not be subjected to critical analysis, Kohler and his colleagues side-stepped the challenges. Recognizing that his definition of Judaism came very close to those of other religions, Kohler insisted that what marked Judaism was its moderation. While the Hebrew Bible contained some problematic accounts of miracles, it had nothing in scope to rival those claimed by the New Testament. Judaism's emotional religiosity might also be reflected in Hinduism, but, Kohler argued, the Hindu's immoderate religiosity (in his definition) was due to the excessively hot weather of India, while Judaism's tempered religiosity was due to its emphasis on moral sobriety.

Defining Judaism too closely in line with America's own self-understanding led to peculiar conflict. Following their Puritan heritage, as Michael Kramer explained in the previous chapter, Americans had long championed themselves via the language of the Hebrew Bible as the New Israel, a chosen people. On one hand, such concepts were a golden opportunity for Jews to demonstrate their own suitability for America, for "trumpeting a symbolic definition of self which Jews and Americans shared" (Eisen, *The Chosen People*, 6). On the other hand, were that true, what was left of Jewish uniqueness, of the singularity of Judaism's religious message? Why be Jewish if simply being American represented the same message? Unintentionally, Reform Jewish thinkers carved a path out of Judaism. If Judaism were but one of many possible roads to moral excellence, there was no self-evident reason to remain within its fold. The religious thought of liberal Jewish thinkers, culminating in Kohler, implied that Jewish teachings were an elaborate metaphor, lovely and poetic, but without the singularity of truth claims.

If Judaism could not be identified by exclusive truths, Reform Jewish thinkers turned instead to the status of the Jew: Jewish chosenness was defined not as indicating a supernatural quality inherent in Jews, but as signaling an obligatory Jewish mission of spreading biblical monotheism to the pagan world. Even while touting the significance of the Jewish mission, however, Reform thinkers rejected Jewish nationalism, removing any hints of present-day or eschatological peoplehood from its liturgy and theology. Mordecai Kaplan, on the other hand, "intended to take the Jewish response to Emancipation represented by Kohler and carefully turn it on its head... While the Reform accepted chosenness in the form of mission and denied Jewish peoplehood, Kaplan did precisely the opposite. He accepted peoplehood and denied chosenness" (Eisen, *The Chosen People*, 2).

Kaplan represents a new stage in American Jewish thought, primarily because of his rootedness in social scientific, functionalist approaches to religion, rather than the philosophical and historical scholarship that formed the basis of nineteenth-century Jewish thought. Like earlier generations, however, Kaplan sought to shape a Judaism distinctive to America, making Jewish values accord with American; the story of the Exodus from Egypt, for example, functioned for Jews, Kaplan argued, analogous to the functioning of the Declaration of Independence in American public life (Scult, *Judaism Faces the Twentieth Century*, 252). For Kaplan, himself an immigrant from East Europe, America was not a melting pot, but an opportunity to live in a Jewish subcommunity, a "cultural nationhood" that embodied the values of American democracy, even to the extent that Americanism took precedence over Judaism. Indeed, one of the motivations for his rejection of Jewish chosenness was democracy, which Kaplan, following John Dewey, viewed as a religion that helped people achieve self-realization, his designation of salvation. For Kaplan, understanding Jewish peoplehood as the central pivot made Judaism the creation of Jewish civilization, its language and culture, and he viewed its various religious manifestations as the sancta (holy things) through which the Jews expressed their identity and which functioned, in turn, to preserve their identity through centuries of diaspora. God, too, is such a sanctum, not the supernatural deity of traditional Judaism. Following the Chicago school of theology that had translated Dewey's pragmatism into theological categories, Kaplan described God as the power that makes for salvation. Neither God nor religious practice had any dogmatic or philosophical significance, but a functionalist one. God does not intervene in history, in response to human pleas, but is part of nature and its processes, and functions as an expression of the highest human values. Kaplan writes, "Divinity is that aspect of the whole of nature, both in the universe and in man, which impels mankind to create a better and happier world and every individual to make the most of his own life" (*The Religion of Ethical Nationhood*, 75).

Kaplan's assertion that Torah is the product of Jewish civilization meant that revision of religious practice no longer threatened divine authority or wisdom. Indeed, Kaplan's elimination of the *Kol Nidre*, *Aleinu*, and other prayers, and his published revised prayerbook and Passover *Haggadah* were just some of his most notorious alterations. Viewing Judaism as the product of Jewish civilization gave an historical impetus to Kaplan's cultural Zionism without suggesting a negation of diasporic life, and the dynamic view of Jewish society contributed to Kaplan's endorsement of religious life as active, not passive. For Kaplan and a growing number of Jews in the 1920s, Zionism would not conflict with Jewish American loyalties, but revitalize them.

Kaplan's impact on Jewish American self-understanding was enormous. Indeed, his vision of Judaism was institutionalized, not only in the Reconstructionist movement based on his teachings that took shape in the 1960s, but in the massive building project ("edifice complex") of synagogues and Jewish community centers that occurred in the post-World War II era. Yet Kaplan's Judaism, as much as it met the needs of the second-generation of upwardly mobile Jewish immigrants moving to the suburbs, created the dilemmas that plagued the last decades of the twentieth century, which saw a disintegration of Jewish identity and commitment. Kaplan's emphasis on changing Jewish religious practice, doctrine, and liturgy in conformity with modernity was part of a larger fetish of change in American life during the first half of the twentieth century (Diggins, *The Promise of Pragmatism*, 34). The result, according to sociologist Samuel Heilman, was that the suburban synagogue became a perfect reflection of the ambivalence of American Jews...Looked at analytically, the synagogue could be either a propaedeutic [preparatory instruction] to assimilation (if it was like a church) or else a brake against it as an ethnic and religious enclave in which a separate cultural life was nurtured under the protective cover of religious freedom (if the synagogue was like the ghetto).

(Diggins, *The Promise of Pragmatism*, 30–31)

In the aftermath of World War II and the Holocaust, sociologist Will Herberg voiced the pessimistic conclusion that "Everything modern man has touched has turned to ashes; every achievement of his has been transformed before his eyes into a demonic force of destruction" (Goldy, *The Emergence of Jewish Theology*, 55). The only answer, for Herberg, was a return to religion. Initially, in *Judaism and Modern Man*, published in 1951, Herberg emphasized the existential significance of faith, regardless of the particular beliefs; Herberg himself went no further than asserting the existence of a universal spiritual force. His 1955 best-seller, *Protestant, Catholic, Jew*, is famous for placing all three religions on the same level, thus accomplishing what so many Jewish thinkers had striven to achieve. Herberg argued that religion, whichever one it may be, would offer consolation for the miseries and alienation of modernity, though he also warned that unbelief was less of a problem than the hypocrisy of secularized pieties that equated American patriotism with religion.

Herberg's warning was prescient. Increasingly after 1960, large numbers of American Jews rejected assimilation and turned instead to a revival of religious observance and belief. The problem was that most had lost their connection to Judaism. Assimilation had been not only outward, with many Jews abandoning their Jewishness as a result of secularism, materialism, religious indifference, and anti-intellectualism, but it was also vectored inward, bringing Christian values and customs into Judaism. The new intrusion of the Christian within Judaism helped make Jews strangers to themselves, and it was now not the Gentile world, but Judaism that had become foreign. Belief that they needed to restore the authenticity of Jewish identity and revive Judaism as a religion became the concern of the post-World War II generation, and for that they turned to the European Judaism that had been destroyed in the Holocaust, and in particular to East European religious traditions.

Two features distinguish the Jewish theology of the post-World War II era most radically from prior modern Jewish thought: first, a return to aspects of classical Judaism that modern Jews had denied, and, second, a radically changed attitude to Christianity and America. The religious thought that emerged in the last decades of the twentieth century sought a recovery of precisely those aspects of Judaism that had been vociferously rejected by the preceding generations of the modern period: Hasidic pietism, kabbalistic symbols and customs, and midrashic literature. One outcome of the recovery was also a turn away from assimilation and toward more traditional religious observance, which brought with it a new valorization of physical expressions of Jewishness and, concomitantly, of the Jewish body. A post-Holocaust disgust with the outcome of Western civilization led to a turn away from Christianity. Gone was the desire to win approbation from Christian theologians, as well as the desire to undermine Christian claims; Christianity was seen as essentially irrelevant to a theology of Judaism. Kaplan's concern to eliminate Jewish claims to chosenness as part of an effort to assuage antisemitism now seemed trivial and even absurd, in light of the massive antisemitism that produced Auschwitz. America, too, seemed less a source of sustenance for Jews than a needy, dispirited, and even corrupt society. Previous efforts to demonstrate that Judaism and American democracy held the same principles were abandoned. Now, both Christianity and America were viewed as in need of moral and spiritual cleansing and regeneration, which Judaism might provide.

The most important American Jewish thinker of the post-World War II era was Abraham Joshua Heschel, whose work exemplifies both trends of Jewish thought. Scion of a distinguished family of Hasidic Rebbes, he was born in Warsaw and earned a doctorate at the University of Berlin before arriving in the United States in 1940. His theology was built on categories drawn from midrashic, kabbalistic, and Hasidic ideas, and he radically changed the position of Judaism in relation to Christianity: now it was Christian theologians, both Catholic and Protestant, who drew inspiration from the Judaism he delineated. Central to Heschel's opus is the category he terms "divine pathos" (*The Prophets*, 221–231) based on the Kabbalistic idea of *zoreh gavoha*, divine need, that God is affected by human deeds. God is not the detached, unmoved mover of the Aristotelian tradition, but the most moved mover, deeply affected by human deeds. What characterizes the God of the Bible, Heschel argues, is passion, a constant involvement in human history, an emotional engagement with human beings: God suffers when human beings are hurt, so that when I hurt another person, I injure God. Heschel's understanding of divine pathos was appropriated by numerous Christian theologians, such as Jürgen Moltmann, despite the fact that theopaschism (the suffering of God) had been condemned as heretical by the early church. For Jews, divine pathos lent a new significance to the observance of religious commandments, as affecting God's inner life, marking a change in direction from the efforts of prior Jewish thinkers to modify Jewish observance or explain its significance in strictly rationalist terms. Heschel also shifted the weight of Judaism away from the abstract principles touted by Reform Jewish thinkers and toward an embodied Judaism that emphasized emotional and physical expression of religion.

Another shift marked by Heschel's work was his pungent critique of the Jewish community. Heschel argued that American Jews had focused excessively on survival of the Jews, building institutions, conducting demographic surveys, all of which distracted attention from the religious goals of Judaism. Instead, he wrote, the community should "create an atmosphere of learning, a climate of reverence... Our disease is loss of character and commitment, and the cure of our plight cannot be derived from charts and diagrams" (*Moral Grandeur*, 29). Judaism's true goal should not be assimilation into secular society, but "spiritual effrontery," subverting secular values and providing "a source of spiritual wealth, a source of meaning relevant to all peoples" (30, 31). He applied a similar critique to the United States, writing that its major problem was "the loss of reverence, the liquidation of enthusiasm for the attainment of moral and spiritual goals... How can adjustment to society be an inspiration to our youth, if that society persists in squandering the material resources of the world on luxuries in a world where more than a billion people go to bed hungry every night?" (30, 31).

Heschel's religious thought began not with structures of formal theology, but with phenomenological observations concerning religious life. He emphasized the uniqueness of religious experience and the futility of understanding it in the categories of philosophy or the social sciences. His work was praised by Reinhold Niebuhr as a "masterly analysis of faith" (Niebuhr, "Masterly Analysis of Faith"), and Heschel himself claimed that people of all religions have similar experiences of faith, even if their theologies stand in conflict. Beginning with descriptions of awe, wonder, and radical amazement, which he views as some of the initial paths to religious awareness, Heschel constructs his understanding of Judaism as an expression of the religiosity intrinsic to human nature.

A similar phenomenological starting-point characterizes the work of Heschel's contemporary, Orthodox Rabbi Joseph Soloveitchik. Born in Lithuania to a distinguished family of Talmudic scholars, Soloveitchik earned his doctorate at the University of Berlin under some of the same professors as Heschel, before immigrating to the United States in 1932. Like Heschel, Soloveitchik's work begins with the conviction that Judaism is best understood by describing the Orthodox Jew's religious life, rather than by reconciling its teachings with science, social science, or philosophy. Observance of Jewish law was not an experience of subjugation, as Reform Jews commonly held, but a means to express and soothe the yearnings and inner conflicts that beset the inner life, and to alleviate the sorrow and loneliness that mark human existence. Soloveitchik's published writings, though small in number, helped spark a renascence of modern Orthodoxy among American Jews. No longer was Orthodox observance to be viewed as an outmoded, confining lifestyle of East Europe with no relevance to the modern world, but as an authentic way to express the existential conflicts that define human life at its most profound level.

The fascination with East European religious life was further stimulated among American Jews by the enormously popular musical, *Fiddler on the Roof*, and by the writings of Elie Wiesel, which often include reworked folktales of Jewish life in the *shtetl* (the small Jewish villages of pre-World War II East Europe). Increasing numbers of American Jews, starting in the 1970s, turned to a neo-Hasidic or *haredi* life, and Chabad became a major force, especially on college campuses. The popularity of Yiddish theatre gave way to *klezmer* music, and by the 1960s, Shlomo Carlebach replaced Herberg and Kaplan as the inspiration of young Jewish college students. Given the extraordinary disparity between pious Orthodoxy and contemporary American society, the valorization of East European Judaism lent a performative quality to being a Jew. In a sense, too, the romance with East European Jewish life was a substitute for Zionism: an inspiring memory that would salvage the Jews from assimilation and disappearance.

Most historians agree that the 1967 Middle East war became an important moment for American Jews, who, emboldened by Israel's military victory, began to speak publicly about the Holocaust. Yet the victory celebrated in 1967 did not last long; by 1973, the vision of Israel as a beacon of political morality was shattered by the realities of the occupation, Palestinian demands for independence, and the devastating Yom Kippur war. Nor did the establishment of the State of Israel have a significant influence on Jewish religious thought in America. Zionism's vision of renewed Jewish physicality was similarly deflected by the American Jewish reappropriation, beginning in the 1970s, of East European clothing and religiosity with its aggressive insistence on the corporeal existence of the Jew as a religious figure. While Zionism played an important role within the American Jewish community, it was widely understood as a political commitment that did not conflict with American citizenship and loyalties, except for the relatively small number who made *aliyah* (emigrated to live in the State of Israel).

Jewish physicality loomed as a major question not only because of anti-semitism and Zionism, but, most important, the Holocaust, whose theological challenge was spelled out most forcefully by Richard Rubenstein, the first American-born and educated Jewish theologian. Rubenstein made the challenge central to both Jews and Christians, insisting that neither religion could continue with its traditional theological constructs of God as an actor in history after Auschwitz. A Protestant theologian in Germany, Heinrich Gruber, himself a survivor of a concentration camp, had told Rubenstein in 1961 that, on the basis of biblical teachings, the Holocaust must be understood as an act of divine punishment, with Germany serving merely as the instrument of God's wrath toward the Jews. From that encounter, Rubenstein concluded that classical theism was no longer tenable as a theological construct for Judaism or Christianity in light of the Holocaust, since it would inevitably lead to the conclusions drawn by Gruber. Jews could no longer believe in an omnipotent God who stood in covenantal relation with them, since such a deity would have sanctioned their murder. God, in the traditional theistic formulation, was dead, and the future of Jewish theology rested on whether a new way of conceiving religion could be developed.

While most Jews may have privately agreed with Rubenstein's articulation of the challenge posed by the Holocaust to traditional belief, his views were publicly condemned as destructive to Judaism. Yet they could not be refuted. One of the strongest responses to Rubenstein came from the rather simple, pietistic pleas of Emil Fackenheim not to grant Hitler a "posthumous victory" by abandoning Judaism. No modern thinker had so forcefully challenged the conventional assumptions of Judaism as Rubenstein, and none had so violated the niceties of the liberal theological formulation. Rubenstein recognized that the confidence of liberal Jewish thinkers of the nineteenth century, who spoke of Jews as "the Messiah of the nations," and the optimism of Kaplan's belief that eliminating Jewish chosenness would overcome antisemitism, could not be viable in face of the slaughter of six million Jews.

The collapse of Jewish optimism in light of the Middle East and the Holocaust coincided with broader trends in American culture. Despite the Eisenhower era's success in the 1950s in inserting God into civic discourse, Protestantism underwent a steady decline as a voice of moral authority and guidance in American culture and politics. America itself experienced the end of its "victory culture" with the war in Vietnam, and with it the confidence in its noble leadership in the world. For theologians, this translated into a loss of confidence in the certainty of religious teachings, and of the long-standing effort to synthesize theology with American political traditions. Protestantism no longer appealed to Jewish thinkers as the standard against which to measure their American success. It was now identified with traditions of anti-Judaism that had contributed to the Nazi genocide. The rise of a new subjectivity in the 1960s, with its emphasis on immediacy, confrontation, and personal witness, inspired Jews to reclaim the spiritual dimensions of East European Orthodox Judaism. Political movements, particularly the anti-war movement and Civil Rights, took on prophetic voices of challenge to the mainstream religious institutions, which were now accused of failing to abate the plagues of American society: racism, the Cold War, nuclear build-up, and the military adventures in Korea and Southeast Asia.

Political movements seem to have lit the spark for most young Jews, beginning with the effort to free Soviet Jewry in the early 1960s, and continuing with the Civil Rights movement, which provided a model to Jews on the Right and the Left for asserting Jewish ethnic identity. On the Right, Meir Kahane, founder of the Jewish Defense League, frequently invoked the Black Power movement as a example for Jews who, he argued, needed to make similarly assertive, physical claims to their rights in American society and, especially, to Israel's over the Palestinians'. Kahane marked the onset of a new kind of Judaism, one with little interest in the prophets or any other universal, liberal elements. Instead, nationhood rooted in shared religious law, rather than beliefs, defined Judaism and established its sharply defined boundaries. The messianic era was not to be awaited or hastened in a post-millenial sense, but established politically and religiously with a theocracy in a State of Israel whose borders were to set by biblical claims, not diplomatic negotiation. Jews should work for the rights of Jews, Kahane insisted, not on behalf of Blacks, Vietnamese, or other non-Jews. Kahane and the Orthodox Judaism of the 1950s and 1960s influenced large contingents of American Jews to join the Gush Emunim movement in Israel, which began establishing Jewish settlements in the West Bank in the mid-1970s and helped bring the right-wing Likud party to power in the Israeli government.

On the Left, it was several of Heschel's students who became major figures in the Jewish religious movements that took shape after his death in 1972. Arthur Green founded the Havurah movement, Michael Lerner established *Tikkun* magazine, and Arthur Waskow, along with Zalman Schachter-Shalomi, organized the Jewish Renewal movement. All shared Heschel's critique of American Judaism, and of Jews who set aside their religion in favor of accommodating secular, materialist values. Lerner, in particular, put forward a platform critical of the Americanization of Judaism for imitating the dominant ethos of post-World War II materialist greed, and of the American government for failing to temper its power with compassion for the poor and powerless. The assimilation that characterized most of American Jewish life resulted, Lerner argued, in ignoring Judaism's subversive elements that demand major changes in the social, economic, and political reality. Jews, according to Lerner, had put aside those aspects of their religion that might bring them into conflict with the dominant society.

While Rubenstein was confronting the foundations of Jewish theology from the perspective of the Holocaust, and Heschel was issuing his critique of American Jewish life, women were subjecting both Jewish theology and practice to a devastating critique of their sexism. Women's exclusion from much of Jewish learning and religious life was clear, but interpretations of the causes of their subordination differed, as did proposed solutions. For some feminists, such as Blu Greenberg, sexism was an accretion of history, while for others, such as Judith Plaskow, it was intrinsic to Jewish theology. Other differences include whether feminism's goals should be ending different roles for men and women, or whether sex-role differences should be acceptable as long as they are not hierarchical; whether women should be granted full inclusion in all aspects of Jewish life now limited to men, or whether Judaism itself should be radically transformed.

While the main thrust of American Judaism had long been to modify or eliminate large elements of Jewish observance, most Jewish feminists have sought to create new rituals and to find halakhic justifications for women to observe aspects of Judaism from which they were exempt. The liberation from patriarchy would be achieved not by minimizing women's involvement in Judaism, but by increasing it – but on their own terms. New rituals include celebrating Rosh Hodesh, the new moon, as a women's holiday; placing an orange on the *seder* plate in recognition of the marginalization of lesbians and gay men; and creating blessings for occasions in women's lives, such as childbirth and menstruation. More common are the assumption by women of rituals previously limited to men, such as wearing phylacteries (small leather boxes containing verses of Scipture that are worn by Jewish men during morning worship), prayer shawl, and head covering during prayer.

Feminists have also developed new interpretations of biblical and rabbinic texts. For example, Drorah Setel has argued that underlying the teachings of the prophet Hosea is an ideology of pornography that identifies the sinning Israel with Gomer, his adulterous wife. Others have looked for positive feminine imagery in Jewish literature, particularly the figure in kabbalistic literature of the *Shekhinah*, the feminine aspect of God. The emphasis on study of rabbinic texts as empowering women to understand the legal arguments behind their subordination has also resulted in a new position within the Orthodox community for women who act as *halakhic* (Jewish legal) advisors to other women, particularly in regard to Jewish divorce law and the laws of menstrual impurity. The ordination of women rabbis in non-Orthodox Judaism has raised the question of whether women rabbis should function in the same way as their male counterparts, or whether they should create a new kind of rabbinic role.

Jewish feminism is very much an American phenomenon, exported to Jewish communities in other countries, and in many ways is a development that only could have occurred in the United States. Clearly, it grows out of the broader feminist movement and out of political movements for radical social change associated with the struggle against racism. In addition, the absence of strong traditions of anti-Judaism in America permits the severe feminist critique of Judaism's sexism that would be inhibited in European countries. Finally, the religious pluralism that is fostered in the United States, compared to Europe and Israel, generally welcomes the creation of new feminist religious practices as a sign of great engagement in Judaism, rather than as an abdication of tradition.

In the decades following World War II, a century after Jewish thought first took root in America, major transformations occurred. The optimism Jews felt about America dissipated after Hiroshima, the wars in Korea and Vietnam, and the domestic racist violence of the Civil Rights era. Similarly, the State of Israel gradually came to be seen less as a source of political redemption than as a place of civil turmoil and incessant threats of war. The Jewish celebration of America as a site of liberation from Europe also shifted, as European Jewishness, particularly East European religious forms, came to be valorized as the source of authentic Jewish identity. Given that Europe's Jewish communities had been destroyed by the Nazis, that valorization had the problematic consequence of being rooted in an imaginative reconstruction, rather than a living reality. The earlier Jewish American effort to liberalize religious practice also reversed itself, as American Jews in the latter decades of the twentieth century reclaimed traditional Judaism, even as dramatically increasing numbers of Jews intermarried.

The reliance of American Judaism on European immigrants for its leaders for the past two hundred years has tended to undermine the construction of an authentic Jewish tradition on American soil. Too often, the authenticity of Judaism was linked to its European expressions, with American Jews viewed as its pale imitators. America's tradition of pluralism has permitted the flourishing of a uniquely multiform Judaism, and the openness of America's multicultural society has encouraged a mixture of identities. Yet the cultural boundaries in America are so porous that Jewishness has become a free-floating signifier open to appropriation by non-Jews as well. The problematic side of American openness is that the high rates of intermarriage, combined with the wider cultural appreciation (and, often, appropriation) of Jewishness, has led to the dissolution of boundaries between Jew and non-Jew. The result is a mixture of the Jewish with the Gentile that sometimes blurs the distinction between them, and obfuscates the nature of Jewish identity. Just as Jews appropriated "blackface" in the early part of the twentieth century to assimilate into American society and assure their position as whites, American Jews toward the end of the century appropriated a "Jewface," a kind of "imitatio Iudei," an imitation of the Jewish, an impersonation of European Judaism in the absence of an inner sense of American Jewish authenticity.

NOTE

My thanks to several colleagues who gave me valuable suggestions and criticisms: Yaakov Ariel, Darryl Caterine, Richard Cogley, Karla Goldman, Susan Gubar, Martha Lannoch, Alan Levenson, Marilyn Reizbaum, and, especially, my close friend and colleague, the late Susanne Zantop.

REFERENCES AND SUGGESTED FURTHER READINGS

Cohen, Elliot, "An Act of Affirmation: Editorial Statement." *Commentary* 1 (November, 1945–June, 1946): 2.

Diggins, John Patrick. *The Promise of Pragmatism: Modernism and the Crisis of Knowledge and Authority*. Chicago: University of Chicago Press, 1994.

Diner, Hasia. *A Time for Gathering: The Second Migration, 1820–1880*. Baltimore: Johns Hopkins University Press, 1992.

Eisen, Arnold M. *The Chosen People in America: A Study in Jewish Religious Ideology*. Bloomington: Indiana University Press, 1983.

Fackenheim, Emil L. *God's Presence in History: Jewish Affirmations and Philosophical Reflections*. New York: Harper, 1972.

Farber, Roberta Rosenberg and Chaim I. Waxman, eds. *Jews in America: A Contemporary Reader*. Hanover, NH: University Press of New England, 1999.

Goldy, Robert G. *The Emergence of Jewish Theology in America*. Bloomington: Indiana University Press, 1990.

Heilman, Samuel C. *Portrait of American Jews: The Last Half of the 20th Century*. Seattle and London: University of Washington Press, 1995.

Heschel, Abraham J. *The Prophets*. New York: Harper and Row, 1962.

    Moral Grandeur and Spiritual Audacity: Essays. Ed. Susannah Heschel. New York: Farrar, Straus and Giroux, 1996.

Heschel, Susannah, ed. *On Being a Jewish Feminist*. New York: Schocken Books, 1983.

Jick, Leon. *The Americanization of the Synagogue, 1820–1870*. Hanover, NH: University Press of New England, 1992.

Kaplan, Mordecai M. *Judaism as Civilization: Toward a Reconstruction of American-Jewish Life*. New York: Macmillan, 1934.

    Not So Random Thoughts. New York: Reconstructionist Press, 1966.

    The Religion of Ethical Nationhood: Judaism's Contribution to World Peace. New York: Doubleday, 1970.

Kohler, Kaufmann. *Hebrew Union College and Other Addresses*. Cincinnati: Ark Publishing Co., 1916.

Marty, Martin. *Righteous Empire: The Protestant Experience in America*. New York: Dial Press, 1970.

Mead, Sidney. *The Lively Experiment: The Shaping of Christianity in America*. New York: Harper and Row, 1963.

Melville, Herman. *Redburn, White Jacket, Moby Dick*. Ed. G. Thomas Tanselle, New York: Library of America, 1983.

Meyer, Michael. *Response to Modernity: A History of the Reform Movement in Judaism*. New York: Oxford University Press, 1988.

Moorhead, James H. *World Without End: Mainstream Protestant Visions of the Last Things*. Bloomington, IN: Indiana University Press, 1999.

Niebuhr, Reinhold. "Masterly Analysis of Faith." *New York Herald Tribune Book Review*, April 1, 1951.

Philipson, David. *The Reform Movement in Judaism*. New York: Macmillan, 1907.

Rubenstein, Richard L. *After Auschwitz: Radical Theology and Contemporary Judaism*. Indianapolis, IN: Bobbs Merrill, 1966.

Sarna, Jonathan D. "American Anti-Semitism." In *History and Hate: The Dimensions of Anti-Semitism*. Ed. David Berger. Philadelphia: Jewish Publication Society, 1986.

"Converts to Zionism in the American Reform Movement." *Zionism and Religion*. Eds. Shmuel Almog, Jehuda Reinharz, and Anita Shapira. Hanover, NH and London: Brandeis University Press, 1998.

Scult, Mel. *Judaism Faces the Twentieth Century: A Biography of Mordecai M. Kaplan*. Detroit: Wayne State University Press, 1993.

Soloveitchik, Joseph B. *Halakhic Man*. Trans. Lawrence Kaplan. Philadelphia: Jewish Publication Society, 1983.

The Lonely Man of Faith (1965). New York: Doubleday, 1992.

Turner, James. *Without God, Without Creed: The Origins of Unbelief in America*. Baltimore: Johns Hopkins University Press, 1985.

3

PRISCILLA WALD

Of crucibles and grandfathers: the East European immigrants

"America is God's Crucible," explains Russian Jewish immigrant David Quixano, protagonist of Israel Zangwill's 1908 play, *The Melting-Pot*, "... where all the races of Europe are melting and re-forming" (37). As he tells his Uncle Mendel, "the real American has not yet arrived. He is only in the Crucible ... he will be the fusion of all races, the coming superman" (37–38). At the play's first performance at Washington's Columbia Theatre, Theodore Roosevelt listened approvingly to David's impassioned speech. The proper course for the immigrant was not in question for Roosevelt, who, a decade and a half prior to the performance, had cautioned the readership of *The Forum* that "the man who does not become Americanized nevertheless fails to remain a European, and becomes nothing at all" ("True Americanism," 26). At the same time, the President did not extend his welcome indiscriminately, finding it "urgently necessary" both "to keep out laborers who tend to depress the labor market, and to keep out races which do not assimilate readily with our own" (27). While popular opinion of the time might well have put David Quixano in both categories, Roosevelt wholeheartedly approved the explicit message of the British Jewish writer's play.

From the political platform to the popular press, from the pens of reformers and sociologists, Americanization – the concept and its terms – was among the most hotly debated topics of the first half of the twentieth century. In a nation in which the foreign-born rose from 16.5 percent of the population in 1880 to 21.5 percent in 1920, such debates are not surprising (Higham, *Send These to Me*, 15). For those who sought to restrict immigration, eugenics arguments were almost as frequent as economic ones; they feared that the South and East European immigrants who dominated the influx in the late nineteenth and early twentieth centuries would dilute both the labor pool and the bloodlines. But for those social reformers and settlement workers who viewed immigration as an ethical obligation, the immigrants could become productive, even invigorating, members of society if they were efficiently and thoroughly Americanized – assimilated, that is, into the values and spirit of America. About what those values were and about how to transmit them, however, there was disagreement.

The literature of East European Jewish immigrants from this period registers both the uncertainties of the dominant culture and their own ambivalent responses to assimilation. Zangwill captures it in the very play that popularized the term and modeled the paradigm of "the melting-pot," a play authored, ironically, by a Zionist who himself never immigrated to the US. Neither Roosevelt nor many subsequent readers and critics appear to have noticed the complexities of the concept that the play made a by-word. The play centers on the romance between David and Vera Revendal, a settlement worker of Russian noble birth. David has come to New York to live with Mendel and Mendel's mother after witnessing the murder of his family, and being wounded himself, in a notorious pogrom in Kishnev. He meets Vera when she hears him play his violin; she is enchanted both by his music and by the symphony that he is composing. Passionate about America, he dreams of a symphony that will express the spirit of the crucible and capture "the fusion of all races" that is, to him, the power and beauty of America.

Zangwill humorously, but movingly, depicts immigrant patterns in his portrait of the three generations living in Mendel's household. The play opens with their frustrated Irish Catholic servant Kathleen's complaining to Mendel about the difficulty of learning the family's ways when their religious observances are so diverse: " 'To-night being yer Sabbath, you'll be blowing out yer bedroom candle, though ye won't light it; Mr. David'll light his and blow it out too; and the mishtress won't even touch the candleshtick. There's three religions in this house, not wan' " (*The Melting-Pot*, 7). Kathleen colorfully underscores a familiar pattern of immigration, in which youth is most receptive to the new culture and the older generations cling ever more tightly to their traditions. David, of whom Mendel says "a sunbeam took human shape when he was born" (42), accomplishes in life what he envisions for his music. He talks Kathleen so thoroughly out of her resolution never to "take service again with haythen Jews" (4) that she not only masters the kashrut laws, but actually begins to refer to "we Jews." And to the initially antisemitic Vera, he proves irresistible.

Yet David is beset by fits of melancholy, bordering on madness, whenever he is reminded of Kishinev. Most haunting to him is the face of the man who oversaw the pogrom and to whom he refers as "the butcher." The crisis of the play comes when Vera's estranged father arrives in New York to reconcile with his daughter and prevent her impending wedding to a Jew (in anticipation of which Mendel has turned David out of his house). Vera persuades her father at least to meet David, but their encounter dissolves into calamity when a horrified David recognizes in the face of his future father-in-law the butcher of Kishinev. Renouncing his betrothal, he returns to his family, but gloom has replaced the sunbeam, and his vision of America falters in his encounter with his past. The vision is strong, however, and David recalls it when his symphony is performed at Vera's settlement house. While it meets with a mixed reception among critics, the people – David's cherished representatives of democracy – understand and love it, as does the famous conductor, Herr Pappelmeister, himself a German immigrant, who was responsible for its production. On the roof of the settlement house, David wonders how he could have written the symphony and be himself so tied to his past. He asks Vera to return to him, to which she expresses her concern, in the very terms with which he had reviled her, that she will ever invoke the memory of Kishinev. A kiss, he insists, will make him forget, and she agrees to kiss him "as we Russians kiss at Easter – three kisses of peace," kisses that the stage directions describe "as in ritual solemnity" (198). For David, the irony of her choice confirms his assurance that he is ready to forget the past: "Easter was the date of the massacre – see I am at peace" (198). Yet his words register his remembering. The stage directions suggest that they have made a ritual (designed to commemorate) precisely where they intended an erasure. Even Vera is skeptical, responding to David's declaration that he is at peace with the words, "God grant it endure!" (198).

On the surface, the play confirms the vision of America – and the paradigm of assimilation – articulated by Roosevelt, and indeed he sent enthusiastic congratulations to its author. Yet Vera's skepticism is infectious; the stage directions troubling. Violence is implicit in his very metaphors – of "the great Melting-Pot...roaring and bubbling...stirring and...seething" and "the great Alchemist melt[ing] and fus[ing the immigrants] with his purging flame!" (198–199). Violence lingers in the "grinding" of the crucible, like the memory David cannot fully repress. The grinding itself marks both the compulsion to forget and the impossibility of doing so.

That impossibility runs thematically through East European Jewish immigrant literature. David's memories surface not only with any mention of Kishinev, but with each twinge of the scar that a Russian bullet left in his shoulder (the violinist's left shoulder) as a physical reminder of the massacre. "Ah, Vera," he proclaims as they reconcile, "What is the glory of Rome and Jerusalem where all nations and races come to worship and look back, compared with the glory of America, where all races and nations come to labour and look forward!" (199). Yet such denial of the past merely begs for its uncanny return, as is evident in the work of David Quixano's real-life compatriots.

Mary Antin, for example, like David, proclaims her own sea change, the death of an earlier, Russian-Jewish, self and her remaking as an American, in the introduction to her well-known celebration of assimilation, *The Promised Land*: "I am just as much out of the way as if I were dead," she writes, "for I am absolutely other than the person whose story I have to tell" (xxii). Yet her celebration rests on a wish, which also could be David's:

> I long to forget. I think I have thoroughly assimilated my past – I have done its bidding – I want now to be of to-day. It is painful to be consciously of two worlds. The Wandering Jew in me seeks forgetfulness. I am not afraid to live on and on, if only I do not have to remember too much.   (xxii)

Precisely in her insistence on her complete remaking she unleashes the Wandering Jew who haunts the very processes of her Americanization, the uncanny reminder of the impossibility of her obituary for an earlier self who is neither "dead," nor even "absolutely other." The expression of longing countermands the exuberant claims of complete Americanization that she makes throughout the work. She is no more "thoroughly assimilated" than is her past.

The denial of the past called for by David Quixano and Mary Antin meant a renunciation of the early affiliations that, however painful, were still the stuff of childhood memory. Nostalgia finds expression in the work of East European Jews often indirectly, emerging in an isolated memory, or an unexpectedly lavish description, as Antin offers of the taste of cherries from her girlhood that she has been unable to replicate since her arrival in America. It could lead variously to the reclaiming of traditions long abandoned and other times to the alienation attendant upon the failure to do so. A sense of loss, an experience typically described in the language of melancholy, infuses the experience of assimilation.

Antin's general ambivalence did not go unremarked even in her own time. Horace Kallen, a Jewish immigrant who popularized the term "cultural pluralism," included her among a group of foreign-born celebrants of assimilation whom he describes as "more excessively and self-consciously American than the Americans." Pointing to the false notes of the work, he complains that they "protest too much, they are too self-conscious and self-centered, their 'Americanization' appears too much like an achievement, a *tour de force*, too little like a growth." In their work "one senses, underneath the excellent writing, a dualism and the strain to overcome it" ("Democracy Versus the Melting-Pot," 193). Significantly, for Kallen, the dualism makes clear a similar dualism, with an even stronger strain to overcome it, in US culture. Not surprisingly, the strain, which finds the most obvious expressions in nativist movements such as the Know-Nothing party of the 1850s and the patriotic societies formed in the late nineteenth century, is most apparent during periods of increased immigration. The ambivalence in the immigrants' work, in other words, resonates with an analogous ambivalence in US culture; both reflect the uncertainty of exactly what "American" means and exactly what is supposed to happen in the process of Americanization.

In attempting to understand that process, the immigrant writers have apparently thrown into relief that latent uncertainty. Kallen cites a letter in which one of his most influential professors describes the recent immigration as " 'a conquest so complete that the very name of us means something not ourselves...I feel as I should think an Indian might feel in the face of ourselves that were' " (194). For Kallen's interlocutor, the literary critic and Harvard professor Barrett Wendell, immigration does violence to the culture and meaning of "America." But, as Kallen recognizes and the analogy to the Indian suggests, the violence inheres in the instability of the term, exacerbated, perhaps, but not introduced by the massive influx of immigrants of the period.

Kallen finds in Wendell's letter evidence that the new immigrants are disturbing in large part because they remind native-born white Americans that they, too, were once immigrants, that "a hyphen attaches, in things of the Spirit, also to the 'pure' English American" (217). The immigrants embody the displacement – and the attendant sense of loss – intrinsic to a settler colony. For him "*natio* is what underlies the vehemence of the 'Americanized' and the spiritual and political unrest of the Americans" (194). *Natio* is inseparable from, and carries the emotional impact of, *natal* as much as *nation*. The question of ethnic loyalty, as he understands it, cannot be divorced from geographic location and family. All the childhood memories that comprise adult selves are inextricably bound up with the location and situation in which they were raised. "The fact is," observes Kallen,

> that similarity of class rests upon no inevitable external condition, while similarity of nationality is inevitably intrinsic. Hence the poor of two different peoples tend to be less like-minded than the poor and the rich of the same peoples...Behind [the immigrant] in time and tremendously in him in quality are his ancestors; around him in space are his relatives and kin, looking back with him to a remoter common ancestry. In all these he lives and has his being. They constitute his, literally, *natio*...whatever else he changes, he cannot change his grandfather. (194)

A nation of settlers, Kallen's US sees its own history in the immigrant experience. Generations seem to melt away as *natio* is troubled both by the memories the immigrants evoke and the changes they threaten. Thus Kallen explains the logic of US nationalism as well as the unacknowledged ambivalence that he identifies in the work of immigrant writers like Antin, who championed a fully assimilative Americanization.

Kallen finds nationalism inseparable from the experience of family; the emotional bonds are stronger than class affiliations. For assimilationists like Roosevelt who believed that preserving ethnic affiliations against the ideology of the melting-pot threatened US democracy, Kallen's cultural pluralism was anathema. Yet against the background of class struggle and revolution in Russia, which he implicitly summoned in his comparison of class and ethnic affiliation, Kallen subtly offered cultural pluralism as a conservative ideology, one certainly compatible with US democracy. The task for the US, according to Kallen, is first to recognize that "the older America, whose voice and whose spirit was New England, is gone beyond recall," and second, to decide what will take its place. "At the present time there is no dominant American mind," he observes,

> Our spirit is inarticulate, not a voice, but a chorus of many voices each singing rather a different tune. How to get order out of this cacophony is the question for all those who are concerned about those things which alone justify wealth and power, concerned about justice, the arts, literature, philosophy, science. What must, what *shall* this cacophony become – a unison or a harmony?
>
> (217)

The choice as Kallen imagines it involves the exact nature of the vision of the US according to which strategies of assimilation would be fashioned. His powerful sense of *natio* as a force in ontological experience – that "Jews or Poles or Anglo-Saxons, in order to cease being Jews or Poles or Anglo-Saxons, would have to cease to be" (220) – yields harmony as the only viable choice. Although this influential essay has been read as imagining an alternative to assimilation, in fact it argues for a particular model of cultural integration, one based on the plural but harmonic coexistence of group affiliations. It was one of many models advanced in the first quarter of the twentieth century, and implicit in each was a vision of native and immigrant cultures that perpetuated and extended, as it reflected, the phantasms through which groups came to know each other.

East European Jewish immigrants seemed particularly eager to share their experiences with each other and with the American public more broadly. They wrote essays, tracts and short stories, novels, plays, poetry, and autobiographies, some of which they published in English, many of which filled the pages of the Yiddish publications that served the emigrant Jewish community. Registered in this work is the difficulty of telling these stories against the images of the Jewish ghetto and other stereotypes recorded variously in the work of reformers, journalists and, somewhat later, sociologists. Among the most influential of those images was Jacob Riis' depiction of "Jewtown" in his acclaimed 1890 work, *How the Other Half Lives: Studies Among the Tenements of New York.* "Typhus and small-pox are bred here," he intones, and "only the demand of religious custom has power to make [Jewish] parents clean up at stated intervals" (89, 91). Their aversion to hygiene is curiously coupled with their avariciousness in Riis' account. "Thrift is the watchword of Jewtown, as of its people the world over. Money is their God. Life itself is of little value compared with even the leanest bank account. In no other spot does life wear so intensely bald and materialistic an aspect as in Ludlow Street" (86). And the Jewish facility for mathematics that he believes he has identified he attributes to their "instinct of dollars and cents" (91).

Not all the depictions were unfavorable. Although it did not circulate widely, journalist Hutchins Hapgood's sentimental portrait of Jewish life in *The Spirit of the Ghetto: Studies of the Jewish Quarter of New York* (1902) was familiar to the writers and sociologists who wrote about the ghetto. Perhaps with Riis' work in mind, Hapgood begins his study by noting that "the Jewish quarter of New York is generally supposed to be a place of poverty, dirt, ignorance and immorality – the seat of the sweatshop, the tenement house, where 'red-lights' sparkle at night, where people are queer and repulsive" (5). By contrast, Hapgood was motivated to write about "Yiddish New York" because of "the charm [he] felt in men and things there" (5). The "ghetto" of Hapgood's experience is "picturesque," and he writes in the hope that this quality will be retained throughout the Americanizing process. "The ideal situation" for a "young Jew," he writes, "would be that where he could become an integral part of American life without losing the seriousness of nature developed by Hebraic tradition and education" (34). Less pernicious than Riis' tenement, Hapgood's romanticized Jewish ghetto nonetheless set in place terms that affected the perception, hence the experience, both of its denizens and of other cultural observers. While the poverty and disease of Riis' slums were not lost on the school of urban sociologists that developed at the University of Chicago in the early decades of the twentieth century, Hapgood's "ghetto" was more central to their writings on assimilation.

Throughout his prolific and influential career, University of Chicago sociologist Robert E. Park struggled to find a cogent definition of "assimilation." His interest in the social cohesion of groups made it a logical term of inquiry. In a work he co-authored with his colleague Ernest W. Burgess in 1921, he described assimilation as "a process of interpenetration and fusion in which persons and groups acquire the memories, sentiments, and attitudes of other persons or groups, and, by sharing their experience and history, are incorporated with them in a common cultural life" (*Introduction to the Science of Sociology*, 735). The impact of the assimilated group on the dominant culture was a national topic of particular concern. Assimilation posed a paradox for many cultural observers in the US: insufficient assimilation could produce the ethnic enclaves that they found corrosive of national solidarity, yet the "interpenetration and fusion" could mean the nation's transformation into something unfamiliar, expressed by Barrett Wendell as the fear that the immigrants make "the very name of us mean something not ourselves." Park turned to the Jews and their quarters for a solution. More than half a decade after he defined assimilation in this way, Park contended that "the relation of the ghetto Jew to the larger community in which he lived" was "symbiotic rather than social" ("Human Migration," 141). While "interpenetration and fusion" suggests a mutual change in being, organisms in a "symbiotic" relationship retain their integrity. Even the "emancipated Jew" of Park's formulation remains apart, "historically and typically the marginal man, the first cosmopolite and citizen of the world. He is, par excellence, the 'stranger' . . . who ranges widely, and lives preferably in a hotel" ("Human Migration," 141).

From this image of the Jew, Park could construct a Jewish enclave in symbiotic relationship with the larger community, its integrity reflecting both its components' ostensible divestiture from their national pasts and their simultaneous segregation from and incorporation into their adopted nation. This notion of assimilation reflected neither the fully integrative vision of the melting-pot, nor the mutually transforming harmonic entities of cultural pluralism. Rather, it reflected the spatial logic of the Indian reservation, itself modeled on the nineteenth-century idea of the asylum, in which the socially inassimilable were set apart in order to be rehabilitated and reintegrated (Findlay, "An Elusive Institution"). The idea in the nineteenth century was that such spaces would be temporary. By the twentieth century, they had come to reflect not a transitional space on the way to assimilation into the mainstream, but a liminal space that marked the denizens' desire to remain segregated. The sociologists made the East European Jews of "Yiddish New York" paradigmatic of this adjusted model of assimilation. The expansion of the term "ghetto," originally denoting a Jewish enclave, into a synonym for tenement resulted from the work of Park and his associates and attests to the representative status they conferred upon the Jews. Park's German Jewish student Louis Wirth, in his landmark work *The Ghetto*, contended that the Jews typically chose to remain in such ethnic enclaves (Wald, "Geographics").

So powerful were all of these images that they shaped the immigrants' experiences of themselves and their surroundings. Evident in their literature are the authors' efforts to refute Riis' depictions, but those of Park and Wirth were more complicated. Wirth's Yiddish New York was nostalgic and almost as picturesque as Hapgood's, offering an antidote to Riis' filthy and godless tenement. And most powerfully, this alternative model of assimilation seemed to reflect the immigrants' own ambivalent relationship to their surroundings. Yet the ghetto of Park and Wirth had a cohesiveness that the immigrants sought at least to complicate if not fully repudiate in their literature. For, implicit in that cohesiveness they still discerned the injunction to forget.

Writing in 1896, nearly two decades in anticipation of Park's earliest efforts to articulate a theory of assimilation, the Lithuanian immigrant socialist writer and editor Abraham Cahan penned his own analysis of assimilation in the Jewish ghetto in his novella *Yekl: A Tale of the New York Ghetto*. Offering an extensive description of the variety of nationalities, occupations, classes, and reasons for emigration found in the Jewish ghetto, he underscores "the whimsical metamorphoses" to which they have all been subjected "by the vicissitudes of life in this their Promised Land..." The only common experience in this description is the experience of transformation: "Jews born to plenty" have been "delivered up to the clutches of penury" while "Jews reared in the straits of need... have here risen to prosperity"; "good people" are "degraded in the struggle for success amid an unwonted environment" while "moral outcasts" are "lifted from the mire, purified, and imbued with self-respect" (14). While Riis depicts the degradation of tenement life and moral turpitude of the Jews, Cahan captures the poignancy of its denizens' experience in an environment that they do not control. Those overwhelmed by their surroundings – the "good people... degraded," the "educated men and women with their intellectual polish tarnished in the inclement weather of adversity" (14) – have his sympathy. With the passive construction, his description suggests that responsibility for the "whimsical metamorphoses" – the successes and failures alike – is not fully in human hands.

The ghetto of Cahan's description is a melting-pot of sorts: "people with all sorts of antecedents, tastes, habits, inclinations, and speaking all sorts of subdialects of the same jargon, thrown pellmell into one social caldron – a human hodgepodge with its component parts changed but not yet fused into one homogeneous whole" (14). Cahan's social caldron is not quite Zangwill's melting-pot. The alchemy is incomplete. Instead, Cahan underscores the experience of dislocation, of being severed from a defining past. The resulting instability constitutes the common experience – even perhaps bond – of the inhabitants of Yiddish New York. For the Chicago sociologists, the instability is preparatory to Americanization. In Cahan's description, however, the uncertainty of what they will become remains, as they are "not yet fused into one homogeneous whole." Nowhere does he suggest that Americanization per se is attendant upon the whimsical metamorphoses The plot of *Yekl* revolves around the struggle of the eponymous protagonist to become a "*regely* Yankee" (Cahan, *The Rise of David Levinsky*, 8. But his vision of what that means is filtered comically, even pathetically, through the prism of Yiddish New York. The ominous conclusion of the story confirms that he will not find what he is looking for in his impending marriage to a woman for whom he has left his "greenhorn" wife. The new wife's longer time in New York has imparted to her the air of worldliness – or, of Americanness – at least in the eyes of Yekl (or Jake, as he likes to be called). But the end of the novella finds him as trapped, and as far from his goal, as he has ever been.

In his marriage not to an American but to a more Americanized Jew, Yekl/Jake lives the pattern of assimilation as Cahan understands it. Americanization does not mean complete incorporation into the "homogeneous whole" of America. The process does entail a divestiture from their particular pasts, but they are not assimilated into the larger culture as individuals. Rather, the "Lithuanian Jews, Volhynian Jews, south Russian Jews, Bessarabian Jews" (14) of Cahan's ghetto are Americanized by becoming "American Jews" – or, in more common parlance, "Jewish Americans." Thus Cahan captures (and anticipates) the nuances of the sociologists' concept. Assimilation, for the sociologists, describes an inevitable social process. For Cahan, by contrast, it is a cultural dynamic. Mainstream culture, in his formulation, imagines an identity into which Jewish immigrants are socialized. Cahan, like many immigrant authors of the period, is interested both in describing that process and in exploring its psychological effects on immigrants.

The vague unhappiness of many of the apparently successful protagonists in the literature of these authors can be traced to the failure to appreciate the distinction that Cahan describes. For characters like Cahan's David Levinsky (*The Rise of David Levinsky* [1917]) and Anzia Yezierska's Sonya Vrunsky (*Salome of the Tenements* [1923]), the success that they are taught to want comes at a price that they cannot afford. The plot of these narratives is familiar from the story of any crossing of social boundaries – class, race, even region. William Dean Howells' Silas Lapham (*The Rise of Silas Lapham*), Levinsky's literary progenitor, finds the social world into which his financial success propels him an unfriendly and unethical place. His temporary adoption of its values nearly costs him his wife and family. If the high society in which Silas Lapham finds himself seems foreign, that into which the Jewish immigrant Sonya Vrunsky marries is doubly so. For the immigrant protagonist, the return home is complicated by the fact that "home" is itself an uncertainty, and unfamiliarity is already the condition of existence. Where Silas Lapham can choose to return home, the immigrant protagonists typically find their return complicated by that unfamiliarity.

Of course, responses to the reversals in fortune and the opportunities offered by the New World register the authors' differing circumstances. Women writers tend to stress the possibilities for change and positive self-creation, while their male counterparts are often more ambivalent about the relocation. The more someone had to lose, of course, the more the changes seem disadvantageous. Skepticism rings through the words of the humorist Sholom Aleichem, who, disappointed in America's response to him and his work during his lifetime, represents one extreme. The disingenuous young narrator of his unfinished immigrant novel, *Adventures of Mottel the Cantor's Son*, for instance, marvels that "only in a country like America can such miracles take place – the small can become big, the lowly great, and the dead practically come to life" (248). The irony is more biting when he describes the class reversals that America enables:

> There's nothing a man can't do in America. In America you can learn any kind of a job, and get used to it. For example, the job of a rabbi. Being a rabbi surely requires deep learning which cannot be mastered by everybody. A rabbi has to be ordained; he's got to know something about Jewish law. And yet in America, you find rabbis, who are called *reverends*, who in the old country used to be ritual slaughterers. (279)

At the opposite extreme were the early film moguls of the next generation, many born in the US, who found in Hollywood the opportunity – or so they believed – to assimilate fully into mainstream culture. While they, too, felt the tug of the past, the message and medium of Hollywood at least explicitly espoused the religion of self-making. Not surprisingly, the breakthrough technology of the first talking picture was introduced in 1927 in an assimilation narrative entitled *The Jazz Singer*. The descendant of a long line of cantors, Jaky Rabinowitz finds himself attracted to American music before he comes to know native-born Americans. Refusing to follow in his ancestors' footsteps and become a cantor, he changes his name, becomes a vaudeville star and falls in love with a Christian woman. Disowned by his father, he nonetheless retains deep ties to home and yearns for reconciliation. The crisis of the film comes when he must choose between the opportunity to move into mainstream theater and the duty to perform the holy *Kol Nidre* service in his dying father's place. In an implausible resolution, he chooses duty but is not penalized for missing the opening night of a sold-out show. For Jack Robins, assimilation is not only possible, but it does not entail any sacrifice or loss. Yet the fact that he performs in blackface does call the hopeful ending into question. It at once underscores – and demonstrates his participation in – the very bigotry that he believes he has left behind and highlights the marginality of his own "American" identity (Rogin, *Blackface White Noise*). The narrative of stardom drew not only from Horatio Alger's rags-to-riches formulation, but also from the assimilation narrative. In *The Jazz Singer*, as in Hollywood itself, the disregarded claims of the past and the complexities of the present haunt the narratives to such an extent that the hauntings actually became the subject of important Hollywood films.

The tradition of socialism nurtured in the Jewish ghettos and advocated by such powerful and compelling figures as Abraham Cahan served as a counterpoint to the narrative of assimilation represented in *The Jazz Singer*. (For more on early Jewish cinema, see Donald Weber's account in chapter 7.) Peter Kvidera has written persuasively about how for activist writers such as Theresa Malkiel and Rose Schneiderman the collectivism fostered by the labor movement serves as an alternative to traditional models of Americanization. Through their activism, workers are socialized into a group identity that is at once "American" and sharply critical of US society. The Jewish immigrants about whom they write find expression for their Jewish identities in their commitments to justice and social activism; they are cultural rather than religious affiliations, but they refuse the terms of Jewish American identity articulated by mainstream US society. Assimilation in Malkiel's 1915 *Diary of a Shirtwaist Striker*, for example, works in reverse as the Christian narrator, Mary, gradually bonds with her Jewish co-workers whose passion and heroism during the 1912 labor strike sensitize her to the class and gender injustices she had been trained not to see. Class bonds sometimes prove even stronger than religious ones in stories like Yiddish writer Leon Kobrin's "A Common Language." The narrator, a Jewish immigrant working as a night watchman, finds that he has more in common with an Italian immigrant whom he catches stealing wood to warm his impoverished family than with his wealthy Jewish boss.

Yet conspicuous in the stories of East European immigrants in the late nineteenth and early twentieth centuries are reminders of the difficulties of refusing identification with their compatriots. In her autobiographical *Out of the Shadow: A Russian Jewish Girlhood on the Lower East Side* (1918), Rose Cohen describes the gradual loosening of traditions to which she and her father slowly submitted when faced with long hours of work and unrelenting impoverishment in their early years in New York. Her extended stay in a hospital makes her grow "to know and understand and love the people all about [her]" with the consequence that she begins to lose her "intense nationalism" (242). But Cohen is reminded that she is an outsider when a trusted friend and mentor maintains her belief that Jews of old sacrificed Christian children on Passover despite Rose's insistence to the contrary. "That night," recounts Cohen, "Miss Farly and Irene and the two coloured women and all the children were together and I felt alone, a stranger in the house that had been a home to me. In that hour I longed for my own people whose hearts I knew" (267).

Stories from the Yiddish press are full of Jews compelled to identify themselves as such against threats of violence and bigotry. The Jewish passengers of a New York streetcar try to look the other way when a street gang harasses a Jewish peddler in Joseph Opatoshu's "How the Fight Began." But when a woman proudly identifying herself as Jewish comes to his defense, "the Jews behind their newspapers threw them away and clenched their fists" (140). The narrator of Kobrin's "Little Souls" recounts his experience as one of three Jewish immigrants passing for Christian in order to get employment in a cigar factory, owned, ironically, by a German Jew but run by an antisemitic foreman. Forced to hire a Jewish worker during a busy season, the foreman teases him mercilessly while the passing Jews look on. Far from coming to his defense, the passers join in the general laughter inspired by the foreman's constant ridicule until the narrator can stand it no longer. Leaping from his "chair half-crazed with anger and humiliation," he cries out in Yiddish, " 'Bentzi! Moishe!...Say something! Who cut out your tongues! They're hurting a Jew! You're Jews yourselves!' " (61). While Opatoshu's story ends with an expression of Jewish consciousness, however, Kobrin's ends with the narrator's isolation. Not only do Bentzi and Moishe not come to his defense, but Nochem Treitle, the foreman's victim, is furious that the narrator's actions lead to the loss of his lucrative job. Kobrin captures the extremes – the self-denial and loss of dignity – to which the penurious circumstances of Jewish immigrants might lead them.

Of the Jewish immigrant writers in this period, few enjoyed (or currently enjoy) a significant mainstream US readership. Championed by William Dean Howells, Cahan was an exception, as was the younger Russian Jewish immigrant Anzia Yezierska. Although she even made it to Hollywood, she died in relative obscurity. However, the compatibility of her work with the particular interest in ethnicity and in women writers resulted in her reincarnation in the late twentieth century. Offering mainstream culture its most sustained view of Jewish women immigrants, her work also sets forth a version of assimilation reminiscent both of Wirth's formulations and of those of some of the most prominent theorists of ethnicity in the 1970s and 1980s. Her wonderfully engaging strong female characters are not always immediately likeable, but they offer important insight into the struggle for bread and for dignity in Yiddish New York. The pages of *Hungry Hearts*, the short story collection that got her to Hollywood, are filled with female characters who become the prototypes for her later heroines. They represent a range of types, from the ever-despairing Hannah Breinah, a familiar figure in Jewish immigrant literature although probably least typical of Yezierska's female characters, to Shenah Pessah, who declares that " 'the hunger to make [her]self a person...can't be crushed by nothing – nor nobody – the life higher!' " (*Hungry Hearts*, 42).

Like Cahan's David Levinsky, Hannah Breinah cannot find a comfortable place in the New World. She deplores her povery and her Lower East Side surroundings, but when a change in fortune allows her to move, she finds her more materially comfortable Upper West Side existence lonely and alienating. Accustoming herself to luxury, she becomes unfamiliar to herself. She finds that she cannot return to the squalor of Delancey Street, yet she feels completely alien on Riverside Drive. She comes to understand not only that her children have outgrown her, but that "she had outgrown her past" (*Hungry Hearts*, 136). Nothing can bridge the distance because, as the striking spatial metaphors of the story attest, there is no place for someone like her. She does not even have words for what such a place would be.

Finding expression, through words or other outlets, for their longing saves many of the most colorful of Yezierska's female immigrant protagonists from the fate of Hannah Breinah. Yezierska is intrigued by what she calls the "hunger" in the hearts of women who want opportunities that they believe their new country will afford them, and her protagonists who fare best are those who, unlike Hannah Breinah, channel their ineffable longings for self-expression into the desire to create. Often, the women have to struggle to understand the creative nature of their desire. Sometimes they experience it initially as love for a man (typically a teacher or prominent figure who is not Jewish) who represents to them the cultivation for which they strive. But ultimately that love – whether requited or not – finds a richer expression as inspiration, as Shenah Pessah's words attest.

The desire that she expresses of making herself a person runs as a refrain throughout much of Yezierska's work, including her most celebrated fictionalized autobiography, *Bread Givers*. The phrase registers the extent to which the characters experience their very personhood as contingent upon the remaking that is taking place in the New World (Americanization). But by replacing the external goals – financial success, the unattainable love object – with the goal of self-expression, they can take pleasure in the hunger itself and in the quest to express it. For them, immigration indeed offers possibilities not available in the Old World. "According to the traditions of her people," for example, twenty-two-year-old Shenah Pessah would be "condemned to be shelved aside as an unmated thing – a creature of pity and ridicule." In the US, however, she knows that "if a girl earns her living she can be fifty years old and without a man, and nobody pities her" (*Hungry Hearts*, 6, 13). Freed from one set of expectations, she discovers that she need not replace them with another; she can thus enjoy the whimsy of Cahan's whimsical metamorphoses.

The hunger makes these women different from their peers, and the American-born men in Yezierska's stories respond variously, but always strongly, to them. Some are troubled by their forthrightness or disturbed by their pathos, but more commonly they are drawn to their passion and spontaneity, which they see as an antidote to their own " 'age-long repressions' " (*Hungry Hearts*, 87), as one man puts it.

But Yezierska's heroines do not provide such an antidote, and her vision of assimilation finds expression in the failure of just such relationships. While her young immigrant women's relationships to their male mentors in *Hungry Hearts* are modeled on Yezierska's own romantic relationship with the famous educator John Dewey, the marriage of Sonya Vrunsky and the wealthy philanthropist John Manning in *Salome of the Tenements* more directly evokes that of Yezierska's immigrant friend Rose Pastor and philanthropist Graham Stokes (Wilentz, Introduction, *Salome of the Tenements*). Sonya is not, like Pastor, a labor and women's rights activist; Yezierska is more interested in how the heroine finds fulfillment by discovering the proper medium for self-expression. Sonya becomes a fashion designer. And with the happiness she finds, Yezierska offers her own narrative of assimilation.

Sonya is not in any conventional way a golddigger. She is drawn to Manning's millions, but Yezierska carefully depicts her interest in beautiful things as a kind of artistic self-expression, a vision that grows out of the hunger that distinguishes Yezierska's worthy protagonists. For Sonya, Manning is above the mean things of the earth, and his settlement work emblematizes the ideals that she wants to be able to embrace. Money would free her to do good works, to bring beauty to the settlements. In Sonya's longings, Yezierska captures the sense of imprisonment experienced by many of her heroines who understand their poverty not just as financial limitation, but also as the most palpable expression of their distance from American culture. For Sonya, the ghetto marks her distance from higher truths, which she believes Manning can reveal to her. With his money, he even holds the continued means to her self-expression in his grasp.

Conversely, Sonya embodies for him a new possibility for self-expression. Manning curses "the thing within him that held him from being himself –

from saying the things he wanted to say" (*Salome of the Tenements*, 97). And Sonya sees "that this man was bound in with centuries of inhibitions that would take a cataclysmic love to break down" (36). In his experience of her as natural and liberating, Manning conforms to the familiar class narrative. But the heavily spatialized vocabulary through which Yezierska expresses his constraint suggests that part of Sonya's appeal might lie in the literal border-crossing with which she is associated. The national borders that she has crossed as an immigrant suggest to him the freedom from the constraints of an established identity. He believes that she has a more fluid relationship to identity, and he imagines that fluidity to be liberating. With Sonya, he has "the sensation of being swept out of himself upon strange sunlit shores. The bleak land of merely intellectual perception lay behind him" (34). Attracted and afraid, he both worries and marvels "that she knew him better than he could ever know himself" (35).

From the outset, their relationship is mediated by preconceptions derived from cultural stereotypes. Where Manning insists on seeing their marriage in terms that resonate with David Quixano's vision – " 'the mingling of the races ... The oriental mystery and the Anglo-Saxon clarity that will pioneer a new race of men' " (108) – Sonya is suspicious of the racialized language of the melting-pot. She is annoyed that he insists on dragging " 'in high words from sociology books in happiness so perfect as' " theirs (108). Yet, the language with which she replaces it – the language of love – is equally conventional: " 'I can't think. I only feel that we are for each other as the sun is for the earth. Races and classes and creeds, the religion of your people and my people melt like mist in our togetherness ... We are the sphinx – the eternal riddle of life – man and woman in love' " (108).

Both, however, quickly learn that something crucial is lost in the translation. Like Hannah Breinah, Sonya finds she cannot speak to anyone, cannot communicate directly. As Mrs. Manning, she is not only distanced from experience by language, but she is distanced from the experience of language itself. And her distance from language marks her isolation. What Sonya calls the language of sociology returns in Yezierska's description of their life together: "Sonya and Manning, tricked into matrimony, were the oriental and the Anglo-Saxon trying to find a common language" (132). With this description, Yezierska underscores that they have already been shaped by cultural stereotypes; they have become "the oriental" and "the Anglo-Saxon." And they are consequently separated by the language through which they are constituted and by the languages into which they have been socialized. In fact, the very language of sociology, inscribing both their difference and the attraction between them, has "tricked them into matrimony."

The disastrous marriage does not satisfy Sonya's hunger. Only the act of creation can do that. Leaving Manning enables Sonya to find her true calling as a fashion designer and her perfect male counterpart. Jacques Hollins, né Jaky Solomon, had worked his way as a tailor through the shops of unappreciative employers until earning enough to study in Paris. When Jaky Solomon became Jacques Hollins, New York's famous Four Hundred had their newest and most exclusive designer, and Sonya had her man. The end of *Salome* reinforces the stereotype of America as a land of opportunity.

Like the sociologists, Yezierska imagines a cultural assimilation – Americanization – that transpires not through intermarriage (Sonya and Manning), but through the marriage of like-minded immigrants (Sonya and Hollins). *Salome* is not a passing story; Solomon/Hollins does not try to hide his past. He simply knows that the Four Hundred will buy more comfortably from Hollins than from Solomon, and he does not experience his self-creation as a severing from the past. Sonya does not seek "forgetfulness of the past" (*Salome of the Tenements*, 183) in this new marriage. With Hollins, she need not sever her past from the present, and, in turn, she bridges Jaky Solomon and Jacques Hollins.

Sonya experiences an intense "closeness of spiritual identification" (183) in her parting meeting with Manning and wistfully muses that " 'We kill the divine in us. We kill the beauty in those we love. But the very killing makes immortal the contact' " (183). Thus she understands the violence implicit in cross-cultural contact. By contrast, assimilation comes out of finding and accepting one's place. Like *Salome*, Yezierska's *Bread Givers* (1925) ends with the heroine's betrothal to her landsman, and the principal of the school where she teaches, who reconciles the New World daughter to her Old World father. While Yekl/Jake ends realizing his choices have not brought him closer to the full-fledged American he hopes to be, Yezierska's heroines are comfortable in their identities as Jewish Americans. Although they experience some rupture with the past, their unions in the end mark some kind of return and reconciliation; assimilation, as in Wirth's formulations, does not mean total absorption.

Chronicling the longings of displaced people and the struggles to make a living, this literature captures the fascinating strangeness – the art – of life in a new place. Yezierska's Sophie Sapinsky, the aspiring writer protagonist of "My Own People," epitomizes this theme when she discovers her subject precisely in the experiences she had initially deemed disturbances. Sophie knows she wants to write, but the words will not live on the page. Taking a room in search of quiet, she is annoyed by the constant interruptions of her landlady, Hannah Breinah (before the move uptown), and the other lodgers.

But as she is pulled into their celebrations and traumas, she realizes that she has found in her neighbors what she had sought in her solitude. Sophie begins to write, thinking triumphantly, " 'At last it writes itself in me!...It's not me – it's their cries – my own people – crying in me! Hannah Breinah, Shmendrik, they will not be stilled in me, till all America stops to listen' " (*Hungry Hearts*, 151).

Sophie's real-life counterparts seem to have found the same inspiration, as they wrote their triumphs and tribulations in Yiddish and English, in prose, poetry, drama, autobiography, and even early cinema. In doing so, they left a record of life in the Jewish ghetto of New York at the turn of the twentieth century. Henry James was drawn to this world, as well as Jacob Riis and Hutchins Hapgood, for it represented the human spirit laid bare by adversity and estrangement and wondrous in its ability to give voice to sorrows and passions, to the injustices and kindness that they encountered as they became, in their various ways, Jewish Americans. The stories are not always unique to Jewish America. They resonate with those of other immigrant groups. But in the sheer volume of their writing, these authors tell the story of the complex shaping of group identities in the United States. Some contemporary critics have expressed dismay at the interest in ethnic literature and culture, wondering why ostensibly assimilated Americans continue to identify with their ethnic roots. This literature might shed some light on that question. The sense of alienation that arises from the pressure (internal or external) to forget bears witness to more than the contemporary terms of identity in the US. It attests to the childhood memories of family and place from which we derive our sense of being human and of belonging in and to the world. We can move away from that, of course, but we cannot forget. The literature of Yiddish New York tells the story of the memories and movements of people for whom family and place, however uncertain, nonetheless formed the basis of the identities that they were asked to build anew.

REFERENCES AND SUGGESTED FURTHER READINGS

Antin, Mary. *The Promised Land*. New York: Houghton Mifflin, 1925.

Cahan, Abraham. *The Rise of David Levinsky*. (1917). New York: Harper, 1960.
Yekl and the Imported Bridegroom and Other Stories of the New York Ghetto. New York: Dover, 1970.

Cohen, Rose. *Out of the Shadow: A Russian Jewish Girlhood on the Lower East Side*. (1918). Ithaca: Cornell University Press, 1995.

Ewen, Elizabeth. *Immigrant Women in the Land of Dollars: Life and Culture on the Lower East Side, 1890–1925*. New Feminist Library. New York: Monthly Review Press, 1985.

Findlay, John M. "An Elusive Institution: The Birth of Indian Reservations in Gold Rush California." In *State and Reservation: New Perspectives on Federal Indian*

Policy. Eds. George Pierre Castile and Robert L. Bee. Tucson: University of Arizona Press, 1992.

Glenn, Susan. *Daughters of the Shtetl: Life and Labor in the Immigrant Generation.* Ithaca: Cornell University Press, 1990.

Female Spectacle: The Theatrical Roots of Modern Feminism. Cambridge, MA: Harvard University Press, 2000.

Hapgood, Hutchins. *The Spirit of the Ghetto: Studies of the Jewish Quarter of New York.* (1902). Ed. Moses Rischin. Cambridge, MA: Harvard University Press, 1967.

Higham, John. *Strangers in the Land; Patterns of American Nativism, 1860–1925.* New Brunswick, NJ, Rutgers University Press, 1955.

Send These to Me: Immigrants in Urban America. Rev. edn. Baltimore: Johns Hopkins University Press, 1984.

Kallen, Horace. "Democracy Versus the Melting-Pot." *The Nation* (February 18 and 25, 1915): 190–194, 217–220.

Kobrin, Leon. "A Common Language." In *Pushcarts and Dreamers and Other Stories of Jewish Life in America.* Ed. and trans. Max Rosenfeld. Philadelphia: Sholom Aleichem Club Press, 1967; reprt. 1993.

"Little Souls." In *Pushcarts and Dreamers and Other Stories of Jewish Life in America.* Ed. and trans. Max Rosenfeld. Philadelphia: Sholom Aleichem Club Press, 1967; reprt. 1993.

Kraut, Alan M. *Silent Travelers : Germs, Genes, and the "Immigrant Menace."* New York: BasicBooks, 1994.

Kvidera, Peter. *Narrating Americanization: Space and Form in US Immigrant Writing, 1890–1927.* Doctoral dissertation, University of Washington, 1999.

Malkiel, Theresa. *Diary of a Shirtwaist Striker.* (1915). New York: Henry Schuman, 1953.

Opatoshu, Joseph. "How the Fight Began." In *Pushcarts and Dreamers and Other Stories of Jewish Life in America.* Ed. and trans. Max Rosenfeld. Philadelphia: Sholom Aleichem Club Press, 1967; reprt. 1993.

Park, Robert E. "The City: Suggestions for the Investigation of Human Behavior in the Urban Environment." *American Journal of Sociology* 20.5 (March 1915): 577–612.

"Human Migration and Marginal Man." (1928). In *Classic Essays on the Culture of Cities.* Ed. Richard Sennett. Englewood, NJ: Prentice Hall, 1969.

Park, Robert E. and Ernest W. Burgess. *Introduction to the Science of Sociology.* Chicago: University of Chicago Press, 1921.

Riis, Jacob. *How the Other Half Lives: Studies Among the Tenements of New York.* (1890). New York: Dover, 1971.

Rogin, Michael Paul. *Blackface, White Noise: Jewish Immigrants in the Hollywood Melting Pot.* Berkeley: University of California Press, 1996.

Roosevelt, Theodore. "True Americanism." In *The Works of Theodore Roosevelt.* National Edition. New York: Scribner's, 1926.

Sholem Aleichem. *Adventures of Mottel the Cantor's Son.* Trans. Tamara Kahana. New York and Oxford: Collier Books, 1961.

Sollors, Werner. *Beyond Ethnicity: Consent and Descent in American Culture.* New York and Oxford: Oxford University Press, 1936.

Sollors, Werner., ed. *The Invention of Ethnicity*. New York and Oxford: Oxford University Press, 1989.

Wald, Priscilla. "Communicable Americanism: Contagion, Geographic Fictions, and the Sociological Legacy of Robert E. Park." *American Literary History* 14.4 (Winter 2002): 653–85.

Wilentz, Gay. Introduction. *Salome of the Tenements*. (1923). Urbana and Chicago: University of Illinois Press, 1995.

Yezierska, Anzia. *Bread Givers*. (1925). Introd. Alice Kessler Harris. New York: Persea Books, 1975.

Salome of the Tenements. (1923). Urbana and Chicago: University of Illinois Press, 1995.

Hungry Hearts. (1920). Introd. Blanche Gelfant. New York: Penguin, 1997.

Zangwill, Israel. *The Melting-Pot*. (1914 edition). New York: Arno Press, 1975.

4

DAVID G. ROSKIES

Coney Island, USA: America in the Yiddish literary imagination

These days, the lingua franca on the Boardwalk in Brighton Beach is Russian. For every ice cream parlor there are two Gastronoms named after another city in the former Soviet Union. On any given morning, rain or shine, winter or summer, you can see a group of Russian Jews doing calesthenics on the beach. For some, the boardwalk joining Brighton Beach to Sea Gate via Coney Island represents Odessa. For others, its Russian restaurants, nightclubs, fruit stands, and bookstores represent their ethnic haven in the New World, within earshot of the ubiquitous El (New York elevated railway).

These Russian Jews have closed the circle of the mass immigration to America, not only because the beaches and baths, Luna Park and Dreamland, Thousand-and-One-Nights and Tower of Seville were the first taste of paradise for millions of their coreligionists, but also because, with their backs to America and their faces to the ocean, the new immigrants have replicated a whole era in Jewish American culture. By the first decade of the twentieth century, Coney Island became the physical and psychological boundary between the Old World and the New, a liminal, conflictual space where one's longing – and loathing – for the Old World were experienced most keenly; where, awash in the sea of humanity, or as pilgrim to this mecca of mass amusement, the Jewish newcomer sometimes felt more alone than anywhere else. On the beach itself, a million footsteps and a thousand sand castles are washed away daily with the tide. So too the Jewish cultural experiment whose bold contours were highlighted so clearly against the backdrop of Brighton Beach and Coney Island. It has vanished, with nary a trace, so that each generation is left to repeat the cycle all over again: from exile, to deliverance, to exile.

From Castle Garden they were thrust headlong not into a melting pot, but a *keslgrub*, a whirlpool as much linguistic as socioeconomic. Never before had so many Yiddish-speaking Jews been forced to rub shoulders with other Jews from different regions and speaking different dialects. Historically,

the "Litvaks" came first, those from Posen, Kurland, and Suwalki, who
spoke a heavily Germanicized Yiddish, and those from (Jewish) Lithuania,
whose pronunciation was closest to an imagined, privileged, standard.
But the "Rumener" were not far behind, speaking a variant of Ukrainian
(Southeastern) Yiddish, not to speak of the much-maligned "Galitsyaner",
who shared a Southwestern dialect with the Polish Jews, and who because
of their extreme poverty, got saddled with a worse reputation, and unlike
the Rumanians, had no matinee idol named Aaron Lebedeff to sing their
praises. Besides breeding mutual contempt, living in such close quarters
sharpened one's ear for the particular sources of one's language, especially the
Slavic component. Litvaks fused more Russian into their speech; the others,
more Polish and Ukrainian. Thus New York's Lower East Side, and later,
Brownsville and Harlem, were something of a linguistic pressure chamber,
cultural differences further reinforced by the presence of Goyim, who spoke
their own local variant of Low Goyish (Italian, Irish Brogue, Pigeon English)
or High Goyish (Public School English).

Every Yiddish-speaker already came endowed with what Max Weinreich
called "component-consciousness," an intuitive grasp of the three language
groups that together shape modern Yiddish – Hebrew-Aramaic (what Jews
call *loshn-koydesh*), Germanic, and Slavic – each carrying a specific affective
load (Weinreich, *History of the Yiddish Language*, 592–595, 656–657). In
America, that affective load shifted dramatically. The Hebrew-Aramaic component became, on the one hand, more attenuated, as religious observance
plummeted, and on the other, more precious, as certain key words assumed
an almost talismanic quality: *toyre* (Torah), *Kaddish*, *khevre kedishe* (Hevra
Kadisha, the Burial Society). While among the *landslayt* (people from the
same home town), the Slavic component might conjure up the rustic qualities of the Old Home, it more easily marked one as a greenhorn, someone still
mired in the *shtetl* outback, the moment one strayed beyond the confines of
the *landsmanshaft*, one's home-town society. That left the only unifying – and
dignifying – component of the language, the Germanic. Unifying, because it
was adopted straightaway by the American Yiddish press, some of whose
pioneers just happened to hail from Kurland and environs; and dignifying,
because German was the language of Enlightenment, and its handmaiden,
socialism. The very titles of the leading newspapers betrayed this genetic
link: *Arbayter-tsaytung* (Workers' Newspaper), *Forverts* (Forward), *Fraye
arbayter-shtime* (Free Workers' Voice), *Di varhayt* (The Truth).

All Yiddish writing in America, therefore, whether highbrow or low, and
all Yiddish theater, which with some notable exceptions was unabashedly
low, exploited the components of the language in new ways. What existed before in a state of creative fusion now deconstructed. By isolating or

exaggerating each component, the speaker, writer, or vaudeville performer could either parody that piece of the past that now seemed most outmoded, or elevate that severed link into an object of longing. Built into the very language that every Yiddish-speaker brought from home was a triangular structure rife with emotive possibilities. Each linguistic component, if deconstructed or unmoored, could function independently as a pole of longing, or loathing. The *loshn-koydesh* component could either bespeak one's liberation from the bondage of the religious tradition, or a desire to reconnect to a rescuable part thereof. The Slavic component, by the same token, could signify either good riddance to *shtetl* (Jewish market town of East Europe) backwardness or a nostalgia for one's native, bucolic, landscape. The Germanic component, to the extent that it merged with the vast fund of neologisms that entered into every modern language bespoke an attachment either to the here-and-now or to the imagined future. As we shall see, it was the singular achievement of Yiddish writers in America to raise this triangular structure to a new level of self-consciousness and sophistication. After isolating each component and endowing it with a particular emotional valence, the American Yiddish poets and prose writers added a temporal layer of signification. The Hebrew-Aramaic component stood in for the distant, mythic past; the Slavic, for the recent, severed past; and the Germanic, for the present and future. Here was a linguistic structure for all seasons, especially well suited to chart the dizzying, veritable Coney Island called America.

The poet and prose writer Morris Rosenfeld (1862–1923) captured the hearts and minds of the newly proletarianized Jewish urban masses by articulating their sense of triple banishment: exiled from home, from nature, and by extension, from God. As Rosenfeld repeatedly stresses, nowhere in the New World can one find a physical space that mediates between the poles of desire. "Nit zukh mikh vu di mirtn grinen," begins one of his most famous poems, set to an exquisitely poignant melody.

> Gefinst mikh dortn nit, mayn shats.
> Vu lebns velkn bay mashinen
> Dortn iz mayn rueplats.
>> ("My Resting Place," 150–151)

> (Look for me not where myrtles green!
> Not there, my darling, shall I be.
> Where lives are lost at the machine
> that's the only place for me.)
>> ("My Place," 78–79)

Once displaced by the machine, there is no return to nature; once enslaved by capitalist servitude, there is no hope of achieving individual freedom. One's only *rueplats*, or resting place, lies in the private domain, in the arms of one's true love.

While Rosenfeld wrote lyric evocations of traditional Jewish life in his native Lithuanian village of Boshka, and on occasion conjured up a Promised Land that he never stepped foot on, his landscape was thoroughly American. When he did venture forth from the Lower East Side, he discovered the enigma of Niagara Falls ("Who will triumph: the Primeval Spirit of the Falls or the factories that harness its might?"), and perceived God in the "sublime seriousness" of the southwestern Catskills (*Geveylte shriftn* II, 99–159). These dreamscapes exist out there, as distant objects of desire, while at the core of the Jewish American experience lay the urban jungle. Rosenfeld was the first Yiddish writer to confront that urban landscape and to exploit the Yiddish language to render its particularity.

> Korner vey un elnt shteyt an alte hayzl:
> untn iz a shenkl, oybn iz a klayzl.
> Untn kumen lumpn oyfton nor neveyles,
> oybn kumen yidn, klogn afn goles.

> Corner of Pain and Anguish, there's a worn old house:
> tavern on the street floor, Bible room upstairs.
> Scoundrels sit below, and all day long they souse.
> On the floor above them, Jews sob out their prayers.

At the crossroads of two personified but generalized expressions of sorrow stands an old and semi-mythic house. We know the house is somewhere in urban America because of the first word, *korner*. *Korner* is an Americanism, one of only two such linguistic markers in the whole poem. *Vey*, or pain, is more social; *elnt*, loneliness, more personal. The house itself is subdivided: on the ground floor are the low-lives, presumably Gentiles, "practicing debauchery." On the second floor are the Jews, pouring out their hearts to God. Together they express a differentiated response to the same condition of uprootedness, as they are audibly yoked together by the Hebraic and semantically laden off-rhyme of *neveyles/goles*, heinousness and exile.

> Higher on the third floor, there's another room:
> not a single window welcomes in the sun.
> Seldom does it know the blessing of a broom.
> Rottenness and filth are blended into one.

The higher you go, the more filth you collect. In the new social order, floor is ceiling.

> Ot in dizn mokem arbetn zikh flaysik
> un tsufridn, dakht zikh, bay an erekh draysik
> opgetserte mener, opgetserte vayber,
> mit tsiterdike gayster un farvelkte layber.

> Toiling without letup in that sunless den:
> nimble-fingered and (or so it seems) content,
> sit some thirty blighted women, blighted men,
> with their spirits broken, and their bodies spent.

Mokem means place, from the Hebrew, *makom*, only in Yiddish it carries the additional meaning of the non-Jewish part of town. So when Rosenfeld introduces the third floor with the super-emphatic "ot in dizn mokem," in this very place, and casts an admiring look upon these (young) men and women working so industriously – at least someone in this old house is doing productive labor – we are startled to see their true physical state. To whom are they beholden? What power binds them to that terrible "place"?

> Scurf-head struts among them: always with a frown,
> acting like His Royal Highness in a play;
> for the shop is his, and here he wears the crown,
> and they must obey him, silently obey.
>
> ("The Sweatshop," 84–85)

King of the shop, the crown of creation, who occupies the highest rung in the new social order is the only named person in the poem, Motke Parkh – no doubt his ugly nickname in the *shtetl*. For the scum of the Old World now reigns over the New, and if you don't like it, there's nothing you can do, as the closing couplet makes eminently clear: "un di shap iz zayne...muz men folgn, folgn on a tayne" (for the shop is his...and they must obey him, silently obey).

In his poetry, Rosenfeld exploits the components of the language in new ways. For him, *loshn-koydesh* is the domain of transcendental values rooted in Scripture and the liturgy, hence the didactic force of rhyming *goles*, *Galut*, exile, with *neveyles*, debauchery, from the Hebrew root, *n-b-l*, to behave scandalously. Rosenfeld stood at the forefront of a movement of cultural revolutionaries for whom German was the embodiment of universal, secular values, whether drawn from the realm of science, socialism, or aesthetics. By rhyming such dignified, High German, words as *mayn shats*, my darling, with *rueplats*, he bespeaks a world of new aspirations. As for the Slavic component of Yiddish, Rosenfeld uses it very sparingly, usually to denote the realia of the old rural lifestyle. *Parkh* (scurf-head) is a Polish loan word.

To be a Yiddish writer in the New World was to chronicle the depradations of exile and the dreams that failed. By creating a poeticized landscape out of the sweatshop and slums, Rosenfeld introduced a species of romantic realism. By staking out what he saw to be the heart of urban darkness, and by creating a synthetic and modern poetic diction, Rosenfeld also heralded the emancipation of Yiddish. There is nothing parochial about his oeuvre. He never adopts the stance of a minority poet, of a beggar standing at the gates of high culture. In America, and only in America, could a Jew speak for all Americans by speaking as a Jew. But given the social realities of his day, the only way Rosenfeld could be mainstreamed was as a poet of the "ghetto." In 1898, six years after the publication of Israel Zangwill's best-selling novel, *Children of the Ghetto*, Leo Wiener, an instructor in the Slavic languages at Harvard University, issued a bilingual selection of Rosenfeld's *Songs from the Ghetto* with the Yiddish rendered into German spelling and Gothic script and the English rendered into prose. On the strength of this little book, Rosenfeld became the first Yiddish celebrity on American college campuses and, at the height of his fame, was feted by European nobility.

So quickly did Rosenfeld fall from grace, however, that his monumental achievement is easily obscured. His subject was the inhuman social conditions of the sweatshop – the locus of alienation from one's past, one's family, and one's own self. Within that center of alienation there flowed vectors of desire: back to the natural and covenantal landscape of one's youth and forward to the day of universal liberation and national return. Though never given the credit, Rosenfeld enshrined what was to become the structure of triangular desire for all of American Yiddish writing to come.

By the time of Sholem Asch's (1880–1957) first visit to America, in 1909, there was already in place a body of prose fiction and serious drama that employed that structure. Most famous were the melodramas of Jacob Gordin (1853–1909), then at the peak of his career. Gordin's classic, *God, Man, and Devil* (1900), for example, presents a marriage paradigm in which a childless middle-aged man marries his niece in order to sire children, even while a more suitable bachelor waits in the wings (29–95).

The bare bones of *Uncle Moses* (1918), the second novel Asch wrote about America, adopts this marriage paradigm with only minor variation. As befits the New World, Moses Melnik is a ruthless capitalist who (unlike Gordin's Hershele Dubrovner) needs no divine intervention to make him sin. As the owner of a sweatshop that employs, or rather, enslaves, all of former Kuzmin, Uncle Moses can have the pick of the crop. And so he plies his virginal "niece" Masha with lavish gifts until she is ready to be plucked. Charlie is the young bachelor waiting on the sidelines. He possesses considerably more class consciousness than his Old World prototype, the *tallis* weaver, Motl, but is similarly naive when it comes to women. In both Gordin's play and Asch's novel, the misalliance signals a breach both of natural continuity and of social justice. From Gordin, in other words, Asch learned how to combine in the same cast of characters the twin themes of class and generational conflict that so preoccupied American Yiddish audiences and readers throughout the whole period of mass immigration.

The novel opens with the sun setting over downtown New York, described as "a devastated Babylon," the cityscape dominated by the Williamsburg Bridge, an "iron giant" with "a mighty Hand" (*Uncle Moses*, 3) Completing the picture are the subway cars, described as steel monsters with flaming heads. This is an industrial landscape endowed with mythic grandeur and elemental force. As the main reference point on the spatial compass, it signifies the universal might of nature and technology.

The second point is the sweatshop. By 1918, most of Asch's readers no longer worked under such primitive, pre-unionized, conditions. Most sweatshops, moreover, were of the type where Uncle Berl works, lowscale shops where even the most Orthodox Jew must rub shoulders with non-Jews. In the shop of Uncle Moses, atypically, men and women do not work alongside each other, and the boss hires only Jewish workers, all of whom hail from his native town of Kuzmin. So the shop is really a New World *shtetl*, where everyone is still known by his nickname, where cantorial pieces are sung to wile away the time, and where Yiddish is the lingua franca. Skillfully exploiting his workers' memories of the Old Country, Moses Melnik provides for them from cradle to grave, all the while paying them slave wages and fooling them into working even on the Sabbath. Behind his back, they call him Pharaoh.

In 1918, the East European heartland lay in ruins, and Asch was using this novel of the recent past to tell his readers what they needed to hear: you can't go home again. The *shtetl* – the third point on the compass – was dead and about to be buried. In the novel, two characters return to Kuzmin, to die. And lest anyone think that the *shtetl* can be Americanized, Asch has this to say: "Uncle Moses made all the citizens of Kuzmin equals. There were no more fashionables, no elders and no tradesmen, no Talmudic scholars and no dunces...all of them now served one god, all were doing the same kind of work – they were sewing trousers" (*Uncle Moses*, 47). Yes, these men still "remembered Kuzmin with love and longing as they sat there, holding their work in their hands" (48), but equality in the present meant the equality of the oppressed. The site of true equality and freedom was not the sweatshop, but...Coney Island.

Nature for Asch, as for the poet, Morris Rosenfeld before him, is the counternorm, the inexhaustible source of renewal. The Kuzminer are transported by their longing for the mighty Vistula of their youth, but only for a fleeting moment. For their children, Masha and Charlie, Kuzmin is a distant memory, and so they extricate themselves of a Sunday from the teeming streets of Harlem, and hop a subway ride to the beach. Asch devotes three whole chapters to their day in Coney Island, the ideological centerpiece of the novel.

These youngsters, who are forced to bear a heavy burden of responsibility, are returned to a state of nature in Coney Island. Always exposed to the sight of people working, suffering, and sorrowing together, Charlie is exhilarated by the startling sight of the same masses enjoying life together, just having a good time. Stimulated by the oceanic experience of the waves, and by the physical contact with the family of man, Charlie waxes rhapsodic:

> There are those who dislike Coney Island, because Coney Island is the place of the raw masses, who pollute the ocean with the trash from their picnics and crowd out the beach with their ungainly, ugly bodies . . . But I would be bored enjoying myself all alone . . . or spending my time only with fortunate people, with the chosen few, who have the opportunity to enjoy life. True enjoyment can be had only here, when one sees how the great masses are having fun. Then it seems as if there were no longer any evil or suffering in the world, that this joy is meant for everyone. (*Onkl Mozes* [Yiddish], 151)[1]

For Charlie, the budding ideologue, Coney Island is a place not only to enjoy, but also to argue for. Those who gainsay its value are not, interestingly enough, his comrades on the Left, who, like Art Young, later pictured Coney Island as belonging to the Devil, seducing the masses with tinsel and cheap thrills, but members of the moneyed elite, people of privilege for whom Coney Island was once a fashionable resort. Asch, swept away by Charlie's rambling monologue, then rhapsodizes in his own voice about the Edenic pleasure of so many almost-naked bodies rubbing up against each other. Walking unself-consciously hand-in-hand, Charlie and Masha "had the feeling that a great Messiah had come and annuled all prohibitions, permitting everything, so that everywhere in the world one person could freely mix with another . . ." (*Onkl Mozes*, 156).

As in the novel's opening scene, on the Williamburg Bridge, the universal landscape of nature is coupled with the magic of modern technology. But whereas only the narrator was privy to the opening epiphany, here, in Coney Island, the magic is apprehendable by all. Masha and Charlie are "stupefied" by their ride on the giant roller-coaster. As the sun begins to set, Coney Island is transformed into a dream-city, a picture-book world. And their day-trip ends as follows:

> Proud turrets, of a fantastic other-worldly beauty, brilliantly lighted turrets, towered above the shining buildings. They were like the towers of sacred temples, descended from the heavens. The flashing lights in the bright streets, the

blazing turrets suggested the heights of Olympus, the holy cities of Mecca or Jerusalem. Majestic, radiant, compelling – a wonder-city, this Coney Island – a city for which to be infinitely grateful, because it brought gaiety, happiness, release from the crassness of reality to millions and millions of people.

(*Onkl Mozes* 165; *Uncle Moses*, 109)

So Coney Island is a necessary catharsis and a foretaste of true democracy. Whatever social, religious, or sexual barriers the ocean and the beach do not break down, the amusement park is there to purge the last vestige of earth-bound inhibition. Its thousand and one nights allow all visitors to play out their most elemental fantasies, to imagine a paradise-on-earth, to achieve communion in a New Jerusalem.

Twenty years elapsed between the publication of *Uncle Moses* and its re-working into English, in 1938. How the world, America, and the Jews had changed in that period of time! Against the backdrop of rising antisemitism in Europe, Asch expunged much of the novel's gross sexuality, as well as the more innocent passages about close body contact on the crowded beach. Meanwhile, back in America, the New Deal was in full swing, and Asch had become a firm believer in the three worlds of American Jewry: *di velt*, this world, *yene velt*, the world-to-come, and *Roosevelt*. Against this backdrop, Charlie's revolutionary rhetoric was passé, if not downright subversive. America had become the crucible of Asch's most fervent ecumenical hopes, and the escapist pleasures offered by Coney Island he would eventually replace with the social integration achieved on the banks of the *East River* (1946).

Having witnessed the failed revolution of 1905 – the dream of a New Russia followed by the nightmare of new pogroms – a whole generation of Jewish intellectuals emigrated to America. Some, the fledgling poets and prose writers among them, displaced their radical politics by ushering in an aesthetic revolution. These so-called *Yunge*, or youngsters, summarily rejected the didactic, collectivist voice of organized labor, and strove instead to achieve the still small voice of Yiddish poetry. To signal their separation from the street below, these young poets typically positioned themselves at a window, and proceeded to cultivate a mood. To signal the independence of the poem from the poet, they adopted masks, the more exotic the better. So while Rosenfeld, the Romantic poet, had used the lyric "I" to represent an authentic authorial voice, which spoke, in turn, of an experience typical of any lover, worker, or father, *Di Yunge* introduced a Symbolist poetics of strangeness.

No persona was more at odds with his surroundings than Moyshe-Leyb Halpern's (1886–1932) "Street Drummer," marching to his own angry beat, and nowhere was the poet's alienation from the masses more pronounced than on the crowded beach at Coney Island, at around ten in the morning.

> Un az Moyshe-Leyb, der poet, vet dertseyln,
> az er hot dem toyt af di khvalyes gezen,
> azoy vi men zet zikh aleyn in a shpigl,
> un dos in der fri gor, azoy arum tsen –
> tsi vet men dos gleybn Moyshe-Leybn?

> Un az Moyshe-Leyb hot dem toyt fun der vaytn
> bagrist mit a hant un gefregt vi es geyt?
> Un davke beys s'hobn mentshn fil toyznt
> in vaser zikh vild mit dem lebn gefreyt –
> tsi vet men dos gleybn Moyshe-Leybn?

> (And if Moyshe-Leyb, Poet, recounted how
> He's glimpsed Death in the breaking waves, the way
> You catch that sight of yourself in the mirror
> At about 10:00 A.M. on some actual day,
> Who would be able to believe Moyshe-Leybl?

> And if Moyshe-Leyb greeted Death from afar,
> With a wave of his hand, asking, "Thing's all right?"
> At the moment when many a thousand people
> Lived there in the water, wild with delight,
> Who would be able to believe Moyshe-Leybl?)
> ("Memento Mori," trans. John Hollander)

This is the poet's "Memento Mori," its high-sounding title emblazoned in the Latin alphabet, no less. Comically at odds with the morbid, otherworldly conventions of the genre, in which the poet contemplates his mortality in the dead of night, the speaker in this poem adopts a playful, ironic, conversational tone, "the voice of Yiddish culture itself," as Harold Bloom once put it, and with seemingly effortless rhymes, evokes a landscape at once banal and bizarre. Coney Island is nowhere mentioned by name, but where else would a Yiddish poet be carousing in the water with "many a thousand people... wild with delight" at about ten in the morning? He sees what the multitude cannot. Only the poet sees death in the midst of life as something familiar, seductive, and in the fourth and final stanza, dazzling. Is it any wonder that no one would believe him?

Who is this Moyshe-Leyb, Poet, anyway? Presumably, some uprooted young Jewish immigrant, a *talush* in bathing trunks, so disenchanted with life that he contemplates suicide. What is *more* ludicrous: yearning for death on a Coney Island summer's day, or writing a carefully wrought poem in the

Yiddish language and with a Latin title amidst the shouts and wild laughter of the urban masses?

The poet at the seashore is one of two major tropes in Halpern's oeuvre, both of them parodic. The first is the city eclogue, or urban pastoral, which opens his first book of poems, *In New York* (1919).

> What a garden, where the tree is
> Bare, but for its seven leaves,
> And it seems it is amazed:
> "Who has set me in this place?"
> What a garden, what a garden –
> It takes a magnifying glass
> Just to see a little grass.
> Is this garden here our own,
> As it is, in light of dawn?
> Sure, it's our garden. What, not our garden?
>   ("Our Garden," 194–195)

Gone is the pathos of Morris Rosenfeld's "*Mayn rueplats.*" The binary opposition between the bounties and solace of nature and the depradations of urban life is here a given. The attempt to render the alienation of the urban metropolis in a high poetic diction is here replaced with the ironic inflection of the spoken idiom, what Benjamin Harshav calls "talk verse."

Halpern replaces Rosenfeld's semi-mythic and emotionally fraught landscape, "korner vey un elnt," with a mock-mythic Garden of Eden, inspired by Hester Park on the Lower East Side of Manhattan, the one bit of foliage and grass the Yiddish-speaking immigrant is likeliest to see (Wisse, *A Little Love*, 101). There follows a cycle of poems that play the conventions of pastoral poetry off the tenements, drying laundry, and garbage cans of Lower Manhattan. Left unfinished at the end of his short life was a poetic sequence called "*Shtotgortn*," modeled, this time, on Central Park.

Pockets of nature within the metropolis are where Halpern dilates upon the nature of his own poetry and his own nature as a poet. Here, every tree, every statue, every passerby stimulates another rumination. But the seashore is something else, a setting at once more social (being that we are still in Coney Island) and universal. For Halpern, it marks the outer boundary of exile.

Never for a moment did Halpern forget that the Jewish master narrative was bounded at one end by *kriyes yam-suf*, the miraculous splitting of the sea of reeds, and by the fateful ocean crossing to America, at the other. Somewhere in between, there was the Yiddish love song about a golden peacock who came flying across the ocean from a distant land. She had lost her golden feather along the way, because she carried bitter tidings from a newly wedded daughter to her parents back home ("The Golden Peacock").

Halpern turned the golden peacock into an emblem of loss, a symbol of unrequited longing, or, worse yet, into an icon of all one's debased dreams and idolatrous desires. Whosoever stood at the seashore looking back was likewise reminded of the home left behind, of lost love, of the divine promises that were never kept. From every shore, the ocean crossing was dead-ended.

Di goldene pave (1924), Halpern's second book of poems, is a modernist mock-epic about exile, "an ontology of homelessness," in Ruth Wisse's astute formulation (*A Little Love*, 136). It begins "*Fun yener zayt yam*," at the far side of the ocean, i.e., in Eastern Europe, and ends with two poetic sequences, one starring the familiar rascal, Moyshe-Leyb, the other starring his side-kick, a philosopher-beach-bum named Zarkhi, both of whom smoke a pipe, lust after women, and spend all their time at the seashore in Coney Island. Moyshe-Leyb is usually there by day. Zarkhi can be seen only at night.

It is no easier to define what Halpern means by exile than to characterize the precise nature of his modernism. Neither is there any consensus about who Zarkhi represents and where he comes from. Is he modeled on one of the Coney Island neighborhood peddlers, or on a character from an other-wise unmemorable story by Herman Gold? Is the name Zarkhi supposed to resonate – ironically, to be sure – with the Hebrew "dawn" or "brightness," or is he Zerah of the Bible, twin brother to Peretz, born from the union of Tamar and her father-in-law, Judah?

One thing is certain: Zarkhi is the distillation of all of Halpern's longing and loathing, and that is why he lives and dies on the seashore at Coney Island, his back to America, his face to the sea.

> Oh Zarkhi, Zarkhi, you cannot cause
> A bridge to be built straight across
> Over the sea, to go there and back –
> And your longing stands on the other side
> With red-raised paws, and calls and cries
> Like a village broad who needs a man –
> > Needs a man,
> > Needs a man.
> > ("Zarkhi to Himself," 421)

The longing is eroticized, and also rendered debased and vulgar by its per-sonification as a man-starved village broad with fat ugly hands. Throughout the Zarkhi cycle, Halpern mocks the very concept of a bridge of longing, when all desire is in fact debased, crass, unattainable, and absurd; when that which lies on the other side is in many ways even uglier than what lies here.

It is the mockery of all sancta – whether religious, cultural, or aesthetic – that is most shocking about this cycle of poems, and that which distinguishes Halpern from among his contemporaries. It may very well be, as Wisse argues, that Halpern's sense of reality coincided at this critical point with the editorial thrust of the communist *Frayhayt*: "the first step toward the realization of a new social order is the destruction of false beliefs" (*A Little Love*, 117). But a poetry so complicated, contradictory, fragmentary, and shockingly obscene, cannot possibly be enlisted in the cause of a new social order.

The Zarkhi poems are more than an allegory of exile. They enact its condition: the condition of an intellectual amidst the craving for material pleasure; the condition of an aesthete amidst the ugliness and slime; the condition of an immigrant whose life is lived only at night amidst people of his own imaginings; the condition of a Jew, who hates the world that craves his blood and whose own civilization is morally bankrupt.

Even death holds out no solace. Zarkhi dies, is buried in "the covenantal community of New York, Nineteen Hundred and Twenty-Three" (epigraph to canto XXIII), and his epitaph fittingly ends with a parody of Halpern's "Memento Mori."

When daybreak finally comes, it finds the poet alone with his beloved wife. And here is the most startling moment of all, brilliantly rendered into English by Benjamin and Barbara Harshav. The woman in this poem represents a rejection of intellectuality. The playfulness represents a rejection of modernist angst. The lullaby represents a return to Rosenfeld's "*Mayn rueplats*".

> So I ask my dear wife
> How to finish the affair
> Of my little booky –
> Says she: Let happiness leave on a train
> And wave back with a hanky.
> Says I: Hanky-panky –
> Says she: Booky-shmooky –
> And asks me whether I'd like
> With my coffee a cooky.
> Says I: Cooky-shmooky –
> And tell her to put a case on my pillow
> And not to play hooky.
> Says she: Hooky-shmooky.
> And tells me to repair her shoe
> By hook or by crooky.
> Says I: Crooky-shmooky.
> So she jumps up, and points at my head:
> I am bald and spooky.
> Says I:
> Spooky-crooky-hooky-cooky-hanky-panky-booky-shmooky.
> But she cannot say it as fast as I can, as fast as I can:

Spooky-crooky-hooky-cooky-hanky-panky-booky-shmooky.
So we laugh together –
Laugh so nice.
Till she closes my eyes –
Closes my eyes.
And rocks me with a song of rain and light,
Rain and light,
That you sing to little children at night
Children at night.   ("The End of the Book," 429)

Notice that as Yiddish in America increasingly becomes a language of exile, its greatest poet turns ever more inward, finding internal resources heretofore untapped. It is as if the language itself became the surrogate for the structure of triangular loathing and longing. For Halpern, as we have seen, the loathing far outstrips the longing, as he pits one linguistic realm against the other. He returns Hebrew-Aramaic to its *Sizt-im-Leben*, the study house and *shul*, in order to parody the form and substance of the Jewish intellectual tradition. Whole chapters of the Zarkhi cycle are written in the language of *lernen*, of Torah study, and they are wickedly funny. If *loshn-koydesh* is the realm of Jacob, then Slavic is the language of Esau, the bloodthirsty, drunken goy. No love lost for the earthiness of the Lithuanian village, for the sounds of the mighty Vistula, for the village broad with her red-raised paws. That leaves the Germanic component, which Halpern also uses against itself. His hallmark is the monosyllabic rhyme – *boym:koym, gloz:groz, zayt:shrayt, brik:tsurik* – or the doggerel that in Yiddish is associated with the *badkhn*, the professional wedding jester: *orglen:gorglen, unter:arunter*. In rare moments of reprieve, he returns to the only unadulterated domain of language, that of lullaby and nonsense rhymes.

America was the measure of Halpern's modernism, the locus of the here-and-now, the reason the components of his Yiddish invariably short-circuited one another. With the rarest exception, he allowed for no escape. However many days, weeks, or months Moyshe-Leyb, Poet, and his sidekick Zarkhi, spent on Coney Island, they stayed rooted to the seashore and never once frequented the rides. (Did either have a nickel to spare?) And however long they ruminated about the East European past, that past was enlivened only within narrow poetic confines, and only for parodic ends: his ode to "Zlochew, My Home"; his subversive ballads; his "Slavic Motifs." The destruction of Galicia in World War I moved him to look back in anguish, but what Halpern saw was a three-thousand-year-long funeral cortege – the unbroken legacy of shattered Jewish dreams – and the way he saw it was through the private hell of a nightmare. Halpern's stubborn, punishing, refusal to countenance a usable past singled him out from among all his contemporaries, for even the most radical among them, either routinely or eventually, divided their time between the New World and the Old.

This was most pronounced among the poets, beginning with his arch-rival and alter-ego, Mani Leyb (1883–1953). In 1918, the annus mirabilis of his career, Mani Leyb published three volumes of his collected verse, each celebrating the expressive possibilities of a different component of Yiddish: the personal and daringly erotic lyric poems gathered together in *Lider* used the Germanic component almost exclusively; the *Ballads* introduced *loshn-koydesh* to add an archaic, epic quality; and the *Jewish and Slavic Motifs* (so wickedly parodied by Halpern), luxuriated upon the Slavic elements in his Ukrainian Yiddish. Soon to follow were lavishly illustrated volumes of children's verse, which conjured up a perfect, poetic, childhood by harmonizing all the components.

Discarding the recent achievements of Yiddish writing in Russia–Poland as neo-romantic pabulum for the unlettered masses, the young H. Leivick (1888–1962) set out to reinvent a tragic-messianic past that stretched from Siberian exile back to the Golem of Prague, and farther still, to Jesus and the Messiah, son of David ("Di–on traditsye," 12–21). Leivick worked his transhistorical magic by means of free rhythmic concatenations and a proto-archaic diction that hearkened back to the *khumesh-taytsh* tradition of old. Indeed, the greatest single achievement of American Yiddish poetry turned out to be the complete, and annotated, Bible translation of Leivick's fellow-Litvak, Yehoash (Solomon Bloomgarten, 1872–1927). Before rehabilitating the biblical landscape for a generation consigned to wander the urban American desert, Yehoash sought and found a new poetic language to render nature, the Orient, and Native American landscapes. And so the search for new expressive possibilities led the poets back to the wellsprings of Jewish culture: to the Bible, the liturgy, the language of learning, hasidic lore. Even Zishe Landau (1889–1937), the chief ideologue of *Di Yunge*, who cultivated a phlegmatic, dandified persona, eventually discovered positive aesthetic uses for the spiritual legacy of his hasidic grandparents.

And what of the women poets? Coney Island and the Atlantic seaboard they apparently left to the men. Does this suggest that they abdicated the American landscape altogether, choosing realms of solipsism instead? By applying our triangular model – selective and schematic by design – to American Yiddish writing by women, the student will discover that Anna Margolin (1887–1952), for example, described "Girls in Crotona Park" in the Bronx and Malka Heifetz-Tussman (1896–1987) staked out the deserts and waterways of the American West in order to map alternative vectors of desire and eroticized states of exile. Almost unique among American Yiddish poets,

Kadya Molodowsky (1894–1975) sojourned in the original Promised Land and sang praises thereto.

Of the prose writers, America demanded realism, and the dictates of critical realism mandated that they chart the complex and rapidly changing social landscape of America: the revolution in sexual mores, in politics, in culture. But once the wave of mass immigration had peaked, and Eastern Europe became the Old Country, *di alte heym*, even writers who were not (yet) affiliated with one or another of the New York Yiddish dailies felt obliged to memorialize the abandoned *shtetl*. David Ignatoff (1885–1954) tried to straddle New York's seething *Cauldron* (1918) and the *Legends of Old Prague* (1920). For Isaac Raboy (1882–1944), who hailed from the Bessarabian outback, horses were the chief link to the past. After describing his exotic life as a stud farmer in North Dakota in *Her Goldenbarg* (1916), Raboy rendered his *Bessarabian Jews* (1922–1923) as salt of the earth. For Joseph Opatoshu (1887–1954), no such seamless transition was possible. As a died-in-the-wool naturalist, Opatoshu exposed moral depravity in *From the New York Ghetto* (1914), these slices-of-life rendered so stenographically that he had to append a glossary of American Yiddish slang for the benefit of readers back home. In contrast, the *shtetl* was a place where even horse thieves had hearts of gold (*Romance of a Horse Thief*, 1912), and every forest was redolent of legend and heroism *In Polish Woods* (1921). This split deepened over time, when the politics of the Left alienated Opatoshu still further from the American present and his triumphant visits to Poland and the USSR intensified his search for exemplars of Jewish heroism.

For Lamed Shapiro (1878–1948), the master of the short story, it was the legacy of murder, rape, and trauma that made the ocean crossing, and in the wake of World War I and the Ukrainian Civil War, Shapiro further elevated the pogrom to the status of Apocalypse. Gradually, however, Shapiro applied his impressionist technique to more humble themes: the life cycle of an exemplary Jewish merchant ("Smoke," 1915), the aesthetic awakening of a yeshiva student ("Eating Days," 1925–1926). Turning, definitively, to America, Shapiro captured the elusive dreamscape of the metropolis in "Newyorkish," followed by "Doc," the story of an uprooted Russian Jewish immigrant with the incongruous name of Benny Milgroym (Pomegranate). Virtually unique in Shapiro's oeuvre, "Doc" contains an hilarious episode on Coney Island, where, in a heavy-handed attempt to ensnare him into matrimony, Bennie is forced to take a camel ride along with his fellow-boarder, Sadie. While the camel named "Aaron" completes its prescribed thirty-foot circle without a hitch, Benny's "Moses" runs amuck, threatening to drag its frightened rider to an uncharted wilderness – or Promised Land. No home in *this* fake Mecca for the serious Yiddish muse!

After the gates had closed and the dreams for prosperity crashed, finding a new home for Yiddish became an ever more desperate problem. *Di Yunge*, who had launched the aesthetic revolution in such journals as *Di naye heym* (The new home) and *East Broadway*, issued their collective swansong in the appropriately titled *Der indzl* (The island, 1925–1926). The modernists, narrowing the domain of Yiddish to the poet's individual psyche, issued *In zikh* (In the self, 1920–1940), heralded by a manifesto with the off-putting title "Introspectivism" (translated by Anita Norich; Harshav and Harshav, *American Yiddish Poetry*, 774–784). Those who took their marching orders from Moscow signaled their allegiance with such titles as *Der hamer* (The hammer, 1926–1938) *Masn* (The masses, 1934), and *Signal* (1933–1936). The only middle ground, between the extremes of high modernism and revolutionary politics, was in the literary supplements and op-ed pages of the Yiddish daily press. Here it was possible for the arch-modernist Jacob Glatstein (1896–1971) to engage all topics literary and political, general and Jewish, and to forge a new synthetic style, at once idiomatic and thoroughly secular.

Were one to follow that secular trajectory, Glatstein would represent the sum and substance of Yiddish writing in America. As Halpern's heir apparent, he structured his first book of poems, *Yankev Glatshteyn* (1921), according to Halpern's dismal plan. In bold, incremental stages, Glatstein moved from *Fraye ferzn* (Free verses, 1926), to *Credos* (1929), to the high-water mark of Yiddish modernist experimentation, *Yidishtaytshn* (Yiddish meanings, 1937). And then he returned to Poland, just long enough to see Polish Jewry in its cultural death throes. Thanks to his prescience, independence of mind, and commanding intellect, Glatstein charted the road back: back to a moral engagement with the fate of the Jews, back to the indigenous core of Yiddish culture, "back to the ghetto."

But not back to Coney Island.

Coney Island continued to belie all initiatives to create a self-sustaining Yiddish secular culture in America. And no one understood this better than a thirty-one-year-old Polish Jew named Yitskhok Bashevis (1904–1991),[2] one of the fortunate few to get a visa to America in the midst of the Depression and to land a lucrative job writing for the *Jewish Daily Forward*. Despite the plethora of such newspapers, despite the network of schools, the *landsman-shaftn* (home-town associations), labor unions, high- and lowbrow theater, Bashevis was convinced that Yiddish secularism had failed, and one had only to listen to American Jews talking – from Brighton Beach to Miami Beach – to realize that Yiddish had ceased to be a universal Jewish language. So what was left?

By 1943, Bashevis had found the answer, and let his literary colleagues know it, in a manifesto innocently titled "Problems of Yiddish Prose in America." Bashevis argued that because the old language, replete with such quaint Slavicisms as *vetshere, podeshve, kholeve,* and *zavyase,* sounds utterly absurd in an American context; and because the language actually spoken by American Jews was a vulgar patois, a creole, the only alternative for a writer of Yiddish prose was to return to a reimagined past. He called on the surviving Yiddish writers to turn their backs on America, and to reclaim a world in which Yiddish was inseparable from *yiddishkcyt* (Jewishness).

Having delivered the radically conservative message, Bashevis then delivered the modernist goods. He perfected an art of demonic realism, grounded in the lexicon of Torah, Talmud, and Zohar; in the cadences of Yiddish folk-speech; in a minutely realized prewar Polish landscape; and in the fantastically complex triangular drama of Id, Ego, and Superego. Faithfully adhering to the rigorous terms of his own manifesto, he produced some of his greatest work (Roskies, *A Bridge of Longing,* chapter 10).

But as in his fiction, so in life, such rules were made only to be broken. "Like the libertines of his stories who require a social context of propriety," to quote Ruth Wisse, "Singer defines a thoroughly conservative norm which he may then bedevil and transgress" ("Singer's Paradoxical Progress," 152). This is what happened to Bashevis in the early Thirties, and it happened again, in January 1957, when he began to serialize in the *Jewish Daily Forward* a huge novel set in Manhattan and Miami Beach that would take a year's worth of installments to complete. If Sholem Asch had enshrined a working class, multi-ethnic enclave on 48th Street, next to the East River, then Bashevis laid claim to the other side of town, where Jews lived in fancy apartments and each Jew spoke many languages.

Shadows on the Hudson is a rambling novel that recycles Singer's favorite plot of one extremely brainy man simultaneously involved with three women, but who still finds time for lengthy philosophical ruminations. The American setting is as yet hardly more than a tease, and Manhattan is but a shadow of Warsaw. By 1960, however, Bashevis hit his stride, and no longer needed a parodic foil to stimulate his American Yiddish muse. He had found his own way of superimposing the two triangles of desire, the one erotic, the other, geographic. In *Enemies: A Love Story* (1966), each woman lives in a different borough of Greater New York, and each borough represents a distinctly different realm of desire.

The main locale, as many may remember, if not from reading the novel then from seeing Paul Mazursky's superb screen version of 1989, is Coney Island, a perfect choice, because the Yiddish-speaking immigrants have moved in en masse, even as the amusement park has gone downhill. The year is 1946.

Here is Herman Broder standing at the window, just as alienated from his surroundings as Zarkhi before him, and for good reason, because everything about Herman is fake. As a ghost writer for a fake rabbi, he peddles ideas he does not believe in, and lives with a fake-Jewish wife in a fake-Jewish home.

> A few blocks away, the ocean heaved. From the Boardwalk and Surf Avenue came the noises of a Coney Island summer morning. Yet, on the little street between Mermaid and Neptune Avenues, everything was quiet. A light breeze was blowing; a few trees grew there. Birds twittered in the branches. The incoming tide brought with it a smell of fish, and something undefinable, a stench of putrefaction. When Herman put his head out of the window, he could see old shipwrecks that had been abandoned in the bay. Armored creatures had attached themselves to the slimy hulls – half alive, half sunk in primeval sleep.
>
> (*Enemies*, 15)

So something is rotten in the borough of Brooklyn. Whatever moments of serenity Herman will experience with Jadwiga, the Polish peasant woman who saved him from the Nazis, America itself will never meet his spiritual needs. For all his paranoia, however, Herman realizes the difference between Europe and America. Inside the subway, on his way to Rabbi Milton Lampert's office, Herman concludes that "here the young seemed dominated by lust for enjoyment rather than for mischief" (18).

A kind of mischief bedevils Herman's life, however. Her name is Masha, and she lives in a semi-abandoned house in a derelict part of the Bronx. The subway ride there is akin to a descent into Hell. "What would happen," Herman wonders as he walks up the rickety stairs to the apartment that Masha shares with her survivor-mother, Shifra-Puah, "if the earth were to split into two parts, exactly between the Bronx and Brooklyn? He would have to remain here" (32). Here, where Shifra-Puah, dressed in black, constantly complains that something is burning, and where Masha's red hair is described as "fire and pitch" and a cigarette always dangles between her full lips – here is literally the abode of the demons. When Masha fails to drag him down to Hell at novel's end, he is consigned to Purgatory instead.

In between, Herman's first wife Tamara, presumably killed by the Nazis, rises from the dead and finds her way to the Lower East Side. So Herman is caught within a structure of triangular desire that looks something like this:

Tamara, whom he meets in the home of a real rabbi, where the smells and the rhythms are the same as they were in Poland, preserves the memory of their two murdered children, and thus represents the immediate, severed past.

Masha, who lives in a haunted house in the Bronx, inhabits the demonic present.

And Jadwiga, the Righteous Gentile, who lives in Coney Island, represents an all-too-perfect future. Jadwiga, following upon her heartfelt conversion to Judaism, gets pregnant with Herman's only living progeny.

In *Enemies*, therefore, the structure of triangular desire is rendered that much more tangible, inevitable, by a substratum of irrational, demonic, forces. Of course, it takes a hopelessly neurotic, hyper-intellectual, and traumatized Holocaust survivor to experience the three boroughs of New York City in quite the way that Herman Broder does, and it comes as no surprise that he ultimately quits the scene, leaving two out of the three women to raise his newborn daughter.

No one would confuse *Enemies* with a novel by Sholem Asch. For Asch, we recall, each point on the compass had an "objective," historical, reality. Kuzmin was the seat of the dead past as Uncle Moses' sweatshop embodied the unredeemed present, as Coney Island represented the messianic future. Asch's allegorical landscape was populist, in keeping with the conventions of Yiddish popular fiction. Bashevis Singer, writing for Asch's old paper – soon to be the only Yiddish secular daily, then weekly, in America – exploits the same conventions for opposite ends. Herman Broder inhabits a subjective-demonic landscape which, if anything, hearkens back to Zarkhi's song of the Coney Island seashore. Singer's triangular romance is a soft-core version of Halpern's ontology of exile.

From beginning to end, during a hundred years of solicitude, Yiddish literature in America gave voice to an anxious present caught between a severed past and an unattainable future.

From beginning to end, Yiddish poets, playwrights, and prose writers, exploiting a language that was itself the sum and substance of three different cultural realms, found new means to render this structure of triangular desire: from the forbidding *mokem, korner vey un elnt* (Off-limits...corner pain and anguish) which straddles the distant Lithuanian village and even more distant Promised Land of socialist brotherhood and national rebirth; to the sweatshop of Uncle Moses, located midway between Kuzmin and the beach-cum-amusement-park at Coney Island; to the Coney Island seashore after dark, as opposed to the seashore in the light of day, and the seashore after death; to the Boardwalk, located midway between the Bronx and the Lower East Side.

Whether they stand with their backs to America and their faces to the sea, or face the opposite direction; whether together or alone; whether in longing or loathing, the immigrants and exiles who populate the pages of American Yiddish literature occupy a unique, liminal space.

Is this Boardwalk here their own,
As it is, in light of dawn?
Sure, it's their Boardwalk. What, not their Boardwalk?

NOTES

1. Note the absence of certain key passages from the English edition.
2. Referred to as Yitskhok Bashevis in the Yiddish literary world, and as Isaac Bashevis Singer in the non-Yiddish literary world.

REFERENCES AND SUGGESTED FURTHER READINGS

Asch, Sholem. *Onkl Mozes.* (1918). Ed. Shmuel Rozhansky. Buenos Aires: Ateneo Literario en el IWO, 1973; *Uncle Moses.* In *Three Novels*, trans. Elsa Krauch. New York: Putnam's, 1938.

Bloom, Harold. "Still Haunted by Covenant." *New York Times Book Review*, January 31, 1988.

Cox, Richard. "Coney Island: Urban Symbol in American Art." In *Brooklyn USA: the Fourth Largest City in America*. Ed. Rita Seiden Miller. New York: Brooklyn College Press, 1979. 137–148.

"The Golden Peacock/Di goldene pave." Ed. Eleanor Gordon Mlotek. *Mir trogn a gezang/The New Book of Yiddish Songs*. 2nd rev. edn. New York: Workmen's Circle, 1977.

Gordin, Jacob. *God, Man, and Devil: Yiddish Plays in Translation.* Ed. Nahma Sandrow. Syracuse, NY: Syracuse University Press, 1999.

Halpern, Moyshe-Leyb. "Our Garden/Undzer gortn." Trans. Benjamin and Barbara Harshav. In *American Yiddish Poetry: A Bilingual Anthology*. Ed. Benjamin and Barbara Harshav. Berkeley: University of California Press, 1986.

"The End of the Book." In *American Yiddish Poetry: A Bilingual Anthology*. Ed. Benjamin and Barbara Harshav. Berkeley: University of California Press, 1986.

"Zarkhi to Himself." In *American Yiddish Poetry: A Bilingual Anthology*. Ed. Benjamin and Barbara Harshav. Berkeley: University of California Press, 1986.

"The Street Drummer/Der gasnpoyker", "Memento Mori." In *The Penguin Book of Modern Yiddish Verse*. Eds. Irving Howe, Ruth Wisse, and Khone Shmeruk. New York: Viking, 1987.

Harshav, Benjamin. *The Meaning of Yiddish.* Berkeley: University of California Press, 1990.

Harshav, Benjamin and Barbara Harshav, eds. *American Yiddish Poetry: A Bilingual Anthology.* Berkeley: University of California Press, 1986.

Howe, Irving, Ruth Wisse, and Khone Shmeruk, eds. *The Penguin Book of Modern Yiddish Verse.* New York: Viking, 1987.

Ignatoff, David. *In keslgrub.* New York: Inzl, 1918.

Kobrin, Leon. "From 'Daytchmerish' to Yiddish in America." (1943). Trans. Joseph Landis. *Yiddish* 2.2–3 (1976): 37–48.

Krutikov, Mikhail. *Yiddish Fiction and the Crisis of Modernity, 1905–1914.* Stanford, CA: Stanford University Press, 2001.

Leivick, H. "Di–on traditsye." *Der inzl,* January 1918.

Opatoshu, Joseph. *Romance of a Horse Thief*. In *A Shtetl and Other Yiddish Novellas*. 2nd. rev. edn. Ed. Ruth R. Wisse. Detroit: Wayne State University Press, 1986.

Rosenfeld, Morris. *Songs from the Ghetto*. 2nd edn. Ed. Leo Weiner. Boston: Small, Maynard and Company, 1900.

"Fun di Ketskils," in *Geveylte shriftn*. New York: Forverts. 1912.

"My Resting Place." *Mir trogn a gezang / The New Book of Yiddish Songs*. 2nd rev. edn. Ed. Eleanor Gordon Mlotek. New York: Workmen's Circle, 1977; trans. as "My Place" by Aaron Kramer in *A Treasury of Yiddish Poetry*. Eds. Irving Howe and Eliezer Greenberg. New York: Holt Reinhart and Winston, 1969.

"The Sweatshop/Der svet-shap." Trans. Aaron Kramer in *The Penguin Book of Modern Yiddish Verse*. Eds. Irving Howe, Ruth R. Wisse, and Khone Shmeruk. New York: Viking, 1987.

Roskies, David G. *Against the Apocalypse: Responses to Catastrophe in Modern Jewish Culture*. Cambridge, MA: Harvard University Press, 1984.

A Bridge of Longing: The Lost Art of Yiddish Storytelling. Cambridge, MA: Harvard University Press, 1995.

The Jewish Search for a Usable Past. Bloomington: University of Indiana Press, 1999.

Shapiro, Lamed. "Doc." In *Newyorkish un andere zakhn*. New York: Farlag Aleyn.

"Eating Days" and "Smoke." In *A Treasury of Yiddish Stories*, 2nd rev. edn. Eds. Irving Howe and Eliezer Greenberg. New York: Viking, 1989.

"Newyorkish." In *New Yorkish and Other American Yiddish Stories*. Ed. Max Rosenfeld. Philadelphia, PA: Sholom Aleichem Club Press, 1995.

Singer, Isaac Bashevis. *Enemies: A Love Story*. (1966). Trans. Aliza Shevrin and Elizabeth Shub. New York: Farrar Straus and Giroux, 1972.

"Problems of Yiddish Prose in America." Trans. Robert H. Wolf. *Prooftexts* 9 (1989): 5–12.

Shadows on the Hudson. Trans. Joseph Sherman. New York: Farrar Straus and Giroux, 1998.

Weinreich, Max. *History of the Yiddish Language*. Trans. Shlomo Noble. Chicago and London: University of Chicago Press, 1980.

Wisse, Ruth R. "Singer's Paradoxical Progress." *Studies in American Jewish Literature* 1 (1981): 152.

A Little Love in Big Manhattan: Two Yiddish Poets. Cambridge, MA: Harvard University Press, 1988.

5

ALAN MINTZ

Hebrew literature in America

The existence of a substantial body of Hebrew literature written on American shores is one of the best-kept secrets of Jewish American cultural history. In 1927, there were 110 Hebrew authors living in the United States, according to Daniel Persky, a columnist for the Hebrew-language newspaper *Hadoar*, which had been published in New York since 1922. Among this large number were at least a dozen Hebrew poets with serious bodies of published work and a smaller yet still substantial number of major prose writers, dramatists, and essayists. There were Hebrew publishing houses, Hebrew literary clubs and writers associations, and many Hebrew periodicals and literary journals that appeared over the course of the twentieth century. Hebrew belles-lettres were allied to a cultural and educational movement that established a network of Hebrew colleges and Hebrew summer camps and exerted enormous influence on the development of Jewish education in America.

There are many obvious reasons why Hebrew culture failed to thrive in America, but the reasons why its struggles and achievements have been forgotten are less obvious. This question, which is essentially a question about cultural memory, is entangled with the sad fate of Yiddish in America and the brilliant success of Hebrew in Israel. In contrast to Hebrew, Yiddish had a firm basis in the Jewish immigrant masses – in the music halls and the tabloids, at home and in the streets. When Yiddish declined under the force of galloping Americanization, it was the remembrance of popular culture that became the substance of nostalgia during the last quarter of the twentieth century. The teeming immigrant culture evoked by Irving Howe in his seminal *The World of Our Fathers* became for many American Jews the record of the collective past, a touchstone for family memories put aside in the rush of acculturation. In this great Jewish American narrative, there was little room for Hebrew, the preoccupation of a small elite and a language more written than spoken.

Even though American Jewry was reluctant to dwell on the victimization of Jews in the Holocaust, it proved eager to celebrate and support the emergence of the new State of Israel with its image of very different kinds of Jews. Jewish organizations and sectors of the community that formerly had opposed Zionism now gave their approval to the struggles for the Jewish state as a refuge for Holocaust survivors and for the victims of Arab nationalism. Israeli military pluck, agricultural innovations, and the appurtenances of statehood exerted a fascination on American Jews; and so, to a much more limited but palpable extent, did Israeli Hebrew. To the degree that American Jews wanted to learn Hebrew they wanted to learn Israeli Hebrew in the Israeli accent and through the *ulpan* method, which stressed conversational skills used in everyday life in the new country. When Hebrew was eventually admitted to the curriculum of major American universities, it was on the strength of its being a "foreign language," the language of a contemporary Middle Eastern country, in addition to its ancient pedigree and the rise of ethnic studies. In all the renewed interest in Hebrew brought about by the establishment of Israel, there was little awareness that Hebrew culture had long before been revived in Eastern Europe and produced a great literature there. And there was utterly no awareness of the fact that a branch of that culture had been planted in America and struggled valiantly, with not insignificant moments of success, to thrive there.

Still, Hebrew literature in America is an unexpected, even exotic, development, one whose contrariant presence can be easily missed in the sweeping generalizations made about Jewish American life and culture. American Hebraism was the activity of a small elite, an implant from abroad rather than a native growth, cultural in nature rather than religious. It represented a pocket of resistance, not to modernity (which it embraced), but to the monopoly of American culture and language over the life of the educated Jew. It is, in short, a phenomenon that calls for explanation.

Its origins lie in the distinction between Zionism, as the term is generally used today, and Hebrew nationalism. As a political movement, Zionism did not become a force until the 1890s, and it set as its main goal the development of the Jewish settlement in Palestine. The revival of Hebrew as a modern literature began much earlier in the nineteenth century. The writing of the first lyric and epic poetry and novels in Hebrew began as an expression of the Enlightenment vision of the *maskilim* but soon became a vehicle for national aspirations. Like most nationalisms of the time, the Jewish national idea encompassed two central pillars: territory and language. The revival of Hebrew as a language for social criticism, cultural discourse, political debate, as well as a language for poetry, fiction, and drama was part and parcel of the Jewish national enterprise. It was in fact the component of Jewish nationalism that could be developed here and now, as opposed to the nearly insuperable obstacles that faced the territorial agenda of the political Zionists. And indeed, by the first decade of the twentieth century, when there were but a few motley colonies in Palestine, Hebrew literature had already brought forth the sophisticated achievements of Abramowitch (Mendele Mocher Seforim), Bialik, Tchernichovsky, Berdichevsky, and Brenner, to name but a few.

Ahad Ha'am (the pen name of Asher Ginzburg) was the East European intellectual who best articulated this side of the Zionist-nationalist equation. Writing at the end of the nineteenth century, he saw the present hour not only as a crisis for Jews (their physical survival under worsening conditions of Tsarist persecution) but also as a crisis for Judaism (the survival of Jewish culture under the force of emancipation and modernity). Traditional Jewish learning and belief, now exposed to the modern world, were unraveling rapidly. To recoup this loss, Ahad Ha'am proposed a vision of Jewish culture and civilization (*tarbut*) that would conserve the best of classical Jewish thought and morality and, at the same time, engage the best ideas of modern literature, history, and science. The key to this ambitious enterprise of cultural synthesis was Hebrew, the organic glue that would hold the ancient and the modern together. The deeply conservative nature of language, with its multiple layers of historical associations, would help to carry over the meanings of the past, while the critical absorption of worthy ideas from European culture into the Hebrew language would domesticate them within a Jewish milieu.

Ahad Ha'am's ideas, together with the larger enterprise of Hebrew literature, fired the imagination of a generation of East European young people at the turn of the century who had left behind traditional homes to enter the turbulent social and ideological currents of the times. Although they could no longer believe in the God of their fathers, they identified with the fate of the Jewish people, conceived in terms of nationhood, and they seized upon Hebrew revived as the medium in which Jewish destiny, both collective and individual, would be worked out. The outstanding advantage of this position was that it was portable, and Ahad Ha'am had in fact declared that the Hebrew cultural revival would necessarily have to begin and continue in diaspora Jewish communities. With the break-up of the centers of Jewish life in Russia during war and revolution, young people committed to Hebrew nationalism set off to three destinations: European cities like Warsaw, Vilna, and Vienna outside Soviet control; Palestine (whose difficulties and privations were legendary); and America. A large number of Hebrew writers and littérateurs were among the trickle of Jews who made their way to Palestine, and a proportionally tiny number among the millions who emigrated to America. Yet there was still, in absolute terms, a substantial kernel of Hebrew cultural activists whose families or fates brought them to New York rather than Jaffa or Warsaw. During World War I, when the centers of Hebrew cultural production both in Europe and Palestine had been shut down, and when such figures as David Ben-Gurion, Yitshak Ben-Zvi, and Eliezer Ben-Yehuda were living in New York, it did not seem so improbable that a center of Hebrew culture could emerge in America.

The achievements of the Hebrew movement in America can be divided into two spheres: culture and education, on one hand; literature, on the other. The two are really part of the same phenomenon; for the writers were often educators (as were their readers), and their activity took place around schools and Hebrew colleges. Yet at the same time, the writers made a point of keeping belletristic writing separate from journalism and ideological discussions. Even if the setting of the literature was the cultural and educational circles of the Hebrew movement, literature was literature, and it was written according to the canons of other fine literature in Hebrew and European languages. Hebrew *literature* in America forms the main subject of this chapter. But in terms of influence on the wider course of American Jewish life, it is the areas of culture and education that have had the greatest impact and also deserve mention.

As an ideology, Hebraism, or *Tarbut Ivrit*, as it was called by its adherents, located itself in a position between religion and politics as totalizing definitions of Judaism. Religion could be blind to modern man's need for beauty and deaf to the dimension of the beautiful in its own classical sacred literature; and it rejected a historical understanding of the development of the institutions of Judaism. Politics – both political Zionism and the left-wing causes to which Jewish young people were attracted in the twenties in massive numbers – dismissed out of hand the vast repository of Jewish spiritual creativity during the great ages of faith. *Tarbut Ivrit* rejected the reductiveness of religion and politics rather than the validity of their claims per se. It posited the existence of a Jewish culture which, developing over the centuries, absorbed the creations of political and religious genius into a larger whole. This whole was called by the name *tarbut*, a disused biblical word that was revived to serve as an equivalent to the French *civilisation* and the German *Kultur*. The identity and integrity of this whole was guaranteed by Hebrew, the historical tongue of Jewish national creativity. Even if important works had been composed in, say, Aramaic and Arabic, their enduring impact was secured by their translation or absorption into Hebrew. Early in the twentieth century, when Hebrew had been reborn as a literary language and was beginning to become again a spoken language, a great opportunity had been created for Hebrew to assume its rightful role as the world language of the Jewish people at this moment of dislocation and dispersion. At this time of the rapid disintegration of religious observance, the spread of assimilation, and the assertion of political ideologies, Hebrew was uniquely positioned to serve as the bridge between the classical heritage from the age of faith and the culture of modernity.

In practice, the Hebraist position entailed a great deal of pride and very little power. Imagine New York's Lower East Side, the cradle of the Hebraist movement, during World War I and in the decade that followed. The young Hebraists, mostly Hebrew teachers and Talmud Torah principals, looked around them with withering scorn at what passed for Jewish culture and leadership. The vulgarity of the Yiddish press and the music-hall culture of Second Avenue disgusted them. Socialism, Bundism and labor union organizing betrayed the idea of Jewish peoplehood and its national aspirations. With the exception of Meir Berlin and his Mizrahi movement, Orthodoxy could make no claims on the soul of a modern young person. Many of the American rabbis trained in Solomon Schechter's uptown Jewish Theological Seminary delivered their silver-tongued oratory to their philistine congregations but were wholly illiterate in modern Hebrew and its rich literature. The greatest scorn was reserved for those closest to home. American Zionism, led by Louis Brandeis, may have rallied to the idea of Zion as a refuge for the persecuted Jews of Europe, but it had no interest in Zionism as a movement of cultural renewal with Hebrew as its life blood. The rightness – and righteousness – of all of these critiques of Jewish American culture did not disguise the fact that the Hebraists remained a small and rather powerless elite whose capacity to broadcast its message was limited, ironically, by its very commitment to Hebrew.

There is one significant exception to the general picture of Hebraist marginality. The vast majority of afternoon Jewish schools (schools that were supplemental to public schools) in twentieth-century America were called "Hebrew" schools. In that appellation, a meaningful rather than a semantic distinction, lies the story of an unlikely revolution in Jewish education – a story that can only be suggested here in brief. Given the largely non-nationalist and non-Hebraic nature of the development of synagogue life in America between the two world wars, it was to have been expected that Jewish schools would have been essentially religious schools that aimed at transmitting beliefs, customs, and synagogue skills. Yet in addition, the educational institutions that widely came into being were Hebraist to the core. They taught modern spoken Hebrew, conveyed a Zionist interpretation of Jewish history, and generally suffused the schools with the culture of the *Yishuv* (the Zionist settlement in Palestine), with a generous dose of modern Hebrew folk songs and folk dances. The diffuse and far-ranging effects of this Hebraist "kidnapping" of Jewish American education have yet to be explored and appreciated. Suffice it to say that the often remarked-upon sudden Zionization of American Jewry after World War II was made possible by the values absorbed by generations of American Jews during the long afternoon hours they sat, willingly or unwillingly, in Hebrew school.

The classroom was left far behind, however, when the Hebraists sat down to write their poems and stories. For them, art was art and education was education. The body of artistic work they produced is considerable, although, as with any serious cultural phenomenon, it is not easy to take its measure. First, the question of size.[1] The broadest vein of creativity in Hebrew writing was found in poetry. The poets who wrote and published estimable bodies of verse include Hillel Bavli, Israel Efros, Shimon Ginsberg, Shimon Halkin, Moshe Feinshtein, H. A. Friedland, E. E. Lisitzky, Gavriel Preil, Avraham Regelson, Isig Silberschlag, and Benjamin Silkiner. The important prose writers are A. A. Arieli, S. L. Blank, Halkin, Bernard Isaacs, Lisitzky, Avraham Shoyer, and Reuven Wallenrod. Important essayists include Avraham Epstein, Daniel Persky, Menahem Ribalow. The sole major playwright in Hebrew is Harry Seckler. In the absence of any agreed-upon standard for gauging the weight of literary communities, it is safe to say that America was a substantial, if modest, center of Hebrew literature. The major center between the world wars, to be sure, was Palestine; but as in Poland, Hebrew literary creativity in America was firmly rooted in its native ground.

Taking the qualitative measure of Hebrew literature in America is even more difficult. There were many writers and many temperaments. Yet it may serve to attempt a gross characterization by referring to parallel developments in Hebrew literature elsewhere. In the first two decades of the century, Hebrew poetry – the preeminent literary form on the American scene – was dominated in East Europe by the poetics of Hayyim Nahman Bialik and his contemporaries. The sway of this poetics was to be severely challenged in the 1920s by the symbolist modernism of Avraham Shlonsky, the violent expessionism of Uri Zvi Greenberg, and the imagistic minimalism of David Fogel. Yet the American Hebrew poets carried the banner of Bialikian poetics rather than revolting against it. They had brought this loyalty with them when they had come from Europe as very young men. In their formative educations in American high schools and universities, their chief exposure had been to the great English and American romantic poets rather than to T. S. Eliot, Ezra Pound, and Hart Crane.

The poetic world of the Bialik generation was poised somewhere between late romanticism and modernism. From these romantic origins came the fundamental assumption of a possible rapport between the soul of the poet and the *anima mundi*, the soul of the world, a sympathetic vibration that once existed between the sensitive soul of the child and an animate universe. In the Jewish-Hebraic version of this privileged moment, the soul of the child is embraced and inspired by the more real-than-life legends and stories of the Bible and rabbinic literature and by the poetry of ritual and sacred time. The loss of this nurturing rapport comes about not only because of the exile from childhood but also because this loss is taking place at a time when tradition has collapsed generally and the locus of Jewish life has moved from the countryside to the cities. Rather than compensating for these losses, the unsuccessful longing for romantic love only exposes the impoverishment of the self. Failed attempts to reconnect with the vibrancy of childhood and the nurturance of the religious tradition similarly end in underscoring the essential aloneness of man.

Despite the collapse of religious tradition, Hebrew remained a poetic idiom inextricably and productively rooted in the past. Raised in the textual culture of the *beit midrash* (the study house), the poets of Bialik's generation – and their readers – could exploit the rich, allusive potential of Hebrew for ironic purposes. As a modern literary medium, Hebrew had the power simultaneously to invoke and subvert the dense authority of received traditions. Yet this subversion had its own consequences; for once meanings behind and beneath the words were no longer guaranteed by religious truth, the void beneath became doubly threatening.

Alongside this essentially lyric mode existed another posture altogether: prophecy. The poet's calling as a Hebrew poet obliged him to address the fate of the Jewish people in hours of emergency. In the tradition of Hebrew prophecy, the poet's reproach is directed not at the external enemy but at an internal target: the cowardice and evasions of his own people. The greatest instance of this prophetic rebuke is Bialik's epic poem "In the City of Slaughter," which blames the victims of the Kishenev pogrom for complicity in their own victimization. Without adopting the same prophetic stance, the poetry of Bialik's contemporaries, Saul Tchernichovsky and Zalman Schneour, also engages contemporary realities, especially political upheavals and scientific revolutions.

This poetic model, consolidated by 1910, was adopted by American Hebrew poets and perpetuated into mid-century, a time when Hebrew verse in Palestine was being roiled and transformed by a variety of European modernisms. The proponents and practitioners of the new poetry in *Eretz Yisrael* were quick to accuse the Americans of a pallid classicism; and the Americans in turn were quick to defend their enterprise. As early as 1924, Shimon Halkin, who was only twenty-five years old at the time,[2] wrote that the poetry of his counterparts in *Eretz Yisrael* was imitative and permeated with "neurosis, an uneven style, an obscurantism of content, and a striving toward the outlandish." It reiterates the mood of *ennui* and lacks the " 'religiosity' that is expressed in true lyric poetry." American Hebrew poetry, on the other hand, is "straightforward, speaks simply, and tries to crystallize and refine emotions rather than befog them." Moreover, "it strives to return man to poetry and poetry to man" (Halkin, "Hashirah ha'ivrit," 10–12).[3]

Discounting some of their defensive zeal, Halkin's terms bring the American achievement into sharper focus. The American Hebrew poets did indeed remain loyal to what had already become, within the accelerated development of modern Hebrew verse, a classical standard. Yet theirs was a loyalty with a definite revisionist slant; the paradigm of Bialik's late romanticism held, but in a domesticated version. Pushed to the margins, to begin with, was the resounding authority of the prophetic voice; the American Hebrew poets did not aspire to spiritual leadership in the national arena. They stressed the aloneness of the lyric voice in part because of the reality of their situation: they had no mass audience in America. That aloneness was a profound exile within the bustling immigrant milieu, and it led to melancholy as a modal poetic mood. Given the limitations imposed on them, the American poets made a virtue out of necessity and cultivated the lyric voice's potential for straightforwardness, lucidity, and serenity. At moments, this classicism even reaches back in time, evoking the *Haskalah* poetry that preceded Bialik with its meditations on such timeless categories as beauty, truth, and love. This is a poetry of refinement and subtlety rather than stormy emotions and strong effects, as Menachem Ribalow stressed in the introduction to his 1938 anthology of American Hebrew poetry.

The contemplation of nature was especially cultivated by the Americans, often in the form of simple observation of the external world or as a stimulus to states of mood and feeling. For several American Hebrew poets, notably Halkin and Avraham Regelson, the contemplation of the vast reaches of the American landscape gave rise to more ambitious metaphysical and transcendental speculations. The simultaneous and paradoxical rejection of Judaism and the experience of aching loss that followed its collapse was the hallmark of European poetry of Bialik's generation. For the Americans, however, this was a crisis that was long taken for granted. Their metaphysical flights, often taking the form of a search for God within or through nature, are religious without being specifically Judaic, despite the biblically tinged Hebrew in which these explorations are expressed. This is true of the stylistic register of American Hebrew poetry in general, which flexibly integrates later periods of Hebrew onto a biblical base without generally engaging in the complex, knotted allusions to classical sources common to the earlier, European style.[4]

The assessment of the conservatism of American Hebrew poetry has differed markedly in Israel and America. In Israel, where the successive waves of modernism had pushed poetry through several generational transformations during the twentieth century, the American scene was often viewed as a provincial backwater frozen in time. Although early in the century there had been expectations for a dynamic literary center, the weight of America had prevailed, and the hoped-for dynamism never emerged. The Americans, in contrast, viewed their conservatism as a badge of honor and as a principled classicism. Their poetic practice took up a stance against the barbarisms of European literary imports and adhered to what was perceived to be the normative and native Judaic–biblical voice of Hebrew verse that had emerged from within East European Jewry at the turn of the century.

A third, arguably more productive way to view American Hebrew literature remains. Rather than charting it on a continuum between conservative and avant-garde poetics or gauging the degree of its remove from the main literary center – all of which stress what it is not rather than what it is – it is far more interesting to focus on the Americanness of American Hebrew literature. American Hebrew literature can be thought of as an epiphenomenon of the Hebrew literary system, which was centered in Palestine between the two world wars, or it can be thought of as an elite experiment within the context of Jewish American cultural history. To take the latter approach means to take the American Hebrew writers as American writers with roots in the Hebrew nationalism of East Europe who seek to engage the American milieu through the lens of Hebrew. Much American Hebrew literature, especially lyric poetry, contemplates such universal themes of nature, beauty, and loneliness. But much explores America; and precisely because there is so much of America to explore, there is considerable fascination in discovering which aspects of the American experience attracted the American Hebrew imagination and which did not.

This engagement, we should note, was encouraged, even demanded, by Hebrew writers and critics in the literary center in *Eretz Yisrael*. Reviewing an early collection of writings by Americans (*Senunit*, edited by Reuven Brainin in 1910), Yosef Haim Brenner, the most influential literary voice in literary circles in Palestine before World War I, expressed extreme impatience with the scarcity of American themes in the poems before him. Like the Americans, Brenner had emigrated from East Europe but had come to Jaffa rather than New York, and what the Americans could potentially contribute to the new Hebrew literature, in his view, was not a pallid replication of European themes but a vibrant representation of the American milieu – a request repeated often by Hebrew writers in Palestine over the next twenty years (Govrin, "The Call for 'Americanness',").

In time American Hebrew writers did turn toward American themes but in ways that were ironically at odds with the expectations expressed from abroad; and it is far from certain that they were responding to anything other than their own internal promptings. Brenner and others had wished for a window onto the struggles of Jewish immigrants to come to terms with the New World that took them beyond the tales of business collars, and "bluff" that they could read in the Yiddish tabloids. In prose fiction, especially in Halkin's *Ad mashber* (*Crisis*, 1945) and Wallendrod's stories and novels, this expectation was met, although at a considerable lag in time. Yet poetry turned its back on the immigrant scene and reached toward the America of different eras and locales. Silkiner wrote an epic about American Indians during the period of the Spanish conquest. Efros composed a book-length narrative poem on the California gold rush. Halkin translated Whitman's *Leaves of Grass* and composed poem cycles set in Santa Barbara and in the Michigan dunes Lisitzky, who settled in New Orleans, wrote a book of linked poems based on Negro spirituals. Bavli offered poetic portraits of figures from the New England countryside. Ginsburg translated William Cullen Bryant, Edgar Allen Poe, and Edward Arlington Robinson. Regelson wrote essays about Longfellow. To give some specificity to this general picture, I will focus on one illustrative topic: the American Indian epics in American Hebrew literature.

Native Americans are the quintessential American subject, yet no English reader – or no Hebrew reader, for that matter – would fail to find it strange to encounter, albeit in print, Hebrew-speaking and Hebrew-thinking Indians. Yet for the American Hebrew poets it was a strangeness that was staged with great deliberateness and not for its own sake. For a resonant affinity exists between the high nobility and sad fortunes of the Indians and those of the dwindling tribe of Hebrew writers on the American continent. The subject, moreover, was far from marginal. No fewer than three book-length epic compositions appeared in Hebrew in America: *Mul ohel Timura* (*Before the Tent of Timura*, 1910) by Benjamin Silkiner, *Vigvamim shotkim* (*Silent Wigwams*, 1933) by Israel Efros and *Medurot do'akhot* (*Smouldering Campfires*, 1937) by Ephraim Lisitzky.[5] Of the three, Silkiner's work is chiefly remarkable for its earliness. A Bible instructor at the Teacher's Institute of the Jewish Theological Seminary in New York, Silkiner stood at the center of a circle of idealistic, young Hebraists even before the movement came into its own during the First World War.[6] Even before Brenner issued his famous complaint about the dearth of Americanness in American Hebrew poetry, Silkiner had created a full-fledged work on an exotic American topic Although its appearence was widely noted, *Mul ohel Timura* was awkwardly structured and hard to read, and even within the intimate world of American Hebraism it remained an esteemed, but largely unread, pioneering effort. It appeared a year or two before the great poet Shaul Tchernichovsky's Hebrew translation of Longfellow's *Hiawatha*, the ur-text of American romantic writing about Native Americans, and although no great sensation was stirred up in the republic of Hebrew letters, the appearance of Silkiner's poem and Tchernichovsky's translation created a climate of legitimacy for this subject matter.

With the appearance in 1933 of Israel Efros' lambent and affecting book-length poem *Silent Wigwams*, it was clear to all that the American theme of American Hebrew poetry had at last come into its own. Born in Ostrog, Ukraine, Efros (1891–1981) came to America in 1905, studied in *yeshivot*, and received a doctorate in philosophy.[7] Efros' long career – whose last phase (from 1955) took place in Israel, where he served as the rector of the newly established Tel Aviv University – was marked by a commitment to lyric poetry of intense musicality interrupted by occasional major projects of poetic narrative. *Silent Wigwams* was followed in 1942 by *Zahav* (*Gold*), which is set during the California Gold Rush.

Because *Silent Wigwams* is a work that is unfamiliar even to most students of Hebrew literature, it is worth giving a brief description of the story line. The setting is Maryland's Chesapeake Peninsula; the time, the end of the seventeenth century or the beginning of the eighteenth. Tom, an English artist who has been brutally assaulted and cast out of the English settlement of Talbot because of his quiet ways, is taken in and nursed back to health by Lalari, the daughter of the *sachem* of the local Indian nation. By night Tom listens to the legends told by the elders around the campfire, and by day he fashions beautiful images of Indian life and lore. He and Lalari fall in love, despite the disapproval of her father and the jealous enmity of a tribal warrior who has been too shy to express his feelings for Lalari. The couple moves to another village, but their relationship begins to unravel when Tom becomes absorbed in memories of a highborn lady in England who had scorned his love because he was a penniless artist. Lalari realizes that she cannot forestall his melancholy, and shows him the wreck of a Spanish galleon with an undiscovered strongbox of gold. After Tom sails for England with the treasure, Lalari discovers she is pregnant and gives birth in isolation to a stillborn child. Lalari's father counsels revenge against Tom, who in the meantime has returned disillusioned from abroad and has sought to return to Lalari. Ennobled by suffering and love, Lalari chooses instead to commit suicide and to be gathered unto her ancestors. Unconsoled by a concomitant belief in the continuity between life and death, Tom looks on at her funeral rites, consumed by remorse and despair.

From the outset, *Silent Wigwams* is based on the generalizing premise of an encounter between Indian and European worldviews. Yet there is no ulti-mate aspiration toward typicality. Both Lalari and Tom are singular in their relationship to their respective societies; they each embody qualities that are unique to their cultures but uncommonly realized. Lalari stands apart from the braves' preoccupation with hunting and battle and from the women's submissive domesticity. Instead, she is given to contemplative communion with nature during solitary retreats in the forests, and she is curious about and receptive to higher European culture, beyond trinkets, weapons, and firewater. For his part, Tom as an artist is at odds with English society, first with the class snobbery at home and then with the rowdy philistinism of the English settlers, who victimize him because they cannot abide his artistic reticence.

At the center of the poem is a dialectic between the aboriginal sublime and the representational capacities of Western art. The vigor of Indian culture already exists under the sign of fated decline and disappearance. As a member of the colonizing power responsible for the destruction, Tom admits collective guilt; but as an artist in their midst he can offer a sort of restitution. He addresses Lalari:

"My people are guilty. The day will come when we shall wish
To repair the damage but we shall not be able to.
Yet from sea to sea sanctuaries will arise
To rescue your beautiful objects, to collect them and preserve them."
"But what?" asks Lalari, "But what will you save then?"
He sits quietly without speaking while his thoughts give the answer:
Blankets and wampum, colored feathers,
Pairs of moccasins and nothing more, nothing more.   (37)

As a preliterate and unselfconscious society, the Indians cannot represent themselves in art or literature; the poetry of their songs, rites, and legends is destined to remain self-enclosed and not to survive them. The canvases Tom paints of Indian life, although first scorned, are eventually accepted and honored by the tribe, and thus his gift of self-representation is accepted, if only for the short period of his dwelling among them.

Lalari and Tom are ostensibly joined in their singularity by an affirmation of silence. Tom's silent ways and his refusal to talk about himself and dispel the mystery that surrounds his appearance in the town provoke his brutal beating at the hands of the English settlers. For her part, Lalari is a creature entirely at peace with muteness. She is accustomed to "opening the door of her heart silently / And entering on tiptoes and sitting / For hours on end in the room of silence / Within the secret company of musings and reflections" (21). Yet when the couple removes to the new, alien village, the nature of their capacities for silence is revealed to be deeply divergent. Removed from his art and living under conditions of adversity and enforced idleness, Tom's silence is unmasked as a cruel withholding of emotions, a sign of the shallow construction of the social self. But Lalari's silence proves itself to be the genuine fruit of an empathic openness to man and nature, an expression of abiding faithfulness.

With the apotheosis of Lalari, Efros offers more than another version of the superiority of the genuinely primitive over the falsely civilized. He delivers, through a reverie of identification, a *cri de coeur* about the fate of his own embattled tribe: the Hebrew poets of America. Already in the early 1930s it was abundantly clear to Efros that the high hopes once entertained for a vibrant and prestigious center of Hebrew creativity on these shores would not be realized. The isolation of these aristocrats of Hebrew aesthetics within the business-mindedness of immigrant and Americanizing Jewish life was acute. It is not farfetched to hear a wider allegory in the words of Lalari when Tom finds her contemplating the setting sun.

> So sit we all. Sunset facing sunset,
> The decline of a nation facing the decline of the sun.
>
> (37)

In Hebrew the notions of sunset and decline are incorporated in the same word *sheqi'ah*, so that the two declines/sunsets encountering one another (*sheqi'ah mul sheqi'ah*) are extremely evocative. The tragic nobility of the setting sun of American Hebraism receives a kind of epic grandeur from the implied association with the great American instance of conquest and sacrifice. The object of the association is not only to appropriate some of the moral mystique of the lost Indian cause but also to reach for a model of consolation and a way to be reconciled to the failure of a noble dream.

Yet *Silent Wigwams*, a hauntingly beautiful poem that holds up very well in retrospective readings, is by no means only about submission to fate. In the years after World War I, the superiority of the Hebrew cultural center in *Eretz Yisrael* became indisputable, while at the same time the American Hebraists worked to demonstrate that America, as a worthy if weaker partner, has something of its own to contribute to the larger enterprise of Hebrew literature. *Silent Wigwams* asserts that this contribution is made up of something more substantial and challenging than the trappings of exotic locales and the display of wampum and wigwams, moccasins and feathered headdresses. In the brief preface to the poem, Efros observes that among American folk materials there is nothing like the lyric poems and songs of the Indians for the qualities of "pictorial precision, the abundance of color, and a depth of emotion that is at the same time controlled, restrained and hushed" (5). These programmatic intentions, represented by Lalari's outlook, are realized with a notable degree of success in the poem itself. Recalling Halkin's critique of the raucous modernism of contemporary Hebrew poetry, one can appreciate the subversive edge of Efros' American offering of precision, nuance, and tonality.

In 1937, four years after the appearance of Efros' poem, Ephraim Lisitzky published his *Medurot do'akhot (Dying Campfires)*, the third of the American Hebrew Indian epics. Lisitzky (1885–1962) was born in Minsk and came to America at the age of fifteen. After wanderings in Boston, New York, Milwaukee, and Canada, where he spent three years in a remote village, Lisitzky settled in New Orleans, where he directed the Hebrew school. He was a prolific poet who composed many large compositions, including *Be'ohalei Kush (In the Tents of Kush*, 1953), which utilized Negro spirituals and folksongs. Lisitzky is also the author of one of the most powerful Hebrew prose works written in America, *Eleh toldot adam* (1949; translated as *In the Grip of Cross-Currents*, 1959), which is an autobiographical narrative of his early years in America. At 321 pages, Lisitzky's Indian poem is more than twice the length of Efros', and in the imaginative world it attempts to encompass it has greater aspirations toward the epic than its predecessor.

The plot revolves around the rivalry between the Vulture Tribe and the Viper Tribe. The lives of the Vultures have been disrupted by a drought that forces them to seek new territory and by internal conflict. The medicine man Yahahadza and his son Hanugahi work stealthily to usurp the authority of the chief Hutonton and his son Midainga. Hanugahi is exiled for falling in love with a woman from another tribe; and Midainga is put through a solitary ordeal to ready him for leadership. Midainga is then dispatched by his tribe to assassinate Nanpivati, the Vulture chief, but instead of fulfilling his mission he falls in love with the enemy chief's daughter Genitaska, who is drowned by her father in rage and shame. The calamity leads to a reconciliation between the two tribes, which now join in counsel to deal with a new common problem: the growing incursions of the white man. In a trance, the medicine man is visited by a black vision of the future in which the Indian tribes are dispersed and destroyed by the Europeans. Meanwhile, Midainga falls in love with Osnat, the sister of Boaz Smith, leader of the English forces, who claims that his people have come to share the land with the Indians. Midainga is briefly taken in by the rhetoric of coexistence before he is taken prisoner and it is revealed that white men are interested only in conquest. Nanpivati, the Vulture chief, commits suicide in despair over the deaths of his family and tribe. Escaping captivity, Midainga sets out in a canoe to rendezvous with his beloved Genetaska in the afterlife in the Blessed Isles.

This bald outline cannot suggest the substantial portions of *Dying Campfires* that are made up of mythic materials and lyric songs that make no contribution to the plot. Lisitzky is less interested in advancing the narrative about the two tribes than he is in erecting an armature on which he can hang the rich tapestry of Indian creation legends about how nature and animals came to be they way they are. The forward movement is frequently interrupted also by songs sung as expressions of joy, mourning, and longing. These are signs of the programmatic intention Lisitzky describes in his prefatory note. Rather than presuming to be writing history or ethnology, with the incumbent obligations toward accuracy and verisimilitude, Lisitsky states that he has taken license to make his two Indian tribes generally representative of time and place in the manner of poetic truths. For his great aim, he avers, is to "infiltrate and record within Hebrew literature an echo of the poetry of the lost Indians" (3).[8] Having sojourned in the Canadian woods and the American Great Lakes and writing from New Orleans, Lisitzky represents his Indian poem as a contribution to the enlargement of the international enterprise of Hebrew literature by incorporating a source of spiritual and literary vitality available nowhere else. The language Lisitzky uses to describe the manner in which he offers his contribution (*lahaflit ulehaqlit*, "to infiltrate and to record") suggests the forcefulness he deems necessary for a writer working at the extreme geographical margins of the Hebrew literary system to get his offering accepted at its center. The assertiveness was indeed necessary and appropriate but, alas, in the end, unavailing; for the American Indian epics failed to elicit much response from the literary community in Palestine. Perhaps the need for romantic aboriginal subjects had been fulfilled closer to home in the literary construction of the Arab. In any event, it was the destiny of these Hebrew poems to be read not by their intended readers in Europe and Palestine but by colleagues in New York and Chicago, who had more direct means of discovering the resonant soulfulness of Native American culture.

If Lisitzky joins Efros in this unrequited aspiration, he tries to accomplish something quite different in his poems. Efros cares little for the mythic structure of Indian culture. He indicates that Lalari's pantheistic connection to the natural world enables her to escape the dread of death and to anticipate a return to a benevolent world beyond the grave, but we hear of no exotic deities and their colorful intrigues in that realm. The world of the poem is entirely naturalistic, with melodrama but no violations of natural law. Lisitzky, in contrast, locates the action of his poem *within* the mythological time-world of Indian lore. At the outset of the poem, for example, Nanpivarti falls in love with and impregnates a maiden goddess who has been lowered in a basket from heaven, and there his troubles begin. *Dying Campfires* is replete with creation stories, hoary legends, mythological creatures, rites, and rituals – all with their attendant songs and visions. Lisitzky's allegiance to the inner perspective of Indian experience applies as well to the scope of his canvas. Although the White Man makes a decisive and apocalyptic appearance in the second half of the poem, *Dying Campfires* is largely focused on developments within and between the two Indian tribes. Efros' *Silent Wigwams*, however, turns entirely on the relationship between Tom and Lalari. The poem's founding premise is, as we would say today, cross-cultural, turning on the fate of an intermarriage.

Taken linguistically, intermarriage is a way of thinking about the peculiar identity of the American Hebrew Indian epics. For Hebrew readers in Europe and Palestine, these poems – part of the vast enterprise of translating the world's literature into Hebrew – functioned as a way of catching a glimpse of the exotic life of the first Americans. Yet for Hebrew readers *in America*, who would have known something about Native American legends and customs, the experience of reading about Indians in Hebrew must have been marked by a degree of strangeness; it thus constituted a particular instance of defamiliarization, the literary theoretical term for making the familiar strange and thus "deautomatizing" it. Writing in a modern classical Hebrew style that relied heavily on the Bible, neither Efros nor Lisitzky attempted to de-Judaize the language they employed. In introducing an episode set in the spring time, for example, Efros says simply, "It was an Iyyar evening" (*Silent Wigwams*, 105), using the Hebrew month without any attempt to find a cognate Indian time marker. When an Indian speaker in Lisitzky's poem remembers the sadnesses of the past, he begins his speech with "Eleh ezkera" ("This do I recall"), unavoidably invoking in the ears of any literate reader Psalms 42:5 and the opening words of the martyrological poem read in the synagogue on the afternoon of Yom Kippur.

Efros and Lisitzky were not trying to make their Indians into Hebrew-speaking prophets dressed in beads and moccasins; yet the use of Hebrew in this register encourages an implied affinity from which they did not take pains to flee. Before being gathered to his people, the medicine man in *Dying Campfires* declaims this prophecy:

> I have seen in a vision
> What awaits us in the end of days:
>
> . . .
>
> I see the remnants of tribes,
> The last lonely survivors
> Saved from the multitudes of the Red Face
> Scattered to the four winds
> Like fallen leaves and desert sands.   (147)

The points of identification between the American Hebrew writers and the saga of the American Indians were many, as we have seen. On the grandest level, however, there was a link not only to the fate of the dwindling Hebrew loyalists in America but also to the great arc of Jewish history and the foundational experience of exile. Ironically, the duality of Indian civilization – the beauty and nobility of its culture in its heyday and the profundity of its calamitous destruction – could perhaps best be caught only in the native Hebrew idiom of Jewish civilization.

NOTES

1. Among the names in the following lists are figures who emigrated to Israel at a later stage in their career or moved back and forth between the two communities. Efros and Halkin, for example, went to Israel later in their lives and continued to produce important work there. I have not included a figure like T. Carmi who grew and was educated in America but made his literary career in Israel.
2. Halkin was born in Russia in 1899 and came to America with his family at the age of fifteen. He emigrated to Palestine in 1932 after completing university studies. He returned to America in 1939 and settled permanently in Israel in 1949.
3. The translations are taken from Ezra Spicehandler, "*Ameriqu'iyut* in American Hebrew Literature" in Mintz, *Hebrew in America*, 78–79.
4. This is a highly generalized model, and there are, needless to say, many exceptions and variants. Perhaps the greatest of these is the poetry of Gabriel Preil, one of the latest and youngest of the active Hebrew poets on the American scene. Because of his exposure to Yiddish modernism in America, Preil developed a distinctive imagistic style that was much admired by Israeli readers in the era of Yehuda Amichai and Natan Zach.
5. I render the transcription according to standard Israeli Hebrew, although it should be kept in mind throughout that the poems were written and read according to various forms of the Ashkenazic scansion; thus Lissitzky's title would sound closer to *MeDUros do'Akhos*.
6. Silkiner was born in Vilkija, near Kovno, in Lithuania in 1882 and emigrated to America in 1904 after spending four years in Odessa, the current center of Hebrew literary creativity.
7. Efros was an authority on medieval Jewish philosophy. The landscape and history of Maryland, it should be noted in reference to *Silent Wigwams*, were far from unfamiliar to Efros; he founded the Baltimore Hebrew College in 1918 and taught at Johns Hopkins University between 1917 and 1928.
8. In this introduction, Lisitzky also goes to great lengths to defend himself against the charge that he has made a derivative copy of Longfellow's great Indian poem because he uses the same meter, which had often been cruelly parodied even during Longfellow's lifetime. Lisitzky states that the epic material simply requires this meter, which, in any case, Longfellow had borrowed from the Finnish epics that had begun to be known in his time.

REFERENCES AND SUGGESTED FURTHER READINGS

Arazi, Ruth. *The American Indian in American Hebrew Poetry*. New York University dissertation, 1987.
Efros, Israel. *Vigvamim shotkim (Silent Wigwams)*. Tel Aviv: Mitspeh, 1933.

Feldman, Yael S. *Modernism and Cultural Transfer: Gabriel Preil and the Tradition of Jewish Literary Bilingualism*. Cincinnati: Hebrew Union College Press, 1987.

Govrin, Nurit. "The Call for 'Americanness' and its Realization in American Hebrew Literature." (Hebrew). In *Migvan*. Ed. Stanley Nash. Lod, Israel: Machon Haberman, 1988.

Halkin, Shimon. "Hashirah ha'ivrit ba'ameriqah" (Hebrew poetry in America), *Hadoar* 4.4 (November 28, 1924): 10–12.

Kabakoff, Jacob. "B. N. Silkiner and His Circle: The Genesis of the New Hebrew Literature in America." *Judaism* 29.1 (Winter 1990): 97–103.

Lisitzky, Ephraim. *Medurot do'akhot (Dying Campfires)*. New York: Ogen, 1937.

Longfellow, H. V. *Shirat Hi'avatah* (Hebrew). Trans. Shaul Tchernichovsky. 2nd edn. Jerusalem and Berlin: Moriah, 1922.

Mintz, Alan, ed. *Hebrew in America: Perspectives and Prospects*. Detroit: Wayne State University Press, 1993.

Nash, Stanley, ed. *Migvan: mehkarim besifrut ha'ivrit uvegiluyeha ha'ameriqaniim mugahim leYaakov Qabaqov (Migvan: Studies in Hebrew Literature and its American Manifestations)*. Lod, Israel: Machon Haberman, 1988.

Persky, Daniel. "The New Literature in America" (Hebrew). In *Sefer hayovel shel hadoar (Hadoar Jubilee Volume)*. Ed. Menachem Ribalow. New York: Hahistadrut Ha'ivrit B'america (Hebrew Federation of America), 1927.

Ribalow, Menachem, ed. *Antologiyah shel hashirah ha'ivrit ba'ameriqah*. New York: Ogen, 1938.

Shaked, Gershon. *Modern Hebrew Fiction*. Bloomington and Indianapolis: Indiana University Press, 2000.

6

HANA WIRTH-NESHER

Traces of the past: multilingual Jewish American writing

Take an old Jewish book – take the Bible, the most famous of all books – and you will see that one language has never been enough for the Jewish people.
(Shmuel Niger, *Bilingualism in the History of Jewish Literature*, 11)

Far beyond the lights of Jersey,
Jerusalem still beckons us, in tongues.
(Linda Pastan, "Passover," *Jewish-American Literature*, 432)

For decades, a New York-based radio station whose multilingual broadcasts served the needs of immigrant communities would identify itself in the following words: "This is WEVD, the station that speaks *your* language." For most of the Jewish listeners, this meant Yiddish. During the first half of the twentieth century, Yiddish fueled the immigrant and second-generation community, with daily newspapers, theatres, novels, poetry, folksongs, and radio programs such as those on WEVD. All of this has been well documented, and all of this is history. In recent years, New York City subways have displayed bold posters of the American flag in the shape of an Aleph (first letter of the Hebrew alphabet), sporting a banner with the words, "Read Hebrew America." By dialing a simple toll-free number, 1-800-444-HEBRE(W), anyone can acquire information at any time about free classes in "the language of our people." But what does "speaking your language" mean in these two advertisements, or in Jewish American culture more generally over the past century? In one case, Yiddish is a sign of the Old World, of an immigrant community tuning in to WEVD as a form of nostalgia. In the other, Hebrew is a sign of an even older identity, not of family history but of ancient history, not of relatives but of ancestors. One is listening, the other is reading; one is remembering, the other is re-enacting; one is *Yiddishkeit*, the other is Judaism. WEVD caters to an audience for whom Yiddish is palpably present; "Read Hebrew" addresses a public for whom Hebrew is conspicuously absent. One community's linguistic home is still Yiddish, the other's home is English, and only a moral or ideological imperative – "Read Hebrew America" – proposes to alter that.

Nowadays, the primary language of American Jewry is neither Yiddish nor Hebrew. Despite impressive bodies of literature in both of these languages in America, the language of American Jewry has become English, so much so that Cynthia Ozick has at one time suggested that English be referred to as the New Yiddish. Still, it would be misleading to talk about American Jewry as entirely monolingual. Jewish American literature offers testimony of multilingual awareness not only among immigrant writers where we would expect this to be the case, but also among their descendants who retained attachments to languages other than English, despite their meager knowledge of them. In fact, sometimes the mere sound of the language or the sight of a letter from the Hebrew alphabet has been sufficient to trigger powerful feelings of belonging.

Reading Jewish American literature with an awareness of multilingualism means that the historical, social, cultural, thematic, and poetic questions that we regularly bring to artistic works will foreground issues of language. When reading works by immigrant writers, for example, language acquisition emerges as a central theme, not only in the actions and dialogues of the characters, but also in the registers and translation strategies of the narrator, and in the textual codes that mark inclusion and exclusion of a divided readership. In the spirit of the recent renewed interest in transnational American literature (exemplified by Werner Sollors' *Multilingual America*), I will be focusing on the uniqueness of Jewish multilingualism marked by issues of sacred and secular, exile and home, mourning for and reification of language through prayer and art, as well as the translation practices that have characterized Jewish culture. Multilingual reading is an historical endeavor when it restores the language concerns and voices of any period, but it is also a poetic endeavor in its ear and eye for the representation of the "foreign."

Multilingualism has always been a prominent feature of Jewish civilization. In Warsaw at the turn of the century, a Jew might have spoken Yiddish at home, prayed and studied holy books in the Beit Midrash in Hebrew and Aramaic, transacted business in Polish, and read world literature in Russian or in German. In Alexandria in the same period, a Jew might have spoken French at home, prayed and studied in Hebrew and Aramaic, read a Ladino newspaper, and conducted his professional life in Arabic. Even the *shtetl* dweller with little formal secular education, such as Sholem Aleichem's Tevye, negotiated between the *mame-loshen* (mother tongue) of domestic and worldy Yiddish and *loshn-koydesh*, the holy tongue of Hebrew-Aramaic. By necessity, he would also acquire enough Ukrainian to secure his income as a dairyman.

European Jewish culture was constituted of the rich symbiosis of these languages, of their complementary and hierarchical relation to each other. Insofar as Hebrew tended to define the sphere of prayer, ritual, study, and law, it occupied a "masculine" position in Diasporic Jewish culture; insofar as Yiddish was generally confined to the more mundane spheres of the home and the marketplace, it was often defined as a "feminine" world (Seidman, *A Marriage Made in Heaven*). But there were many exceptions to this polarization, particularly in the emergence of a flourishing and wide-ranging modernist Yiddish literature whose themes and readership cut across gender lines. European Jewish immigrants brought this linguistic legacy with them to the United States, where their experience was bound to alter their attitudes toward and their practice of these tongues. Immigration to America dramatically altered the need for bilingualism: separation of church and state on one hand and the melting pot ideology on the other made Jewish affiliation a matter of individual conscience. Webster's standardized American English forged a nation through linguistic uniformity; it was the Jewish immigrant's ticket to success.

For immigrant writers, English language acquisition became a passion, and often a dominant theme in their writings. In the novels of Abraham Cahan and Anzia Yezierska, to name two celebrated immigrant authors, seasoned English speakers take on the sensual charm of Henry Higgins in romantic scenes that revolve around diction. In Cahan's *The Rise of David Levinsky* (1917), lovers quarrel over correct pronunciation and grammer: Dora gloats over Levinsky when he utters an English phrase in a "Talmudic singsong" and Levinsky retaliates by pointing out that "she had said 'nice' where 'nicely' was in order" (254). In Yezierska's *Bread Givers*, Sara Smolinsky nearly swoons in front of the schoolchildren in her classroom, when the principal, Hugo Seelig, places the tips of his fingers on her throat to teach her the muscular control necessary to pronounce "sing" rather than "sing-gg" (272).

When Mary Antin wrote in her autobiography *The Promised Land* (1912) that she had reached the stage where she could "dream my dreams in English phrases" (156), and "at least to think in English without an accent" (282), she admitted that it was easier to write and dream in English than it was to speak in her new language. For the immigrant intent on passing as an American, speech is the critical hurdle, since a language acquired past childhood retains traces of native speech habits. Accent attests to the body as a memory site, as the interface of the physical and the cultural. Because the written page holds out the promise of accentless self-presentation, of linguistic "passing," it is intriguing that immigrant writers retained, even accentuated, speech on the silent page of the written text. Jewish immigrant writers in America from the late nineteenth century up to the First World War encountered two prevailing attitudes toward accent, represented most dramatically by Henry James and Mark Twain. Aiming for a language of consciousness that transcended ethnicity or race, and eschewing any representation of speech difference in his novels, James feared the imprint of immigrants on his beleaguered English, particularly the marks of Jewish immigrant pronunciation. "East side cafés," James wrote, were "torture-rooms of the living idiom" and "portents of lacerations to come" (*The American Scene*, 139). In contrast, representation of dialect was hailed as one of realism's central features, a democratizing poetic that gave rise to local color writing as practiced by Twain. "Give us the people as they actually are," wrote Fred Patee. "Give us their talk as they actually talk it" (*A History of American Literature*. 15). As a result, Jewish immigrant writers could choose between representing accented speech in the framework of local color writing or exploiting the disembodied act of writing in order to bypass the problem of speech. The works of Abraham Cahan and Mary Antin offer striking examples of these two extremes.

Caught up in the spirit of regional writing and encouraged by William Dean Howells, Abraham Cahan composed *Yekl: A Tale of the New York Ghetto*, in which his characters' speech is standard English when they converse in Yiddish and dialect when they speak English. This technique produces comical wordplay that enriches the themes of immigration and acculturation. "America for a country and *'dod'll do'* [that'll do] for a language!" (21) exclaims one of the sweatshop workers, an interlingual pun that requires both phonetic and semantic processing. Since Cahan cannot rely on his readers' familiarity with Yiddish-accented English, he provides the explanation in brackets. But his American readers will be able to process "dod'll do" as both a rooster crowing in English (his Jewish readers would recognize the "translation" from "coco-rico"), and as the language of Yankee Doodle. By using "dod'll do" as a synonym for American English, Cahan is referring both to the comic sound of the words to his characters' "foreign" ears, as they associate American speech with the English rendering of a crowing rooster, and with their own stumbling efforts to utter those sounds. In short, whatever they succeed in pronouncing will simply "have to do," will have to serve as English (Wirth-Nesher, " 'Shpeaking Plain' ").

The attention to speech on the printed page is also conveyed in bilingual puns requiring bilingual readers, a common feature of ethnic or minority writing that divides readers into outsiders and insiders, unless the author chooses to explain as in the case of Cahan's *Yekl*. After changing his own name to Jake, for example, Yekl renames his pious wife Gitl as Gertie, which he pronounces as "Goitie," a word phonetically akin to Yiddish for "Gentile" according to the author's note. For the Anglophone reader, it also carries the unflattering association with "goiter." By transforming the name of his stubbornly un-Americanized wife into a word meaning "Gentile," Jake deals a blow to her pride every time he addresses her. Whereas this type of wordplay depends upon knowledge of Yiddish, Cahan's eye dialect is a function of the discordance between what the reader hears and what he reads: when Yekl brags about his American prize-fighting knowledge, he claims that one boxer "leaked" another. Although the American reader will process "leak" back into "lick," the association with urination will already have accentuated Jake's coarseness.

In contrast, Mary Antin's reverence for English – "it seems to me that in any other language happiness is not so sweet, logic is not so clear" (*The Promised Land*, 164) – accounts for her startling detour into the third person in her account of shameful mispronunciation of her beloved English in her autobiography. In an incident in which she nearly drowned shortly after her arrival in Boston, the American boy with whom she was swimming taunts her, "You was scared, warn't you?" "The girl understands so much," wrote Antin about herself, quoting her clumsy reply, "You can shwimmen, I not." Her accent sparks the boy's mocking retort, "Betcher life I can schwimmen" (153). Having immigrated to the United States at the age of twelve and writing at a time when "passing" in racial or social terms was a major topic of concern for American nativists, Antin strove for linguistic passing. She devoted several sections of her book to her efforts to eradicate accent from her speech, to rid herself of that "buzzing sound of the dreadful English *th*" (164). After elocution lessons, after publication of her writings, after her nation-wide fame as an exemplary immigrant, Antin admitted that years later she "passed as an American among Americans" (156), she could "dream [her] dreams in English phrases" (156), and she "learned at least to think in English without an accent" (282). In other words, Antin could write, think, and dream in English, but when she spoke, she did so with a tell-tale trace of her native tongue, because her remembering body could not transcend the physical limits inscribed by her formative years as a Jew in Russia. Antin was so preoccupied with speech, that she even appended a *Guide to Pronunciation* for her Gentile readers, in addition to a Glossary of foreign terms. A tool to enable access to outsiders, the Guide ironically placed these readers in the linguistic space of the immigrants about whom they were reading; impeded by strange sounds, they would reenact the struggles of immigrants willy-nilly each time they attempted to say the unfamiliar words.

First-generation Jewish American writers, the sons and daughters of immigrants, sometimes forged their own distinctive voices by inscribing traces of immigrant speech into their writing, by retaining an "accent" of ethnicity. Among the finest of these writers whose first language was Yiddish are Henry

Roth, Bernard Malamud, Saul Bellow, Delmore Schwartz, Isaac Rosenfeld, Grace Paley, and Cynthia Ozick. With English as a native language but not their only linguistic home, these authors are all translators in the broadest cultural sense. In their writings, the search for a distinctive poetic "voice" sometimes expresses itself in mutual translation between their two (or more) native languages and their two cultural homes. The bilingualism of immigration, often characterized by translation in one direction – from the Old World source to the New World target – is replaced by the bilingualism of ethnicity, dual sources mutually translated into a new, in-between space enriching American literature.

Huck Finn's colloquial speech slides into Augie March's brassy tones in Bellow's groundbreaking novel, *The Adventures of Augie March* (1953). The same character who is "read the riot act" by his mother – "Gedank, Augie, wenn ich bin todt" (27) – introduces himself in the confident breezy voice of Whitman and Emerson. "I am an American, Chicago born – Chicago, that somber city – and go at things as I have taught myself, free-style, and will make the record in my own way"(3), Bellow's prose echoing "Walt Whitman, a kosmos, of Manhattan the son" (Whitman, "Song of Myself,") and "And I will report all heroism from an American point of view" (Whitman, "Starting from Paumanok"). Taking on a celebrated public voice such as Whitman's is an act of translation in which the Jewish writer impersonates a distinctive form of American rhetoric, but with an ethnic difference. When the novel is constituted of both artful imitation of canonical American voices and ruptures of other languages onto the English page, such as Yiddish, German, and Hebrew in Bellow's fiction, an altogether new voice is forged.

Grace Paley's distinctive Jewish American accent comes on the scene in the 1950s as well, in her collection of stories *The Little Disturbances of Man*. "The Loudest Voice," a story whose wry title alludes to the stereotype of the strident Jewish voice, counters Mary Antin's correct and mannered prose by mocking the speech of the WASP grammar school teachers, Mr. Hilton and Miss Glacé, as they patronize the children of immigrants, "my dear, dear child." One of these children, the narrator Shirley Abramowitz, recalls her New York childhood where a grocer bearing the name of the most revered of modern Hebrew poets, Bialik, joins her mother in pleading with Shirley to tone down her loud voice. Shirley's father Misha, on the other hand, dotes on his daughter's loudness, a sure sign for him of her self-confidence in the New World. According to Shirley's mother, "if you say to her or her father 'Ssh,' they say, 'In the grave it will be quiet.'" ("The Loudest Voice," 55). Mrs. Abramowitz's transposed syntax signals Yiddish as her native tongue, just as her silencing gesture signals her lingering unease among Gentiles, remnant of her life in Russia. In contrast, her husband's remarks indicate that he no longer feels the need to speak in muted tones out of concern for his safety. He is vindicated in this American story, for Shirley's loud voice is no liability in a meritocracy. On the contrary, it qualifies her for the most coveted role in the Christmas pageant, the voice of Christ himself. In a parody of the Nativity in which "Celia Kornbluh lay in the straw with Cindy Lou, her favorite doll" (61), the children of Jewish immigrants, coached by their Gentile teachers, dramatize the full Gospel, from nativity to crucifixion, with one crucial deviation: "the soldiers who were sheiks grabbed poor Marty to pin him up to die, but he wrenched free, turned again to the audience, and spread his arms aloft to show despair" (62). Marty refuses to be crucified, and therefore cannot be resurrected. Instead, he gestures melodramatically as if on a vaudeville stage, as Shirley's booming voice delivers the final words of the script: "I shall have life eternal" (20). The extension of the Christmas Nativity pageant to the Crucifixion, normally performed only on Easter, serves as a compressed lesson on the New Testament to accelerate the immigrant children's Americanization. The zany finale featuring Christ wresting himself free of his captors rewrites the Gospels into a Hollywood script with requisite happy ending, omitting the crucial act that marked the Jews as Christ-killers, and that generated Christianity. Moreover, the "famous moment" of Judas' betrayal, in Shirley's words "the terrible deceit of Abie Stock" (62), is performed by a boy whose very name encapsulates the line of descent of "the stock of Abraham" that Christianity claimed to transcend. Judas and Jesus, *both* descendants of "the stock of Abraham," now melt into the stock of the new American, with a reminder that Gentiles have tended to see the Jew as the shopkeeper "Abie" with his "stock." Shirley's mother concludes that Christmas, after all, is a Christian commodity: "Christmas... the whole piece of goods... they own it" (62). But not in America, Paley suggests, where her loud Jewish voice feels entitled to English and makes its own claims on the national culture.

Multilingualism in Paley's story is evident not only in artful Yiddish traces that convey the immigrant milieu, but also in cultural literacy. As minority discourse, "The Loudest Voice" hones in on the most highly charged event for Jewish children in Christian culture, Christmas, and reads it from a newly secured Jewish perspective, in which the life of Christ is humanized – "It was a long story and it was a sad story" (61) – and also Judaized, in that it stops short of the Resurrection. Knowledge of the New Testament is essential to understanding Paley's subversion of it, but knowledge of Jewish religious practice is also necessary to understand the closing scene, for Shirley's recitation of the Hebrew monotheistic credo, "Hear, O Israel" on her knees and with folded hands, is a Christian practice. In Paley's words, "Two ears, one for literature, one for home, are useful for writers" (x).

Another child of Yiddish-speaking immigrants who came onto the literary scene in the 1950s, Bernard Malamud also parodies and Judaizes Gentile literature. In "The Jewbird" (1963), a skinny "black-type longbeaked bird" (322) flies into Harry Cohen's apartment on First Avenue, perches on the top of the kitchen door, flaps his bedraggled wings, and caws hoarsely, "Gevalt, a pogrom!" "It's a talking bird," observes Edie Cohen "In Jewish," adds her son Maurie (323). Invoking Edgar Allen Poe's "The Raven," Malamud's "Jewbird" replaces Poe's noble fowl and his mournful lament – "spoke the raven 'Nevermore!' " – with a crow named Schwartz. A sharp-tongued bird critical of the Cohen family's Americanization, he embodies Jewish types from the past who were dwindling in the America of the 1960s: Schwartz calls himself "an old radical" (323), one of the last of the old-time communists, but his actions betray his words as he begins "*dovening*," rocking back and forth as if he were a black-frocked pious Jew from the *shtetl*. Furthermore, his habits – from playing chess and listening to the violin to eating herring with schnapps and reading the *Jewish Morning Journal* – are familiar traits of Jewish refugees from East Europe. Like the raven, or like Melville's well-known "Bartleby the Scrivener," Schwartz becomes an immovable squatter, until Cohen, in a fit of rage, whirls the bird around his head and "flings him into the night" (329). Since Harry kills Schwartz on the day after his mother's death in the Bronx and minutes after his son leaves for a violin lesson, the Jewbird's murder signifies Cohen's violent erasure of his Jewishness in the family's disregard of traditional mourning rites. Malamud's parody is double-edged in this story, for Schwartz is not only an ignoble version of "The Raven," he is also a parody of the fowl in the Old World *kapara* ritual before Yom Kippur, in which the whirling of a fowl around a penitent's head displaces the sins onto the bird. Schwartz attempts to defend himself by catching Cohen's nose in his beak until he cries out in pain and "pulled his nose free" (329). Writing in the postwar period of upward social mobility for American Jews, Malamud creates, in the figure of Schwartz, a trope for the East European culture that was annihilated in the Holocaust and that was also rejected by the children of immigrants. For self-hating Harry Cohen, despite the priestly lineage of his surname, the crow is an obstacle to his Americanization. Schwartz's tenacity in latching hold of Cohen's nose with his own beak is a reminder that Cohen has little chance of passing as a Gentile, the very word "Jewbird" echoing the anti-Semitic "Jewboy." Searching for the creature after the winter snows have melted, mother and child discover the skeleton, wings broken, neck twisted and eyes plucked clean. "Who did it to you, Mr. Schwartz?" Maurie wept. 'Anti-Semeets,' Edie admits, imitating the bird's own Yiddish accent (330). Ironically, her accusing finger is pointed at Harry. Malamud's "The Jewbird" is a site of mutual translation aimed at a readership familiar with both American and Jewish sources. Schwartz, which means "black" in Yiddish, is perceived to be the dark shadow of the Jewish past that Harry Cohen violently evicts from his home, while also hinting at the complex relation between "Jewboy" and "black boy" in the 1960s (Wright's *Black Boy* [1937] serving as yet another American intertext beyond Poe's elegy). Like "The Raven," it is a story of mourning, but in a different key. Poe's raven metamorphoses into a Yiddish-speaking refugee victimized by an assimilating Jewish American, and the story's fantastic and vaudevillian tone barely masks the neurotic laughter of the Jewish American writer only beginning to come to terms with the Holocaust in his art.

Post-Holocaust sensibility and responsibility redraw the map of Jewish languages for American Jews. The fierce drive away from Yiddish that marked many immigrant writers has been partly replaced by a romanticizing or reifying of Yiddish as a sacred touchstone of Jewish collective identity. Cynthia Ozick's novella *The Shawl* illustrates this shift as her searing account of a mother's witness to the murder of her infant daughter in a concentration camp also serves as a metafiction about her Jewish American reader's relation to both the Holocaust and multilingual Jewish culture. Many years after Rosa Lublin's trauma as a refugee in the United States, she retains her class snobbery and assimilationist attitudes in denying any knowledge of Yiddish, which she associates with poor uncultivated Jews, while she simultaneously remembers her grandmother's Yiddish "cradle croonings" (*The Shawl*, 19) from Goldfaden's operetta "Roshinkes mit Mandeln" (Raisins and almonds). Rosa's adulation of Polish, akin to Ozick's Jewish readers' total embrace of English, and her repressed nostalgia for a Yiddish melody from her childhood, are depicted as self-deluding betrayal of authentic Jewishness signified by the Yiddish language. Ozick's treatment of the place of languages in post-Holocaust Jewish American identity finds its most sophisticated expression in her story "Envy – Or Yiddish in America," a satirical elegy about the effects of linguistic loss, personal and collective. Edelshtein, the Yiddish poet in Ozick's story, sums up the inevitable cultural loss in translation:

> please remember that when a goy from Columbus, Ohio, says, "Elijah the Prophet" he's not talking about Eliahu Hanovi. Eliahu is one of us, a folk-mensh, running around in second hand clothes. Theirs is God knows what. The same biblical figure with exactly the same history, once he puts on a name from King James, COMES OUT A DIFFERENT PERSON.
>
> (Ozick, *The Pagan Rabbi*, 82)

That the annihilation of the Yiddish language meant the annihilation of the culture that it expressed has inspired some Jewish American writers to weave Yiddish into their works as a memorial to the dead, as in the historical novel *Inventing Memory* by Erica Jong, which has a *Glossary of Yiddish Terms* at the end. Unlike Paley, Malamud, and Ozick, who are the children of immigrants, Jong, like Philip Roth, is two generations removed from the Old World. Unlike Jong, Roth does not attempt to reinstate what he and his characters admittedly do not understand. So intent is Roth on portraying the barrier between American English-speaking Jews and their European past that in his story about Jewish Americans' ethical unease regarding their European brethren, "Eli, the Fanatic," he focuses on the untranslatability of both the trauma of the Holocaust and the culture of the survivors. American-born Eli, assimilated suburban lawyer, is so desperate to communicate with the mute refugee who is his double that he collars him and pleads, "Say something, speak *English*" (10). But the story dramatizes the chasm of this language barrier, that is also a cultural and experiential barrier.

Hebrew is another story. Since the exile from Judea to Babylon in the 6th century BCE, Babylon has been the trope of longing for the lost home of Zion and for the Hebrew language, the very name of Babylon signifying confusion of tongues, the fall into a linguistic Babel of languages – "How shall we sing the Lord's song in a strange land?" (Psalm 137). The return "home" to the Promised Land has always meant a return to Hebrew. Yet America as the new Promised Land challenged the notion that Jews were still in exile; indeed, Mary Antin declared that English had replaced Hebrew as a sacred tongue. However, once immigration shifted from personal experience to collective memory in the minds of native-born Americans, once Yiddish receded (except in the ultra-Orthodox community), and once English became a birthright, American Jews redefined their relationship to Hebrew. Whereas the fall into language and the constitution of the self for American Jews take place in English, the ethnic identity that America has required of its citizens after the melting pot gave way to cultural pluralism (or multiculturalism) is partly derived from the Hebrew alphabet as mark of difference, letters that are as "other" as they are "self," as foreign as they are home.

Although Jewish American writing shares many features with other ethnic literature in the United States, its singularity is that it also entails a religious and theological dimension. The Emancipation of Europe's Jews and the Re-form movement in Germany in the nineteenth century laid the groundwork for a redefinition of Jewish identity as a faith rather than as a civilization. Separation of church and state in the United States transformed Jews into adherents of Judaism, the third religion in America after Protestantism and Catholicism. The only language that has been a continuous integral feature of Jewish life no matter what the country of origin for Jews has been Hebrew, almost exclusively in the context of religious practice. At rites of passage in the life of the individual and at communal observance of holy days, at weddings and at funerals, at circumcision and naming ceremonies, at Bar and Bat Mitzvah, Jews assemble to hear and to recite Hebrew prayers. Whether or not they understand the words, the liturgy ushers in defining moments for American Jews through its familiarity and its foreignness. American Jews have found themselves in the paradoxical situation of acknowledging a language of home that seemed more foreign than familiar, of affirming the primacy of Hebrew as an "original" language while simultaneously experiencing its texts largely in translation into their native language, English. Ozick's fiction provides a rich sampling of this phenomenon, which also marks the works of a younger generation of writers, such as Aryeh Lev Stollman's *The Far Euphrates* and *The Illuminated Soul* and Myla Goldberg's *Bee Season*.

The Judaization of American and Christian texts in Malamud's and Paley's stories has its counterpart in the Americanization of Jewish sources. In Cynthia Ozick's *Puttermesser Papers*, a female *golem* brings about the downfall of the Mayor of New York, Malachy Mavett (meaning "angel of death" in Hebrew), and masterminds a plan "for the resuscitation, reformation, reinvigoration, and redemption of the city of New York" (67). The *golem's* ingenuity brings about a short-lived urban paradise under the mayoralty of her creator, Ruth Puttermesser, until the *golem* lurches out of control. An artificially created human being, a *golem's* life force results from the utterance of sacred Hebrew words. Drawing on the famed *Golem* of Prague, Ozick combines Jewish mysticism and American mayhem when Rabbi Judah Loew of Prague is replaced by Ruth Puttermesser ("butterknife" in Yiddish), who molds the *golem* out of the soil of her houseplants. Puttermesser recalls, "To begin with, he [Rabbi Loew] entered a dream of Heaven, wherein he asked the angels to advise him. The answer came in alphabetical order: *afar, esh, mayim ruach*; earth, fire, water, wraith" (45).

The climactic moment of investing the *golem* with spirit requires that Puttermesser pronounce "a single primeval Hebrew word, shimmering with its lightning holiness, the Name of Names, that which one dare not take in vain. Aloud she uttered it" (40). Ozick literally reproduces the word in Hebrew letters on the page, isolated and untranslated in a space cleared for them: "*Hashem*." The creature springs to life at the moment of Hebraic rupture into the English text. Ozick depends on her reader's linguistic as well as cultural literacy, for the printed word facing the reader cannot be the word before Puttermesser in the fictional world, which would have to be the unsayable tetragrammaton, "Yahweh." In *The Puttermesser Papers*, Ozick offers a metafictional commentary on the very act of writing fiction, for Puttermesser gives birth to the *golem* as Ozick gives birth to her "papers" through the medium of English, with traces of the "primal" language of Hebrew. In her essay on the New Yiddish, Ozick has claimed that art is "the religion of the Gentile nations" ("Toward a New Yiddish," 156) and that the worship of aesthetic objects is, from the Jewish perspective, a worship of graven images. Therefore, in to this comic parable of Mayor Puttermesser's plan for the redemption of New York City through the creation of a *golem*, Ozick inserts Hebrew letters as counterpoint to her work of fiction comprised of the Roman alphabet. When the *golem* runs amok, she has to be destroyed by erasure of one letter of the sacred alphabet, the "aleph" from the word "emet" on her forehead, transforming it from the word "truth" to the word "death." The Hebrew typeface underscores the boundary between sacred and secular invocations of God's name, between use of the holy tongue in religious ritual and in secular fiction.

The story of the place of Hebrew in Jewish American literature would not be complete without modern Hebrew as the secular national language of the Jewish state, Israel. In Johanna Kaplan's story "Sour or Suntanned, It Makes No Difference" (1975), Hebrew is represented as accent and transposed syntax just as Yiddish had once been. An Israeli playwright in an American summer camp produces a script that takes place in the Warsaw ghetto, and therefore requires a girl camper who knows enough Yiddish to sing a song before the final curtain. "Little girl," he asks Miriam, who is chosen for the part, "which languages you are speaking?" (190). At first Miriam is very pleased with her part. "I'm practically the only one who doesn't turn out to be killed" (200). But the rehearsals of the death of children remind her of the stories she has heard at home. Amnon, the Israeli playwright, notices the change in her, "Look here, Mir*iam*, say me what's wrong." "Nothing," she says. "Why you are saying me 'Nothing' when I see you are crying?" When the curtain goes down on "a little girl in braids and too-long dress who would end up not dead," she braces herself for Amnon's refrain, "Say me what's wrong, Mir*ia*m. Mir*iam*, say me the matter." Amnon's voice, his Hebrew pronunciation of her name, makes her vow "that never again in her life would anyone look at her face and see in it what Amnon did" (201). She yearns to fortify herself with flawless English, to sever herself from the painful familial and collective memories that Amnon reads on her face, the memories that, significantly, are associated with Israel and with the Hebrew pronunciation of her name.

Whereas the significance of Yiddish and Hebrew have shifted over time in response to historical forces, Aramaic has always been a marker of prayer, liturgy, and Jewish tradition, making its appearance in Jewish literature most often in phrases from the *Kaddish*, the mourners' prayer recited by the son of a deceased parent during the eleven months after the funeral. Jews in

America have been so devoted to "saying *Kaddish*," that appeals to recite it in English translation have always failed, the Aramaic text serving as a mystical touchstone, even if read from a transliteration. So widespread is the sudden rupture of the foreign words of the *Kaddish* into Jewish American literature that *Yisgadal v'yiskadash* (its opening line) has become a mantra, a signifier of Jewish identification intensified after the Holocaust. Although Allen Ginsberg's poem by that name may be the most often cited of these works along with Charles Reznikoff's moving pastiche "Kaddish," and most recently Leon Wieseltier's extensive intellectual memoir *Kaddish*, many other writers have invoked or partially reprinted it in their works. Due to the traditional restriction of the recitation to males, for women writers the *Kaddish* has served to illustrate the problem of creating space for the Jewish woman, the theme of E. M. Broner's memoir, *Mornings and Mourning: A Kaddish Journal*. The last page of Thane Rosenbaum's novel *Second Hand Smoke* reprints the full mourners' *Kaddish* in bold Hebrew typeface. Appearing at the end of a book in which the American son of Holocaust survivors has been obsessed with the enigmatic numbers tatooed on his mother's arm, the Hebrew print on the page is a defiant act of remembrance, exclusion, and identification. Although Yiddish, Hebrew, and Aramaic figure prominently, other languages have left their mark as well, such as Ladino and Arabic in the works of Andre Aciman, Victor Perrera, and Ruth Setton, Spanish in Ilan Stavans, French in Raymond Federman, or German in Lore Segal.

By looking closely at a short section from Henry Roth's monumental novel *Call It Sleep* (1934), I would like to demonstrate in greater detail what is entailed by writing and reading multilingually. Born in Austria, Henry Roth immigrated to the United States at the age of two, grew up in a Yiddish-speaking household, studied Hebrew as a child, and later majored in English literature at the City College of New York. Combining naturalism and symbolism in his story of an immigrant child's journey toward Americanization, Roth produced a novel that has been hailed as a classic of Jewish, American, and modernist literature. Roth's prose encompasses all of the aspects of multilingual writing that I have mentioned (and more): dialect, reproduction of "foreign" languages, internal translation and untranslatability, cultural literacy through non-English triggers, interlingual puns, liturgy, sacred and secular language, linguistic home and exile.

Seeking refuge from a grim and menacing urban world, eight-year-old David Schearl thrusts his father's zinc milk dipper between the street car tracks to release the sparks that he identifies with God, and suffers electrocution from the short circuit. Before he regains consciousness in this story of immigration as symbolic death and rebirth, his prostrate body on the cobblestones will draw out the "huddled masses" of his poor neighborhood, setting off a chorus of ethnic accents bemoaning what appears to be the tragic death of a child. "Bambino! Madre mia!" wails one onlooker; "Oy, sis a kind," cries another. Amidst this multilingual din, one outcry is striking for the way in which it encapsulates the book, "Christ, it's a kid!"

In the panorama that Roth describes just prior to David's nearly fatal act, characters speak in colorful, often crude street idiom as they check their hand in a pinochle game, confide their troubles to each other in a saloon, down another pint of beer. Insofar as "Christ, it's a kid!" is an expression of American slang in a naturalistic Lower East Side setting in the 1930s, it blends in seamlessly with the rest of the speech. But Roth is aiming for more than naturalism. By the time this phrase appears, the word "kid" has become a recurring motif in the book, and a multilingual marker of Jewish American writing.

As Passover approaches, the rabbi has been drilling his rowdy class in the liturgy of the festival, specifically the *Haggadah*. After their recitation of the traditional Four Questions, the rabbi commands, "now the chad godyaw." The children obey. "'Chad godyaw, chad godyaw, chad godyaw,' they bayed raggedly. 'disabin abaw bis rai zuzaw, chad godyaw, chad godyaw'" (*Call It Sleep*, 232). When they complete the Aramaic chant, the rabbi asks for a rendition into Yiddish; David earns his teacher's praise for reciting the song in full, its Yiddish "translation" represented as standard English. David's recitation in Yiddish is identical to the English translation found in bilingual editions of the *Haggadah* that would have been familiar to Jewish American readers. "One kid, one only kid...that my father bought for two zuzim. One kid, one only kid" (233). David is able to chant the entire song in one breathless sweep, the lyrics describing a chain of power that culminates in the ultimate force, the one that David later seeks between the car tracks. "'Blessed be He,' he repeated hurriedly, 'killed the angel of death, who killed the butcher, who killed the ox, who drank the water, that quenched the fire, that burned the stick, that beat the dog, that bit the cat that ate the kid, that my father bought for two zuzim. One kid, one only kid!'" (233).

From this moment, the refrain "one kid, one only kid" is inscribed into David's consciousness, just as the reader registers "the kid" as an analogue of the child, weak and vulnerable, at the bottom of the power chain. Bullied by street boys, terrorized by his father, and overwhelmed by his city surroundings, David identifies with the solitary kid of the song. Although the kid is eaten by the cat, the cat in turn is punished by the dog, with each successive victimizer paying a price for his aggression until the supreme power of the universe vanquishes the Angel of Death himself. Despite the kid's fate as sacrifice, he is vindicated by "Blessed is He," who intercedes again and again in the *Haggadah* narrative as the God who with an outstretched arm and a mighty sword freed the Children of Israel from bondage in Egypt. Their descendants are commanded to recite the story of the Exodus at each Passover *seder* as if they too had been slaves in Egypt. The Aramaic "Chad Godya" is sung after the full text of the *Haggadah* has been recited and after the ceremonial four cups of wine have been drunk; it is usually the song that caps the *seder* and is therefore sung with gusto, particularly among the children.

Why did the father buy a goat for two zuzim? Presumably to slaughter it for Passover to commemorate the sacrifice of the kid whose blood on the door post signaled a Hebrew home for the Almighty to pass over as he slew the first-born Egyptians (Exodus 12:5). Moreover, Jesus' celebration of the Passover *seder* is transformed into the Last Supper in the New Testament, as Jesus is himself transformed into Christ, and as Easter displaces Passover. (Celebrating Passover was deemed an act of heresy by the First Council of Nicea.) "Christ, it's a kid!" also refers, then, to the Christian God's kid, the one sacrificed to redeem mankind, the Messiah whose rejection by the Jews led to centuries of persecution in Europe. Insofar as David's injury, his near death by electrocution, is a consequence of his brutal environment, "Christ, it's a kid!" is a lament spawned by his surroundings. It is verisimilitude in a naturalistic setting. Insofar as David has died out of that world and will be reborn into a somewhat different world, insofar as he has died out of bondage into a modicum of freedom, the cry "Christ, it's a kid!" serves as an intersection of competing narratives, of Passover and Easter, of Judaism and Christianity. After his recitation of the Chad Godya earlier in the book, his daydream on the riverbank is pierced by a vision of a large muscular male on a tugboat calling out to him, "Wake up, Kid!" This memory resurfaces as he regains consciousness at the end of the novel, the capitalization of "Kid" underscoring its symbolic and anthropomorphic dimension. That David *is* the "kid" is clear enough; what this might signify for the reader is less obvious. Does his Americanization require a death and rebirth, an abandoning of the kid of the *seder* for the Kid of Easter, a Christianizing that is inherent in the acquisition of English? Regardless of what we make of this climactic ending, "Christ, it's a kid!" is evocative in *Call It Sleep* because it partakes both of American slang and of a familiar English translation of an Aramaic song in a Jewish ritual. The phrase enables multilingual and intertextual wordplay *because* it is in English.

Yet Roth does not stop with the collapse of boundaries between high and low culture, sacred and profane, Jewish and Christian. The dual influence of Joyce on one hand and of Jewish liturgy on the other emboldened him in his language experiments. For illustration, we need only return to the Chad Godya, first transliterated as the rabbi's utterance, "chad godyaw." When he snarls at one of the boys for laughing through the recitation, David notes the reason for the boy's amusement: "someone had been chanting 'fot God Yaw' instead of Chad-Godyaw" (232). To recognize sacrilege here, the reader will have to process "fot" as the immigrant or lower East Side pronunciation of "fart." Transliteration of the same Aramaic phrase differs here according to the accent of the speaker, and the design of the novelist. Because the rabbi does not hear English word play in the religious texts, the transliteration of his recitation is lower case. Because David is aware of English interference, his transliteration is capitalized, so that the reader can *see* what he *hears*, namely God. In David's semi-conscious state after the electrocution, he imagines his own death: "Not himself was there, not even in the last and least of the infinite mirrors, but the cheder wall ... sunlit, white-washed. 'Chadgodya' ... 'one kid, one only kid' " (427). Here the deity associated with the "one only kid" has been secularized to lower case, and converted into a bilingual pun – "godya," namely "gotya" or "got you." As this expression is an idiom for defeating another, then someone has gotten David. In fact, it was his father's intention "to get" David that launched his panicked flight to the street. Just as each perpetrator in the Chad Godya song is "gotten," so his father is also eventually defeated for having wanted to defeat the kid.

Yet another way of reading the eye dialect of "godya" is God – ya!, an affirmation of the existence of God. This is precisely what the song Chad Godya rehearses, the chain of command that places God at the apex. Paradoxically, this playful affirmation of God is expressed through a violation of Jewish practice, namely the taboo of writing God's name on any surface other than special parchment in order to prevent sacrilege by defacement. Whereas this taboo refers to the writing of God's full name in *Hebrew*, Anglophone Jews have sometimes extended it to the English word "God," by omitting the middle letter. In these transliterations of the Chad Godya, then, God is both present and absent, affirmed and ridiculed. He gets lost in the translation, the eye dialect itself performing one of the main themes of the novel, the perilous journey of the Jewish immigrant to America. The cry "Christ, it's a kid!" foregrounds the American Christian God, but ironically in an expletive, while simultaneously signaling the Jewish deity in the "kid" and its association with Chad Godya. Multilingual wordplay in this extraordinary passage encompasses several levels of Jewish American experience: immigrant accent, ethnic intertextuality, religious ritual. The Hebrew "chad" together with the English "god" in *Chad Godya* is a bilingual way of stating that "God is One" ("chad" being the Aramaic equivalent of the Hebrew "echad"). As such, it alludes to the Jewish monotheistic credo, the *Shema* (Hear O Israel! The Lord our God. The Lord is One) which escapes Red Yidel's lips at the first sound of thunder: " 'Shma Yisroel!' the rabbi ducked his head" (234).

Given the role of Moses in the Passover *Haggadah*, it is not surprising to find him mentioned in Roth's novel as well. When the police arrive at the scene of David's injury, they part the crowd with a wave of their clubs, addressing the Jewish immigrants generically. " 'Back up youz! Back up! Didja hea'me, Moses? Beat it! Gwan!' They fell back before the perilous arc of the club" (423). Like Christ, whom he prefigures in Christian hermeneutics, Moses is invoked in an epithet. "Hooray! Hully Muzzis!" (229) shouts Izzy after the rabbi has ridiculed David's quest for God between the railway tracks. The final appearance of Moses, this time by inference, requires the same kind of translation back from American into Jewish culture that characterized the word "kid." In David's hallucinations after the electrocution, his father's voice thunders, "Go down! Go down!" (428). With these familiar words, his flight to freedom merges with the biblical "Go down, Moses," mediated through the language of African American spirituals, the indigenous *American* story of slavery and freedom. "When Israel was in Egypt's land," begins the spiritual that ends with "Let us all from bondage flee, And let us all in Christ be free!"

Irish cops bring David back to his tenement flat, admonishing him, "Dat'll loin yuh a lesson, kid" (433). His parents are instructed to take him to the Holy Name Hospital if he does not feel well the next day. The intern examines him one last time, " 'Well, how's the kid'?" (436). The New York street, a modern collage of speech fragments, yields to the intimate space of mother and child. After offering him the simple maternal nourishment of warm milk and a boiled egg, she gently addresses him, "Sleepy, beloved?" (441). In this book of many voices, the reader may recall that "beloved" in Hebrew is the identical word as – David. The story of the deliverance from Egypt will find its redemptive closure in the Messiah, descendant of the House of David. "No kiddin!" (431) is the final English comment from the awestruck crowd when David is revived. Few Jewish American writers have crossed so many linguistic and cultural boundaries in so few words. Roth's stunning dialogue between "Chad Godya" and "Christ, it's a kid" exemplifies Walter Benjamin's claim that in translation if the sentence is the wall, words are the arcade.

Multilingual Jewish American literature, such as *Call It Sleep*, complicates the slogans with which I began this chapter, namely "the station that speaks *your* language" (Yiddish) and "Read Hebrew America, the language of our people." There is surely a significant difference between the addressee of the first, the Yiddish-speaking immigrant nostalgic for the sonorous mother tongue and the addressee of the second, the monolingual American Jew spiritually or historically bound to an "original" language that he or she no longer knows. But WEVD's appeal these days is as much to the native-born English speaker who might nod in assent to Yiddish being "your language" as it is to the immigrant. Similarly, the American Jew who would dial a toll-free number to learn "the language of our people" could do so as much in the name of being American as of being Jewish. Insofar as multiculturalism assumes that American culture is truly an amalgamation of cultures and languages, then Jewish American literature has opened up a new cultural and linguistic arena in American letters, where, in Benjamin's terms, the original and the translation become "recognizable fragments of a greater language" ("The Task of the Translator," 78). Multilingual reading enables us to experience translation at the heart of every communicative act and the foreignness of language itself.

REFERENCES AND SELECTED FURTHER READINGS

Antin, Mary. *The Promised Land*. (1912). New York: Penguin, 1997.

Baal-Makhshoves. "One Literature in Two Languages." Trans. Hana Wirth-Nesher. In *What is Jewish Literature?* Ed. Hana Wirth-Nesher Philadelphia: Jewish Publication Society, 1994.

Bellow, Saul. *The Adventures of Augie March*. (1953). New York: Penguin, 1996.

Benjamin, Walter. "The Task of the Translator." In *Illuminations*. New York: Schocken, 1969.

Broner, E. M. *Mornings and Mourning: A Kaddish Journal*. San Francisco: Harper, 1994.

Cahan, Abraham. *The Rise of David Levinsky*. (1917). New York: Harper, 1960.
  Yekl: A Tale of the New York Ghetto. (1896). Reprinted in *Yekl & The Imported Bridegroom*. New York: Dover, 1970.

Goldberg, Myla. *Bee Season*. New York: Random House, 2000.

Harshav, Benjamin. *The Meaning of Yiddish*. Stanford, CA: Stanford University Press, 1990.

Hoffman, Eva. *Lost in Translation: A Life in a New Language*. New York: Penguin, 1989.

Hollander, John. "The Question of American Jewish Poetry." *Tikkun* 3 (May–June 1988): 33–37.

James, Henry. *The American Scene*. (1904). Bloomington: Indiana University Press, 1968.

Jong, Erica. *Inventing Memory*. New York: Harper Collins, 1997.

Kaplan, Johanna, "Sour or Suntanned, It Makes No Difference." In *America and I*. Ed. Joyce Antler. Boston: Beacon Press, 1990.

Kellman, Steven. *The Translingual Imagination*. Lincoln: University of Nebraska Press, 2000.

Malamud, Bernard, *The Complete Stories*. New York: Farrar, Straus, Giroux, 1997.

Niger, Shmuel. *Bilingualism in the History of Jewish Literature*. Trans. Joshua A. Fogel. New York: University Press of America, 1990.

Ozick, Cynthia. "America: Toward Yavneh." *Judaism* 19 (Summer 1970): 264–282.
  The Pagan Rabbi and Other Stories. New York: Schocken, 1976.
  "Toward a New Yiddish." In *On Art and Ardor: Essays*. New York: E. P. Dutton, 1983.

The Shawl. New York: Random House, 1990.

The Puttermesser Papers. New York: Knopf, 1997.

Paley, Grace. *The Little Disturbances of Man*. New York: Penguin, 1959.

Pastan, Linda. "Passover." In *Jewish-American Literature: An Anthology*. Ed. Abraham Chapman. New York: Signet, 1974.

Patee, Fred Lewis. *A History of American Literature Since 1870*. New York: The Century, 1915.

Roth, Henry. *Call It Sleep*. (1934). New York: Farrar, Straus, and Giroux, 1991.

Roth, Philip, "Eli, the Fanatic." In *Goodbye, Columbus*. New York: Meridian Press, 1962.

Seidman, Naomi. *A Marriage Made in Heaven: The Sexual Politics of Hebrew and Yiddish*. Berkeley: University of California Press, 1997.

Sollors, Werner, ed. *Multilingual America: Transnationalism, Ethnicity, and the Languages of American Literature*. New York: New York University Press, 1998.

Stavans, Ilan. *The Inveterate Dreamer: Essays and Conversations on Jewish Culture*. Lincoln: University of Nebraska Press, 2001.

Stollman, Aryeh Lev. *The Far Euphrates*. New York: Riverhead, 1997.

Weinreich, Max. *History of the Yiddish Language*. Chicago: University of Chicago Press, 1980.

Whitman, Walt. "Song of Myself" and "Starting from Paumanok." In *Anthology of American Literature*. Ed. George McMichael. New York: Macmillan, 1980.

Wieseltier, Leon. *Kaddish*. New York: Knopf, 1998.

Wirth-Nesher, Hana. "The Languages of Memory: Cynthia Ozick's *The Shawl*." In *Multilingual America: Transnationalism, Ethnicity, and the Languages of American Literature*. Ed. Werner Sollors. New York: New York University Press, 1998.

"Language as Homeland in Jewish American Literature." In *Insider/Outsider: American Jews and Multiculturalism*. Eds. David Biale, Michael Galchinsky, and Susannah Heschel. Berkeley: University of California Press, 1998.

" 'Shpeaking Plain' and Writing Foreign: Abraham Cahan's *Yekl*." *Poetics Today* 22.1 (Spring 2000): 41–63.

"One Kid, Only One Kid." *Princeton University Library Chronicle* 63.1–2 (Autumn 2001–Winter 2002): 341–349.

Wisse, Ruth R. *The Modern Jewish Canon: A Journey through Language and Culture*. New York: The Free Press, 1994.

Yezierska, Anzia. *Bread Givers*. New York: Persea, 1925.

7

DONALD WEBER

Accents of the future: Jewish American popular culture

Returning to his American homeland in 1904, after more than twenty years of living abroad, Henry James discovered to his astonishment that the physical and cultural landscape of his "old neighborhood" had been utterly transformed by the palpable signs of immigration. The sounds and smells of the new New York City startled his refined sensibilities. Observing the picturesque urban spectacle of the Lower East Side, James was both fascinated and appalled by the overflowing scene of recently arrived humanity. Walking the ghetto's streets on a "warm June twilight," James reports in *The American Scene* (1907) the sensation of "a great swarming, a swarming that had begun to thicken, infinitely, as soon as we had crossed to the East side." James' response to what he called the "Hebrew conquest of New York" is indeed telling: "the scene here bristled, at every step, with the signs and sounds, immitigable, unmistakable, of a Jewry that had burst all bounds... where multiplication, multiplication of everything, was the dominant note... here was multiplication with a vengeance" (*The American Scene*, 131–132).

Most striking about James' views on immigration is his deep consciousness of a profound change looming in American speech, and thus in American culture in general. Taking in the strange sounds issuing from the ghetto streets, James heard, with nervous anticipation, the "Accent of the Future," the tones of rhetorical newness – the grafting of immigrant speech onto English, the "accent of the very ultimate future, in the States" – which he associates with the realm of the popular. Genteel to the core, a man of letters "anguished" by the fate of speech in this new America James nonetheless recognized amidst the intense café culture of the Lower East Side an emerging urban audience, "the germ of a 'public'": "a new thing under the sun" (*The American Scene*, 138–139).

As many cultural historians have shown, the story of twentieth-century American culture – a world that James caught a glimpse of in New York in 1904 – is the story of how immigrants shaped popular tastes as they transformed a variety of established and emergent forms of entertainment: film, music, theater, vaudeville, radio, television. In the case of the Jews who migrated in extraordinary numbers to America, a majority settling in New York, the narrative of their contribution to popular culture is so rich, their impact so pervasive, it is impossible to describe fully even a modest zone of cultural influence. Rather than striving for encyclopedic breadth, this chapter highlights the core themes of Jewish American popular culture through analyses of a few key texts, including early immigrant cinema, 1950s television shows (the heyday of Jewish cultural expression), and the rich traditions of Jewish comedy, including dialect humor, "Yinglish" parodies, and various styles of Jewish standup.

If, as scholars assert, popular culture expresses a subculture's desires, fears, longings, and dissent; if, that is, popular culture both enables the psychosocial ordeal of "Americanization" and provides opportunities for cultural dissonance, then Jewish American popular culture offers a rich testament to *how* that complex dialectic of acculturation and resistance works. Jewish artists in America both appropriated the existing popular media to address the concerns of their audiences and helped shape – indeed invented – a vision of the country to help their fellow "aliens" negotiate the often bewildering new world in which they now resided. In this respect, Jewish American popular culture sounds everywhere with the troubling "accent of the future" James heard among the immigrants flooding the Lower East Side.

In the early twentieth century, the now legendary Lower East Side was a vibrant scene of nickelodeons, Yiddish theaters, literary cafés, and, above all, an audience primed to experience new forms of entertainment. The intensity of migration helped nourish this lively street culture, generating a particular urban energy, a desire to engage the new world, and with it, dreams of self reinvention. "The streets are crucial," Irving Howe noted. "[F]orming each day a great fair of Jewish life, they became the training ground for Jewish actors, comics, and singers" (*World of Our Fathers*, 558). Similarly, Alfred Kazin claimed that "the positive creative role of the Jew as modern American...was in the first years of this century being prepared not in the universities...but in the vaudeville theaters, music halls, and burlesque houses where the pent-up eagerness of penniless immigrant youngsters met the raw urban scene on its own terms" ("The Jew as Modern American Writer," 588–589). Early popular entertainers like Al Jolson and Fannie Brice imbibed the pent-up energy of the streets; according to the early pop-culture critic Gilbert Seldes their performances were "surcharged with vital energy," expressive of what he termed, in the early 1920s, "the daemonic" in American theater ("The Daemonic in the American Theatre," 200).

Why was the creative reaction between America and immigrant so potentially explosive? For Seldes, the answer had to do with what we now often term cultural "difference": with the perception – both by the official, "dominant" culture and by the artists themselves – of Jewish entertainers as "other" ("The Daemonic in the American Theatre," 20c). It may be difficult, in our own time, to recover the electricity of a tireless Jolson in concert at the Winter Garden Theater ("You ain't heard nothin' yet!" was his signature expression, refusing to let his audience go home) or the "insider" pleasure of hearing Fannie Brice perform dialect routines like "Mrs. Cohen at the Beach" (1927) or Yiddish-inflected songs like "I'm an Indian" (1921); we may even assess the "fine carelessness" of their "art" (Seldes, "The Daemonic in the American Theatre," 200) as less than brilliant. For Seldes, their status as ethnic outsiders enabled them to transgress boundaries of civility, at least for the implied genteel audiences who could afford to attend shows at the Winter Garden and Ziegfeld theaters.

For the large immigrant population and (especially) their children still living, through the 1920s and 1930s, on the Lower East Side, Yiddish theater and the movies were the preferred modes of entertainment; in these venues – either live on stages along Second Avenue (where most of the Yiddish theaters were located) or on screen (movie houses were initially concentrated in ethnic neighborhoods) – audiences watched their deepest anxieties and desires literally enacted, displayed before their eyes. Rescreening early immigrant cinema enables us, eighty years later, to fathom the affective costs of Americanization; in the process, the films continue to speak to us, not merely as sentimental artifacts indulging our own needy nostalgia, but rather as texts that open up a world where the claims of memory, the rawness of generational struggle, the rivening impact of shame remain palpable. In this respect immigrant movies depict the combustible reaction of street versus home, English versus Yiddish (or "potato Yiddish," as the less than perfect rhetoric of *shund* [trashy] theater was derisively styled), of "civilized" America and the nation's linguistically mongrel future. Out of that exhilarating encounter much popular culture in America was forged.

At the beginning of the 1920s, movies drew heavily on existing literary materials, often adapting short stories from popular magazines or by translating plays from the Yiddish theater directly to the screen. There is a rich history of this "primitive" immigrant cinema, helpfully cataloged by scholars of Jewish film such as Lester D. Friedman and Patricia Erens. The few very early examples that survive suggest that movie houses were dominated by brief film comedies, on the order of "The Cohens and the Kellys" – a continuing series of silent features chronicling how deeply stereotypic ethnic families learn both how to negotiate the new world and to overcome the superficial differences between them – along with historical spectacles, melodramas, and historical movies based on recent history ("pogrom" films, in Erens' taxonomy [*The Jew in American Cinema*, 57]).

Among the most important directors in the silent era was Edward Sloman, who between 1922 and 1928 made five features, including *His People* (1925) and *Surrender* (1927) – both of which survive – and *We Americans* (1928). As a strong example of silent immigrant cinema, *His People*, based on a short story, "The Jew" by Isadore Bernstein, stands out for the intensity of the acting and the resonance of its depiction of the Jewish American family undergoing Americanization. Refracting the core dilemmas of immigrant family life, the film concerns a pious father and his two sons, an ungrateful yet favored son who seeks an *alrightnik* lifestyle away from his grimy Lower East Side origins, and a faithful yet unappreciated son who boxes professionally under an Irish name, "Battling Rooney." Looking back forty years later, Sloman recalled his warm feelings for *His People*: "This is my favorite film . . . because it was such a sure-fire picture. I knew when I started that it was going to be a great hit" (Brownlow, *Behind the Mask of Innocence*, 409).

His People remains powerful because of tour de force performances by Rudolph Shildkraut – a star of German theater who emigrated to Hollywood in the early 1920s – and Rosa Rosanova as Papa and Mama Cominsky, the struggling old world couple on Delancey Street, helpless before their lawyer-son Morris' acculturating new world desire. Rosanova, who plays a mournful, long-suffering, yet ultimately strong Jewish matriarch, made a career playing Jewish mothers, starring as well in the screen adaptation of Anzia Yezierska's *Hungry Hearts* (1922) and Frank Capra's *The Younger Generation* (1929).

The plot of *His People* turns on shame-ridden Morris' almost fatal denial of his father: while dining uptown, with his upscale fiancée's refined family, Morris (now "Maurice") refuses to recognize his downtown Jew of a father, who has surfaced on *alrightnik* row in search of his son – an unbidden figure who represents for Morris the embarrassing ethnic self under repression. ("Remember," the father tells his departing son, "on Fridays we always have gefulte fish." Of course it is the memory of such old world foodway rituals that Morris seeks to forget.) Cut by the son's shocking disavowal, the elder Cominsky staggers out. He is eventually saved by the "good son," Sammy, who takes his brother's place at the side of his father's sickbed, receiving his blessing, and who wins a boxing match in order to pay for his weakened father's treatment in a sanitarium. The father is taken ill when he goes off in a blizzard to pawn his only winter coat, carried over in steerage from Russia, for a more "appropriate" suit for his ungrateful son, who immediately throws the father's worthless gift – and, emblematically, his heritage – into a trash can.

The theme of generational chasm and the question of filial "return" preoccupied immigrant stage and cinema; it is not surprising, in this respect, that Jacob Gordin's Yiddish *King Lear* was a huge success on Second Avenue. The most famous version of the Jewish immigrant story is, of course, the Warner Brothers' production of *The Jazz Singer* (1927), which Priscilla Wald has discussed in chapter 3. A foundational work of American popular culture, it inspired a rival studio's response in Columbia's still relatively unknown half-silent, half-talkie *The Younger Generation* (1929), directed by a young Frank Capra, and a Yiddish counter vision in *The Cantor's Son* (1937), the Yiddish cinema's answer to *The Jazz Singer*.

By the time *The Cantor's Son* opened in the late 1930s, the audience for all modes of Yiddish culture – literature, theater, film – had decreased dramatically, in large measure as a result of the "success" of Jewish assimilation in America. The audience for Yiddish theater declined from over half a million in 1916 to under 250,000 by 1940. During the same period the number of Yiddish theaters dwindled from twenty to just a handful. Similarly, by 1940, "with the exception of a few stock phrases, knowledge of Yiddish had almost totally disappeared among native-born Jews" (Feingold, *A Time for Searching*, 88). In the realm of popular culture the figure of the Jew appeared to have vanished as well, at least in the assessment of Henry Popkin, writing in *Commentary* in 1952. Surveying the cultural scene, Popkin was struck by how large a number of contemporary films and plays had evacuated the Jewish presence from their original sources, a process of "'de-Semitization'" which, he observed, "is now a commonplace in the popular arts." Trying to explain this striking phenomenon, Popkin surmised that the impulse on the part of producers and scriptwriters, beyond a "desire to avoid inciting anti-Semitism," was an unconscious anxiety about appearances, a "desire to prettify, to depict life without discordant, heterogeneous elements. Jews are an intrusion; they do not belong to the pretty picture" ("The Vanishing Jew," 46, 53).

On the evidence of popular culture Popkin's retrospective survey captures the postwar mood of American Jews – after all, by the early 1950s, after World War II and the revelations of the Holocaust – most simply wanted to "fit in" and not be seen as "too Jewish." Still, rather than translating the Jew into an ethnically neutral American everyman, the early 1950s witnessed everywhere an astonishing breakthrough in Jewish American culture; indeed, there was a flowering in highbrow culture (the New York Intellectuals and the arrival of serious writers like Saul Bellow), in middlebrow culture (novelists like Herman Wouk and the hugely popular ethical guide, *Peace of Mind*, by

Rabbi Joshua Loth Leibman), and – most spectacularly – in popular culture. In the case of popular culture, especially Jewish comedy, what accounts for the stunning emergence of stars like Sid Caesar, Gertrude Berg, Milton Berle, Mickey Katz and (by the early 1960s) Mel Brooks, Lenny Bruce, and Woody Allen? More importantly, what is the genealogy of the Jewish comic imagination in America?

In situating Jewish American comedic art it is important to remember that even the "Two-Thousand-Year-Old Man" has antecedents. Mel Brooks' Yiddish-inflected witness to the history of the world represents the culmination of at least two generations of dialect artists, beginning with early figures like Monroe Silver and Joe Hayman, whose numerous novelty recordings beginning with "Cohen on the Telephone" (numerous dates) and including such performances as Hayman's "Cohen on Telephone Etiquette" (1923) and Silver's "Cohen Becomes a Citizen" (1924) draw on the dissonances of immigrant accent and the comedy of malapropism to satirize various American institutions (gas companies, college, the military, etc.). Of course, dialect humor itself has a long history in American popular culture, from minstrel shows and the "German" and "Irish" comics of early vaudeville to Peter Finley Dunne's "Mr. Dooley" and Langston Hughes' "Jesse Simple": in each case a literary character's heavy dialect generates substantial social-political criticism through satire. At the turn of the century the New York publisher Wehman Brothers printed a variety of "dialect" anthologies for popular consumption. *Cooper's Yankee, Italian, and Hebrew Dialect: Readings and Recitations* (1891) gathered a host of selections from popular and anonymous authors, apparently for public performance. By 1943, an "updated" version of such an aural guide was published for the use of a more professional audience: the *Manual of Foreign Dialects for Radio, Stage and Screen* includes phonetic transcriptions and musical notation to a host of dialects, including word and dialogue exercises, designed for those artists in the business of "performing" ethnicity.

In popular literature, Montague Glass' "Potash and Perlmutter" benign dialect sketches ("Abe and Mawruss") about the comic life of partners in the dress business were so popular that their lives were translated into a Broadway show called "Partners Again." Perhaps the most notorious of the print dialect artists was Milt Gross, a satirist-cartoonist whose wicked transcriptions of mangled immigrant speech in collections like *Nize Baby* (1926) and *Dunt Esk!* (1927) can still make readers wince. The linguistic world inscribed in these sketches is indeed raw: scenes of immigrant violence, both to American-born children and to the American language. In this respect there is, perhaps, only a narrow aesthetic-linguistic border separating Gross' thick street argot and the mangled speech we overhear in Henry Roth's stunning dialect evocations in *Call It Sleep* (1934). After all, don't the restless, nasty kids in *cheder* – a "gutter generation," in the words of Roth's disillusioned, bitter Reb Pankower – use Jewish newspaper as toilet paper?

The point, however, is the unmasking potential of dialect itself, the ability of immigrant accents to demystify – through disjunctions of perception, disparities of sound and sense – the high-toned claims (social and political, moral, and aesthetic) of the host culture. The Jewish American artists who most famously incarnate such a radical vision are the Marx Brothers.

Much has been written about the importance of the Marx Brothers for subsequent Jewish American humor, especially on the early career of Woody Allen. Like Groucho, Woody often summons a self-knowing, punning, parodic wise-ass wit to get even with the pious authority of the dominant culture. Like Harpo, Woody's non-stop, adolescent pursuit of unattainable women remains only a comic aim in itself – in the end their characters enact harmless (if wild) "parodies of lechery," in Stanley Cavell's nice phrase ("Nothing Goes Without Saying," 4). In movies such as *Monkey Business* (1931) and *Duck Soup* (1933), the Marx Brothers appropriated traditional vaudeville forms and, with the help of brilliant comic writers like S. J. Perelman, transformed their original touring stage performances into movies of anarchic comic energy, often laced – linguistically and culturally – with (Jewish) insider pleasure.

Consider the opening images of *Monkey Business*, where the stowaway Brothers make a memorable film entrance by popping out of barrels labeled "kippered herring." Such a zany olfactory mode of new-world arrival offers, perhaps, another slant on "steerage." Or, better, think of the exchange between Groucho and Chico (with his signature "Italian American" accent) in the Ship Captain's headquarters:

GROUCHO: A fine sailor you are.
CHICO: Hmm, you bet I'm-a fine sailor. You know, my whole family was a-sailors? My father was a-partners with Columbus.
GROUCHO: Well, what do you think of that, eh? Your father and Columbus were partners?
CHICO: You bet.
GROUCHO: Columbus has been dead four hundred years.
CHICO: Well, they told me it was my father...

(Anobile, *Why a Duck?*, 60–61)

What elevates the Brothers' dialogue beyond its recognizable vaudeville-like tones are the deeper resonances embedded in the exchange itself. For Groucho and Chico's routine is filled with the rich ironies of immigrant culture. If schoolchildren on the Lower East Side were compelled to memorize the sacred story of Columbus in school, the (Yiddish) word at home could be quite different. *A klug tsu Columbus* – a curse on Columbus, for having "discovered" this "wonderful" new world in the first place – was often uttered in the *mama loshen* in ironic response to the nation's official narrative. Columbus and my father were "partners," announces Chico – a wild immigrant fantasy claiming original collaboration in "discovery"!

"On the screen," Michael Wood observes, the Marx Brothers were "a set of immigrants who refused to accept the customs of the new country" ("Vulgar Marxism," 20); indeed, they refused to "swallow" the country's bland fare. Kippered to their core, stewed in the ironizing *tzimmis* of (Jewish) immigrant experience, the Marx Brothers seized on language, parody, and (in the case of Harpo) anarchic gesture to overturn authority. Groucho's elemental rudeness, as is often noted, expresses a necessary defense against new world outrage; his mania for punning launches – perhaps on behalf of all insulted immigrants – a rhetorical attack on new world civilities.

Other modes of popular culture emerged in the 1920s and 1930s, taking hold of the nation's imagination. With the advent of radio, a number of Jewish artists arrived on the scene, gaining national recognition – many, like Jack Benny, eventually making the transition to television in the early 1950s. Among these radio pioneers none was more popular than Gertrude Berg, who created, wrote, and starred in the Jewish family series *The Goldbergs* on radio and film, Broadway and television from 1929 through the mid-1950s. Berg's evocation of Jewish American family life was an immediate hit on radio in the early 1930s, second only to *Amos 'n Andy* in audience. For almost forty years Berg was by far the nation's most familiar, indeed the most recognizable icon of Jewish matriarchy in America. What accounts for Berg's sustained popularity? What did audiences find so appealing in *The Goldbergs*?

Part of Berg's appeal as "Molly" had to do with the historical moment of 1930s America, a time of economic and (no doubt for some) psychic depression. Faced with uncertainty, Americans across the nation listened attentively to *The Goldbergs'* daily fifteen-minute serials and felt reassured by Molly's voice: an accented voice of practical, homespun wisdom *revoicing* American ideals of optimism and resilient, self-reliant striving. Interestingly, in Berg's early (*circa* 1930s) performance as "Molly Goldberg" (American-born herself, Berg had no accent) her alter ego speaks in a *very* thick Yiddish-English dialect, much like the immigrant speech caricatured in Milt Gross' sketches. Berg, however, consciously labored to overturn that unsavory, unflattering vaudeville tradition; in the radio *Goldbergs* the Old World parents may have accents, but their hearts are 100 percent American.

At still another, deeper level of feeling, the radio *Goldbergs* jogged the memories of its Jewish listeners. Indeed, as the numerous letters to Berg attest, the show appears to have to have assuaged shame anxieties over social marginality and cultural difference on the part of its Jewish auditors; for others it helped release long-suppressed or simply forgotten ethnic feelings. A few years into the series Berg would broadcast shows enacting the family's observance of the High Holidays and Passover, a ritual (entertainment?) practice which continued through the early 1950s on television. Berg's "faithful" representation of Jewish faith and observance – in conscious response to the Milt Gross style of raw dialect humor – inspired a certain pride in her Jewish listeners. In the process Berg herself became an emblem of nostalgia, a figure associated with, indeed, the incarnation of ethnic memory itself. Only in her early forties, Berg was nonetheless felt to be of the older generation, a symbol of an earlier mode of life. Although by the 1940s she lived surrounded by high culture on Park Avenue, Berg would occasionally be chauffeured downtown, to the old neighborhood of the Lower East Side (Berg herself was raised in Harlem), culling stories from shopkeepers, soaking up the local culture. By the early 1950s, Gertrude Berg was among the most beloved figures in all of show business.

The sometimes vexed matter of dialect humor – its artistic potential, its relation to Jewish identity – lies at the heart of the era's Jewish pop cultural achievements. If Berg worried over the matter of dialect, figures like the "Yinglish" parodist of Hit Parade tunes Mickey Katz and – by the early 1960s – the comedian-social satirist Mel Brooks (in his Academy Award-winning short film, *The Critic* [1963]) seized the possibilities of dialect as a mode of deep cultural criticism. In the art of Katz and Brooks – and later, of course, the career of Woody Allen – we can observe the substantial powers of Jewish parody during this, the heyday of Jewish American popular culture.

It was the Jewish middlebrow raconteur Sam Levenson who argued in *Commentary* in 1952 (in response to Henry Popkin) that "The Dialect Comedian Should Vanish." Though he was himself fond of dialect humor early in his own performing career, Levenson was troubled by the mainstream audience's reaction to such insider, *haimisch* sounds of Jewish speech. "This may sound extreme," Levenson asserts, but it "is my belief that any Jew who, in humor or otherwise, strengthens the misconceptions and the prejudices against his own people is neither a good Jew nor a responsible human being." As a positive example Levenson cites "Molly Goldberg," "who speaks with an accent yet teaches love, kindliness, honesty, and respect for culture" ("The Dialect Comedian Should Vanish," 168–169). As a negative example of shameful dialect Levenson cites the current (*circa* 1952)

Broadway revues, the Yinglish showcases *Bagels and Yox* and *Borscht Capades* – the latter hosted by and starring Mickey Katz. The figures of Molly and Mickey thus conjure for Levenson opposing visions of Jewish experience in America. If Berg's Molly speaks, even with an accent, on behalf of her people, whom does Mickey Katz represent? What, we might ask, does the cultural work of Yinglish parody accomplish?

In the early 1950s Mickey Katz gained a substantial popular following – for the most part, solely among Jewish audiences – with a series of novelty songs and albums that radically revoiced Hit Parade tunes with a Yinglish twist. Katz's career started out in the 1930s in Cleveland, where he played the clarinet in local bands. He then joined the Spike Jones orchestra, where he learned the art of novelty music. When he recorded, in 1947, a Yinglish version of "Home on the Range" ("Haim afen Range"), Katz recalled that record stores in Times Square sold out ten thousand copies in three days.

What embarrassed Levenson in the early 1950s – and perhaps worried many American Jews who found Katz's Yiddish-filled send-ups "too Jewish" for their self-conscious Americanizing taste – we now hear as irreverent deconstructions of the voice of America, carnivalesque "anti-crooner" (in Josh Kun's phrase) Yinglish performances highlighting the sounds of Jewish difference. Now we hear the utterly unselfconscious, indeed shameless celebration of Jewish modes of (self) expression, taking on, with substantial impudence – for Theodore Reik, writing a few years later, the source of Jewish wit – the dominant whitebread tones of the era. In the tradition of mocking, subversive dialect humor, Katz retells (for example) the popular American story of Davy Crockett, now christened "Duvid Crockett," who must return to Delancey Street after losing his pants gambling in Las Vegas. Thus Katz "hijacks" (one of Kun's keywords) American pop musical standards in order to destabilize, in effect to counter the 1950s Jewish American impulse to forget. Katz's novelty songs thus compelled his Jewish listeners to remember their still uneasy place in America and offered the pleasures of insider tones as a salve against the hurts of outsider status in general.

The source of Katz's parodic imagination flows from the sophisticated musical arrangements themselves, the *klezmer*-inflected breaks of his band, the Kosher-Jammers, the wholesale rupturing of Hit Parade tunes by a jaunty ethnic-inspired Jewish beat. And at the same time, the aural anarchy that drives Katz's musical art issues from the distinctive qualities of his high-pitched, heavily Yiddish intonated "Jewish" voice seeking, through the power of parody, to shake the foundations of society. "Yinglish" is how cultural critics in the early 1950s described this new "hybrid" voice, expressive of "the mixed world of halvah and Hershey almond bar" that had come to characterize Jewish American experience by mid-century (Shack and Shack,

"And Now – Yinglish on Broadway," 588). The emergence of Yinglish tones and energies in the 1950s enabled a group of comic actors and comedy writers to seize the unmasking, demystifying powers latent in Yiddish humor – its ability to see through pretension, its rich potential to expose, to reduce the mighty and awesome through the leveling playfulness of the earthy "other" tongue – and create in the process a parodic art.

The Marx Brothers' creative legacy of zany wordplay and wicked parody may be observed in figures like Mel Brooks and Sid Caesar who, along with a now legendary group of writers and performers (including a very young Woody Allen) collaborated to create *Your Show of Shows* in the early 1950s on television. Caesar himself was a master of invented dialects; at an instant he could launch into a *spritz* of gibberish Italian, French, or German, with some vaguely recognizable words laced between the antic, virtually incomprehensible stream of sound. Each week Caesar appeared as another authority figure – as, say, "Professor Hugo von Gezunheit, medical authority and author of *The Human Body and How to Avoid It*" or "Professor Ludwig von Complex, authority on animal behavior, author of *Animals, Their Habits, Habitat, and Haberdashery*," or "Professor Lapse von Memory, the memory expert, and author of *I Remember Mama – But I Forget Papa*" (Sennett, *Your Show of Shows*, 55).

A very young Mel Brooks worked as a writer on *Your Show of Shows*, and was responsible for some of that show's most memorable movie parodies and satirical sketches. In clear anticipation of the "Two-Thousand-Year-Old Man," Carl Reiner interviews Caesar as "Professor Filthy von Lucre, the financial expert who wrote *Money Talks, So Listen!*". In this routine the Professor explains that in the ice age rocks were used as a medium of exchange because they were so rare ("It was the ice age. Plenty of ice cubes, but no rocks" [Sennett, *Your Show of Shows*, 55].)

The "voice of authority" in most of Caesar's "interlocutor" routines tended to be of "German" extraction; eventually Mel Brooks hijacked the Yiddish of his Brooklyn boyhood and Borscht Belt adolescence and invented the voice of "the Critic" – "some old Yid with phlegm in this throat" – whose "contemptuous common sense" unmasks the pretensions of high level art criticism in the Academy Award winning short film *The Critic*. "Vot da hell is dis?" the bewildered *alter* asks. Watching a "racy" French flick, the Critic inveighs, "Lips . . . doit and filt . . . I don't know much about psychoanalysis, but I'd say dis was a doity picture . . . Dat fella dat made dis . . . Vat does he vaste his time wit dis? A fella like dat, he probably could drive a trock, do somet'ing constructive. Make a shoe" (Yacawar, *Method in Madness*, 68). A richer, if still familiar variation of this voice can be heard in Brooks' "Two-Thousand-Year-Old Man" routine, initially a private *shtick* performed among show business friends in the 1950s. For these routines Brooks' stance is less edgy, more wildly inventive, even capable of wonder: this aged Jewish seer marvels at the miracle of saran wrap, pronounces on the heavenly taste of rotten nectarines ("I'd rather eat a rotten nectarine than a fine plum"), muses on the cosmic differences between comedy and tragedy: "To me tragedy is if I cut my finger... Comedy is if you walk into an open sewer and die. What do I care?" The comedy flows from its *antic*-semitic perspective, its irreverent juxtapositions of Jewish Brighton Beach with the awesome monuments of world history: Christ as a very nervous customer browsing in Two Thousand's store; the revelation that Shakespeare was a "terrible writer" (bad penmanship); Joan of Arc recalled indelibly as "vat a cutie," although her desire for martyrdom was hard to understand: "She used to say, 'I got to save France.' I'd say, 'I got to wash up'" (Yacawar, *Method in Madness*, 56).

With his substantial achievement in TV, recordings, and film Brooks exemplifies one major strain in Jewish American comedy. This mode, according to Howe, expressed a "long-contained vulgarity [which]... broke through the skin of immigrant life. It was a vulgarity in both senses: as urgent, juicy thrust of desire, intent on seizing life by the throat, and as the cheap, corner-of-the-mouth retailing of Yiddish obscenities" (*World of Our Fathers*, 558). Post-immigrant comedians uttered off-color Yiddishisms merely for their shock value, often for the sake of their middlebrow audience's nostalgia, the pleasure of hearing insider language sail over the heads of the deaf and dumb *goyim*. Of a slightly older generation of Jewish entertainers, Milton Berle falls into this "vulgar" category, on the basis of his frequent, always breezy invocation of Yiddish words on the short-lived but hugely popular *Texaco Star Theater* in the late 1940s and early 1950s. Later, numerous dialect comedians like benign raconteur Myron Cohen toured the resort hotels of Miami Beach and the Catskills; but Brooks' dialect art, infused with his parodic sensibility, has proved the most long lasting.

By the middle 1960s, however, Brooks' vaudeville-indebted, show-biz worshipping style of satire and parody (culminating in his 1981 film *History of the World Part 1*, which features a Roman standup named Comicus, who plays – and closes – the *original* Caesar's Palace) gave way to a darker, more dangerous form of comedy in the figure of Lenny Bruce, a comedian who also employed parody and, at times, dialect to indict the hypocrisies of postwar America. Unlike Brooks, Bruce's comedic art also involved a private search for identity through a very public, obsessive effort to locate himself in an alien society unable to tolerate the shaman's unmasking message. As Albert Goldman writes, the Jewish comic of this later era "dare[d] more and more to expose his inner turmoil to self-satire... to ironic mockery of personal

plights... to angry thrusts at broken dreams" (*Freakshow*, 186). By the time
the urban, neurotic, self-mocking comedy of Bruce and, a few years later, of
Woody Allen appeared on the scene, the Jewish voice had fully arrived. The
dialect itself may have become toned down, but the creative, at times even
radical, ranting impulses to which it had served found alternative expression
in the distinctively urban-Jewish sensibilities of Bruce and Allen.

Listening to Lenny Bruce recordings today, his talent as mimic, as pure
performer is less apparent than the sheer shock value of his subject matter.
What drives his comedy is its unabashed "Yidditude" (Damon, "Talking
Yiddish,"), the desire to send up as he deconstructs goyish-American whitebread wholesomeness. Thus in one of Bruce's better routines, the popular
radio (and later, television) hero the Lone Ranger turns out to be an old Jew
who *masks* his ethnicity on 78 rpm records. When his rich, sonorous voice
is played at 33 rpm, the Jewish voice, under repression, reveals itself: "You
vanna svitch it ova from sefenty-eight to toity-tree-und-a-toid? You'll hear
[*imitating slowed down record*], HIGHH YOOOSILLL BERRRR. I sent two
boice to collich. You tink dy even sent me a pustul cud? Hmmm. I got tebble
bucitis of my yarm. Alotta *tsuris* I have, mine friend. *Zugnicht* and *goyim*"
(Cohen, *The Essential Lenny Bruce*, 54).

In radical contrast to Bruce, whose raunchy show-biz mother dragged
him to the burlesque houses off Times Square and nourished his "blue"
sensibility with a vulgarity all her own, what happens when a bright, utterly middle-class Jewish kid from Brooklyn reads comic books, watches the
Marx Brothers, takes philosophy in college, suffers through Hebrew school,
absorbs Kafka, Melville, Bellow, the great Russian and French novelists,
and studies modern art yet always returns to the provincial nest of Brighton
Beach? The result is Woody Allen, who, beginning with a brief turn as a nervous standup in the mid-1960s, fashioned a comedy of ironic, self-deflating
juxtapositions, a wit displaying a self-knowing intellect while at the same
time mocking the pretense to deep knowledge itself.

The figure of Allen as comedian may be less socially dangerous than Bruce,
less "vulgar" than Brooks, but he shares a "Jewish" sensibility shaped by
New York City, the world that mediates his distinctive vision. As he explains
in "My Philosophy," "If only Dionysus were alive! Where would he eat?"
"Can we actually 'know' the universe? My God, it's hard enough finding
your way around in Chinatown" (Sunshine, *The Illustrated Woody Allen
Reader*, 181). Deflating the cosmic via the mundane is the hallmark of Allen's
humor (as is Groucho's, whom Allen greatly admires), and it is a mode of
comedy indebted to a major strain of Yiddish literature. As Mark Shechner
explains, "the particular genius of Yiddish comedy" is "to domesticate the
exalted and cut the marvelous and the awesome down to human scale"

("Woody Allen," 233). God and carpeting, famously announced as Allen's family values, summarizes Allen's mid-1960s vision of the universe.

Where Bruce, in the end, ranted obsessively about his persecution by the government (here the famous quip, "even some paranoids have enemies," appears to have been the case), Allen offers, in early standup routines, his neurotic "self" for collective analysis. "Since I was here last," he told the audience at Mr. Kelly's in Chicago, in March 1964, "a lot of significant things have occurred in my private life that I thought we could go over tonight and, um, evaluate." What follows gives new meaning to group therapy. "My mother's in the corner knitting a chicken. And I said I had to get a divorce. My mother put down her knitting. She got up and she went over to the furnace. She opened the door and got in. Took it rather badly I thought" (Sunshine, *The Illustrated Woody Allen Reader*, 8, 31).

Allen perfected the art of parody in the pages of *The New Yorker* and on film, in movies like *Take the Money and Run* (1969), his send-up of *I Was a Prisoner on a Chain Gang*, and *Love and Death* (1975), his revision of the great Russian novels. There is no parody, we might say, without a secret sympathy with the original, and in a series of literary sketches (collected in *Getting Even*, *Without Feathers*, and *Side Effects*) Allen reveals his knowledge (and admiration) of high culture, invariably reduced by a deflating Jewishness. "What if the Impressionists *had* been dentists?" (emphasis added) one of Allen's parodies asks.

Allen's comic sensibility, drawing deeply on the traditions of Jewish humor and his experience as a very young writer on *Your Show of Shows* (where manic Brooks-Caesar forms of parody reigned), help situate him in relation to the sources of Jewish American popular culture. This work represents only a portion of his creative output, which after thirty-five years of filmmaking now numbers over twenty-five films. In trying to map the shape of Allen's career, most critics highlight Academy Award-winning *Annie Hall* (1977) as the turning point in his creative imagination. *Annie Hall* is indeed Allen's most "personal" film, the work which inaugurates the key transformation of the Allen "character," from *schlemiel*-satirist-parodist to a complicated self seeking answers to questions of faith and identity, Jewishness and morality, art and audience, celebrity and integrity. However difficult, or premature, it may be to speak of a Woody Allen "canon," it is possible to identify those films which stand out for their inventiveness and intelligence as works which speak directly to Allen's core themes.

Following the taxonomies offered by Jeffrey Rubin-Dorsky, we can begin to map the key phases of Allen's career: the revisiting, at times nostalgically, at times with a vengeance, of the Brooklyn world of his youth and the local anthropology of Jewish family life (*Annie Hall*, *Radio Days*). The quest for wisdom and moral order in a soulless world, again often mediated by questions of Jewish identity (*Manhattan, Hannah and Her Sisters, Crimes and Misdemeanors*, even *Broadway Danny Rose*, Allen's "most sweetly Jewish film" [Rubin-Dorsky, "Woody Allen After the Fall"]). The need to turn inward, away from an adoring public, leading to sour meditations on the meaning of celebrity itself (*Stardust Memories, Deconstructing Harry*). But perhaps Allen's most richly suggestive film, the movie that links him to the sources of early twentieth-century popular culture, remains *Zelig* (1981), a "documentary" of the "chameleon man," who can miraculously take on the characteristics of anyone he stands next to. With its evocation of the 1920s culture of acculturation, of Gatsby-like passing; with its use of real-life, talking-head "authorities" (Irving Howe, Susan Sontag, Saul Bellow) who end up parodying their own famous ideas; with its attention to the feel and tone of 1920s society itself (Allen recreates the very texture of old newsreels, sounds, and images) *Zelig* returns us to the century's source of creative energy and context for popular expression in general – the scene of immigration, the ordeal of assimilation, the pain of alienation, the desire for human connection. To the extent that *Zelig* is among Allen's most personal movies as well as an artistic tour de force, it articulates, above all, his vision of Jewishness – really, of the (ethnic) self in general – evoking the unstable, ever shape-shifting struggle of being in the world.

In surveying the scene of Jewish American popular culture over the past twenty years, there are a number of vibrant sites of energy to be noted, including the revival of an older, East European style of popular Jewish music called *klezmer* (a subject demanding separate treatment in its own right) along with the attendant interest in Jewish music in general, notably the emergence of John Zorn and the premier venue for showcasing avant-garde Jewish composers, the Knitting Factory in New York City. We can also observe the rich "memory culture" industry that has sprung up in the Lower East Side – the "central sacred space in American Jewish life," in Hasia Diner's analysis (*Lower East Side Memories*, 181) – in the forms of walking tours, tenement museums, and the marketing of symbolic ethnicity itself. And there are countless web sites and E-zines devoted to aspects of Jewish cultural expression, making the contemporary moment an exciting time in Jewish life in America.

We can assess how representations of Jewish American experience have changed over time, especially for the so-called "post-immigrant" generation, over the past decade, by examining recent network television. As in the case of the *klezmer* revival and Lower East Side memory culture (exemplified in film by Joan Micklin Silver's love letters to that region, *Hester Street* and *Crossing Delancey*), much of the "Jewish" drama on television is driven by nostalgia, with plots turning on matters of ethnic identity, the meaning and relevance of religious ritual, and the possibilities of achieving family in a world of intermarriage and the inexorable loss of individual and collective memory. As a result, the question of "return," of reconnecting with the Jewish past – re-membering one's faith – has occupied some of the strongest television over the past decade, particularly in shows as different in style and content as *Thirtysomething*, *Northern Exposure*, and *Brooklyn Bridge*.

Of these shows, *Brooklyn Bridge* (CBS 1991–1992) tried to be the most "faithful" in recuperating the self-enclosed, provincial Jewish world of Bensonhurst, Brooklyn circa 1956, yet it was also the most short-lived. Although this half-hour comedy-drama received very strong reviews, it never found a loyal audience, in part because the network (at least according to the show's creator, Gary David Goldberg) kept moving the show around, never settling on a consistent time slot. Ironically, its ratings proved higher outside the major twenty-five urban markets which measure viewer popularity, suggesting that this show, which depicts a three-generation family living in adjoining apartments in the same building in multi-ethnic, 1950s Brooklyn – "a neighborhood so far away from Manhattan for us," Goldberg observed, speaking of the deep autobiographical dimension of the show, "it might as well have been Tokyo" (Du Brow, "Family Ties," 18) – ruled over by an old world, Molly Goldberg-inspired grandmother, appealed to a wider, middle American (Gentile) audience.

In creating *Brooklyn Bridge*, Goldberg was interested in exploring an organic world on the threshold of dissolution, before the lure of beatnik Manhattan seduced the rising countercultural generation; before nice Jewish boys fell for beautiful Irish Catholic girls; before the American family itself began breaking apart, leaving the old relatives behind for the more expansive pastures of Long Island; above all, before families broke apart as a result of divorce. "I think there's something very wonderful about having a strong connection with the generation that came before you," Goldberg explained, at the start of *Brooklyn Bridge*'s second (and final) season; "I think there is something very comforting about being that close, and that in touch with your roots, having that sense of personal history" (Kettman, "Gary Goldberg," 41). In this respect *Brooklyn Bridge* is less about the past than the present – about the palpable sense of contemporary anomie and the quest for "roots" and ethnic identity that began in the late 1970s and has continued into the early 1990s and beyond. Nostalgia bridges the gap between the ache for a lost place as it addresses the hurts of contemporary history. With its sweetly reimagined old neighborhood, *Brooklyn Bridge* applied nostalgia's comforting salve to those viewers overwhelmed by assaults on the family in the present, performing, if only for a brief interval, the work of remembering for an implied audience yearning for a return to the organic world of extended family life.

Examples of prime time television that explore the question of Jewish identity in more profound ways can be found in selective episodes of *Thirty-something* and *Northern Exposure*. In "Prelude to a *Bris*" (*Thirtysomething*, 1989), Michael Steadman seeks to resolve the issue of whether to ritually circumcise his newly born son. "This whole *bris* thing" bewilders him; he can't answer his Gentile wife Hope's matter-of-fact question: "Why? Just explain it to me." Michael's dilemma is his inability to explain "it"; he isn't sure what his relation to Jewish ritual law, indeed to "tradition" in general, truly is. The plot of "Prelude to a *Bris*" turns on the *very* Jewish character of his mother's current boyfriend, the retired ophthalmologist Ben Teitelbaum (played by the comedian Alan King) who, impertinently, sends for a *mohel* to perform the ritual and assumes, despite Michael's protest, the role of Michael's surrogate father. After much anger, confusion, and displaced resentment, Michael agrees to his son's *bris*. "I want to be a part of something," he confesses. The King character functions in this respect as an emblem and agent of Jewish memory, therapeutically drawing out what is repressed in Michael (his buried Jewish identity, the pain of a son without a father), and what is desired by Michael (to be a part of something, above all to honor his father's memory). "They remember us," Michael's cousin Melissa tells him, as they pore over old family pictures. By performing the *bris*, the episode implies that Michael's blurred Jewish identity can achieve some focus. Acknowledging the obligations of the covenant confers an ambivalently sought, yet unconsciously buried Jewishness. Thus this *Thirty-something* episode implies that Michael is representative of his spiritually searching but Jewishly lost generation.

The most wackily inventive television series to explore the state of the contemporary Jewish soul in the condition of diaspora was the award-winning *Northern Exposure* (ABC, 1990–1995). Dr. Joel Fleischman has been hired direct from New York City by the frontier town of Cicely, Alaska to be their General Practitioner. The show's energy and comic spirit issues from the encounters between the memorable cast of characters that make up loony Cicely and the indelibly New York-marked Joel. In the moving 1991 episode, "*Kaddish* for Uncle Manny," Joel hears of his favorite uncle's passing and seeks to honor his memory by reciting *Kaddish*, the prayer for the dead. The problem is finding a *minyan* (a required quorum of ten Jews) with whom to pray. Launching into action, the entire town begins seeking Jews in the gentile wilds of Alaska. In a dream sequence Joel, dressed in old-school frontier garb, meets the leader of the "Minyan Rangers," who introduces him to a band of mangy Jewish rough riders, each deputized with a Star of David, including "Levi" and "Strauss," and (in an obvious Hollywood insider joke) "the Co(h?)en Brothers, Ethan and Joel." In the end, Joel comes to recognize that his true family, his real tribe of fellow believers, resides in Cicely. As he chants *Kaddish* for Uncle Manny in the last scene of this episode, he is surrounded comfortably by his new *landsmen*, the only appropriate congregation with whom he can share his grief and fulfill his obligation to mourn. For Jews in exile from New York, even Alaska can begin to feel like home. In the alien yet *haimisch* (Jewishly familiar) world conjured by *Northern Exposure*, Joel discovers, to borrow from Bernard Malamud's "Angel Levine": "A wonderful thing... Believe me... there are Jews everywhere" (Malamud, *The Stories of Bernard Malamud*, 289).

At the start of a new millennium, Jewish American popular culture remains as rich and as vibrant as ever. In film and music, television and performance comedy, a host of artists and performers continue to engage questions of memory and identity, the meaning of Jewish experience and its immigrant legacies, and the relation between dominant culture and subculture. But the extent to which future generations – both audiences and artists – will be able to, or even wish to, incorporate the achievements of the past as they continue to forge their own creative visions remains to be seen. Can we expect, for example, to watch specifically "ethnic" television drama when most Jews no longer live in "old neighborhoods"? The current memory culture suggests that young Jews can be nostalgic for their parents' nostalgia, that they can even move back from the suburbs to the Lower East Side! With the passing of a shared traditional culture – of foodways, accents, common urban–regional experiences, etc. – what can contemporary Jewish comics poke fun at? In potential response, instead of mere "observational" comedy, a static, routinized standup of quips and insights, we now have an emerging cohort of comedians/performance artists dramatizing "the story of my story." It may be that the future of Jewish popular culture resides in the rich potential of such self-ironizing, self-conscious, "post-standup" verbal constructions: of the American Jewish self performing, enacting the story of becoming Jewish. In the words of the French historian Pierre Nora, "The quest for memory is the search for one's identity" ("Between Memory and History," 13). Perhaps such faith-keeping acts of remembering will serve to inspire and generate new accents, sounding the distinctive Jewish voice heard everywhere in the history of popular culture in America.

REFERENCES AND SUGGESTED FURTHER READINGS

His People (1925). National Center for Jewish Film, Brandeis University.
"Kaddish for Uncle Manny." *Northern Exposure* (1991, ABC), video recording.

"Prelude to a Bris." *Thirtysomething* (1989, CBS), video recording.

Anobile, Richard J., ed. *Why a Duck?: Visual and Verbal Gems from the Marx Brothers Movies.* New York: Darien House, 1971.

Brownlow, Kevin. *Behind the Mask of Innocence.* New York: Alfred A. Knopf, 1990.

Cavell, Stanley. "Nothing Goes Without Saying." *London Review of Books* 16 (January 16, 1994): 3–5.

Cohen, John, ed. *The Essential Lenny Bruce.* (1967). New York: Douglas Books, 1970.

Damon, Maria. "Talking Yiddish at the Boundaries." *Cultural Studies* 5 (1991): 14–29.

Diner, Hasia R. *Lower East Side Memories: A Jewish Place in America.* Princeton: Princeton University Press, 2000.

Du Brow, Rick. "Family Ties of 'Bridge' Reach beyond Brooklyn." *Los Angeles Times*, October 12, 1991. F18.

Erens, Patricia. *The Jew in American Cinema.* Bloomington: Indiana University Press, 1984.

Feingold, Henry L. *A Time for Searching: Entering the Mainstream, 1920–1945.* Baltimore: Johns Hopkins University Press, 1992.

Goldman, Albert. *Freakshow.* New York: Atheneum, 1971.

Howe, Irving. *World of Our Fathers.* New York: Harcourt, Brace, Jovanovich, 1976.

James, Henry. *The American Scene.* (1907). Ed. Leon Edel. Bloomington: Indiana University Press, 1968.

Kazin, Alfred. "The Jew as Modern American Writer." In *Jewish American Literature.* Ed. Abraham Chapman. New York: New American Library, 1974.

Kettmann, Steve. "Gary Goldberg Bridges '50s – '90s Gap." *San Francisco Chronicle.* August 30, 1992. Sunday Datebook, 41.

Kun, Josh. "The Yiddish are Coming: Mickey Katz, Antic-Semitism, and the Sound of Jewish Difference." *American Jewish History* 37 (1999): 343–374.

Levenson, Sam. "The Dialect Comedian Should Vanish." *Commentary* 14 (August 1952): 168–170.

Malamud, Bernard. *The Stories of Bernard Malamud.* New York: New American Library, 1983.

Nora, Pierre. "Between Memory and History: Les Lieux de Mémoire." *Representations* 26 (1989): 7–25.

Popkin, Henry. "The Vanishing Jew of Our American Popular Culture." *Commentary* 14 (July 1952): 46–55.

Rubin-Dorsky, Jeffrey. "Woody Allen After the Fall: Literary Gold from Amoral Alchemy." *Shofar,* forthcoming.

Seldes, Gilbert. "The Daemonic in the American Theatre." *The Seven Lively Arts.* New York: Harper and Brothers, 1924.

Sennett, Ted. *Your Show of Shows.* New York: Da Capo Press, 1977.

Shack, William and Sarah Shack. "And Now – Yinglish on Broadway." *Commentary* 12 (December 1951): 586–589.

Shechner, Mark. "Woody Allen: The Failure of the Therapeutic." In *From Hester Street to Hollywood.* Ed. Sarah Blacher Cohen. Bloomington: Indiana University Press, 1983.

Sunshine, Linda, ed. *The Illustrated Woody Allen Reader.* New York: Alfred A. Knopf, 1993.

Weber, Donald. "Taking Jewish American Popular Culture Seriously: The Yinglish Worlds of Gertrude Berg, Milton Berle, and Mickey Katz." *Jewish Social Studies* 5 (Fall 1998/Winter 1999): 124–153.

Whitfield, Stephen J. *In Search of American Jewish Culture.* Hanover, NH and London: Brandeis University Press, 1999.

Wood, Michael. "Vulgar Marxism." *New York Review of Books* 26.3 (March 8, 1979): 20–22.

Yacawar, Maurice. *Method in Madness: The Comic Art of Mel Brooks.* New York: St. Martin's Press, 1981.

8

MAEERA Y. SHREIBER

Jewish American poetry

Introduction

Up until quite recently, when the question of Jewish American poetic practice was raised, it was largely in the interest of declaring the enterprise difficult, if not impossible. Twenty-five years ago, Harold Bloom broached the subject in a now-infamous essay entitled "The Sorrows of American-Jewish Poetry." As the funereal title suggests, Bloom takes a gloomy view of his subject, maintaining that, as a category of analysis, Jewish American poetry has all but withered on the vine before it has even blossomed. Indeed, he argues that the poetic process – which according to Bloom entails an agon, a wrestling, between a would-be poet and his precursor – is fundamentally alien to a Jewish sensibility on at least two counts. To begin with, even the most secularized Jew cannot wholly commit himself to the "pragmatic religion-of-poetry" (251) or to hold a precursor poet in "god-like" esteem (253). The objection is predicated on an essentializing link between Christianity and the poetic, based upon a mutual investment in the "universal" which necessarily precludes Jewishness, a category of being which Bloom sees as bound up with historicity and specificity. Furthermore, Bloom provocatively suggests that a poetic alliance between a Jewish poet and a "Gentile precursor" (such as Milton), a Jewish self mixing with a foreign other, is in some way transgressive – a violation perhaps of a culture deeply committed to keeping its borders intact.

For Cynthia Ozick the question of Jewish American poetry must be necessarily deferred. As she sees it, the future of Jewish American writing depends upon its ability to generate a shared vision of communal well being, grounded in a culturally distinct language – a "New Yiddish." And, while novels that fulfill this vision may well be in the offing, it will take some time before this new language is "ripe enough for poetry" ("America: Toward Yavneh," 32). Such an aesthetic ideology, based upon a potentially coercive principle of cultural/religious unity, certainly complicates the possibility of the poetic, a kind of speech that often serves as the site of strong individuated utterance. But with her focus on language, Ozick identifies what ultimately emerges as a defining feature of Jewish American poetry. This view is most clearly articulated by poet-critic John Hollander, who is perhaps the most optimistic among Jewish American poetry's early diagnosticians. He argues that, writing out of an irrecuperable sense of loss or estrangement from an "original language," the Jewish American poet stands to make a singular contribution to a larger American aesthetic. At the core of Hollander's argument is an allegorical or perhaps midrashic equation between the Jewish exilic position and poetry itself: "every true poet is in a kind of diaspora in his own language" ("The Question of American Jewish Poetry," 43). This sort of comparison potentially leads to the problematic erasure of the specificity of Jewish poetic practice, as the Jew becomes but a trope for the universalized poet; nonetheless, in identifying language, or more precisely the memory of language, as a central feature of Jewish American poetic discourse, Hollander initiates what I take to be requisite in studying this emerging field – the theorizing of its aesthetics. That is, even as we are well on the way to establishing a canon of Jewish American poets, we would do well to specify the material difference Jewishness makes to poetic practice. It is in the interest of such theorizing that I offer this chapter. Rather than making a comprehensive survey of Jewish American poets, I want to discuss some key aesthetic issues characteristic of Jewish American poetry, by concentrating on a selection of poets, grouped chronologically – whose work helps define the various identity positions, aesthetic dilemmas, and formal innovations that distinguish this complex body of writing. In discussing such writing, I want to generate a range of terms to describe the position of outsider, of the marginal – so as to recognize the material specificities of particular, but nevertheless similar and related, cultural situations without risking homogenization.

Yiddish-in-America

Such generalized claims about the primacy of language become concrete upon noting that one of the earliest chapters of Jewish American poetry belongs to Yiddish American verse, which constitutes the single largest body of poetry produced in America written in a language other than English. During much of the twentieth century American Yiddish poets occupied themselves with the details of American urban life, addressing such issues as civil rights and economic injustice. Rather than writing in the interest of perpetuating an illusion of a *shtetl*-like existence, most of these poets sought to traverse such circumscribed models and contribute toward the large-scale modernist projects that we have come to narrowly associate with such artists as

T. S. Eliot and Ezra Pound. The marginalized position assigned to poets such as Moyshe Leyb Halpern, Jacob Glatshteyn, Malka Heifetz Tussman, and Kadya Molodowsky, in respect to the larger story of American writing, attests to the extent to which dominant accounts of literary culture depend upon formulations of "nation" (such as "Americanness") or other stable models of identity (such as those based on ethnicity or race). Writing as part of, but apart from America, Yiddish American modernist poets sound an important warning to those who would celebrate the benefits of multicultural alliances, without attending to its various liabilities, including the loss of ethnic specificity. For the early part of the century finds Yiddish poets mourning an increasing sense of linguistic isolation as the imperative to assimilate translates into a steady retreat from the *mame-loshn*, the mother tongue.

The condition of outsidedness or marginality dominates the imagination of the Yiddish American poet. Consider, for example, Kadya Molodowsky's 1937 volume *In the Country of My Bones*, the first of several collections she writes in America. Writing indeed as if "a stranger in a strange land," a position further aggravated by virtue of her gender, Molodowsky's poems trouble the widely disseminated notion of America as *de goldne medina* – the promised or golden land. In "A White Poet" (a reference to New York Yiddish poet H. Leyvik) Molodowsky represents disenfranchised workers, "the barefoot" who "built New York / Blacks, Italians, Ukrainians, Chinese, Poles and we Jews" (*Paper Bridges*, 339). The complaint intensifies as the speaker, identified as the "white poet," "chokingly" instructs the inhabitants of the city outstretched before him to rise and level one of its signature monuments as a collective expression of disappointment and rage: "Here is the crowbar, the ax, / The Empire State Building should return to clay, / Back to rocky stone" (339).

This rage is fueled by the knowledge that even as America flourishes, enriched by the bodies and souls of a surging immigrant population, Europe is being decimated, with savage consequences for its Yiddish culture. Faced with a now attenuated link between "here" and "there," Yiddish American poets cling even more fiercely to the language itself as a means of keeping the connection alive. Like the prophet Ezekiel who breathes life into dry bones, these poets are committed to breathing life into the language, the bones of Yiddish culture, so that it may live. But this prophetic stance is hard to maintain when faced with the knowledge that it is not simply buildings or institutions that are under Nazi siege – it is a whole people who are subject to annihilation, a people who spoke, studied, and sang in Yiddish. By virtue of its fragility, Yiddish, a deterritorialized language, speaks directly to those theoretical claims about linguistic loss as a founding principle of Jewish American poetic practice. This heartbreaking loss is named by another

Yiddish American modernist, Jacob Glatshteyn, in his 1956 proleptic elegy, "Soon," in which the poem itself becomes a gravesite:

Soon we'll have lost all the words.
The stammer mouths are growing silent.
The heritage-sack is empty . . .
In the dark we compose
Lightning words, fast extinguished.
And ash becomes their meaning
And ash becomes their meaning.

("Soon," 363)

In the wake of the Shoah, a language system that had long been vulnerable was all but annihilated: words themselves are now reduced to burnt bones. As a particularly intense case study of the fate suffered by marginalized literatures, Yiddish American writing illuminates the problems incurred by Jewish American poetry as a category of inquiry. But it also suggests the kind of critical opportunity that such literatures offer, inviting its readers to remap American literary history by thinking through its margins.

Jewish American modernism – with special reference to the Objectivists

The dynamics of marginality and the role it plays in broader accounts of Jewish literary history come into even sharper focus upon considering a group of poets known as the Objectivists, who represent the most sustained example of Jewish poets writing in English. Up until recently this group of writers, whose Jewish members include Charles Reznikoff, Louis Zukofsky, George Oppen, and Carl Rakosi, were viewed as a subset of the avant-garde, or more precisely a subset of a modernist aesthetic defined most notably by Ezra Pound and William Carlos Williams. This account has resulted in largely obscuring what is distinctly Jewish about these writers, both in terms of theme as well as rhetorical predisposition. That is, the history of Objectivism is a clear example of that universalizing impulse that neutralizes the specific experiences of minority writers. Now that the history of this movement is being thoroughly revised, we are in a position to recognize how Objectivism is affiliated not only with mainstream modernist poetics, but also with lesser-known collectives such as the *In Zich* (the Introspectivists) – a band of American Yiddish poets who sought "first of all, to present life as it actually is, with precision" (Blau DuPlessis and Quartermaine, "Introduction," 15). The claim anticipates Louis Zukofsky's own defining essay, "Sincerity and Objectification with Special Reference to the Work of Charles Reznikoff" (1931), in which he writes of a "Desire for what is objectively perfect, inextricably the direction of historic and contemporary particulars" ("An Objective," 12). That said, we should note how even as Objectivism has emerged as a prominent subject in current discussions of Jewish American as well as modernist aesthetics, its founding members, including Zukofsky, routinely expressed a deep ambivalence toward the idea of a group aesthetics. This very resistance may well speak to a certain tension in Jewish aesthetics whereby the "I," the individuated speaker, stands in an aggravated relation to the "we," the collective.

Charles Reznikoff, the most senior member of this diverse "group," is most consistently devoted to exploring the aesthetic implications, indeed obligations, of Jewishness. Consider his 1936 poem entitled "Kaddish," in which he offers a variation on the classical *kaddish d'rabbanan*, redefining the boundaries of *klal yisrael* (the community of Israel) to include a more expansive version of belonging, of community bound by mutual concern. His vision presumes that because of their own history of oppression, Jews must be particularly attuned to the suffering of others:

> upon Israel and upon all who meet with unfriendly glances,
> sticks and stones and names –
> on posters, in newspapers, or in books to last,
>
> chalked on asphalt or in acid on glass,
> shouted from a thousand windows by radio.
> ("Kaddish," *Complete Poems*, I, 85)

Assuming the role of *paytan* (a post-biblical prayer-poet, often anonymous), Reznikoff extends that liturgical strain of Jewish American poetic practice initiated by Penina Moise in the nineteenth century, and practiced more recently by Marcia Falk, Jacqueline Osherow, and Marge Piercy. But Reznikoff hardly adopts a consistently pious agenda. Writing under the rubric of an Objectivist poetics, Reznikoff resists ascribing to the romantic model of poet-as-prophet, which his contemporary Louis Zukofsky describes as the practice of "putting on singing robes to lose himself in the universal" (Blau DuPlessis and Quartermaine, "Introduction," 15). Objectivism's investment in specifics, which makes for an anti-sublime, anti-transcendent, largely secularized perspective, coincides with a commitment to the particularities of history – a prominent concern for many Jewish American poets. (Indeed, Reznikoff's position is a strong example of historian Yosef Yerushalmi's claim that, for the modern secular Jew, history has become a matter of faith – a displaced form of religion.) The burden of history – and by history I mean, here, the irreversible implications of temporal reality – claims Reznikoff's attention for much of his career, as evidenced by his two long poetic projects, *Testimony* and *Holocaust*. The first, which initially appeared in 1932 as a two-volume sequence, is comprised of poems based on federal and state trial records from the late nineteenth and early twentieth centuries. Making one's way through the sequence, one variously reads of factory workers' injuries, the indignities suffered by blacks in Jim Crow America, and tales of domestic abuse. The cumulative effect is one of a profound loss of order. As an artfully constructed text, *Testimony* works to a certain extent to resist the violence it takes as its subject. But when it comes to the Holocaust, this mode of resistance is finally inadequate. If Reznikoff's *Holocaust* comes to teach its readers anything, it is how that catastrophe thoroughly disables such bulwarks of justice as the promise of a compensatory aesthetic. By failing to provide a systemic approach to pain, it effectively amplifies and aggravates the social breakdown which has engendered this desperate state of affairs. Drawn exclusively from the records of the Nuremberg and Eichmann trials, Reznikoff's *Holocaust* compels its readers to wonder if there are indeed circumstances which can utterly overwhelm and ultimately defeat poetry, even of the Objectivist kind. By calling into question the idea of "Holocaust poetry" as a viable aesthetic category, Reznikoff thus makes apparent how the Jewish poet may challenge such cherished genres (as Holocaust poetry) that participate in central paradigms of identity and belonging. As Hilene Flanzbaum has recently argued, during the last decade or so the Holocaust has emerged as a significant, indeed defining, event in the construction of Jewish American identity (*The Americanization of the Holocaust*, 1–17).

That said, the deep sense of loss which saturates Reznikoff's work cannot be simply attributed to immediate historical circumstances. On the contrary, it is a transhistorical predisposition that he rehearses as if his birthright. As early as 1927 Reznikoff expresses a nostalgic attachment to Hebrew as the site of primary, stable meaning – an idealized region from which he is permanently exiled:

> How difficult for me is Hebrew:
> Even the Hebrew for *mother*, for *bread*, for *sun*
> is foreign. How far I have been exiled, Zion.
> (*Complete Poems*, 1, 72)

With these lines Reznikoff returns us to that theoretical paradigm which identifies linguistic severing or loss as a defining feature of Jewish American poetic practice. Although raised in a Yiddish-speaking household, Reznikoff views this linguistic inheritance rather dismissively. While the Yiddish-language poets sought to retain the *mame-loshn*, Reznikoff privileged Hebrew as an eternal language of quasi-religious significance – the language behind all language. This turn away from Yiddish, a language associated with the dailiness of life, toward Hebrew, the holy tongue, certainly complicates his standing as an Objectivist poet. For as we have seen, his is an aesthetics devoted to resisting ahistorical, messianic claims in favor of hard confrontations with the "real." However, rather than diluting Reznikoff's contribution to Jewish American poetics, I would suggest that this complication shores up his interest for us, calling attention to the poet's role as a thoughtful interrogator of categorical accounts of belonging. For to be a Jew in America (particularly during the mid-part of the twentieth century) means confronting the breakdown of cultural transmission and the loneliness which rushes in to fill the vacuum. Reflecting upon his experience as a first-generation American, the son of Polish immigrants, Reznikoff voices the lingering sense of isolation that permeates his vision of Jewishness – a vision at odds with the dominant view of Jewishness as a collective enterprise:

> My parents were of great company
> that went together, hand in hand;
> but I must make my way alone
> over waves and barren land.
> (*Complete Poems*, II, 80)

Throughout his career, Reznikoff remains committed to exploring the aesthetic and thematic implications, indeed obligations, of Jewishness (particularly the imperative to bear witness, to tell the story of the oppressed other). Louis Zukofsky, a principal spokesperson for the Objectivists, and the assimilated child of Russian immigrants who held fast to Orthodox Judaism, takes quite another path. Rather than struggling to write in the service of Jewishness, Zukofsky chooses ultimately to write his way out of whatever aesthetic constraints this ethnic/religious identity might impose. Writing in 1925, Zukofsky queries whether the Jewish past may no longer determine aesthetic practice – since American Jewry has been so thoroughly assimilated:

> Not by art have we lived
> Not by graven images forbidden to us
> Not by letters I fancy,
> Do we dare say
> With Spinoza grinding lenses, *Rabbaisi*
> After living on Cathedral Parkway?
> (*Complete Short Poetry*, 11)

Aligning himself with the seventeenth-century philosopher Baruch Spinoza, a celebrated Jewish heretic, Zukofsky proposes that the time has come to shrug off those religious dicta (such as the biblical prohibition against graven images) which have inhibited poetic production. Elsewhere in the same text ("Poem Beginning 'The'") he defiantly accepts the consequences of his decision: "Assimilation is not hard/And once the Faith's askew/I might as well be a Shagetz [Yiddish for non-Jewish male] just as much as Jew" (*Complete Short Poetry*, 251–253).

These gestures notwithstanding, "Poem Beginning 'The' " represents an important chapter in the story of *Jewish* American poetry. Published in 1928, "Poem" is a self-conscious reply to T. S. Eliot's *The Waste Land* – one of the twentieth century's most cataclysmic literary events. Zukofsky's target is explicit: "And why if the waste land has been explored /... Are there only wrathless skeletons exhumed/new planted in its sacred wood." As Zukofsky later explains to another highly modernist poet, Ezra Pound: "I wanted to tell [Eliot] why, spiritually speaking, a wimpus as opposed to a bang was still possible, and might even bear fruit of another generation" (*Pound/Zukofsky*, 79). That is, while Eliot grieves for the end of Western culture, mourning those crumbling myths which had sustained its foremost institutions, Zukofsky rejects such universalizing tenets, proposing that one mine what is close at hand for its own aesthetic potential. Setting out to question and ultimately challenge the older (and Christian) poet's sense of universalized time and history, Zukofsky dramatizes how, writing from the margins, the Jewish American poet may trouble the mandates of those who occupy the center.

The middle generation: Muriel Rukeyser and Karl Shapiro

Fueled by the modernist tension between the universal and the particular, the demands of history continue to preoccupy the Jewish American poet. In 1938 Muriel Rukeyser publishes her *Book of the Dead*, a long poem documenting a Depression-era disaster that left hundreds of miners dead or disabled from a lung disease, silicosis. Like Reznikoff's *Testimony*, Rukeyser's poem uses "real" materials, including testimonies from congressional hearings, stock reports, letters, newspaper accounts, and interviews with the victims and their families, to tell the story of this West Virginia tragedy. Unlike Reznikoff, however, who consistently maintains a narrative frame by letting the court records speak for themselves, Rukeyser inserts herself, showing her hand as maker of this national allegory: "These are the roads to take when you think of your country/and interested bring down the maps again" (*Book of the Dead*, 71). After taking us on a tour of the destruction, complete with a detailed account of the degenerative nature of "The Disease," Rukeyser instructs her readers thus: "What are three things that can never be done?/Forget. Keep silent. Stand alone" (102). But Rukeyser is more than a documenter or journalist; she is a seer, a prophet taking up a spiritual charge. This role is inscribed in the poem's title, alluding to a sacred Egyptian text.

The Eastern association deepens when Rukeyser interrupts a monologue spoken by a mother who lost three sons to the disaster, with the wisdom of the Egyptian goddess Isis who promises rebirth: "I open out a way, they have covered my sky with crystal / I come forth by day; I am born a second time..." (82). It is a striking move, as Rukeyser – writing from the position of Jew – reaches outside the confines of Western, Judeo-Christian culture to something wholly other; for in the Jewish imagination, Egypt is not only a strong marker of the exilic condition, it belongs to those others who threatened the very existence of a Jewish people. By going outside Jewish culture for powerful images with which to indict America's collective indifference to those who suffer as a result of its labor practices, Rukeyser calls attention to her own otherness, her own marginality as a woman writing out of an ethnic identity and religious tradition which systemically represents the feminine as marginal.

For Muriel Rukeyser, who grew up in an affluent, mostly assimilated Jewish family, Jewishness primarily takes the form of an ongoing commitment to the sociopolitical demands of history. Further, she explicitly insists on making gender part of the equation, understanding it as the third term whereby Jewishness and poetry are linked. Written on the occasion of the Spanish Civil War, "Letter to the Front" (1944) begins with the speaker laying claim to prophecy: "Women and poets see the truth arrive. / Then it is acted out, / The lives are lost and the newsboys shout" (Complete Poems, 235). Grieving the ravages of war, Rukeyser brings to mind that rhetorical tradition which casts women in the role of professional mourners (Shreiber, "Where Are We Mocred?"). In the prophetic book Jeremiah, for example, songs of communal loss are a maternal legacy: "and teach your daughters wailing, and one another lamentation" (Jer. 9:19). But the role Jewishness plays in this aesthetic burden only emerges when, nearly two-thirds into this poetic sequence, one comes upon a sonnet identifying the Jew as tragic survivor:

> To be a Jew in the twentieth century
> Is to be offered a gift. If you refuse,
> Wishing to be invisible, you choose
> Death of the spirit, the stone insanity.
> Accepting take full life...
> (Rukeyser, Complete Poems, 239)

Extracting a powerful lesson from the Holocaust, Rukeyser commits herself, not only as a woman but as a Jew, to "Daring to live for the impossible" (239). In this way, her work has much to say about how the feminine and the Jewish may be figured as two sides of the same coin.

Rukeyser's position is especially striking in contrast to that of Karl Shapiro, another central figure in the story of Jewish American poetry. One year after Rukeyser's "Letter to the Front" is published, Karl Shapiro wins the Pulitzer Prize for *V-Letter*, for this discussion a volume more interesting for what it omits than for what it includes. Written while Shapiro was stationed during World War II in the Pacific Theater, it contains no mention whatsoever of the recent events in Europe. It is not so much a matter of Shapiro disavowing his Jewishness in favor of his Americanness, but that, as he understands it, the latter category of identity absorbs and complements the former. His subsequent attacks on high modernist aesthetic practices (which would have certainly included the work of such "difficult" or anti-lyric poets as Reznikoff and Zukofsky) may be also understood in the context of his wrestling with ethnic specificity. Shapiro could no more claim Jewishness than he could "heave the iambic pentameter" (Pound's famous call for aesthetic revolt) – for both would amount to assuming a marginalized relation to the dominant culture.

As it turns out, the burden of Jewish history presses down inescapably. Working under the long shadow of the Holocaust, Shapiro writes in the preface to his 1958 collection *Poems of A Jew*: "No one has been able to define *Jew*, and in essence this defiance of definition is the central meaning of Jewish consciousness. For to be a Jew is to be certain of a consciousness which is inescapable" (ix). For Shapiro this recognition is devastating on two counts. First, it means admitting to the failure, or at least the limitations, of his own best efforts to belong, to be fully absorbed into the larger national consciousness; he is and will always be Other. Second, this admission makes for certain debilitating consequences; as far as Shapiro is concerned, Jews are an "artless people...a people in dread of the graven image" (x) – a sentiment previously expressed by Zukofsky. The implications are critical: while the "Jew" may serve as an apt metaphor or trope for the wandering Other, the Jew is constitutionally incapable of practicing the art of metaphoric transformation. Ideologically bound to the literal, according to Shapiro, the Jew has a fundamental distrust of the figurative. In a poem entitled "The Synagogue" (a place that he experiences as "dispirited" by contrast to the "swift cathedral" that "palpitates the blood"), Shapiro writes:

> And Zion womanless refuses grace
> To the first woman as to Magdalene,
> But half-remembers Judith or Rahab,
> The shrewd good heart of Esther still,
> And weeps for almost sacred Ruth, but doubts
> Either full harlotry or the faultless birth.

Our wine is wine, our bread is harvest bread
That feeds the body and is not the body...
(*Poems of a Jew*, 9)

The lines suggest that a defining Jewish hostility to metaphoric equivalencies ("our wine is wine") may be linked to a systemic devaluation, indeed steady occlusion, of the feminine (from Eve "the first woman" onwards) – a standard feature of Hebrew biblical as well as rabbinic tradition. For metaphor entails the ability to imaginatively posit a relation between unlike entities. That is, a given metaphor invites consideration of the way something is *not* like, as well as like, the thing to which it is being compared. Inheriting a tradition that resists or suppresses the feminine, which often functions as an extreme mark of difference or otherness, the Jewish poet is thus supposedly at a distinct disadvantage when it comes to deploying one of the standard strategies of his craft. To put it another way, Shapiro seems to be saying that since the feminine is a cultural marker of difference, a group – i.e., Jews – that is unable or unwilling to make room for the feminine is imaginatively handicapped when it comes to metaphor, and is therefore without aptitude for the poetic. It is a striking claim – not so much because it is right, but because it raises the possibility that a specific ethnic orientation may bring with it certain, specific aesthetic implications. Indeed the claim itself may well register as melodramatic, overblown, reductive, and pretty much impossible to sustain. One quick look at Hebrew liturgy, for example, reveals an abundance of metaphoric language generated in the service of imagining a relation to the divine. Nevertheless, this gloomy pronouncement raises important questions about the link between certain formal aesthetic practices and an ethnic/religious/cultural orientation. For Shapiro goes some way in actively diagnosing a religious/cultural bias that may, as I argue below, make for some real aesthetic consequences.

Family matters: Allen Ginsberg and Adrienne Rich

For Shapiro, the failure to fully accommodate the feminine virtually derails all prospects for the poet who would write under the rubric of Jewishness. But for Allen Ginsberg, who comes of age (poetically speaking) around the same time Shapiro is drafting his gloomy reckonings, such liabilities become assets. Restoring the feminine, specifically the lost mother, is central to both of the long poems which make his reputation. "Kaddish," completed in 1958, and dedicated explicitly to "Naomi Ginsberg 1894–1956," makes the mother its foremost concern. But the recovery effort actually begins several years prior to "Kaddish," with the writing of "Howl." Twenty years after completing the poem, Ginsberg confesses as much: " 'Howl' is really about my mother, in her last year in Pilgrim State Hospital – acceptance of her later inscribed in 'Kaddish' " (Stephenson, " 'Howl': A Reading," 389).

With the publication of "Howl" in 1956, Ginsberg bursts upon the poetry scene. It is a long and powerfully expressive grieving for the injuries and injustices suffered by those brilliant, mad young men whose visionary aspirations and agonized compassion for others put them at odds with the button-down values of middle-class America circa 1950. The poem famously begins: "I saw the best minds of my generations destroyed by madness, starving hysterical naked" (Ginsberg, *Selected Poems*, 49). Although the poem is dedicated to Carl Salomon, who is also mentioned in the body of the poem, the loss is not narrowly private or personal. Instead, like Rukeyser's *Book of the Dead*, "Howl" addresses a loss of national significance. In this respect, it may be understood as yet another variation upon the Lament – a kind of verse that may be central to Jewish poetic practice. Unlike Karl Shapiro, who somewhat belatedly and reluctantly acknowledges his outsider status, Ginsberg makes this legacy the very grounds of his poetic genius. As a poet, a Jew, and a homosexual, he is triply other. Indeed his poetry invites us to consider how constructions of sexual difference (homosexuality) and ethnic difference (Jewishness) may implicate as well as illuminate one another. It is in the course of writing "Howl" that Ginsberg discovers his obligation to the elided (Jewish) mother – whose restoration is the central project of "Kaddish," Ginsberg's great contribution to Jewish American poetics.

This long poem, completed in 1959 and dedicated to Naomi Ginsberg, finds the poet once again writing counter to the dominant culture, construed as white, middle-class, Protestant America. But this time the critique is more pointedly grounded in ethnic, rather than sexual, difference, as the poet works to restore the maternal. Long marginalized in the patriarchal history of Jewish identity, the mother emerges as an explicit target of ridicule and abuse as suburban America seeks full access to the New World. Excessive, demanding, and possessive, the stereotype of the Jewish Mother is a notorious construction borne out of anxious self-hatred, blamed for those perpetual feelings of outsidedness that continue to afflict the American Jewish (male) psyche. For his part, Ginsberg takes up this image, giving it a darkly parodic twist, offering a searing portrait of a Jewish mother who can't cook:

Serving me meanwhile, a plate of cold fish – chopped raw cabbage dript with tapwater – smelly tomatoes – week-old health food – grated beets & carrots with leaky juice, warm more and more disconsolate food – I can't eat it for nausea sometimes... (*Selected Poems*, 103)

It is an image designed perhaps to put the brakes on the torrent of Jewish Mother jokes that become commonplace in the fifties and sixties. That is, Naomi's death makes it possible to imagine the end of a certain version of Jewish cultural identity, founded upon gendered distortions.

Generically speaking, "Kaddish" is importantly hard to classify. Although its title alludes to the Jewish mourner's prayer (or as Ginsberg calls it, the "Hebrew Anthem"), there is nothing orthodox or pious about this searing, often harrowing account of Naomi's descent into madness. Nor does the poem conform to the conventions of elegy, the most prominent form of poetic mourning, insofar as "Kaddish" provides little in the way of compensation. Indeed, instead of approaching the poem as an act of mourning, we would do better to read it as an expression of protracted melancholia whereby the poet sorts out the implications of the mother's death. It is one thing to say who has died, it is another to say what that loss means. The poet writes, "Now I've got to cut through – to talk to you – as I didn't when you had a mouth" (*Selected Poems*, 96). Speaking as the son who lives to tell the story of the abject mother, Ginsberg offers a powerful variation on the idea of the Jew as tragic survivor. But such an account is finally too benign, eliding the extent to which the poem is colored by self-interest. As the poem reaches its conclusion, it becomes clear that the poet-son seeks not only to grieve his now-dead mother, but to claim, or even harness, the rhythms of her anguish to his own poetic ends with a last strangled cry, "Lord Lord Lord caw caw caw Lord Lord Lord caw caw caw Lord" (111). It is hard to say whether, with this line, Ginsberg means to register a complaint, or to offer a prayer; for "caw caw caw" may be heard as a guttural translation of "kadosh, kadosh, kadosh" – a communal chant (meaning "holy") recited as part of the "*Kedusah*," a prayer celebrating God and his angels as holy and complete. Again, we see an instance of Jewish American poetry testing the boundary between poetry and prayer. Ultimately, however, this final utterance is well beyond the bounds of conventional liturgical decorum, Jewish or otherwise, as the poet works to imagine a way out of a culture that has done such damage to the feminine.

Ginsberg's preoccupation with Naomi, his dead mother, does not end with "Kaddish." She continues to haunt his imagination (such is perhaps the force of the Jewish Mother). Twenty-six years later he revisits this loss in "White Shroud," where, in a dream he meets "my mother saner than I." While the scene brings with it the suggestion that Ginsberg is acting out of guilt (a motive that would certainly fall within the province of the Jewish poet), such a reading hardly does justice to the poet's tender fantasy: "Those years unsettled – were now over, here I could live/forever, have a home with Naomi, at long last" (*Selected Poems*, 355). Indeed the title itself, "White Shroud," suggests that something more profound is at stake, insofar as it brings to mind the *kittel* – the simple white burial garment which is customarily also worn on Yom Kippur, the Day of Atonement and of Judgment. That is, the Jewish poet-son seeks not only to recover the lost mother, but to make full amends, to do *teshuvah* (penance), as it were, for exploiting her (or her memory) in the interest of his own poetic ambition.

Family attachments are also at issue when turning to consider how Jewishness informs the work of Adrienne Rich, another prominent American poet who emerges in the late fifties and early sixties. While Ginsberg takes it upon himself to tell the mother's story, Rich's interest in questions of Jewishness oblige her to negotiate a relation to the father. For as Rich put it in 1960, she is "Split at the root, neither Gentile nor Jew, / Yankee nor Rebel" (*Adrienne Rich's Poetry*, 224). This condition of in-betweenness stems from a bifurcated lineage. Her father was a Southern Jew (Birmingham, Alabama); her mother was raised Protestant, and Rich herself was raised Episcopalian. In other words, since rabbinic (orthodox and conservative) law maintains that Jewishness is a maternal legacy, Rich is arguably not "really" Jewish at all. Her decision to claim Jewishness thus places her outside the bounds of some dominant religious paradigms; but it also makes for a certain contested relation to the feminist/lesbian models of belonging (another one of Rich's formative rubrics) which maintain that "we think back through our mothers, if we are women" (Rich, citing Virgina Woolf, *Adrienne Rich's Poetry*, 225). That is, by contrast to Ginsberg, Rich initially figures sexual and ethnic difference as oppositional rather than complementary structures of identity. What tips the balance in favor of claiming Jewishness is Rich's abiding commitment to the idea of the artist as a product of, and participant in, history – a commitment to which she feels doubly bound as a woman and a Jew. (As in the case of Rukeyser, we see how Jewishness and the feminine function as entwined identity positions.) For a Jew writing after 1945, "history" means the Holocaust. Recognizing that despite her mixed parentage, she would have been decreed "Mischling, first degree-nonexempt from the Final Solution" ("Split," *Adrienne Rich's Poetry*, 226), Rich sets about claiming her Jewish self. This project is carried out poetically in *Sources* (1986), the volume most explicitly devoted to questions of Jewish identity. There Rich describes how she had long seen her father solely as "the face of patriarchy," without noticing "beneath it the suffering of the Jew" (*Adrienne Rich's Poetry*, 15). This refiguring of the father, by way of the culturally entrenched figure of the Jew as the feminized other, has implications beyond the immediate matter of Rich's specific attachment to Jewishness; for it also calls attention to her vexed relation to an aesthetic tradition in which "fathers" outweigh "mothers." We should note here that Rich first gains national recognition in 1951, when, as a Yale Younger Poet, she is celebrated by W. H. Auden for her kinship with such luminaries as Frost and Yeats (*Adrienne Rich's Poetry*, 278). In this way, we see how an ethnically specific focus may end up illuminating broader concerns. In the case of Rich, for example, the struggle to claim her Jewish father should be viewed in the context of her more generalized struggle to find aesthetic models and forms that are not wholly tainted by their patriarchal origins, and hence unavailable to her.

This search for usable poetic models inspires some of Rich's most interesting contributions to Jewish American poetry and to the culture of Jewish American life at large. In the long poem "Atlas of a Difficult World," Rich pays homage to Muriel Rukeyser's *Book of the Dead*, weaving lines from that poem into her own text. Indeed Rich extends Rukeyser's project which, we recall, was composed in the wake of an industrial tragedy, with national reverberation, crafting a national lament of her own. Writing in response to the 1992 Gulf War Crisis, Rich questions the very idea of "nation" as a principle of belonging: "I am bent on fathoming what it means to love my country" (*Adrienne Rich's Poetry*, 155). But even as Rich takes on the lament as a mode for grieving national/communal despair, she is obliged to reject, indeed evacuate, some of its founding metaphors, including that of the non-nurturant mother. In this way, Rich's poem fulfills what I understand to be another strong function of Jewish American verse – that of problematizing received forms and, by extension, the ideologies or cultural biases informing them.

In another poem from the same volume, "Tattered Kaddish," Rich continues to take a transformative approach to canonical forms of address. As the title suggests, the form in question is that of the *Kaddish* – an utterance that has become central not only to the history of Jewish American liturgy, but also perhaps to its poetic practice, emerging as what Hana Wirth-Nesher recognizes as a "recurrent sign of collective memory and Jewish identity" ("Language as Homeland," 223). In this instance Rich retains the liturgical frame, but to her own subversive or, more precisely, ideologically corrective ends. To begin with, her "tattered" reworking of this ancient Hebrew prayer does not mention God (the subject of the precursor text), but, rather, is dedicated to "all suicides" and to life, "how they loved it, when they could" (*Adrienne Rich's Poetry*, 159–160). Rich thus writes counter to rabbinic law, which denies the suicide the usual honors and liturgical trappings of death. Further, Rich represents the primary speaker of the prayer as feminine, thereby violating the orthodox practice forbidding women publically to lead prayers or to be counted as part of a *minyan* – the requisite prayer quorum of ten. Identifying the speaker as the "Taurean reaper of the wild apple field" (159), Rich indicates, in an accompanying note, that she means to invoke the Kabbalistic figure of *Malkut*, a wisdom figure known also as the *Shekhinah*. A source of "secrets and new meanings of Torah" (159), the *Shekhinah* has, of late, achieved the status of muse in Jewish American poetic practice (Shreiber, "A Flair for Deviation"; Selinger, "Shekhinah in America"). Writing thus under the sign of this enabling presence, Rich – like others before her – traverses the boundary between prayer and poetry, expanding the discursive categories of Jewish American writing, as well as her readers' understanding of Jewish structures of belonging.

The poem in the eye, the poem in the ear: the experimental poetics of Jerome Rothenberg and Irena Klepfisz

Formal experimentation and innovation is central to contemporary Jewish American poetic practice. While the field is happily crowded with numerous, wildly diverse writers who merit attention, I want to conclude this discussion by considering two poets, Jerome Rothenberg and Irena Klepfisz, who take the aesthetic implications of Jewishness to particularly striking ends.

Rothenberg, whose career begins in the sixties, is perhaps best known as one of the founding members of the movement known as "ethnopoetics." This alternative aesthetic places itself counter to or outside the parameters of traditional Western verse culture as exemplified by the lyric, focusing instead on visual and performance (oral) based modes of expression. Further, its practitioners derive inspiration through cross-cultural as well as cross-disciplinary exchange. Rothenberg's earliest collaborators, for example, are cultural anthropologists, not poets. He introduces the term "ethnopoetics" with the publication of his anthology, *Technicians of the Sacred* (1968). Looking at this gathering of "primitive" poetries (Navaho, Inuit, and Aborigine, to name a few), the student of Jewish American writing might well ask: "What is a nice Jewish poet doing in a place like this?" The answer begins with the recognition that Rothenberg, like Ginsberg, is not interested in being nice – that is, correct or decorous. Nor, however, should his turn toward the wisdom literatures of other ancient, mostly non-Western, cultures be narrowly construed as a repudiation or denial of his Jewishness. On the contrary, this move is in direct response to the Marxist philosopher Adorno's famous dictum that "After Auschwitz writing poetry is barbaric"(Rothenberg, "Nokh," 140). As Rothenberg understands it, "poetry" in this instance means "lyric" – a first-person retelling of a subjective experience. The Holocaust – or, as Rothenberg prefers to call it, the *khurban,* Yiddish for "disaster pure & simple, with no false ennoblement" ("Nokh," 140) – renders the lyric suspect on at least two counts: first, devastation of such magnitude dwarfs the power of individuated emotive experience; second, and perhaps more profoundly, the effort to annihilate an entire group of persons, of speaking subjects, amounts to an assault on the very grounds upon which lyric claims to stand – subjective speech. To paraphrase Yeats, after 1945 all is changed, changed utterly, including poetry. This catastrophic event, precipitating a linguistic crisis for the Yiddish American poets, becomes, for Rothenberg, an ideological trauma with aesthetic consequences. As he sees it, the event marks a radical choice for the poet who would write under the rubric of Jewishness. He could ally himself with an emerging, fledgling "Jewish nationalism" (otherwise known as Zionism), a choice which Rothenberg contends leads necessarily to reinscribing some sort of xenophobic and imperialistic urges. Or, he could commit himself to writing against orthodoxies of all kinds (including those sanctioned by Judaism) in the interest of envisioning a more heterogeneous, inclusive version of Jewishness. Rothenberg opts for the latter. In this respect, Rothenberg differs from Ginsberg, who ultimately writes his way out of Judaism through the m/other and claims Buddhism as the right form for his own spiritual practice. For Rothenberg's interest in the other, who resides outside the boundaries of Western culture, leads him to an extended exploration of the imaginative potential of the esoteric, the other who dwells within various Jewish mystical traditions, including those of the Kabbalah, which he treats as a particularly rich poetic resource.

Rothenberg contributes to the field of Jewish American letters both as a poet and as anthologist. *Exiled in the Word: Poems & Other Visions of the Jews from Tribal Times to Present*, a revised version of the earlier, more sprawling anthology *A Big Jewish Book* (1978), brings together that strain in Jewish writing which is perhaps best described as belonging to the avant-garde. It is an eclectic, eccentric, and finally fascinating compilation, including works by twentieth-century poets such as George Oppen, David Meltzer, and Edmond Jabes, as well as translations of ancient heterodox Jewish texts such as poems by the mystics of the thirteenth and sixteenth centuries – Moses De Leon and Issac Luria, respectively. Drawing upon surrealist poet André Breton's idea of *poesis* as "sacred action," Rothenberg calls attention to the ritual function of Jewish poetic texts, many derived from Kabbalistic material. Particularly striking among the various offerings are visual texts such as the sixteenth-century mystic Moses Cordovero's "The Unity of God," comprised of a large image of the letter *alef* (the first letter in the Hebrew alphabet, also signifying the number one), which contains the tetragrammaton – a symbol for the ineffable name of God. Another example of this visual strain may be found in Rothenberg's own "Gematria" (composed in collaboration with Harris Lenowitz). This is a "poetry of numbers" whereby

English texts are generated through a procedure based on the ancient Hebrew practice of coded correspondences between numbers and letters. Such texts function both inside and outside the boundaries of Jewish discursive practice. On the one hand, as "visual" texts, they refute Judaism's anti-iconic bias, which begins with the Second of the Ten Commandments prohibiting the making of graven images. On the other hand, by virtue of their fundamental untranslatability (they are literally unspeakable texts) they dramatize a conception of Hebrew, the Holy Tongue, as "pure language," a wholly transparent system in which word and meaning are of a piece. Furthermore, in these visual texts the author or maker has all but disappeared from her creation, by contrast to the written/spoken text which depends upon the poet's voice and by extension her full presence. In this way, these visual texts reach back to the very origins of Jewish poetry, whose makers were often anonymous, singing not for themselves but for the well being of the collective.

While Rothenberg focuses our attention on the visual text, the bilingual (Yiddish/English) experimental verse of Irena Klepfisz returns us to the region of the voice. Bringing this chapter to a fitting conclusion, Klepfisz returns us to the preoccupation with which we began – a haunting, lingering desire for an originary language. As a non-native speaker of Yiddish (Polish was her native tongue), Klepfisz's project is unique. Rather than taking the poem as an occasion for grieving the loss of East European Jewry – with all of its idealized associations of a bygone period of stability in the construction of Jewish identity – Klepfisz writes in the service of linguistic recovery. Devoting herself to a language that has been routinely pronounced dead, or at least in intensive care, Klepfisz works to reclaim Yiddish, and perhaps even more importantly its vision of a heterogeneous Jewish identity. As a "language of fusion" Yiddish moves in and out of its component languages (German dialect, Old French, Italian, Slavic, and Hebrew), absorbing more or less their various vocabularies, depending on the location of the speaker and on the circumstances of a given exchange (Harshav, "The Semiotics of Yiddish Communication," 146). Yiddish can thus potentially bespeak a more inclusive version of Jewish community, cutting across a number of boundaries, social as well as linguistic. Klepfisz writes that "Yiddish was never the exclusive property of *di groyse gerlente* (the upper class). It was a language of different ideologies, education, commitment, as much the language of gangsters and shopkeepers as that of poets and intellectuals. Never was it a private cult" ("Secular Jewish Identity," 160).

Her commitment to reanimating Yiddish, with particular emphasis on the language's capacity to represent collective diversity, informs the title poem of her 1990 collection, "*Etkhe verter oyf mame-loshn*/A Few Words in the Mother Tongue." Structured as a lexicon, the first section of the poem registers as a (somewhat ironic) concession to Yiddish's imminent demise: virtually any current English translation of a Yiddish text must be necessarily supplemented with such a glossary. But what looks like a concession actually has a pedagogic function: for, two-thirds through the poem, Klepfisz leaves off translating altogether and writes exclusively in Yiddish. Reflecting ten years after their composition, Klepfisz wonders whether these bilingual experiments are wholly successful ("The Pen of the Heart," 329–331). On occasion the use of Yiddish strikes her as artificial, arbitrary rather than necessary. Moreover, rather than bringing her readers closer to a rich linguistic legacy and the rapidly vanishing world to which it belongs, the fragments of Yiddish woven throughout only accentuate the magnitude of the loss. For there is a vast difference between the dense, multivalent poems of her literary forbearers, and the comparatively impoverished Yiddish she is able to offer, both because of her own professed linguistic limitations, and those of her mostly non-Yiddish-speaking readership.

These doubts aside, Klepfisz remains interested in the aesthetic and ideological possibilities bilingual verse stands to offer. Recognizing how Yiddish, as a strange (foreign) tongue, can effect radical thinking by interrupting and disrupting the status quo, she continues to experiment, complicating that view of Jewish American verse as an aesthetics grounded in a nostalgic attachment to the past, crafted out of a language marked by longing and loss. Highly self-conscious of the aesthetically awkward and politically inflammatory nature of her enterprise, Klepfisz persists in wrestling with how the ideological essence, indeed life force, that Yiddish signifies, might be made available. Her vision of Yiddish as a distinctly Jewish, but anational, language, speaks to what the great Jewish philosopher Franz Rosenzweig had in mind when he warns against equating "the earth of one's homeland," which can be measured in square footage, with the "priceless sap of life." He continues, "Whenever a people loves the soil of its native land more than its own life, it is in danger – as all the people of the world are" (Glatzer, *Franz Rosenzweig: His Life and Thought*, 294). For Klepfisz, Yiddish is a dream space "*on grenetsn* without boundaries / *lender* lands" ("The Pen of the Heart," 330). In this way Klepfisz, like other powerful artists whose works comprise the ever-expanding oeuvre of Jewish American poetry, returns us to Ozick's call for a Jewish American poetics whose language is "ripe enough" to represent a complex, ever-shifting category of identity. As Klepfisz herself puts it elsewhere:

> *yidishkayt*   a way of being
> Jewish   always arguable
> ("A Few Words," 330)

REFERENCES AND SELECTED FURTHER READINGS

Barron, Jonathan and Eric Selinger, eds. *Jewish American Poetry: Poems, Commentary and Reflections*. Hanover, NH: University of New England Press, 2000.

Blau DuPlessis, Rachel and Peter Quartermaine. "Introduction." In *The Objectivist Nexus: Essays in Cultural Poetics*. Tuscaloosa: University of Alabama Press, 1999.

Bloom, Harold. "The Sorrows of American Jewish Poetry." In *Figures of Capable Imagination*. New York: Seabury Press, 1976.

Falk, Marcia. *Book of Blessings: New Jewish Prayers for Daily Life, The Sabbath, and the New Moon Festival*. San Francisco: Harper Collins, 1996.

Finkelstein, Norman. *Not One of Them in Place: Modern Poetry and Jewish American Identity*. New York: SUNY Press, 2001.

Flanzbaum, Hilene. *The Americanization of the Holocaust*. Baltimore: Johns Hopkins University Press, 1999.

Fredman, Stephen. *A Menorah for Athena: Charles Reznikoff and the Jewish Dilemma of Objectivist Poetry*. Chicago: University of Chicago Press, 2001.

Ginsberg, Allen. *Selected Poems: 1947–1995*. New York: Harper Collins, 1996.

Glatshteyn, Jacob. "Soon." In *American Yiddish Poetry: A Bilingual Anthology*. Eds. Benjamin and Barbara Harshav. Berkeley: University of California Press, 1986.

Grossman, Allen. "The Jew as an American Poet: The Instance of Ginsberg." In *The Long Schoolroom*. Ann Arbor: University of Michigan Press, 1997.

"Jewish Poetry Considered as a Theophoric Project." In *The Long Schoolroom*. Ann Arbor: University of Michigan Press, 1997.

Harshav, Benjamin. "The Semiotics of Yiddish Communication." In *What is Jewish Literature?* Ed. Hana Wirth-Nesher. New York: Jewish Publication Society, 1994.

Herzog, Anne F., and Janet E. Kaufman, eds. *"How Shall We Tell Each Other of the Poet": The Life and Writing of Muriel Rukeyser*. New York: St. Martin's Press, 1999.

Hollander, John. "The Question of American Jewish Poetry." In *What is Jewish Literature?* Ed. Hana Wirth-Nesher. New York: Jewish Publication Society, 1994.

Klepfisz, Irena. "Secular Jewish Identity: *Yidishkayt* in America." In *Dreams of an Insomniac: Jewish Feminist Essays, Speeches, and Diatribes*. Portland: The Eighth Mountain Press, 1990.

"The Pen of the Heart." In *Jewish American Poetry: Poems, Commentary and Reflections*. Eds. Jonathan Barron and Eric Selinger. Hanover, NH: University of New England Press, 2000.

"A Few Words in the Mother Tongue." In *A Few Words in the Mother Tongue: Poems Selected and New (1971–1990)*. Portland: The Eighth Mountain Press, 1990.

Molodowsky, Kadya. *Paper Bridges: Selected Poems of Kadya Molodowsky*. Trans. Kathryn Hellerstein. Detroit: Wayne State University Press, 1999.

Osherow, Jacqueline. *Dead Man's Praise*. New York: Grove Press, 1999.

Ozick, Cynthia. "America: Toward Yavneh." In *What is Jewish Literature?* Ed. Hana Wirth-Nesher. New York: Jewish Publication Society, 1994.

Piercy, Marge. *The Art of Blessing the Day*. New York: Knopf, 1999.

Pound/Zukofsky: Selected Letters of Ezra Pound and Louis Zukofsky. Ed. Barry Ahearn. New York: New Directions Press, 1987.

Reznikoff, Charles. "Kaddish." In *Poems 1918–1975: The Complete Poems of Charles Reznikoff*. Ed. Seamus Cooney. 2 vols. Santa Rosa: Black Sparrow Press, 1996.

Rich, Adrienne. *Adrienne Rich's Poetry and Prose*. Eds. Barbara Charlesworth Gelpi and Albert Gelpi. New York: Norton, 1993.

Rosenzweig, Franz. *Franz Rosenzweig: His Life and Thought*. Ed. Nahum Glatzer. New York: Schocken Press, 1961.

Rothenberg, Jerome. "Nokh Aushvits After Auschwitz." In *Jewish American Poetry: Poems, Commentary and Reflections*. Eds. Jonathan Barron and Eric Selinger. Hanover, NH: University of New England Press, 2000.

Rothenberg, Jerome and Harris Lenowitz. *Exiled in the Word: Poems and Visions of the Jews from Tribal Times to the Present*. Port Townsend: Copper Canyon Press, 1989.

Rukeyser, Muriel. *The Complete Poems of Muriel Rukeyser*. New York: McGraw Hill, 1978.

Scroggins, Mark. *Louis Zukofsky and the Poetry of Knowledge*. Tuscaloosa: University of Alabama Press, 1998.

Selinger, Eric Murphey. "Shekhinah in America." In *Jewish American Poetry: Poems, Commentary and Reflections*. Eds. Jonathan Barron and Eric Selinger. Hanover, NH: University of New England Press, 2000.

Shapiro, Karl. *Poems of a Jew*. New York: Random House, 1958.

Shreiber, Maeera Y. " 'Where Are We Moored?': Adrienne Rich, Women's Mourning and the Limits of Lament." In *Dwelling in Possibility: Women Poets and Critics on Poetry*. Eds. Yopie Prins and Maeera Y. Shreiber. Ithaca: Cornell University Press, 1997.

"The End of Exile: Jewish Identity and Its Diasporic Poetics." *PMLA* 113.2 (March 1998): 273–287.

"A Flair for Deviation: The Troublesome Potential of Jewish Poetics." In *Jewish American Poetry: Poems, Commentary and Reflections*. Eds. Jonathan Barron and Eric Selinger. Hanover, NH: University of New England Press, 2000.

Stephenson, Gregory. " 'Howl': A Reading." In *On the Poetry of Allen Ginsberg*. Ed. Lewis Hyde. Ann Arbor: University of Michigan Press, 1984.

Wirth-Nesher, Hana. "Language as Homeland in Jewish-American Literature." In *Insider/Ousider: American Jews and Multiculturalism*. Eds. David Biale, Michael Galchinsky, and Susannah Heschel. Berkeley: University of California Press, 1998.

Zukofsky, Louis. "An Objective" (revised version of "Sincerity and Objectification"). *Prepositions*. Berkeley: University of California Press, 1981.

Complete Short Poetry. Baltimore: Johns Hopkins University Press, 1991.

9

ALAN WALD

Jewish American writers on the Left

The appeal of the Left

The literary category of US Writers on the Left was initially delimited by Daniel Aaron in his 1961 *Writers on the Left: Episodes in American Literary Communism*. The genus pertains chiefly to mid-twentieth century authors and literary intellectuals inspired by the ideas of Marxism, most notably through an attraction to the Communist-led cultural movement. During the first two decades, only a modest number of distinguished poets, novelists, critics, and dramatists declared themselves socialists; they fashioned an amorphous, somewhat Bohemian legacy of art in the service of the emancipation of the working class in the pages of publications such as the *Masses* and the *Liberator*. This heritage would be revivified in new form as a repercussion of the social crisis of the 1930s when an extraordinary number of the most gifted writers veered precipitously in the direction of the revolutionary Left. During the 1940s, this tradition of "littérature engagée" evolved as a constituent component of the cultural mainstream, but in the 1950s it was ultimately marginalized by the anti-radical political repression of the McCarthy era.

The Bolshevik rendition of Marxism is the conspicuous political feature at the heart of this legacy. Sundry of the most capable writers were passionately enthralled by the ideals of the 1917 October Revolution in Russia, which they believed to be embodied in the activities and ideology of the Communist Party. Even Left critics of the Stalin regime often based their condemnation on writings by Lenin and Trotsky. The attraction remained potent through World War II but waned as the Cold War began.

In 1956, all but a few of those writers remaining close to the Party were so appalled by Nikita Khrushchev's exposé of Stalin's crimes that they terminated their association. In the 1960s, this Old Left tradition was displaced by new forms of cultural radicalism: the counter-culture, the Black Arts Movement, and the Second Wave of Feminism. Yet respect among literary scholars for the earlier achievement escalated dramatically in the 1980s and after, as new research and theories opened modern perspectives on many neglected writers and their work.

Daniel Aaron profiled only two Jewish Americans in his central cast of a dozen leading Communist cultural figures: Mike Gold (a pseudonym for Irwin Granich, 1893–1967), author of the novel *Jews Without Money* (1930), and Joseph Freeman (1897–1965), author of the autobiography *An American Testament* (1936). Both men served as editors of the Party's *New Masses* magazine during the 1930s; Gold endured as a Party member until his death, while Freeman was cast out in the wake of the Moscow Purge Trials of 1936–1938. A more ample examination of the rank and file as well as secondary leaders of the Communist-led literary movement, suggests a Jewish American presence of close to 50 percent of the aggregate of those who appeared regularly in Party-affiliated publications and joined Party-led organizations such as the John Reed Clubs and League of American Writers. This is a curious number, considering that Jews were approximately 2 or 3 percent of the US population during these decades.

The explanation for such an inordinate Jewish participation may be attributed to divers contingencies. These include the strong roots of the US Communist movement in East European immigrant families who had transported to their new homeland working class and socialist loyalties along with a hatred of Tzarist autocracy. In the ambience of the organized Left were a Jewish People's Fraternal Order, a Jewish Socialist Federation, Jewish workers' choruses, Yiddish-oriented summer camps, a Jewish Workers University, and Yiddish-language newspapers such as the socialist *Jewish Daily Forward* and Communist *Morgen Freiheit*.

In addition, the Communist movement preached a cultural pluralist and internationalist universalism appealing to young men and women breaking free of the shackles of *shtetl* and ghetto isolation. To the stern religious faith of orthodox elders, Communism provided the alternative of a moral life justified by allegedly scientific arguments and analysis. Young people who came of age in an environment marked by the study of holy books and fervent disputations about passages in the Torah, were well equipped for a political movement where sacred texts by Marx and Lenin were heatedly debated as guides to action.

Moreover, as the threat of fascism marched across Europe in the 1930s, the Communist movement was among the most militant in attempting to organize a response. In 1936, a disproportionately large number of young Jewish Americans volunteered to combat the forces of Franco, Hitler, and Mussolini in Spain by joining the Party-led Abraham Lincoln Brigades. Once abroad, they, along with thousands of other Jewish internationalists from Europe and the Middle East, participated in the formation of a people's army through the Communist-led International Brigades.

Jews with Communist sympathies were probably the leading ethnic component of this first effort to stop fascism by military force of arms. Yet the Jewish Lincolns thought of themselves foremost as anti-fascists and partisans of democracy, which is characteristic of the spirit of the Jewish literary Left during the years of the Popular Front. Officers and Political Commissars of the Lincoln Brigade included many Jewish Americans, such as Milton Wolff, the last commander, but more publicity was given to the presence of African Americans in leadership positions, such as Oliver Law, one of the many martyrs to the cause.

Participants in the Communist-led crusade to save the Spanish Republic were naive about Stalin's policies and intentions in Spain and elsewhere, but their actions were prescient and critical in installing an anti-fascist spirit among the US public. Although the Party suffered acute embarrassment when a non-aggression pact was signed between Hitler and Stalin in August 1939, anti-fascism returned as a major Communist theme when Germany invaded the USSR in June 1941. Thus Jewish American and other Communist activists and writers were in the forefront of supporting the Allies in the Second World War.

Left-wing Jewish cultural workers certainly held additional significant beliefs: an egregiously idealized vision of the USSR, an ardent support of the Congress of Industrial Organizations, and a passionate hatred of white supremacy. Yet anti-fascism was at the crux of their convictions. What was unique in the politics of Jewish American left-wing anti-fascism was the form it took: not Jewish nationalism nor a reliance on powerful Western protectors, but a cry for unified armed resistance among all the oppressed, and a sense of sympathy and solidarity with other, non-Jewish, groups suffering analogous persecution, especially through colonialism and white supremacism.

It was furthermore consequential that, starting in the 1930s, New York City, a heavily Jewish-populated city, was the center of the Communist movement (and much of the rest of the US Left). New York was also the headquarters of the US publishing industry. Communism's ability to variously pull into its magazines and protest activities so many leading writers of the day – Ernest Hemingway, Langston Hughes, Theodore Dreiser, John Dos Passos, Thomas Wolfe, Genevieve Taggard, Ruth McKenney, Richard Wright – rendered it exceedingly appealing to the young Jews pouring into the intellectual professions.

The Jewish presence

Before the Great Depression, Jewish American writers allured by socialism included Abraham Cahan (1860–1951), editor of the *Jewish Daily Forward* and author of *The Rise of David Levinsky* (1917; Anzia Yezierska (1885–1970), author of *Bread Givers* (1925); and Samuel Ornitz (1891–1955), author of *Haunch, Paunch and Jowl: An Anonymous Autobiography* (1923). Yet the leading names in socialist literary circles of that era were the non-Jewish Jack London, Upton Sinclair, Floyd Dell, John Reed, and Max Eastman.

In the 1930s, when Communism was at center stage, the situation changed considerably. Mike Gold, hitherto a minor playwright and journalist, achieved national acclaim for *Jews Without Money*, and for his earnest defense of Jewish proletarian culture in his columns, reviews, and debates. Clifford Odets (1906–1963) created an uproar with his proletarian drama *Waiting for Lefty* in 1935 and continued on with the achievements of *Awake and Sing* (1935) and *Golden Boy* (1937). Lillian Hellman (1905–1984) emerged as a popular anti-capitalist playwright with *The Little Foxes* (1939) and an anti-fascist campaigner with *Watch on the Rhine* (1941). Kenneth Fearing (1902–1961) became a major force in US poetry with *Angel Arms* (1929), *Poems* (1935), and *Dead Reckoning* (1938), and Muriel Rukeyser (1913–1980) attained celebrity as a young modernist Left poet with *Theory of Flight* (1935) and *US 1* (1938).

Behind these, another stratum of Jewish Americans was emerging from divers associations with the Communist Left to assume center stage as radical writers in the 1940s. Nelson Algren (born William Abraham, 1909–1981), after struggling through the 1930s with little success, finally gained acclaim as bard of the *lumpenproletariat* for his novels of the Chicago urban underclass, *Never Come Morning* (1942) and *The Man With the Golden Arm* (1949). Irwin Shaw (born Irwin Shamforoff, 1913–1984) launched his career in the 1930s as a left-wing playwright and short fiction writer, achieving best-seller status with his World War II novel *The Young Lions* (1948). Jo Sinclair (born Ruth Seid, 1913–1995) commenced her literary career with a 1936 anti-lynching story in the *New Masses*; ten years later she published a prize-winning attack on homophobia and antisemitism, *Wasteland* (1946). Howard Fast (b. 1914) was sympathetic to Communism when he began publishing historical novels in the 1930s, joining the Party the same year that he issued *Citizen Tom Paine* (1943). Arthur Miller (b. 1915) a struggling Marxist playwright since the late 1930s, won the Pulitzer Prize for *Death of a Salesman* in 1949. Norman Mailer (b. 1923), a Communist fellow-traveler, achieved both popular and critical success with his masterpiece of battle on the Pacific front, *The Naked and the Dead* (1948).

Moreover, Jewish Americans were eminently discernible in the infrastructure of Left institutions. The Communist movement's editor of its publishing house was Alexander Tractenberg (1884–1966); its chair of the Party cultural Commission was V. J. Jerome (born Isaac Jerome Romaine, 1896–1965); and its head of the important Hollywood Party section was playwright and screenwriter John Howard Lawson (1895–1977). Most of the founding members of the New York Party-led journals *Partisan Review* and *Dynamo* in 1934 were Jewish, and there was also substantial Jewish literary presence on the editorial board of the Party's *New Masses* – Gold, Freeman, Stanley Burnshaw (b. 1906), A. B. Magil (b. 1905), and Joseph North (born Joseph Soifer, 1904–1976). The Party's other influential literary magazines, *Mainstream* and *Masses & Mainstream*, were edited by Samuel Sillen (1911–1973) and Charles Humboldt (born Clarence Weinstock, 1910–1964). The Party's theoretical organ, called *The Communist* and then *Political Affairs*, was edited in the late 1940s and early 1950s by Jerome. When the House Committee on Un-American Activities signaled out ten leading Communist screenwriters and directors for harassment in 1947 and eventual imprisonment in 1950, six were Jews – Alvah Bessie (1904–1985), Herbert Biberman (1900–1971), Lester Cole (born Lester Cohn, 1904–1985), John Howard Lawson, Albert Maltz (1908–1985), and Samuel Ornitz.

Most scholarship on the Jewish American literary Left has taken one of two directions. Among scholars preoccupied with the creative arts, the approach is to analyze a small group of texts deservedly acclaimed as classics of the 1930s and 1940s, only a few of which conspicuously dramatize Jewish characters or issues. Among the most ubiquitously deliberated are *Jews Without Money* by Gold, a sentimental tribute to an East European-based Jewish folk culture no longer appropriate to class struggles in New York; *Call It Sleep* (1934) by Henry Roth (1906–1995), a stream-of-consciousness protest against the brutality, ignorance, and sexual frustration of ghetto poverty; *The Day of the Locust* (1939) by Nathanael West (born Nathan Weinstein, 1903–1940), a surrealistic satire of the emptiness of mass culture; *Yonnondio* (written in the 1930s, published in 1974) by Tillie Olsen (born Tillie Lerner, 1913), a skillfully crafted sequence of vignettes about a destitute mid-West working-class family in the late 1920s; *The Unpossessed* (1934) by Tess Slesinger (1905–1945), a wicked satire about urban intellectuals and political commitment; and *The Naked and the Dead* (1948) by Mailer, an unabashed Marxist indictment of the senselessness of war. Left playwrights such as Odets, Hellman, and Miller have also come by extensive treatment.

Among scholars more preoccupied with criticism and literary intellectuals, even more concentration has been devoted to one-time Jewish American leftists who passed through Communism to develop Left critiques of the Soviet Union, often influenced by Trotskyism. In the post-World War II era, this unevenly deradicalizing milieu was ranged around *Partisan Review* and, later, *Commentary* and *Dissent* magazines. Sundry of the writers, eventually called the "New York Intellectuals," achieved noteworthy authority in cultural circles, amply succeeding in constituting their Cold War interpretation of the history of the literary Left as semi-official. In contrast, virtually all the pro-Communist literary intellectuals in academe were fired and blacklisted, including the Jewish Americans Harry Slochower (1900–1991), Morris U. Schappes (b. 1907), and Annette T. Rubinstein (b. 1910).

Among the most prominent cultural figures of the "New York Intellectuals" are the literary critics Lionel Trilling (1905–1975), Philip Rahv (born Ivan Greenberg, 1908–1973), William Phillips (born William Litvinsky, 1907–2002), Leslie Fiedler (b. 1917), Alfred Kazin (1915–1998), and Irving Howe (born Irving Horenstein, 1920–93); the art critics Harold Rosenberg (1906–1978), Meyer Schapiro (1904–1996), and Clement Greenberg (1909–1994); and the creative writers Saul Bellow (b. 1915), Isaac Rosenfeld (1918–1956), Delmore Schwartz (1913–1966), and Harvey Swados (1920–1972). While all owe a considerable portion of their intellectual awakening and social vision to adventures with the Communist and Trotskyist movements, their major attainments lie in their post-revolutionary years. Thus very few of the "New York Intellectuals" of the postwar era are part of the Jewish literary Left as an ongoing tradition.

What is missing from these two reigning corpuses of scholarship is a fair representation of the uncommon scope, breadth, and diversity of Jewish American writers on the Left. A cultural tradition is not exclusively defined by its "classics," and often the more influential writings are in the sphere of popular culture. Moreover, there are authors of considerable merit who have gone unrecognized as part of the Left tradition, due to their disappearance as a result of Cold War repression and/or changing literary fashions. Confounding the matter of reconstructing a tradition is the dilemma of self-identification. A small portion of these Left writers did not identify themselves as Jewish American, sometimes due to ambivalent feelings about their families; this was the case of Kenneth Fearing, whose Jewish mother left him with his non-Jewish father. Many more have been variously secretive or misleading about their Marxist itineraries, due to political embarrassment and an understandable fear of being simplistically labeled in their mature years.

With minimal traversing of old ground, and no pretense of providing comprehensive coverage of a topic still insufficiently researched, this chapter will endeavor to furnish an overview and survey of the literary themes, personnel, and some of the neglected writings of the Jewish American literary Left in the mid-twentieth century. Of particular interest are the range of forms, genres, and styles; the trajectory of political and literary careers; the contribution of women; the relationship of Jewish American radicals to African American issues; and the response to international and domestic fascism. However, this chapter treats only Jewish American writings in English. Beyond its scope is the thriving Left-wing movement of Yiddish authors which lasted from the 1890s through the Cold War, including the "Sweatshop Poets," and the "Proletpen" contributors to *Der Hammer*, *Signal*, and *Yiddishe Kultur*.

Genres of the Left

The issue of Jewishness in specific literary texts cannot be isolated from a panoply of concerns that often over-rode or obscured in innumerable ways the effect on poetry and fiction of the author's religio-ethnic upbringing or family background. Indeed, one representative way of partaking of the Jewish literary Left tradition was the abrogation of both Jewish particularism and assimilation to Christian bourgeois society. Moreover, the legacy of the Jewish literary Left provides no unique resolution to the long-debated questions of "is there a Jewish American poetry aesthetic?" or "is there a Jewish American women's literary tradition?" Whether a large number of Jewish writers, and the full range of their creations, can be organized compellingly around peculiarities of subject, style, or perspective that are attributable to Jewishness rather than to geography, generation, or literary models, remains as contested in the heritage of Left writing as elsewhere in US culture.

As Marxist activists, Left writers diversely expressed their Jewishness as part of an internationalist framework. They were unsympathetic to Zionism, advocating class unity to extirpate antisemitism. Moreover, they saw the struggle against antisemitism as part and parcel of the battle against racism, especially anti-Black racism. Beyond that, generalizations are formidable. In personal background, which contributed heavily to the autobiographical basis of much fiction and poetry, many were from poor, East European families, such as Roth, Gold, and poet Sol Funaroff (1911–1942). Yet others were of the middle and upper classes, such as Rukeyser, Maltz, and Lawson. A few were of German Jewish background, such as poet Walter Lowenfels (1897–1976), and of Sephardic families, such as novelist Vera Caspary (1904–1987).

One perplexing peculiarity for scholarship is that left-wing Jewish writers usually crisscrossed a surfeit of genres. They not only combined the production of novels, plays, poetry, and writing for the movies and television; they also moved from "serious" literature to mass culture. A paradigmatic career of a minor writer is that of Melvin P. Levy (1902–1980). Levy launched his professional life with the novels *Matrix* (1925), *The Wedding* (1927), and *The Last Pioneers* (1934). He then joined the Communist Party and switched to radical theater with *Gold Eagle Guy* (1935), produced by the Group Theater and starring John Garfield and Elia Kazan. In 1937, Levy first commenced writing for Hollywood and relocated there in 1940. His films include *Robin Hood of El Dorado* (1935), *She's a Soldier, Too* (1944), *The Bandit of Sherwood Forest* (1946), and *Calamity Jane and Sam Bass* (1949). In 1952, Levy voluntarily testified before the House Committee on Un-American Activities in Washington, DC during the second round of the motion picture industry probe, informing against nine people. Nevertheless, Levy's career petered off in films and he ended his days returning to fiction and also writing the television series "Wild Bill Hickok," "Daniel Boone," and "Bonanza."

Only a handful of the Left poets wrote poetry principally. Don Gordon (1902–1989), Eli Siegel (1902–1978), Robert Friend (1913–1998), Laurence Fixel (b. 1917), and Aaron Kramer (1921–1997) are five illustrations, albeit the last in due time became an English professor who published on nineteenth-century literature. In contrast, Alfred Hayes (1911–1985) and Ben Maddow (1909–1992) wrote prolifically in poetry, fiction, film, theater, non-fiction, and television. Dorothy Parker (born Dorothy Rothschild, 1893–1967) originated as a satirical poet, but also wrote stories, sketches, plays, and film scripts. Joy Davidman (1915–1960) published symmetrically in poetry and fiction, and did a stint in Hollywood. Isidor Schneider (1896–1977) alternated equally between poetry and fiction, plus he had a lengthy career as a literary critic for the *New Masses*. Robert Gessner (1907–1968) moved successively among poetry, novels, and non-fiction about Native American Indians and Jews, finally becoming a world authority in film criticism. James Neugass (1905–1949), a Southern Jew who served as an ambulance driver in Spain, is known for his poetry but primarily aspired to be a novelist, managing to issue one of his eight unpublished books before his premature death. Norman Rosten (1914–1995) was voluminous in the production of poetry and fiction, but was also engaged in drama and radio plays. Even Party cultural functionary Jerome, who aspired originally to poetry, produced short plays and two autobiographical novels.

Those primarily identified as novelists were equally dexterous. George Sklar (1908–1988), Albert Maltz, and Michael Blankfort (1907–1982) produced radical plays, novels, and film scripts. Guy Endore (born Samuel Goldstein, 1901–1970) wrote horror fiction, historical fiction, mysteries, as well as popular novels and screenplays. Sam Ross (born Samuel Rossen, 1912–1995) shuttled among fiction, film, and television. Daniel Fuchs (1909–1993), Lester Cohen (1901–1963), and Samuel Ornitz wrote fiction early and late in their lives, producing film scripts in between. Abraham Polonsky (1910–1999) published five novels, along with directing classics of *film noir*. John Sanford (born Julian Shapiro, 1904) wrote fiction, screenplays, prose poetry, and autobiography. Laurence Lipton (1898–1975) wrote fiction, poetry, and a famous book about the Beats, *The Holy Barbarians* (1959). Ira Wolfert (1906–1998) alternated between fiction and Pulitzer Prize-winning journalism. Two left-wing playwrights also produced noteworthy fiction, Arthur Miller and Elmer Rice (born Elmer Reizenstein, 1992–1967), while Lillian Hellman published celebrated memoirs.

Yet there were also a sufficiently large number of left-wing Jewish American novelists to constitute a major school of realist-naturalist literature within modern fiction. Budd Schulberg (b. 1914) was author of the controversial *What Makes Sammy Run?* (1941). Albert Halper (1904–1984) wrote numerous books about Chicago, New York, and Miami. Edward Dahlberg (1900–1977) wrote three substantial left-wing novels in the 1930s. Nathan Asch (1902–1964), son of Yiddish writer Sholem Asch, published novels, stories, and non-fiction in the 1920s and 1930s. David Alman (b. 1919), Ben Field (born Moc Bragin, 1901–1986), Ben Appel (1908–1977), and Meyer Levin (1905–1981) were also talented novelists variously connected with the Left.

Equally challenging to the scholar is the uneven political evolution of Left writers. The patterns were far more various than familiar Cold War narratives of seduction at the start of the Great Depression and betrayal with the Hitler–Stalin Pact. Some writers, such as Roth and Burnshaw, were attracted to radical socialist thought as students in the 1920s, and felt loyal to Communism until they deradicalized in the post-World War II decade. Others, such as poet Carl Rakosi (b. 1903) and Rukeyser, were on the Left for their entire lives, with the attraction to Communism constituting a singular but far from all-inclusive phase. Writers such as Dahlberg, Fuchs, Fearing, and Asch may have been politically disillusioned with the Left before the end of the 1930s. Yet Halper, Schulberg, Blankfort, Davidman, Vera Caspary, and Appel remained in the proximity of the movement into the early 1940s. Sklar, Polonsky, Endore, Field, Alman, Kramer, Ross, Ornitz, Maltz, Bessie, Sanford, and Roth were still part of the Communist cultural milieu into the 1950s. Gold, Lawson, and Lowenfels lasted as Party members to the closure of their long lives.

Thus the imprint of one's Left commitment can range from being a lifelong inspirational guide to constituting merely one stage, albeit often a defining one, through which a writer has passed. The centrality of Marxist convictions and activities to creative practice depends on the particular artist and the date of the text at which one is looking. For example, the attitude toward the Left is qualitatively different between the 1936 autobiography and the two post-World War II novels of Joseph Freeman, and between poems of Aaron Kramer before and after the early 1950s, although both men remained radical all of their lives.

From a stylistic point of view, the predominant mode of Left writing in the 1930s was social realism animated by a working-class perspective, even if the characters and events were drawn from other social strata. Yet, earlier many of the Jewish leftists – Mike Gold, Isidor Schneider (1896–1977), John Howard Lawson, Maxwell Bodenheim (1893–1954), Stanley Burnshaw – had close affinities with 1920s modernism. Moreover, some of the younger poets of the 1930s – Edwin Rolfe (born Solomon Fishman, 1909–1954), Muriel Rukeyser, Alfred Hayes, Sol Funaroff, Herman Spector (1905–1959), Joy Davidman, Norman Rosten – were far from immune to the technical influences of T. S. Eliot. Still others, such as the Jewish Marxist "Objectivists" – Louis Zukofsky (1904–1978), George Oppen (1908–1984), and Carl Rakosi – were aloof from the proletarian genre altogether. Perhaps the most outstanding neglected novelist, John Sanford, blended experimental techniques with realism. The best-selling Left novelist, Howard Fast (b. 1914), opted for the genre of the historical novel. Some, such as Ed Lacy (born Leonard S. Zinberg, 1911–1968), became proficient in the mystery novel, while a group of young radicals, known as the Futurians, became pioneers of science fiction – Isaac Asimov (1920–1992), John Michel (1917–1969), and Judith Merrill (1923–1997).

Jewish leftists sometimes wrote directly about Jewish experiences. In the Depression, Mike Gold's Jews Without Money, John Howard Lawson's Success Story (1932), Henry Roth's Call It Sleep, and Isidor Schneider's From the Kingdom of Necessity (1935) were characteristic efforts. In the 1940s and after, Jo Sinclair's Wasteland (1946), Joy Davidman's Anya (1940), Sam Ross's Sidewalks Are Free (1950), Ben Field's Jacob's Son (1971), V. J. Jerome's A Lantern for Jeremy (1952), and John Sanford's five-volume Scenes From the Life of an American Jew (1981–1995) dominated the field. As late as 1974, the Jewish Communist Jean Karsavina (1908–1990) published White Eagle, Dark Skies, a novel of Jewish life in Poland.

Jewish American women

Notwithstanding this imposing record, Jewish American Left writers, female as well as male, more often abjured a primary focus on Jewish material, favoring a broader canvas. Tillie Olsen, Muriel Rukeyser, Lillian Hellman, Tess Slesinger, and Dorothy Parker are the best-known Jewish American radical women writers, all the subjects of dissertations and book-length biographical and critical studies. Yet within this body of writing there are only select novels, poems, and stories that depict Jewish experiences. Slesinger, for example, employed the exclusively Jewish circle of *Menorah Journal* writers as the original for the intellectuals lampooned in *The Unpossessed*, yet only several are fictionalized as Jews.

The pattern is similar with those female Jewish writers who have acquired less attention. Eve Merriam (1916–1992) was intimately associated with Communist organizations and publications in the late 1940s and early 1950s, but later became the highly successful author of adult and juvenile poetry. Her books include *Family Circle* (1946), *Tomorrow Morning* (1953), *Montgomery, Alabama, Money, Mississippi and Other Places* (1957), *The Double Bed: From the Feminine Side* (1958), *The Inner City Mother Goose* (1969), and *The Nixon Poems* (1970). From the outset Merriam greatly admired the work of Archibald MacLeish, and her writing was sharply critical of sexism, as well as especially effective at combining witty wordplay with social commentary.

A second prolific but neglected Jewish American Left writer is Leane Zugsmith (1903–1969), who was ideologically pro-Communist in the 1930s and 1940s. She was born into a German-Jewish family in Kentucky whose roots went back to the early nineteenth century, but she spent most of her childhood in Atlantic City, New Jersey. Zugsmith began working as a copyeditor for the pulp magazines *Detective Stories* and *Western Stories*, then published a first novel, *All Victories Are Alike* (1929), about the loss of a newspaper columnist's ideals. In the 1930s she published *Goodbye and Tomorrow* (1931), portraying a romantic spinster who becomes an artists' patron; *Never Enough* (1932), offering a panoramic view of existence in the 1920s in the United States; *The Reckoning* (1934), about the life of a boy of the New York slums; *A Time to Remember* (1936), depicting a middle-class Jewish woman who goes on strike in a department store in New York; and *The Summer Soldiers* (1938), a collective character sketch of Northern radicals who travel South by train to hold a hearing on the treatment of Black workers. *Home Is Where You Hang Your Childhood* (1937) anthologizes her short stories, many of which are political and have Jewish characters.

The most successful radical female author of her day was Vera Caspary, a premium popular writer of mysteries and romances whose actual political views were not known to her audience until she narrated a rather tame version of her 1930s Communist Party activities in her autobiography, *The Secrets of Grown-Ups* (1979). Earlier she had fictionalized some of her adventures in a novel, *The Rosecrest Cell* (1967). Prior to that time, her reputation had been very solidly that of a skillful suspense writer who excelled at showing personalities under stress, usually due to fear, or as a consequence of a police inquiry. Indeed, for many, her career seemed to begin fifteen years after her first novel, with *Laura* (1943), also a celebrated play and film, featuring a police investigator who falls in love with an alleged murder victim. In *Bedelia* (1945), *The Murder in the Stork Club* (1946), *Stranger Than Truth* (1947), *Thelma* (1952), *False Face* (1954), *Evvie* (1954), *The Husband* (1957), and many others, Caspary usually employs multiple points of view and often features a character dominated by one particular emotion.

Among the very minor Jewish American writers are several women who published poetry and fiction during the Cold War years. The early verse of Martha Millet (b. 1919) appears in the Communist *Young Pioneer* in the 1930s, and she later contributed to *Masses & Mainstream*. Her books are *Thine Alabaster Cities* (1952), a long, dramatic poem, and *Dangerous Jack, A Fantasy in Verse* (1953). Naomi Replansky (b. 1918) published verse in Communist and other publications in the 1940s, sometimes as "Naomi Ripley." Aggressively championed by Marxist modernist Thomas McGrath, she published *Ring Song* in 1952 and *The Dangerous World* in 1995.

A Jewish American fiction writer who was a Communist Party member for over a decade is Wilma Shore (b. 1913), the daughter of Viola Brothers Shore of the Algonquin circle. Her fiction was collected in *Women Should Be Allowed* (1965). Of a greater reputation is Helen Yglesias (born Helen Bassine, 1915), a Party member for about fifteen years who published her first novel, *How She Died* (1972), at age fifty-seven.

An example of a radical writer more removed from the organized Left is Bessie Breuer (1893–1975), who joined the Communist-led League of American Writers in the late 1930s. Breuer's fiction tends to employ experimental styles and to feature women who flounder among disappointing relationships and unsatisfying jobs. She also wrote a play, *Sundown Beach*, about World War II pilots suffering from combat trauma, which was produced by Elia Kazan as an early effort of the left-wing Actors Studio in New York in 1948.

African Americans and Jewish Americans

Starting in the early 1930s, radical Jewish writers began an assault on anti-Black racism. John L. Spivak (1897–1981) addressed the condition of chain gangs in *Georgia Nigger* (1932), while Guy Endore recreated the early period of the Haitian Revolution through the eyes of a kidnapped African in *Babouk* (1934). This literary association reflected the close and supportive relations that Jewish radicals often had to figures such as Langston Hughes (for example, Mike Gold introduced Hughes' 1938 collection, *A New Song*); Richard Wright (Wright married two Jewish Communist women, and he wrote the preface to *Letters from the Tombs* [1941], the prison writings of Morris U. Schappes, a future Communist Jewish cultural leader); Chester Himes (a Jewish radical named Dan Levin published Himes' early left-wing stories and became a model for his most memorable Jewish fictional character, Abe Rosenberg in his 1947 novel, *The Lonely Crusade*); Paul Robeson (Jewish Communists were among his close personal friends); Lorraine Hansberry (Jewish Communist songwriter Robert Nemiroff was her husband); and W. E. B. Du Bois (Marxist Herbert Aptheker was his friend and literary executor). In 1939–1940 Albert Maltz was among the several Jewish Left writers associated with the journal *Equality*. This was launched under Communist Party direction, "To Defend Democratic Rights and Combat Anti-Semitism and Racism." Vera Caspary served on the editorial council of *Equality*, along with Lillian Hellman, and both Tess Slesinger and Dorothy Parker were contributors.

This association between Jewish and Black radicals was not restricted to the 1930s or even the 1940s. Jewish leftists such as the poet Aaron Kramer and Julius Fast (b. 1919), who was the mystery-writing brother of Marxist novelist Howard Fast, were part of the left-wing Harlem Writers Club, and a central figure in the early 1960s Black radical poetry group *Umbra* was the Jewish Communist Art Berger (b. 1920). Moreover, throughout the 1960s and early 1970s, there was no single Euro-American individual who did more to promote African American poetry than Jewish American Communist Party member Walter Lowenfels, who featured Black poets in his highly successful commercial paperback anthologies: *Poets of Today* (1964), *Where is Vietnam* (1967), *In a Time of Revolution: Poets from Our Third World* (1969), *The Writing on the Wall: 108 American Poems of Protest* (1969), and *For Neruda, For Chile* (1975). From the late 1930s until the 1960s, mass-market author Ed Lacy created African American characters in his thrillers and detective novels, and promoted strong anti-racist values.

Nevertheless, such examples should not lead one to idealize Jewish American Old Left radical practice regarding racism in culture, or to conclude that Jewish cultural workers did everything they might have done to foster self-expression by writers of color, or that their literary portraits of Blacks were particularly authentic. What can be established is that a unique relationship existed – Jewish radical writers identified with Blacks whom they thought were playing the same "scapegoat" role in the US that Jews were playing in Europe; and Jewish radical writers wanted to act in solidarity with

African Americans in a manner that they wished the Christians of Europe had acted in solidarity with Jews.

It is also noteworthy that the atmosphere of anti-racism on the Jewish Left was such that it was harder for Jewish American Left writers to caricature or paternalistically depict African Americans, even unconsciously, in novels, poetry, theater, and film, because there were checks and controls. Leftists would have their works carefully scrutinized and sometimes lambasted by their comrades, Black and white, for the ways they depicted people of color or historical situations of racist oppression and rebellion.

There is no doubt that at certain times this tendency to ruthlessly criticize got out of control. The most notorious episode involving literature occurred during the Communist Party's campaign against "white chauvinism" in its own ranks during the 1950s. At that time, Jewish American pro-Communist writer Earl Cohen (1916–1986), who wrote under the name Earl Conrad, was brutally and unfairly denounced as a white chauvinist by black and Jewish Communist reviewers for his novel *Rock Bottom* (1952), which drove him unwillingly out of Party circles.

Conrad can be taken as an example of a once-influential Jewish American Left author of some two dozen novels and nonfiction works, whose career has toppled into obscurity. In the 1930s, as a fledgling writer, he had been a Communist Party member; during the 1940s, when he worked for the New York office of the African American newspaper *Chicago Defender* and published popular books excoriating racism such as *Jim Crow America* (1947) and *Scottsboro Boy* (1950), he was a fellow-traveler. Although Conrad often gave lectures about the problem of anti-Black racism among Jews, and he was generally perceived as Jewish, he never depicted Jewish characters in his novels nor wrote about Jewish matters in his other books. This includes a 1954 book about his father, *Horse Trader*. However, in his notes for the autobiography he was trying to complete when he died in 1986, Conrad started by referring to himself as "A Twentieth Century Abolitionist"; he then made a startling statement, never appearing in any of his published writings: "My interest in the 'underdog,' the submerged or oppressed, in particular the blacks, had Judaic origins" (unpublished manuscript, courtesy Alyse Conrad).

Conrad might be regarded as a characteristic type of the Jewish literary Left. He was not an assimilationist by any fair definition because he did not assume the dominant middle-class Christian culture of his society. But he did not identify as Jewish positively by a fair definition, either, because there are no references to anything in Jewish religion or culture that served him well. His Jewish heritage was mainly felt through an awareness that Jews had been and still were victimized by bigots; this led him to take an internationalist identity that required him to champion the cause of what he believed to be the most oppressed group in his own society, African Americans.

Information about the "Judaic origins" of one of the most famous literary texts about African Americans by a Jewish radical comes from the memories that historical novelist Howard Fast provides in his 1990 autobiography *Being Red*. This concerns his 1944 novel *Freedom Road*, the story of a Black Southerner, Gideon Jackson, under Reconstruction. What had originally propelled Fast to undertake this novel was the combination of four events. First, during his youth he had hoboed through the South, appalled by the racism he witnessed. Second, Fast and his wife had spent an afternoon with novelist Sinclair Lewis and had been horrified to find him expressing genteel antisemitism. Third, while working at the Office of War Information during World War II, Fast had initiated a project to study the possibility of integrating Blacks into the still segregated army. Finally, Fast reveals, "Reports were beginning to filter out of Germany about the destruction of the Jews.... [Hence] all the notes and thinking that I had done for a novel about Reconstruction came together – and every moment I could steal from my work at the OWI was put to writing the new book" (Fast, *Being Red*, 75).

Fast's correlation of antisemitism, in both genteel and vulgar forms, with anti-Black racism, coming from both rich and poor, propelled him to write his celebrated novel of the Reconstruction Era, with Black characters dominating the narrative. *Freedom Road* went on to become a publishing sensation world-wide, and there are claims that it was the most widely printed and read book of the twentieth century. W. E. B. Du Bois wrote a foreword, praising its psychological insight into African Americans, and Paul Robeson proposed playing Gideon Jackson in a Hollywood film version. However, both Fast and Robeson were blacklisted in Hollywood soon after. Fast never wrote another novel with an African American as the central character, and his one effort at a Jewish counterpart to *Freedom Road*, *My Glorious Brothers* (1948), was marred by oddball factual errors that irritated even the sympathetic Communist press.

Among the most prolific and talented of the Jewish American Communist writers whose work has been revived in recent years is John Sanford. Sanford appears to primarily use African American characters to express his own anger and outrage about the US system, and his own utopian dreams of carrying out some action. Sanford was born in Harlem, the only son of Russian immigrants. Falling under the influence of his childhood friend, Nathanael West, he started submitting stories to little magazines such as *Pagany* and *Contact*, and in 1934 he published *The Water Wheel*, a stream-of-consciousness meditation on events in the life of a law clerk in the late 1920s.

In his 1943 anti-racist novel, *The People From Heaven* (reprint, 1996), Sanford creates a Black woman driven to shoot a local white bully and antisemite who has raped her in an upstate New York town. Eight years later, in an act of sheer will, Sanford self-published a four-hundred-page modernist, proletarian narrative in the middle of the witch-hunt called *A Man Without Shoes* (1951). This novel depicts the developing political consciousness of a working-class youth, Dan Johnson, and the events that finally lead him to volunteer to fight with the International Brigades in Spain. The touchstone at every stage in Dan's political development is anti-Black racism, and the main influences on Dan become two African American friends.

A fuller focus on African American life, and one without political ideal-izations, was penned by Warren Miller (1921–1966). Miller was a Jewish American who was in the Communist Party from the late 1940s until the late 1950s, remaining far Left and an ardent supporter of the Cuban Revo-lution until his death at age forty-four of lung cancer. In 1959 he published *The Cool World*, a celebrated first-person narrative of a young Black Harlem gang leader. Yet Miller, though he issued more than a half-dozen other books, never produced anything comparable about Jewish life.

Miller's example is characteristic. Despite the close connections between Blacks and Jews in left-wing circles, it is rare to find a novel that treats equally the interactions between the two groups. One of the few examples is Jo Sinclair's *The Changelings* (1955), originally drafted in her radical youth but completed after she turned hostile to Communism.

Anti-fascism

The powerful anti-fascist convictions of the Jewish American Left urged Jewish American writers into the forefront as chroniclers of the Spanish Civil War. Edwin Rolfe became the "poet Laureate" of the Lincoln Battalion, and Sol Funaroff, Joy Davidman, James Neugass, and others created verse about Spain. From the 1930s to the 1990s, Jewish veterans published a steady stream of autobiographical narratives of the Spanish experience.

The resulting novels by veterans are variegated in perspective. Alvah Bessie's *The Un-Americans* (1957) pictures the heroic and self-sacrificing Abraham Lincoln Brigade veteran Ben Blau persecuted by the House un-American Activities Committee; Spain is unequivocally "the good fight," and McCarthyism is only an extension of Francoism. A contrasting response is by dissident Lincoln veteran, William Herrick (b. 1915). In his violently anti-Stalinist *Hermanos* (1969), Herrick portrays a whole crew of incompetent and sometimes cowardly US officers in the Lincolns whose fanaticism leads them to deploy their troops as canon-fodder for the cause. In *Another Hill* (1994), Milton Wolff (b. 1915) attempts to show some of the tragic aspects of fighting for a good cause under bad conditions; the climax comes when a manly Jewish soldier, Mitch Castle, carries out the execution of a cowardly one, Leo Rogin.

The theme of anti-fascism is pursued in left-wing World War II novels. Albert Maltz published *The Cross and the Arrow* (1944) to provide an explanation of the basis of German support for the Nazis, as well as evidence that some Germans carried out resistance within Germany to Hitler. Stefam Heym (b. 1913), a pro-Communist refugee from Germany, published *Hostages* (1942) about anti-Nazi resistance in Prague, and *The Crusaders* (1948), a best-seller of a thousand pages about the war on Europe. Along with *The Naked and the Dead* (1948) by Norman Mailer, and *The Young Lions* (1948) by Irwin Shaw, Heym's best-seller became one of the most widely read World War II novels.

Other left-wing World War II novelists are less renowned. *The Sun is Silent* (1951) by Saul Levitt (1911–1977), traces the military careers of a group of men from Air Force training through the completion of their bombing raids in Europe. *Face of a Hero* by Lewis Falstein (1909–1995) was intended to show that even a man as unselfconfident as Falstein could survive and carry out his duties. *Spearhead* (1946), by Martin Abzug (1916–1986), later the husband of Congresswoman Bella Abzug, dealt with the retreat of a United States artillery unit during the early days of the Battle of the Bulge. There is also a subgenre of domestic novels published in the 1940s depicting the United States as potentially the site of the growth of its own fascist, antisemitic and racist movements: *Focus* (1945) by Arthur Miller, *Coming Home* (1945) by Lester Cohen, and *Tucker's People* (1943) by Ira Wolfert.

Ambivalent legacy

How central and how characteristic has the Left tradition been to Jewish American writing? In the autumn of 1944, the *Contemporary Jewish Record*, a publication of the American Jewish Committee, published a famous assembly of statements called "Under Forty: A Symposium on American Literature and the Younger Generation of American Jews." The object of the symposium was simply to elicit opinions on the relevance of a Jewish heritage from "a representative group of American authors, all under forty years of age" ("Under Forty," 4). Yet every single participant was left-wing and marked by some personal association with Marxism. Five of the creative writers were from the milieu of the Communist-led cultural movement: Rukeyser, Field,

Halper, Fast, and drama critic Louis Kronenberger (1904–1980). Another five, mostly literary critics, were from the semi-Trotskyist milieu that became the New York Intellectuals: Trilling, Greenberg, Rosenfeld, Schwartz, and Kazin. The eleventh participant, David Daiches, Scottish-born literary scholar, identified himself as a democratic socialist also influenced by Marx.

Yet only in the case of Field was an affirmation of positive Jewishness unambiguously clear and strong. His statement was replete with warm memories of Jewish relatives and neighbors discussing literature and politics on Saturday evenings, the origin of his own attraction to writing. Although Field's "interest in things Jewish" is said to have "slumbered" during the 1930s, he maintains that his early work was nevertheless an "unconscious" Jewish expression evidenced by his "devotion to the underdog, in the wrath against the despoilers of the people, in the mysticism and religious fervor which color the tale of a schoolboy who goes to a country fair"; all these reflected his "heritage as a son of the people of the Book, of the people of the prophets." Later, his feelings came awake in response to Nazi atrocities, and he believes that his novel *The Outside Leaf* (1943) "could only have been written by a writer of Jewish descent" ("Under Forty," 18). At the other extreme to Field is the oft-quoted remark of Lionel Trilling, that "I cannot discover anything in my professional intellectual life which I can specifically trace back to my Jewish birth and rearing" ("Under Forty," 15). Between those two poles, all the participants in the symposium, regardless of precise ideological affinities, negotiate a range of different responses. Some aspects of Jewish culture, past and present, are rejected, while others – usually affiliated to secular movements in modern cultural and radical politics – are embraced.

All of the featured writers in the 1944 symposium continued to publish for the next three or four decades, and a couple lasted even longer. Naturally, their political convictions evolved so that it is difficult to propose a precise date when the Old Left tradition of Jewish literary radicalism finally ended, prerequisite to offering a definitive post-mortem. To the extent that the tradition was bolstered, in a contradictory fashion, by a belief in the Soviet Union and warm feelings toward the Communist Party, the decline set in during the postwar era and hardly survived the 1950s.

Yet the tradition lived on more individualistically and in some ways more richly in the sense of a self-critical consciousness. Novels such as E. L. Doctorow's *The Book of Daniel* (1971), modeled on the children of the executed Julius and Ethel Rosenberg, and even Chaim Potok's *Davita's Harp* (1984), grounded in experiences of Potok's in-laws, sympathetically and yet candidly address the personal and psychological issues that only a few works written from inside the tradition were able to recognize. Arthur Miller's autobiography *Timebends* (1987) is in many ways an extraordinary testament to the integrity and commitment of Jewish American writers on the Left.

Some of the wisest and most artistically compelling ruminations on the Left experience can be discovered in the pages of two later novels by former Party members, *Between the Hills and the Sea* (1971) by Bert Gilden (1915–1971) and Katya Gilden (1914–1991), and *A Walk in the Fire* (1989) by John Sanford. A new generation of Jewish American writers who got their start in the 1960s, such as Grace Paley, Sol Yorick, Philip Levine, and Marge Piercy, is also partially shaped by the older tradition.

Nearly sixty years after the *Contemporary Jewish Literature* symposium, neither the questions nor the compass of responses seem outdated or obsolete. Indeed, the symposium stands as just one of many clues that the Jewish American literary Left was and remains a robust and stimulating force of our time, half-hidden and demonized during the Cold War, but a tradition whose secrets we are now beginning to unlock. The ongoing reassessment of American literature in the new millennium may well conclude that the Jewish American literary Left decisively stands at center stage, not only in Jewish American culture, but also in the entire accomplishment of mid-twentieth century US letters.

REFERENCES AND SELECTED FURTHER READINGS

Aaron, Daniel. *Writers on the Left: Episodes in American Literary Communism.* Reprint. New York: Columbia University Press, 1992.

Chametzsky, Jules. *Our Decentralized Literature: Cultural Mediations in Selected Jewish and Southern Writers.* Amherst: University of Massachusetts Press, 1986.

Dick, Bernard. *Radical Innocence: A Critical Study of the Hollywood Ten.* Lexington: University Press of Kentucky, 1989.

Fast, Howard. *Being Red: A Memoir.* Boston: Houghton Miflin, 1990.

Folsom, Franklin. *Days of Anger, Days of Hope: A Memoir of the League of American Writers, 1937–1942.* Niwot: University Press of Colorado, 1994.

Guttman, Allen. *The Jewish Writer in America: Assimilation and the Crisis of Identity.* New York: Oxford University Press, 1971.

Harap, Louis. *Creative Awakening: The Jewish Presence in Twentieth Century American Literature, 1900–1940s.* New York: Greenwood Press, 1987.

Himelstein, Morgan Y. *When Drama Was a Weapon: The Left-Wing Theater in New York, 1929–1941.* New Brunswick, NJ: Rutgers University Press, 1963.

Homberger, Eric. *American Writers and Radical Politics, 1900–1939: Equivocal Commitments.* New York: St. Martin's Press, 1986.

Liptzin, Sol. *The Jew in American Literature.* New York: Bloch, 1966.

Mullen, Bill and Shetty Linkon. *Radical Revisions: Rereading 1930s Culture.* Urbana and Chicago: University of Illinois Press, 1996.

Rabinowitz, Paula. *Labor and Desire: Women's Revolutionary Fiction in Depression America.* Chapel Hill: University of North Carolina Press, 1991.

Rideout, Walter. *The Radical Novel in the United States, 1900–1954.* Cambridge, MA: Harvard University Press, 1956.

Rubin, Rachel. *Jewish Gangsters of Modern Literature.* Urbana and Chicago: University of Illinois Press, 2000.

Shapiro, Ann R., ed. *Jewish American Women Writers: A Bio-Bibliographical and Critical Sourcebook.* Westport, CT: Greenwood Press, 1994.

Shatzsky, Joel and Michael Taub, eds. *Contemporary Jewish American Novelists: A Bio-Critical Sourcebook.* Westport, CT: Greenwood Press, 1997

Shechner, Mark. *After the Revolution: Studies in the Contemporary Jewish American Imagination.* Bloomington: Indiana University Press, 1987.

"Under Forty: A Symposium on American Literature and the Younger Generation of American Jews." *Contemporary Jewish Record* 3 (February 1944).

Wald, Alan M. *The New York Intellectuals: The Rise and Decline of the Anti-Stalinist Left From the 1930s to the 1980s.* Chapel Hill: University of North Carolina Press, 1987.

Writing From the Left: New Essays on Radical Culture and Politics. London: Verso, 1994.

10

RUTH R. WISSE

Jewish American renaissance

Of the many literary and intellectual groups that fueled the emergence of Jewish literature in America, none was as well situated to take advantage of the country's opportunities as the cohort centered in New York City during World War II. While social conditions alone can never inspire a renaissance, the quality of Jewish culture – and even the language in which it was produced – always depended on the Jews' relations to the surrounding polity. The radical intellectual community dominated by Abraham Cahan between 1897–1917 had drawn tremendous energy from the concentrated mass of Yiddish readers and theatergoers, but the urgent needs of immigrant audiences riveted the writers' attention on crises of security and material subsistence. Subsequent groups of Yiddish poets and writers, like the *Yunge* (Young) and *Inzikhistn* (Introspectivists), managed to distance themselves somewhat from the social and national claims of their immigrant society, yet their reliance on a Yiddish readership put them essentially at odds with English America even as their work responded to its atmosphere. During the 1920s, when American nativism spurred a fear of immigrants and tried to set limits on the advancement of those who had already entered the country, Jewish enthusiasts of the Russian Revolution tried to introduce its egalitarian ethos into America, but their dependence on directives from the Soviet Union limited ever more of their autonomy of mind and spirit the longer they stayed under its ideological influence.

By contrast, the generation born or educated in America that came of age in the 1930s was still close enough to its immigrant roots to know something of the European Jewish past without feeling burdened by any obligation for its protection. Early schooling in English gave children a powerful advantage over their parents, allowing them to exploit or to abandon their native culture at will. Isaac Rosenfeld and Saul Bellow were so proficient in their mother tongue that they could mock both high English culture and their own ambitions of entering it by composing a Yiddish parody of T. S. Eliot. By the time Bellow hit his stride as a novelist, integrating Yiddish cadences and expressions into his narrative style, he was no longer conveying an immigrant sensibility, but rather the acquired ease of a Jew in American literature. Alfred Kazin gave lyrical expression to the Russian Jewish inheritance that had formed him even as his memoir *A Walker in the City* described a one-way trajectory *out* of the immigrant neighborhood into a Christian world.

Through a happy paradox, the 1930s proved to be a propitious breeding time for writers and thinkers. The Depression that left the economy of the country in a shambles discouraged parents from herding their young into the professions to train for a lifetime of putative security. Without the prospect of jobs, youngsters could abandon themselves to the "delight of irrelevant studies" (Barrett, *The Truants*, 209), then find cheap lodgings in Greenwich Village and peck away at their typewriters. By all the Marxist laws (that Jewish youth favored over the religious discipline of their tradition), the Depression should have plunged America into a genuinely revolutionary situation. But as the philosopher William Barrett winningly observes in his memoir of the period, the country was swept instead into a new feeling of social unity as the camaraderie of poverty erased the stigma of being poor (*The Truants*, 209–210). "When poverty is near universal in your universe," said Irving Kristol, "you don't experience it as poverty" (Dorman, *Arguing the World*, 29).

Given the large numbers of Jews in the city, and Judaism's traditional emphasis on the importance of literacy and learning, Jewish youngsters formed a huge majority in New York's City College in the 1930s and constituted a critical mass at Columbia University. Barrett, who crossed the river from Queens to attend City College, describes the "something of shock" he felt at *not* being one of the school's Jewish 95 percent:

> [There] had been very few Jews in the high school I attended, and in the successive neighborhoods to which my family moved, Jews were a very small minority. Now I was suddenly thrown, like Daniel in the den of lions, into a swarm of intense, squabbling, and noisy young Jews. Nevertheless, I seem to have acclimatized myself quickly ... I became assimilated. (*The Truants*, 23)

According to Barrett, the Jewish majority had inverted the normal pattern of acculturation – a shift that would later induce the comedian Lenny Bruce to define all New Yorkers as Jews. And since City College of the late 1930s happened to produce what was probably the largest concentration of intellectuals in modern history, a new Jewish American cultural amalgam was formed there in place of the old Anglo-American ideal.

But the strongest advantage of this intellectual-literary cohort may have been its angled relation to the rest of the Jewish world. No one in the heady early days of Enlightenment and Emancipation could have foreseen how the collapse of traditional society would vastly increase the vulnerability of Jews, forcing them to create new forms of self-protection if they intended to survive. By the late 1930s, antisemitism had reached such a critical point in Europe that it catapulted the Jews to the center of world attention. Having identified the Jews as the scourge of the continent, Hitler began eradicating them with a brutality that broke new historical ground. Communism's ideological assault against religion, though not aimed at the Jews specifically, singled them out nevertheless, attacking Jewish particularism as the most glaring doctrinal divergence from the egalitarian ideal, and making their political status in Russia even more perilous than it had been under the tsars. As the Jewish responses to modernity coalesced around Zionism, the small *yishuv*, the Jewish community of Palestine, began absorbing streams of refugees from Europe. This provoked large-scale attacks from local Arab opposition that would eventually result in an all-out Arab war against the Jewish state. Lionel Trilling's youthful image of the Jewish condition, "Being a Jew is like walking in the wind or swimming: you are touched at all points – conscious everywhere" (notebooks, *Partisan Review*, 496), expressed a vulnerability, a sense of exposure, that was elsewhere charged with actual danger.

American Jews were not only spared the Holocaust, they unwittingly drew from the moral credit that accrued to its victims. The victorious American armies that entered the Nazi death camps discredited antisemitism back home. Conscription forced these writers and intellectuals to join the war against Hitler, but allowed them to benefit from its social consequences. Discrimination against Jews became unpopular, and as the subsidized education of the GI bill sent returning veterans back to college, Jews were offered teaching positions at universities that had recently used quotas to keep them out. Thus, during the same remarkable decade when the Jews lost one third of their numbers and reclaimed their land after two millennia of foreign occupation (and while everywhere else in the Jewish world writers were caught up by the exigency of survival and rescue), American Jews made a dramatic entry into American letters – and did so with almost total oversight of the events that had transformed their people. "There was a striking contrast between our preoccupation with nothing less than the most global problems and our actual intellectual provinciality. New York acquired the qualities of a nation: it was not only the homeland; it took the place of the rest of the world" (Phillips, *A Partisan View*, 185). Not until they began writing their memoirs in their sixties and seventies did these Jewish Americans face up to this neglect.

The cluster of Jewish writers that formed in New York in the 1930s, later joined by a few others from Chicago, constituted America's first – and so far, its only – European-style intelligentsia (Howe, "The New York ntellectuals," 29). Irving Howe accentuated their critical-intellectual function when he dubbed them "The New York Intellectuals," comparing his colleagues to the nineteenth-century Russian vanguard that thought of itself as the "consciousness of the nation." Like the Russian radicals who felt themselves estranged from the society they were trying to reform, these children of East European immigrants wanted to improve the country they were simultaneously eager to impress. And just as the Russian intelligentsia believed that their provincial countrymen would benefit from exposure to Western thought, this Jewish group was initially convinced that socialist ideology imported from Europe would benefit the American people. An intelligentsia by definition believes in the transforming power of ideas, and tries to develop the cultural weaponry to disseminate its own. This group was forged and largely maintained by two magazines that remained active into the twenty-first century.

Partisan Review was founded in 1934 as a monthly organ of the Communist John Reed Club. Dissolved a year later when its editors William Phillips and Philip Rahv defied the orthodoxy of the Party, it was revived in 1937 as "an independent Marxist periodical" (Phillips, *A Partisan View*, 33–45). Its early contributors included Sidney Hook, Lionel Trilling, Diana Trilling, F. W. Dupee, Mary McCarthy, Dwight Macdonald, Meyer Schapiro, Harold Rosenberg, Clement Greenberg, Lionel Abel, and James T. Farrell. Younger by some ten or fifteen years, Saul Bellow, Isaac Rosenfeld, William Barrett, Irving Howe, Elizabeth Hardwick, Delmore Schwartz, Alfred Kazin, Leslie Fiedler, Richard Chase, and Robert Warshow broke into its pages soon after. Daniel Bell and Nathan Glazer pioneered a distinctively American form of sociology as part of this constellation. A third generation included Hilton Kramer, Steven Marcus, Susan Sontag, and Norman Podhoretz, the last of whom characterized the movement as a "Family" of founders with competitive offspring (Wisse, "The New York (Jewish) Intellectuals") Despite the inclusion of a majority of non-Jewish editors on the masthead (perhaps an attempt by the co-editors to "naturalize" their publication), the magazine's Jewish ambience prompted America's premier intellectual Edmund Wilson to dub it *Partisansky Review* (Phillips, *A Partisan View*, 63).

The group's second tribune, *Commentary*, was also the rebellious offspring of earlier publications. The *Menorah Journal* had been the first attempt to cultivate an English-language intellectual Jewish periodical in America. Launched in 1915 as a response to the crisis facing the Jews during World War I, it was formally conceived as an intercollegiate forum for the growing number of Jewish students on American campuses. Some of the Columbia boys began publishing in its pages, and the first editor of *Commentary* rose from its ranks. Twenty years later, facing another such political threat, the

American Jewish Committee founded the *Contemporary Jewish Record*, this time more explicitly to monitor world events and to raise the cultural morale of American Jewry. But in both instances, the intentions of the institutional sponsors were thwarted by some of their contributors, who used the subsidized venue to upend its priorities. This tension increased when the *Contemporary Jewish Record* was dissolved into *Commentary* in 1945. The founding editor Elliot Cohen tried to convince the best young writers through his magazine that "an American Jewish intellectual could live comfortably in both worlds, that there was no necessary contradiction between Jewish particularism and full participation in American life and culture" ("A Short History of *Commentary*," 2). His successor Norman Podhoretz, taking this lesson for granted, set out to create the best magazine in America, one that would feature Jewish topics and angles only to the degree that they were of interest to a general readership.

That each magazine expressed its independence from its original purpose – historical necessity of Communism in one case, urgency of Jewish survival in the other – defined the tone of filial autonomy and set the agenda of critical revisionism. Those who had broken free of Communist dogma never ceased to feel proud of having defied the original mold of political correctness, and since Communist influence remained powerful among the rest of the American cultural elites in the ensuing decades, the anti-Communists continued to refine their arguments against it. The attitude of this intelligentsia toward their native Jewishness was far less ideological and polemical, but the very presence of a highbrow Jewish magazine kept alive the contact with their formative culture. *Commentary*'s periodic symposia on Jews and intellectuals kept reopening questions about their religious and national identity. Together, the two magazines reinforced the sense of an emerging Jewish culture that would not only adapt itself to the American mainstream, but transform the larger culture in the process of self-adaptation. The preferred genre of both magazines – the critical essay of the Anglo-American tradition as developed by Ralph Waldo Emerson and Matthew Arnold, George Orwell and Edmund Wilson – was personalized and toughened by their own hard-won American experience. The group turned reviewing into such a fine art that Norman Podhoretz recalled with some bemusement how his ambition as a young man was to become a literary critic! In that fiercely competitive, mostly male camaraderie, *attention was paid* (Howe, "The New York Intellectuals," 30).

Two members of the pantheon will have to stand for the many bold perspectives that the Jewish American intelligentsia brought to the appreciation of literature and art. Philip Rahv, who was born in Russia, brought by his Zionist family to Palestine, and who then immigrated to America in his early teens, retained both a deep-rooted sense of personal exile (Lelchuk, "Philip Rahv," 204) and an equally powerful streak of cultural independence. Even as he supported Communism in the early 1930s, he warned that its mechanical conception of utility takes its toll in creativity by foisting formulas on writers. This critique accelerated when he broke with the Party, and devoted himself to the "heightened reality of literature" (Hindus, "Philip Rahv," 172). The supreme importance that Rahv invested in literature can be evinced from his signature essay "Paleface and Redskin" (1939) that finds all of American literature hopelessly polarized between two types of writing, one represented by the drawing-room fiction of Henry James, the other by the open-air poems of Walt Whitman. Taking literature as the truest guide to society, he finds the "lowbrow" realism of the frontier and the big city fatally estranged from the "thin, solemn, semiclerical culture of Boston and Concord" (Rahv, *Essays on Literature*, 3–7). Rahv does not condemn the patrician at the expense of the plebeian as he would have been obliged to do when he was a Communist, but rather, he laments the dissociation of mind from experience, the "split personality" of American culture that prevents it from coming to fullest maturity. And how does Rahv know this? Because just as the Jew developed a supreme talent for cleverness to compensate for adverse social conditions and a lost political independence, so the American "paleface" cultivates a talent for refinement to compensate for his country's backward cultural conditions and the lost religious ethic of Christianity. Rahv believes that his own experience in tempering Judaism with Marxism had prepared him to heal the breach in American culture.

Born Ivan Greenberg, Rahv chose for himself a surname meaning "rabbi" with the hope that a modern critic could help to transpose religion into moral sensitivity. His positive models were Leo Tolstoy and the writers of Russia who, he believed, straddled what was still a coherent culture. Rahv defines his own artistic credo when he writes of Tolstoy that he is above all an artist of the normal, "the normal, however, so intensified that it acquires a poetic truth and an emotional fullness which we are astounded to discover in the ordinary situations of life" (*Essays on Literature*, 213). He admires Dostoevsky's ability to sustain the deepest contradictions within himself, and salutes the victory scored "by the imaginative artist in him over the ruthless polemicist" (173). Rahv personified what Russian-Jewish culture might have become had its intelligenstia remained as free as he was in America to redefine his standards of excellence.

Rahv's reverence and love for literature as "felt experience" was shared by Lionel Trilling, the first Jew entrusted by Columbia University with the teaching of English literature and probably the foremost American critic of his generation. Like Rahv, Trilling identified certain weaknesses in American literature, but he was troubled by the roots of these weaknesses in Emancipation itself. "A politics which is presumed to be available to everyone is a relatively new thing in the world." By granting prominence to those who can influence public opinion, it tempts the writer with unprecedented power. "[Those] of us who set store by ideas and ideals have never quite been able to learn that, just because they do have power nowadays, there is a direct connection between their power and... the old, unabashed, cynical power of force" (*The Opposing Self*, 134). Trilling's brief flirtation with Communism in the early 1930s had revealed to him how deeply intellectuals were implicated in consolidating its tyranny, but he also became alert to the much subtler control that liberalism exercises through its optimistic assumptions about progress.

> So far as liberalism is active and positive, so far, that is, as it moves toward organization, it tends to select the emotions and qualities that are most susceptible of organization. As it carries out its active and positive ends it unconsciously limits its view of the world to what it can deal with, and it unconsciously tends to develop theories and principles, particularly in relation to the nature of the human mind, that justify its limitation.   (*The Liberal Imagination*, Preface)

Trilling reaches these conclusions as a literary man. He sees how liberalism cramps the possibilities of great art because as it works toward the rational direction of human life, "it drifts toward a denial of the emotions and the imagination" (*The Liberal Imagination*, xi). He resists not only polemical reductionism in the arts, as does Philip Rahv, but the inhibiting optimism of the modern worldview that cuts literature off from the intimations of transcendence and the knowledge of evil.

In one of his most noted essays, "Wordsworth and the Rabbis," Trilling counter-intuitively compares the British poet to the rabbis of *Pirke Avoth*, *The Ethics of the Fathers*, whom he studied in his boyhood, for the way they both recognize a power higher than themselves while continuing to stand free of that higher power. He suggests that despite the apparent antithesis between the Torah's emphasis on study and Wordsworth's election of Nature as his teacher, both poet and rabbis acknowledge "a great object which is from God and might be said to represent Him as a sort of surrogate." Having been somewhat repelled in his youth by what seemed to him the rabbis' passive "acceptance of cosmic contradiction," he senses the same disappointment among modern readers in Wordsworth's philosophical quietude. Trilling draws on Wordsworth's poetry to argue against his earlier beliefs. The rabbis and the poet are *actively* engaged with this divine source of wisdom, not in negation of life but, on the contrary, in "affirmation of life so complete that it needed no saying" (*The Opposing Self*, 115). Their posture of acceptance engenders a much enlarged "sentiment of Being," that ultimately ennobles rather than reduces both the human being and Art. Trilling kept his social distance from the American Jewish community but he forged a moral aesthetic that moved back in the direction of Judaism.

The Jewish American intellectuals excelled in argument not only with others but with themselves. In the early days, mocking their ideological inconstancy, Tess Slesinger called her *roman-à-clef* about the group *The Unpossessed* – playing on the title of Dostoevsky's novel about the genuine radicals of Russia. Edward Dahlberg spoofed the way *Partisan Review* went about choosing a name: "Lob [Rahv] suggested Self-Love, but Cog Murrain [William Phillips] said that was too introspective, and then he thought Self-Interest might be closer to the Truth... At first it was a Stalinist periodical, then it was Trotskyite, and ultimately High Church Comma" ("Ignorance and Malice," 176). But the targets of this satire defended their self-revision. The qualifying act of moral adulthood, wrote Leslie Fiedler, is "the admission of responsibility for the past and its consequences, however undesired or unforseen" (*An End to Innocence*, 4).

This "admission of responsibility" fueled some of the most important political debates of the Cold War. In fact, the 1948 trial of Alger Hiss pitted the New York intelligentsia against the literary elites in the same way that it set the chief witness against the defendant. When Whittaker Chambers emerged from the Soviet underground in 1938 he had no intention of implicating Hiss, who had been a member of his espionage network, but ten years later, as the facts emerged during the investigation by the House Committee on Un-American Activities, Hiss tried to prove his innocence by discrediting Chambers and, the statute of limitations having passed for treason, he was tried and found guilty of perjury. The prevailing liberal attitude was so far from doubting Communism that Hiss was turned into a liberal martyr – and this was before the vigilante tactics of Senator Joe McCarthy had raised legitimate fears about the protection of civil liberties. Though there was little affection for Chambers among the New York Intellectuals (a couple of whom had befriended him as a fellow student at Columbia), they knew he was telling the truth. This same certainty had prompted Sidney Hook to join the Trotskyists Felix Morrow and Herbert Solow in fighting for the exoneration of Leon Trotsky against Stalin's charges of treason in 1937. "A generation was on trial with Hiss," wrote Fiedler about those who continued to believe that a man of liberal persuasion was incapable of wrong (*An End to Innocence*, 21).

Throughout the trials of Hiss and of Julius and Ethel Rosenberg that followed soon afterward, this Jewish intelligentsia tried to understand how and why so many of their fellow writers were determined to ignore the evidence of Soviet criminality. "That mind is above all terrified of the disorder and evil of history, and it flees the harsh choices which history so often imposes. It fought to save Hiss in order to safeguard its own illusions and to escape the knowledge of its gullibility and chronic refusal of reality" (Rahv, *Essays on Literature*, 323). Robert Warshow, who wrote incisive essays on American mass culture, was fascinated by the meaning that innocence had acquired among adherents of Communism. When Julius Rosenberg writes, "It is obvious that I could never commit the crime I stand convicted of," Warshow does not assume that he is simply lying. "More probably, what he means is something like this: If it were a crime, I could not have done it. Since in the language of the unenlightened what I did is called a crime, and I am forced to speak in that language, the only truthful thing to say is that I did not do it" (*The Immediate Experience*, 36).

Lionel Trilling's novel *Middle of the Journey* (1947) was the anchoring text of this liberal self-critique. The central character John Laskell, recovering from a near-fatal illness, grows disillusioned with his friends, the well-intentioned Crooms, for nervously avoiding the subject of his mortality "as though death itself were politically reactionary" (125). Linked to the Crooms' squeamishness about death is their tolerance of a brutish hired hand who openly deceives them, and their fury with the character modeled on Whittaker Chambers who is trying to extricate himself from the Soviet spy network without being murdered. Laskell is sad to find himself growing estranged from his leftist friends, but he is rewarded for all that he is letting go by a deepened appreciation of life and personal freedom. It is as though Trilling were countering the whole progressive project that culminated in the Russian Revolution with the sobriety of Freud's *Civilization and its Discontents*, a book that stands "like a lion in the path of all hopes of achieving happiness through the radical revision of social life" (Trilling, *Sincerity and Authenticity*, 151). Though some of Trilling's peers felt that his novel did not fully come alive, it captured better than any other single work the interconnected passions and ideas that later converged in "neo-conservatism."

Whether or not Emily Budick is right in her assumption that Trilling's critique of liberalism was an indirect response to the destruction of European Jewry ("The Holocaust," 17–18), the group as a whole began to engage that subject openly in the debate that erupted around Jean-Paul Sartre's *Anti-Semite and Jew*. Sartre's book, which was itself prompted by his recognition of France's complicity in the murder of the Jews, offers dazzling psychological portraits of the fanatic Jew-hater, the ideological antisemite, and of his "feeble protector," the democrat: "The former wishes to destroy [the Jew] as a man and leave nothing in him but the Jew, the pariah, the untouchable; the latter wishes to destroy him as a Jew and leave nothing in him but the man, the abstract and universal subject of the rights of man and the rights of the citizen" (*Anti-Semite and Jew*, 57). Meanwhile, the product of this hostility, the designated Other, tries to parry the attacks against him by losing himself in a Christian world. Judging the attempt to be doomed to failure, as evidenced by Hitler's peremptory round-ups, Sartre urges the marginal Jew to accept his existential situation and to affirm his authenticity by "choosing himself *as Jew* – that is, in realizing his Jewish condition" (136).

Sartre might have found plenty of evidence for his thesis about the reluctant Jew in the postwar culture of America. Laura Hobson and Arthur Miller wrote thesis novels to prove that the American Jew would be undifferentiated from his fellow Americans were it not for the antisemite's hatred of him; Hobson's *Gentlemen's Agreement* did this through the device of a Gentile reporter who assumes a Jewish identity, and Miller's *Focus* through the figure of a mild antisemite who is mistaken for a Jew when he begins wearing glasses. The genre of the war novel (Irwin Shaw's *The Young Lions*; Norman Mailer's *The Naked and the Dead*; George Mandel's *The Wax Boom*) conventionally included a Jewish character whom only antisemitic prejudice distinguishes from his fellow soldiers. Writers with open Zionist sympathies, like Ludwig Lewisohn, Meyer Levin, and Marie Syrkin, had long complained of the prejudice against *them* within Jewish ranks on the part of assimilationists who resented their appeals to Jewish nationalism. Meyer Levin accused Irving Howe of ignoring him as an "undistinguished writer" because of his Zionist passion. But though the New York Intellectuals admitted some accuracy in Sartre's portraiture, they disputed his conclusions. Sidney Hook was horrified by the idea that Jews should respond to antisemitism with increased religious or national fervor. He concedes that "When six million Jews are slaughtered, the remaining Jews cannot but feel uneasy about their own position; when six million Gentiles are slaughtered, the remaining Gentiles do not feel uneasy," but he does not consider this feeling justified, nor does he yet think it warrants any change in Jewish politics ("Reflexions on the Jewish Question," 463–482). From the opposite vantage point, Harold Rosenberg locates Jewish "authenticity" in the original Jewish tradition, while insisting on the Jew's option to assimilate if he so desires:

> Since the Jew possesses a unique identity which springs from his origin and his story, it is possible for him to be any kind of man – rationalist, irrationalist, heroic, cowardly, Zionist or good European – and still be a Jew. The Jew exists but there are no Jewish traits. The Jew who chooses to free his Jewishness does not thereby turn into something other than a man, any more than does an Italian who decides to become an American.   ("Does the Jew Exist?," 23)

Sartre's notion of a reactive Jewish identity elicited from Rosenberg and others important essays on the Jewish question, but they ignored the irony that they had addressed the subject only in response to his provocation.

When Hannah Arendt covered the Eichmann trial in Israel for the *New Yorker* in 1963 she triggered the group's most sustained internal debate, as much for her criticism of Zionism and the Jewish Councils of Europe as for her controversial thesis about the "banality of evil." Arendt, who arrived in America in 1940, represented the ideal of European intellectual cultivation to which the Americans had aspired, so that the perceived wrong-headedness of her analysis touched off a corresponding disillusionment with her tradition of brilliance. The most damning refutation of Arendt was Jacob Robinson's book-length investigation of her factual mistakes, but Lionel Abel and Norman Podhoretz saw in Arendt's thesis a dangerous perversity that required reconsideration of all they had previously admired. "Making use of a tragic history to promote the foolish arguments of Weimar intellectuals," says the disgusted Artur Sammler, speaking for his author Saul Bellow (Bellow, *Mr. Sammler's Planet*, 19). Arendt's contempt for organized Jewry magnified their own earlier indifference to Zionism, and forced the group to reevaluate its attitudes toward the Jewish fate.

In this roundabout way, the group that had been a conduit for European ideas disengaged itself from the European model of the intellectual and began defining a new relationship between the thinking elites and the rest of society. What had begun as censure of Stalin's corruption, and had broadened into a full-scale reevaluation of progressive ideology, now turned into a self-critique of the intellectuals' function as "agents of discontent." "The American artist and intellectual no longer feels 'disinherited,'" announced the *Partisan Review*'s symposium on "Our Country and Our Culture:" "We have obviously come a long way from the earlier rejection of America as spiritually barren, from the attacks of [H. L.] Mencken on the 'booboisie' and the Marxist picture of America in the 1930s as a land of capitalist reaction" (*America and the Intellectuals*, 2–3). Some of that change was attributed to the war that had turned America into the protector of Western civilization, but mostly they were changed by what had happened to them. Daniel Bell demonstrated that the prevailing social theories about America (including those he had upheld in his youth) were mistaken because they had uncritically applied "ambient theories from European sociology to the vastly different experiences of American life" (*The End of Ideology*, 14). With newfound appreciation for their country and for capitalism, the old compulsion of iconoclasm gave way to an image of intellectual citizenship, of sympathetic analysis from within society. Irving Howe observed that "[the] whole idea of the intellectual vocation – the idea of a life dedicated to values *that cannot possibly be realized by a commercial civilization* has gradually lost its allure" ("This Age of Conformity," 11). Howe was almost alone in regretting this change that the others hailed as a mark of maturity.

The group became the more original the more it accepted responsibility for democratic society, chipping away at the image of the intellectual rebel that had prevailed since the beginning of the modern period. Because this "Family" was made up of more than a single literary generation, the "counter-revolt" was repeated more than once (Bell, *The End of Ideology*, 287). Norman Podhoretz, a student and protegé of Trilling's who was appointed editor of *Commentary* at the age of thirty, said that he felt like a "young fogey," middle-aged before his time. Thus, in the late 1950s he was infected by the spirit of radicalism that he had missed out on, and for several years he mounted an assault against the status quo, enlisting the help of contributors like Paul Goodman and Norman Mailer (Podhoretz, *Breaking Ranks*, 30). He then undertook the same process of self-revision against the culture of the sixties that he had seen his elders launch against their former leftism. Although Podhoretz attributes his belated radicalism to a hankering for a missing youth, he may also have been eager for intellectual sins to repent of, having seen that his mentors fought Communism as effectively as they did only because they had once embraced it.

Lionel Trilling coined the phrase "adversary culture" to define the unprecedented phenomenon of modern Western civilization whose cultural elites did not support its values and ideals. Expanding on Trilling's insight, Irving Kristol contrasted the modern adversarial culture which they had so enthusiastically embraced with Judaism's traditional balance between its "rabbinic" and "prophetic" components, the first inviting compliance through reinforcement of values, the latter criticizing in the name of higher ideals. He pointed out that this balance had shifted dangerously toward the latter since the beginning of the nineteenth century, merging with political expectations of universal regeneration ("Liberalism and American Jews," 19–23). But precisely because democratic society was so volatile and open to challenge, it needed intellectual leadership on the model of the rabbi rather than the prophet. The task of the Jewish intellectual was therefore not to exploit his marginality by remaining a critic from without, but to adopt the posture of his rabbinic tradition by assuming responsibility for society from within.

Despite the centrality of intellectual debate in the rise of Jewish American letters, the highest value was ascribed to imaginative literature for its ability to convey a kind of experience that was irreducible to convictions and ideas alone. When *Partisan Review* featured as its lead item Delmore Schwartz's maiden story "In Dreams Begin Responsibilities," it was not only acknowledging a splendid new talent, but expressing its veneration for that *kind* of talent. The young man in Schwartz's story watches, as if in a movie theater, the unfolding courtship of his parents, helplessly subject to the destiny that their mistakes have imposed on him; the modernist story actualizes the young man's inner life that is crying out "against life itself, inconceivable without mistakes" (Howe, Foreword, *In Dreams*, ix). Schwartz's ruptured narrative was much admired for being no mere description of immigrant society, family pathology, or man's existential terror, but for subordinating analysis to the *experience* of these conditions:

> This sense that Schwartz had found both voice and metaphor for our own claustral but intense experience – this, more than any objective judgment of his technical skill – must have been the source of our own strong response. We heard a voice that seemed our own, though it had never really existed until Schwartz invented it: a voice at home with the speech of people not quite at home with English speech. (Howe, Foreword, *In Dreams*, ix)

For capturing the quality of New York life in the 1930s and 1940s Irving Howe called Schwartz the "comedian of alienation" (Foreword, *In Dreams*, ix).

Alienation, which they associated with their Jewishness, did not have for these Jewish American writers the same negative meaning that it did for Karl Marx. Schwartz acknowledged in 1944 "(with gratitude and yet diffidence because it has been so different for other Jews, different to the point of death) that the fact of Jewishness has been nothing but an ever-growing good to me... nothing but a fruitful and inexhaustible inheritance" (Schwartz, "Under Forty," 14). Isaac Rosenfeld made an even larger claim for the Jewish writer. "He is a specialist in alienation (the one international banking system the Jews actually control)," but since nearly all modern sensibility felt itself to be in exile, the Jew's alienation was his qualification for telling the story of everybody: "Out of their recent sufferings one may expect Jewish writers to make certain inevitable moral discoveries. These discoveries, enough to indict the world, may also be crucial to its salvation" (Rosenfeld, "Under Forty," 36).

Surveying the best of Jewish writing in America from the 1930s onward, one can see how its comedy – for it is largely a comic literature – specializes in calibrating the distance between immigrant home and the "host culture," which seems to lessen over time. Nathanael West (born Nathan Weinstein) never experienced the fellowship of Jewish immigrant poverty, hence he identified his well-to-do German Jewish family with the despised bourgeoisie and nouveaux riches. His radical dislike for who he was and where he came from, in which he resembled Europeans like Karl Kraus more than his fellow-Americans, made him alive to the undercurrents of rage in America that seemed to him about to explode into violence. West situates the vulnerable heroes of his novels in vaudeville, in newspaper offices, and in Hollywood, exploiting the media's appetite for sensationalism to warrant his grotesque plots and characters. One of many east coast Jews who took up writing for the movies, West captured in his short novel *The Day of the Locust* (1939) the desperation that the entertainment industry, with its phony facades and transparent imitations, is trying to disguise: "It is hard to laugh at the need for beauty and romance, no matter how tasteless, even horrible, the results of that need are. But it is easy to sigh. Few things are sadder than the truly monstrous" (*Novels and Other Writings*, 243).

Daniel Fuchs also moved to Hollywood in the 1930s, but being West's temperamental opposite, he observed himself and his surroundings with sympathetic irony. He recalls that when he told John Ford that he was a writer of fiction, that great director mocked him in their native Yiddish, "*Mendl, Mendl, kakt in fendl, fun dos makht men a lebn?* (Mendel, Mendel, defecates in a pan, from this one makes a living?)" (*The Apathetic Bookie*, 9–10). The most modest of writers, Fuchs honed a refined literature out of coarse and crazy lives. In *The Williamsburg Trilogy*, three novels that Fuchs wrote about the neighborhood of his childhood, he tried to compensate for the diminished life of its residents by according them the fullest artistic respect: "At seven o'clock the streets of Williamsburg were barely awake, there was no humiliation, no indignity, and it was possible . . . to feel a man, living in great times, with grandeur and significance" (12–13). In Hollywood, he discovered more manic personalities. The masterful short story "Twilight in Southern California" follows the increasingly frantic efforts of a Hungarian Jewish immigrant to stay afloat in Hollywood's mercurial economy. The American dream does not turn into nightmare for Fuchs' characters as it does for West's, but they look comically small against the vast promise of the country (*The Apathetic Bookie*, 60–78).

Younger than West by eleven years, than Fuchs by five, Bernard Malamud seemed to capture an "authentic" Jewish American style by transposing the crises and sufferings of his characters back into the confined spaces and Yiddish cadences of his immigrant childhood. His work gained mythic resonance from its atmosphere of old world poverty and from characters who manifested an old world conscience. For example, in his novel *The Assistant*, Malamud reverses the gender roles of his own intermarriage to tell the delicate love story of an Italian small-time crook for the daughter of a Brooklyn Jewish grocer; the love of the father and his Catholic assistant for the same "Helen" implicitly unites their religions as well. Malamud is most perfect in tragicomic short stories like "The Magic Barrel" and "The Jewbird," which extend the boundaries of immigrant fiction into magic realism. Because Malamud identified the Jewish condition with suffering and guilt, he wrote best about these themes, but the troubling corollary of this proposition was that he identified the Jewish condition exclusively with suffering and guilt. He was far less artistically persuasive when he set his fiction in the acculturated milieu in which he actually lived his adult life.

Not every Jewish writer played up the comic incongruities of the Jewish American condition. Herman Wouk, the best of Jewish middlebrow novelists and later, Chaim Potok, achieved best-seller status by turning Jewish problems into standard narratives, drawing no attention to any difficulty in telling such a story. Alfred Kazin, and later, Norman Podhoretz, wrote superlative literary autobiographies from the perspective of immigrant sons who had resolved the problems they were now describing in retrospect. Irving Howe provided one of the most influential interpretations of the immigrant experience in his classic, *World of Our Fathers*, and he also culled "the sacred texts of secular Jewishness" (Alexander, *Irving Howe*, 78), in a series of anthologies of Yiddish and Jewish American writings (see Bibliography at end of chapter). But Howe, too, was always on the lookout for the "felt experience" that he thought fiction could best provide, and one of the highlights of his critical career came during the making of the anthology *A Treasury of Yiddish Stories*, when he and his co-editor the Yiddish poet Eliezer Greenberg got Saul Bellow to translate the story "Gimpel the Fool." The editors of *Partisan Review* featured this discovered masterpiece as their lead item (as they had done with Schwartz's story), launching the Yiddish writer Isaac Bashevis Singer on the American career that would result in a Nobel Prize for Literature. The translator of "Gimpel the Fool" won the Prize in 1976; Bashevis Singer in 1978. Both these writers excelled in the art of comic incongruity.

Indeed, Saul Bellow said that literature is Jewish when "laughter and trembling are so curiously mingled that it is not easy to determine the relations of the two" ("Introduction," *Great Jewish Short Stories*, 12). (Substituting "laughter" for Kierkegaard's "fear" is Bellow's way of acknowledging his intellectual affinity to Christian civilization while affirming his Jewish divergence from it.) After writing two very good novels and a number of short stories that do not really fit this description, Bellow felt that he broke through as a novelist in 1953 when he invented the voice of Augie March, a Jewish street-tough from Chicago who fearlessly embarks upon American adventure. Later, Bellow developed a way of staying very close to the perspective of a protagonist like himself, while allowing for a slightly ironic distance from that character. "When it came to concealing his troubles, Tommy Wilhelm was not less capable than the next fellow. So at least he thought, and there was a certain amount of evidence to back him up" (*Seize the Day*, 3). "If I am out of my mind, it's all right with me, thought Moses Herzog" (*Herzog*, 1). Bellow sets the subjective judgment of his protagonist against the rest of the world's, admitting – without succumbing to – the anxiety which is the special bonus of the thinking animal.

Bellow was the novelist the Jewish intelligentsia had hoped to put into contention with the likes of Dostoevsky and Balzac. As though to exemplify Philip Rahv's ideal of an American culture that joins the patrician and the plebeian, Herzog sitting in the garden of his Massachusetts estate, discussing the decay of Western civilization with his childhood friend Shapiro, berates his fellow scholar for offering a merely aesthetic critique of modern history. "After the wars and mass killings! You are too intelligent for this. You inherited rich blood. Your father peddled apples" (*Herzog*, 75). As Herzog descends from the grand historical outcry to the homey admonition, Bellow is *ascending* from the acquired mastery of Western culture to the truest knowledge that is gained through experience: anyone privileged to know life right off the applecart should not waste himself in theoretical sophistication. Along these lines, the remorseful founder of the Mnemosyne Institute in Bellow's *The Bellarosa Connection* is a man professionally dedicated to the retention of memory, who comes to recognize that his failure to stay in touch with his Jewish relations has hollowed out his life.

The most celebrated American author of the twentieth century, Bellow objected during the first part of his career to being designated a "Jewish writer," but it was he who demonstrated how a Jewish voice could speak for an integrated America. With Bellow, Jewishness moved in from the immigrant margins to become a new form of American regionalism. Yet he did not have to write about Jews in order to write as a Jew. Bellow's curious mingling of laughter and trembling is particularly manifest in his novel *Henderson the Rain King*, that follows an archetypal Protestant American into mythic Africa. Bellow not only influenced and paved the way for other American Jewish writers like Philip Roth and Cynthia Ozick, but naturalized the immigrant voice: the American novel came to seem freshly authentic when it spoke in the voice of one of its discernible minorities.

In order to take the full measure of the American Jewish renaissance, we may recall the positive image of the Jewish intellectual that was presented to Europe in 1779 by Gotthold Ephraim Lessing. Nathan the Wise was the intended antidote to Shylock the usurer, his generosity extending from philanthropy to religious philosophy. When asked, "What human faith, what theological law / Hath struck you as the truest and the best?" (Lessing, *Nathan the Wise*, 250), Nathan demonstrates through the parable of three rings that, far from favoring his chosen people, God loves Jew, Christian, and Muslim alike. In Lessing's ecumenical atmosphere of a fictionalized Jerusalem, the only villains are the scheming Christians, while gentle Nathan insists that the category of Man has replaced earlier ethnic and sectarian distinctions, and argues for Jewish loyalty only on historical grounds "Why should I less rely / Upon my ancestors than you on yours; / Or can I ask of you to give the lie / To your forefathers, merely to agree / With mine?" (250). But there is no need to worry about Jewishness at all since Nathan has no Jewish descendants. After surviving the slaughter of his wife and seven sons, he had raised an adopted Gentile orphan, but once he reunites this adopted daughter with her biological family, he is terminally alone. In sum, Lessing renders the Jew harmless and impotent as the price of his acceptance – an omen of what Europe meant by Emancipation.

America was different, as we may see from three outstanding works of the year 2000. Saul Bellow's novel *Ravelstein*, inspired by the author's close friendship with Allan Bloom (as Lessing's work was by his friendship with Moses Mendelssohn), also presents the Jew as the quintessential intellectual, but turns the intellectual into an American hero. The Jewish narrator explains that he is writing this book as homage to his deceased friend who, though childless, like Nathan, was attended by three or four generations of students who staff their country's institutions as historians, teachers, journalists, experts, civil servants, think tankers. "Inevitably Ravelstein was seen by the young men he was training as the intellectual counterpart to [Michael] Jordan" (57). America's outstanding athlete is Black and its outstanding intellectual is Jewish, and (to continue the sports metaphor) each is coming off of a very strong bench. If Ravelstein, like Nathan, has his share of enemies, they react to his philosophic influence rather than to his being a Jew, and they do not interfere with his enjoyment of life or stop him from using his intellect to become enviably rich. Nor does Bellow have to neuter the Jewish intellectual to make him acceptable: "He was sure of himself, as de Gaulle had said about the Jews" (62). Europe's negative judgment of the Jew is appropriated as a compliment.

Norman Podhoretz's *My Love Affair with America: The Cautionary Tale of a Cheerful Conservative* lifts the theme of "our country and our culture" to a new pitch of enthusiasm. Using his education as an illustrative text, Podhoretz offers his thanks to those who, by teaching him the English language and insisting that he speak "like a classier and more cultivated person than [he] actually was," enabled him to become one of America's leading intellectuals and to turn *Commentary* into the most influential Jewish magazine in history. Podhoretz feels none of the anxieties over success that beset the immigrant hero in Abraham Cahan's classic *The Rise of David Levinsky*, and he expresses none of the disappointment in America that one finds in *The Education of Henry Adams*. Indeed, Podhoretz exposes and refutes many of the major critical assaults on America – regretfully admitting that some of them were launched in his own magazine – and insists on *celebrating* its freedoms and strengths. "America is not God, but it declared its independence as a nation by an appeal to 'the laws of Nature and Nature's God,' and the Constitution its founders wrote and ratified for that new nation uses the word '*blessings*' in its very first paragraph" (*Love Affair*, 232–233). To express his own gratitude he ends with *Dayyenu*, paraphrasing the Passover hymn that thanks God for His bounty (234–235): pledging allegiance to America in the language of Jewish liberation, Podhoretz demonstrates how his country rewards its citizens for remaining true to their tradition.

The most complicated exploration of these themes is Philip Roth's novel *The Human Stain*, which ascribes to a light-skinned Black intellectual the dilemma that once confronted the Jews of whether or not to pass. Coleman Silk's option is not equally available to all African Americans, but America does extend the choice, at least in principle, to all the children of its immigrants. Coleman balks when his father insists that he attend a Negro college, thereby confining him intolerably to the fate of his group:

> Overnight the raw I was part of a we with all of the we's overbearing solidity, and he didn't want anything to do with it or with the next oppressive we that came along either. You finally leave home, the Ur of we, and you find *another* we? Another place that's just like that, the *substitute* for that? Growing up in East Orange, he was of course a Negro, very much of their small community of five thousand or so, but boxing, running, studying, at everything he did concentrating and succeeding, roaming around on his own all over the Oranges and . . . down across the Newark line, he was, without thinking about it, everything else as well. He was Coleman, the greatest of the great *pioneers* of the I. (*The Human Stain*, 108)

Never in his own voice or in the voices of his Jewish protagonists had Philip Roth unleashed a protest as candid as Coleman's against the pressure exerted by the familial community on the singular hero who could otherwise be free in the land of the free. Coleman *is* able to pass for a white man, and by cutting himself off from his family he manages to flourish in the assumed identity of a nominal Jew. Roth's hero cleverly identifies himself with the group that is famed for its marginality, and Roth even more cleverly enfolds his own Jewish subject matter within the currently more exigent subject of

Black America: Lessing's emblematic outsider, the Jew in Europe, has become Roth's emblematic insider, the American Jew in academe. Silk becomes a professor of classics, the dean of faculty, the kind of academic that might have flourished in a novel by David Lodge.

But the greatest of the great pioneers of the I is destroyed by his success. Once his power at the university has begun to wane, when he is accused of racism for a slur against Blacks, his own camouflage prevents him from taking the high ground against his accusers. Instead of turning the tables in a comical come-uppance, the professor is tragically upended by the genius of his self-invention. Roth's picture of America is bleaker and darker than that of Bellow or Podhoretz. He sees the country growing more violent the more it aspires to tolerance. A society that allows a man to repudiate his loving family will also dispossess him; both processes employ the skills of deception to further individual ambitions. Roth is far from preaching against (Jewish/Black) self-hatred, the sin he stood most accused of when he started out as a writer, but no American novel has ever exacted such a high price from its protagonist for betraying his origins. While Roth concedes that the novel is itself an imagined new life, Silk fails America as much as America fails him by misapprehending its terms of engagement. The intellectual and the writer especially must keep faith with truth.

By force of their numbers, energy, and accomplishment, the Jewish intellectual and literary cohort of the 1940s and 1950s introduced the hyphen into American letters, creating the fact of an American Jewish literature and a new standard of cultural authenticity. As they gradually abandoned the European models of an adversarial intelligentsia and the posture of a Jewry forever on trial, they assumed for America the kind of responsibility that Jewish tradition had always demanded of its learned and literary elites.

REFERENCES AND SELECTED FURTHER READINGS

Abel, Lionel. "The Aesthetics of Evil: Hannah Arendt on Eichmann and the Jews." *Partisan Review* (1963): 211–230.

Alexander, Edward. *Irving Howe: Socialist, Critic, Jew.* Bloomington and Indianapolis: Indiana University Press, 1998.

America and the Intellectuals: A Symposium (Reprint of the 1952 symposium *Our Country and Our Culture*). *Partisan Review* (1953).

Barrett, William. *The Truants: Adventures Among the Intellectuals.* Garden City, NY: Anchor Books, 1983.

Bell, Daniel. *The End of Ideology.* Glencoe, IL: Free Press, 1960.

Bellow, Saul. *Seize the Day.* New York: Viking, 1956.

    "Introduction." *Great Jewish Short Stories.* New York: Dell, 1963.

    Herzog. New York: Viking, 1964.

    Mr. Sammler's Planet. New York: Viking, 1970.

The Bellarosa Connection. New York: Penguin, 1989.

Ravelstein. New York: Viking, 2000.

Budick, Emily. "The Holocaust and the Construction of Modern American Literary Criticism: The Case of Lionel Trilling." Working Paper 61, Berlin: John F. Kennedy-Institut fur Nordamerikastudien, abteilung fur Kultur, 1993.

Commentary editors. "A Short History of *Commentary.*" *What Commentary Has Wrought* (May 2, 1995): 2.

Dahlberg, Edward. "Ignorance and Malice at the *New.*" In *Samuel Beckett's Wake and Other Uncollected Prose.* Ed. Steven Moore. Elmwood Park, IL: Dalkey Archive Press, 1989.

Dorman, Joseph. *Arguing the World: The New York Intellectuals in Their Own Words.* New York: Free Press, 2000.

Fiedler, Leslie A. *An End to Innocence: Essays on Culture and Politics.* Boston: Beacon Press, 1952.

Fuchs, Daniel. Author's Foreword to *The Apathetic Bookie Joint.* New York: Methuen, 1970.

The Williamsburg Trilogy. New York: Avon, 1972.

Hindus, Milton. "Philip Rahv." In *Images and Ideas in American Culture: The Functions of Criticism. Essays in Memory of Philip Rahv.* Ed. Arthur Edelstein. Hanover, NH: Brandeis University Press, 1979.

Hobson, Laura. *Gentleman's Agreement.* New York: Simon and Schuster, 1947.

Hook, Sidney. "Reflections on the Jewish Question." *Partisan Review* (May 1949): 463–482.

Howe, Irving. "This Age of Conformity." *Partisan Review* (January–February 1954): 7–33.

"The New York Intellectuals: A Chronicle & A Critique." *Commentary* (October 1968): 29–52.

"Foreword." In *In Dreams Begin Responsibilities and Other Stories.* New York: New Directions, 1978.

Howe, Irving and Eliezer Greenberg, eds. *A Treasury of Yiddish Stories.* New York: Viking, 1954.

A Treasury of Yiddish Poetry. New York: Holt, Rinehart and Winston, 1969.

Voices from the Yiddish: Essays, Memoirs, Diaries. New York: Schocken Books, 1972.

Selected Stories: I. L. Peretz. New York: Schocken Books, 1974.

Yiddish Stories Old and New. New York: Holiday House, 1974.

Ashes Out of Hope: Fiction by Soviet-Jewish Writers. New York: Schocken Books, 1977.

Howe, Irving and Ruth R. Wisse, eds. *The Best of Sholem Aleichem.* London: Weidenfeld and Nicolson, 1979.

Howe, Irving, Ruth R. Wisse and Khone Shmeruk, eds. *The Penguin Book of Modern Yiddish Verse.* New York: Viking, 1987.

Kazin, Alfred. *A Walker in the City.* New York: Grove Press, 1951.

Kristol, Irving. "Liberalism and American Jews." *Commentary* (October 1988): 19–23.

Lelchuk, Alan. "Philip Rahv: The Last Years." In *Images and Ideas in American Culture: The Functions of Criticism. Essays in Memory of Philip Rahv.* Ed. Arthur Edelstein. Hanover, NH: Brandeis University Press, 1979.

Lessing, Gotthold Ephraim. *Nathan the Wise: A Dramatic Poem*. (1779). Trans. Patrick Maxwell. Ed. George Alexander Kohut. New York: Bloch Publishing Company, 1939.

Mailer, Norman. *The Naked and the Dead*. New York: Grosset & Dunlap, 1948.

Mandel, George. *The Wax Boom*. New York: Random House, 1962.

Miller, Arthur. *Focus*. New York: Reynal and Hitchcock, 1945.

Phillips, William. *A Partisan View: Five Decades of the Literary Life*. New York: Stein and Day, 1983.

Podhoretz, Norman. "Hannah Arendt on Eichmann: A Study in the Perversity of Brilliance." *Commentary* (1963): 201–208.

Breaking Ranks: A Political Memoir. New York: Harper and Row, 1979.

My Love Affair with America: The Cautionary Tale of a Cheerful Conservative. New York: Free Press, 2000.

Rahv, Philip. *Essays on Literature & Politics 1932–1972*. Eds. Arabel J. Porter and Andrew J. Dvosin. Boston: Houghton Mifflin Company, 1978.

Robinson, Jacob. *And the Crooked Shall Be Made Straight: The Eichmann Trial, the Jewish Catastrophe and Hannah Arendt's Narrative*. Philadelphia: Jewish Publication Society, 1965.

Rosenberg, Harold. "Does the Jew Exist?" Reprinted in *Arguments and Doctrines: A Reader of Jewish Thinking in the Aftermath of the Holocaust*. Ed. Arthur A. Cohen. Philadelphia: Jewish Publication Society, 1970.

Rosenfeld, Isaac. "Under Forty: A Symposium on American Literature and the Younger Generation of American Jews." *Contemporary Jewish Record* (February 1944): 34–36.

Roth, Philip. *The Human Stain*. New York: Houghton Mifflin, 2000.

Sartre, Jean-Paul. *Réflexions sur la Question Juive* (1944). Trans. as *Anti-Semite and Jew* by George J. Becker. New York: Schocken Books, 1946.

Schwartz, Delmore. "In Dreams Begin Responsibilities." *Partisan Review* (December 1937): 5–11.

"Under Forty: A Symposium on American Literature and the Younger Generation of American Jews." *Contemporary Jewish Record* (February 1944): 12–14.

Shaw, Irwin. *The Young Lions*. New York: Random House, 1948.

Slesinger, Tess. *The Unpossessed*. New York: Simon and Schuster, 1934.

Trilling, Lionel. *The Opposing Self*. New York: Harcourt Brace Jovanovich, 1955.

Sincerity and Authenticity: The Charles Eliot Norton Lectures, 1969–1970. Cambridge, MA: Harvard University Press, 1972.

Middle of the Journey. (1947). New York: Harcourt Brace Jovanovich, 1975.

The Liberal Imagination: Essays on Literature and Society. New York: Harcourt Brace Jovanovitch, 1978.

1928 selection from his notebooks by Christopher Zinn, in *Partisan Review*, 50th anniversary issue (1984–1985).

Warshow, Robert. *The Immediate Experience: Movies, Comics, Theatre, and Other Aspects of Popular Culture*. Garden City, NJ: Anchor Books, 1964.

West, Nathanael. *Novels and Other Writings*. Ed. Sacvan Bercovitch. New York: The Library of America, 1997.

Wisse, Ruth. "The New York (Jewish) Intellectuals." *Commentary* (November 1987): 28–38.

"Jewish Writers on the New Diaspora." In *The Americanization of the Jews*. Eds. Robert M. Seltzer and Norman J. Cohen. New York: New York University Press, 1995.

"Language as Fate: Reflections on Jewish Literature in America." In *Literary Strategies: Jewish Texts and Contexts*, vol. XII, *Studies in Contemporary Jewry*. Ed. Ezra Mendelsohn. New York: Oxford University Press, 1996.

"The Maturing of *Commentary* and of the Jewish Intellectual." *Jewish Social Studies* (Winter 1997): 29–41.

11

EMILY MILLER BUDICK

The Holocaust in the Jewish American
literary imagination

In the third of the Zuckerman novels, Philip Roth includes the following poignant detail concerning the protagonist's dying mother:

> A year after his [father's] death she developed a brain tumor. [F]our months later, when they admitted her again, she was able to recognize her neurologist when he came by the room, but when he asked if she could write her name for him on a piece of paper, she took the pen from his hand and instead of "Selma" wrote the word "Holocaust" perfectly spelled. This was in Miami Beach in 1970, inscribed by a woman whose writings otherwise consisted of recipes on index cards, several thousand thank-you notes, and a voluminous file of knitting instructions. Zuckerman was pretty sure that before that morning she'd never even spoken the word aloud. Her responsibility wasn't brooding on horrors but sitting at night getting the knitting done and planning the next day's chores. But she had a tumor in her head the size of a lemon, and it seemed to have forced out everything except the one word. That it couldn't dislodge. It must have been there all the time without their even knowing.
>
> (*Zuckerman Bound*, 447–448)

Roth's figure of the Holocaust lodged in the brain of the American-born Jewish mother in a 1985 Jewish American novel that seems in no way a work of Holocaust fiction can be taken as a measure of the place of the Holocaust in the Jewish American imagination. As Norma Rosen puts it in the foreword to the recent republication of her 1969 novel *Touching Evil*: "As safe Americans we were not there. Since then, in imagination, we are seldom anywhere else" (Preface, 3). For most Jewish Americans (and many non-Jewish Americans as well: Rosen's own novel deals with non-Jews as does Emily Praeger's even more recent *Eve's Tattoo* [1998]), this Holocaust consciousness is largely unspoken and, as compared with the daily concerns of ordinary life, it is almost of radical disconcern. Nonetheless there "it" is, all the time, without anyone, even the person him- or herself, knowing it is there. Yet, as the sliding referent for the word *it* in Roth's last sentence suggests, "it" is, perhaps, at least for many Americans, nothing less than

212

a cancerous growth that just might dislodge everything else in its mortally destructive insistence, a "murdered eye," as Cynthia Ozick puts it in *The Messiah of Stockholm*, through which the Jewish orphan-refugee-survivor is condemned to see the world (3).

Roth's image, like Ozick's, likely shocks the reader. Nonetheless it accurately reproduces the Jewish American's problematical relationship to Jewish history, in particular that of the survivor children/first-generation Americans, like Art Spiegelman of *Maus* (published from 1973–1991), the child Stefan in Lev Raphael's *Winter Eyes* (1992), the protagonist-narrator Ben in part two of Anne Michaels' *Fugitive Pieces* (1996), and Duncan Katz in Thane Rosenbaum's *Second Hand Smoke* (1999), whose tormented survivor mother also dies, like Zuckerman's, of a cancerous growth. In the first and probably most famous of the Zuckerman books, *The Ghost Writer* (1979), in which Roth creates his alter-ego Nathan Zuckerman and, telling the story of the young Jewish American writer starting out, mounts his response to his readership's fierce objection to what they take to be the self-hating stance of his earlier fiction, Roth already puts at the center of his critique the Jewish community's fascination with the Holocaust. He represents this fascination through the community's idealization and idolization (fetishizing) of Anne Frank. Resurrecting the dead martyr and rewriting her *Diary* in the process (rather accurately as it turns out from later republications of the unexpurgated text), Roth interrogates the community's Holocaust-inflected script of itself, which the novel presents as a melodramatic and hysterical expression of misplaced and rather absurd Jewish tribalism.

The object of Roth's attack is by no means the project of historical knowledge. Rather, anticipating recent moves in the American intellectual debate (Walter Benn Michaels, for example, and Dominick LaCapra), he calls into question the community's way of constructing personal and communal identity on the basis of a trauma not even their own, which is taken on retrospectively for just the purpose of what has come to be called identity politics. In so doing, Roth not only predicts contemporary views concerning such identity politics, but recent critiques of the popularization of the *Diary* itself. For many people, the *Diary* has come to seem more a sentimentalized falsification of the events than an accurate and significant confrontation with the catastrophe and horror of the Holocaust.

The burden of historical remembering and the potential distortions it produces in the second, often American-born, generation of Jews is a subject that galvanizes not only Roth's *Ghost Writer* but Art Spiegelman's more explicitly Holocaust-focused *Maus: A Survivor's Tale*, volume 1 of which is not-so-innocently subtitled: "*My Father Bleeds History.*" *Maus* is a doubly dual narrative. It is autobiography and biography both, and as both it serves the primary function of almost all Holocaust fiction: to document or witness the experience of the Holocaust which the author would bring to the attention of an unenlightened public. In this it is like the many memoirs written by survivor immigrants to the United States and Canada – Eva Hoffman's *Lost in Translation* (1989), for example, which, though not about the Holocaust per se, is Holocaust-linked; Gerda Weissman's *All But My Life* (1957), and Isabella Leitner's *Fragments of Isabella* (1978). All of these texts participate in one major genre of American writing from the early twentieth century on, the immigrant or refugee novel, many of which, we are reminded by these books, are also autobiographical.

In the less strictly memoiristic *Maus* (narrated as much by the son as by the father), we are presented, not so much with Vladek Spiegelman's immigrant experience in America as with his life preceding and during the Holocaust, including in the camps themselves. Like other such narratives, in particular non-American authored works like Primo Levi's *Survival at Auschwitz*, Spiegelman brings out what is most compelling about the Holocaust: the atrocities perpetrated against innocent human beings in the name of some distorted national ideological vision, and the violent and total perversion and illogic of a world that seems anything but the world as we know it.

At the same time, however, *Maus* adds a feature that has of necessity only entered Holocaust writing fairly recently. Like the other survivors'-children narratives cited above, it records the son's experience of growing up a child of survivors. It is the son's memoir as much as the father's, and the story of the son is also part of Spiegelman's program to inform. Yet it is this second story that also possibly compromises the text, even as it lays the foundations for a particularly American form of Holocaust fiction. Spiegelman's autobiographical self-concern transforms his telling of his father's history from an act of objective historicism into a form of private, psychotherapeutic intervention. Like much American fiction, Jewish and non-Jewish (and this is part of what makes *Maus*, like *The Ghost Writer* and other Holocaust-related texts characteristically *American* texts), *Maus* has to do with the individual in the struggle to achieve personal identity against societal demands and restraints. Art Spiegelman would excise the cancer that threatens his and his children's and, for that matter, his community's viability and vitality both. And he would do this by some act of severing the present from the historical past – even while signaling the inescapable link of past to present, as of father to son.

To add paradox to paradox: while, to be sure, *Maus* serves a documentary, historical function, at the same time, however, and to some degree in acknowledgment of the distortions that the son's traumatized telling necessarily imports into the otherwise factual, historical text, the book is also, if only because of its comic-book format, a consummate, even heightened, work of fiction. One of its deep concerns, which it shares with the project of Philip Roth's life's work (both Spiegelman and Roth create artist-protagonists), is whether there is a story for this son to tell, which is to say, whether there is for American Jews any specifically American story whatsoever worth their while telling (a major focus of Cynthia Ozick's *The Messiah of Stockholm* as well). Excise the cancer, get rid of the trauma, these texts seem to say, and not only does the patient die, but their progeny have nothing to write about. For this reason, perhaps, the book is self-consciously, self-reflexively fictional rather than straightforwardly factual, as if to place the new story in the realm of ever-inventing imagination rather than the real world of real occurrences. Not only is the story drawn (as opposed to told), comic-book style with the characters represented as animals, but we are constantly being made conscious (in these and other ways) of the variety of rhetorical and literary strategies out of which the text is being constructed by its author. For the son-narrator-protagonist of this work, the question encoded in the title, which recalls Roth's own earlier anxieties concerning American Holocaust consciousness, is not simply whether his father can survive the hemorrhage that is his post-Auschwitz existence, but whether he, the son, who is the survivor of his father's survival, can survive this bleeding of the past into the lifeblood of the present. This is the reason the text begins, not with the father's story, but with the son's, which continues throughout the two volumes literally to "frame" the narrative – in more ways than one. Yet without his father's story, which threatens to overwhelm his, Spiegelman has no story at all.

In many ways *Maus* is atypical of American Jewish fiction, and not only because of its cartoon-book style. Given the centrality of the Holocaust in Jewish American social, religious, and cultural life, and the way in which it persistently flits in and out of many literary texts, there is actually relatively little serious fiction that has been written directly concerning the events in Europe, in the ghettos and in the camps. Indeed, most Jewish American consciousness concerning these events derives from European-authored texts (most of them nonfictional), such as the works of Primo Levi, Elie Wiesel, Tadeusz Borowski, and from the handful of more popular epic novels that appeared in the decades immediately following the war, books by such authors as Herman Wouk, Meyer Levin, and Leon Uris (Uris' *Mila 18*, for example, and Levin's *Eva*). In addition to these, and of a somewhat more nuanced and philosophical nature are, in more or less the same time-frame: Jerzy Kosinski's very painful artistic masterpiece *The Painted Bird* (1965), Susan Schaeffer's *Anya* (1974), and Leslie Epstein's *King of the Jews* (1979), with only a very few such texts being written in the very recent past, namely: Cynthia Ozick's short story entitled "The Shawl," first published in 1983, now collected in the novella of that same title (1989); the long first part of Anne Michaels' quite beautiful and extraordinarily affecting *Fugitive Pieces*, and a Kafkaesque, phantasmagoric recent short story by Nathan Englander called "The Tumblers" in his book *Unbearable Urges* (1999). The by-far larger and more significant group of American fictions are those (also like *Maus*) that deal explicitly with the survivor experience, though they may contain flashbacks to the events themselves. This group includes, most notably Roth's "Eli, the Fanatic" (1959), Edward Wallant's *The Pawnbroker* (1961), Bellow's *Mr. Sammler's Planet* (1970), Isaac Bashevis Singer's *Enemies, A Love Story* (1972), Ozick's *Cannibal Galaxy* (1983), *The Messiah of Stockholm* (1985), and "Rosa," part II of *The Shawl* (first published in 1980), Rebecca Goldstein's *Late Summer Passion of a Woman of Mind* (1989) and "Legacy of Raizel Kaidish" (1993), Louis Begley's *Wartime Lies* (1991), Lev Raphael's *Winter Eyes* (1992), Aryeh Lev Stollman's *The Far Euphrates* (1997), Michaels' *Fugitive Pieces*, and Rosenbaum's *Second Hand Smoke*. In this same line, but constituting a third even more extensive, and sometimes even more intriguing group of texts, are those fictions that are Holocaust-inflected rather than about the Holocaust per se. These texts inscribe the Holocaust sometimes silently, sometimes marginally – often in an allusion or phrase or set of images – in their pursuit of their other, more primary agendas, including, and even typically, Jewish identity in the United States. Thus, for example, many of Bellow's novels, from the early *Dangling Man* (1944), *The Victim* (1947), and *Seize the Day* (1956) through the much later *Bella Rosa Connection* (1989) and *Ravelstein* (1999), all constitute forms of thinking about the Holocaust, as do many of the writings of Cynthia Ozick, from her first novel *Trust* (1966) through such stories as "The Pagan Rabbi," "Envy," and "The Suitcase" in *The Pagan Rabbi, and Other Stories* (1971) or the works "A Mercenary" (1974) and "Bloodshed" (1970). Similarly, much of the fiction of Isaac Bashevis Singer and of Bernard Malamud resonates with Holocaust consciousness: for example, in the case of Malamud, two of the stories printed in *The Magic Barrel* (1957) – "Lady of the Lake" and "The Last Mohican" – "The German Refugee" in *Idiots First* (1963), *The Assistant* (1957), *The Fixer* (1966), and *God's Grace* (1982), while, as the Jewish American literary canon has expanded, so have the contributions to the field of Holocaust fiction: Rebecca Goldstein, Allegra Goodman, Melvin Bukiet, Lev Raphael, Nathan Englander, and Thane Rosenbaum all write post-Holocaust, Holocaust-inflected texts, in pursuit of their often different but collectively Jewish – and most importantly *American* – concerns (see Berger, *Children of Job*). For the way that the Holocaust gets taken up in Jewish American writing is part and parcel of the project of creating a

Jewish *American* tradition distinct from any other national Jewish (or, for that matter, ethnic American) tradition.

That American authors should be reluctant to deal head-on with the facts of life in the ghettos and camps is not exactly surprising, since Americans, including American Jews, occupy an oblique and distant relation to the events of the catastrophe. Furthermore, America, where they reside, is for many Jews not only not the cause or continuation of historical antisemitism, but, quite the contrary, its solution. For the most part Jewish Americans are not eye-witnesses in any sense of the term, and their restraint in the face of their lack of direct knowledge or experience has to be held admirable. But there is a further reason for the American obliquity in relation to what is clearly European and not American Jewish history. A major subject, both explicit and implicit, informing these Jewish American fictions is the new American reality of the Jew, in which European history is relevant background but not the primary story itself. Indeed the story of the American Jew, in order to get itself going, may well have to rid itself of the past that binds it to Jewish realities no longer pertinent or desirable.

A cancer in the brain serves as one image for the Holocaust lodged in the consciousness of Jewish American writers. Another is figured in the frame from *Maus* in which Spiegelman draws himself drawing his comic strip, corpses strewn under his writing table and concentration camp installments clearly and anachronistically visible outside his window (*Maus*, II, 41). From at least one perspective Jewish American writing might seem a whole-scale writing out of secondary or inherited trauma, what psychoanalysts Nicholas Abraham and Maria Torok have called *encryptment*, whereby a trauma not one's own becomes the basis for repressed, hysterical behavior (Thane Rosenbaum calls this "second hand smoke"). "The most problematic aspect of *Maus*" itself, argues Dominick LaCapra,

> may be the subject-position of the child of the survivor or more generally, of the Jew of a later generation, especially someone tempted to convert the Holocaust into a founding trauma and thus a paradoxical, perhaps impossible source of meaning and identity. [I]n certain ways, [Art/ie] becomes a Jew or assumes a Jewish identity through his concern with the Holocaust – a concern that nonetheless escapes sufficient critical examination.
>
> (*History and Memory*, 177)

Spiegelman, I think, is more conscious of what he is doing than LaCapra allows. Nonetheless, LaCapra's basic insight concerning the construction of Jewish identity on the basis of trauma touches an important issue, the implications of which extend far beyond Spiegelman's *Maus*. Jewish identity, in other words, may be quintessentially defined by an experience that, in order to maintain that identity, has to be excised. Or, the opposite: preserved. According to some cultural critics, Walter Benn Michaels among them, Jewish Americans have tended to convert history into memory as part of a "project of sustaining identity" (" 'You who never was there,' " 8). For these American Jews what is threatened with extinction in the forgetting of the Holocaust is not merely the events themselves, with their historical meanings and lessons, but Jewish identity itself. French writer Alain Finkielkraut's "imaginary Jew" is the figure for this construction of identity around history transformed into memory, which captures the fragility and problematics of such self-definition. Geoffrey Hartman has argued that, as the Holocaust fades from view, "the question of what sustains Jewish identity is raised with a new urgency" (*Holocaust Remembrance*, 7). To some extent LaCapra and Michaels are reformulating in more post-modernist terms what is a fundamental objection to Holocaust writing in general, and Holocaust fiction in particular: what Lawrence Langer calls "preempting the Holocaust." Langer means by this "using – and perhaps abusing – its grim details to fortify a prior commitment to an ideal of moral reality, community responsibility, or religious belief that leaves us with space to retain faith in their pristine value in a post-Holocaust world" (*Preempting the Holocaust*, 1). Yet, how can Jewish writers construct identity without recourse to the Holocaust? Jewish American fiction would seem to be caught in a no-win bind. Forget the past and the Jewish component falls away. Remember the past and you write European rather than American fiction.

The best American Holocaust fiction, I suggest, understands just this problem and thereby offers considerable resistance to preempting the Holocaust to some other agenda. At the same time, however, even as it respects the inviolable inaccessibility of the past itself – indeed, perhaps *because* it respects the past's pastness – it discovers a relationship to this event which serves the needs of the specifically American story Jewish American writers have to tell. One fact about the Holocaust that these texts refuse to dismiss, and this is what prevents their use of it from becoming illegitimate exploitation, is that the extermination of the Jewish people was a primary objective of Hitler's genocide. How can any response to the catastrophe not take on, then, as one of its purposes, the preservation of Jewish life and identity, in America as elsewhere? "You ain't got a life?" one character chastises another in Cynthia Ozick's *The Shawl*, one of the most extraordinary of American Holocaust fictions; to which the protagonist-survivor Rosa responds, over and over again, and in many different ways, that she does not: "Thieves took it," she says simply enough (28, 33, cf. 20).

A major trajectory of American Holocaust fiction constitutes an attempt to retrieve these stolen lives, both by preserving and clarifying the events in which those lives consisted, and, equally important, and in line with a major trajectory of American writing from the nineteenth century on, also by restoring individual voice and identity to those who lived them, and to their descendants. This is the great achievement of Ozick's *The Shawl*, which tells the story of the survivor Rosa, her survivor-niece Stella, and her child Magda, who perished in the camp and whose death is described in the first, flashback, part of the novel. Quite against our expectations, and reminiscent of Bellow's hero in *Mr. Sammler's Planet* and Spiegelman's father in *Maus* (and also recalling elements of Roth's strategy in relation to Anne Frank), Rosa is an almost thoroughly unlikable character. She not only exhibits many of the familiar symptoms of trauma that might explain or excuse her behavior (also like Sammler and Vladek), but she is almost a compendium of Nazi stereotypes of the Jew: grotesque, arrogant, obnoxious, mean-minded, overly intellectual, intent upon assimilating into a culture that despises her, and contemptuous of her fellow Jews and her fellow Poles both. "My Warsaw isn't your Warsaw," she tells the refugee Persky on more than one occasion (19, 22). "Imagine confining *us* with teaming Moskowiczes and Rabinowiczes, and Perskys and Finkelsteins, with all their bad-smelling grandfathers and their hordes of feeble children. [W]e were furious because we had to be billeted with such a class, with these old Jew peasants worn out from their rituals and their superstitions" (66–67). Like her father "she is a Pole by right": a self-hating Jew and an anti-Zionist: were it not for her "they would have shipped Stella with a boatload of orphans to Palestine, to become God knows what, to live God knows how" (40).

Yet for all this, indeed *because* of all this, Rosa is a human being, whose fate was in no way commensurate with her "crime" of being an unlikable person, even an auto-antisemite. Therefore, it is given to her in the story to articulate for us what in the post-Holocaust condition perpetuates rather than undoes the travesty perpetrated against the Jews of Europe. Speaking of those good-intentioned individuals (like us readers of Holocaust fiction perhaps) who have set themselves the task of comprehending and even helping the victims of the Holocaust, she rails out,

> Consider also the special word they used: *survivor*. Something new. As long as they didn't have to say *human being*. A name like a number – counted apart from the ordinary swarm. Blue digits on the arm, what difference? They don't call you a woman anyhow. *Survivor*. Even when your bones get melted into the grains of the earth, still they'll forget *human being*. (*The Shawl*, 36–37)

It is one Dr. Tree who is researching what he calls "repressed animation" syndrome, who writes to Rosa out of his "concern" as a "human being" for survivors like Rosa: "for himself," Rosa observes with appropriate contempt, "he didn't forget this word *human being*" (37). This paradox of a humanitarian, humanistic impulse that dehumanizes, or at least, de-individualizes the specific human being, captures the problem of one major trajectory of post-modernist discourse concerning what Elizabeth Bellamy labels "after Auschwitz." "Real Jews," she writes, "have tended to be transformed into tropes or signifiers for the decentered, destablized post-modern subject in a theoretical system that persists in defining (or "fetishizing") them from without" (*Affective Genealogies*, 17–18, 31). "The Holocaust," writes Dominick LaCapra, "has often tended to be repressed or encrypted as a specific series of events and to be displaced onto such general questions as language, nomadism, unrepresentability, silence, and so forth." "Such reactions," LaCapra warns, "inhibit processes of working-through and learning from the past" (*Representing the Holocaust*, 209–210).

One challenge of American Holocaust fiction is exactly not to evade dealing with "real Jews," not as a form of celebration or special pleading or identity politics, but in acknowledgment of the individual Jews who lost their lives in Hitler's attempt to annihilate both them and their culture. To be sure Rosa (like Vladek) suffers from just such repression as Dr. Tree would ascribe to her. And Dr. Tree would both try to explain this and, perhaps, even to cure the angry, eternally mourning Rosa. But, like the father in *Maus*, Rosa does not ask for this help, and the question that the text raises in relation to the present's relationship to the past's traumas is that same question raised in *Maus*, or, for that matter in Roth's *Ghost Writer*: not, do we have a responsibility to the past, but does the past have a responsibility to *us*, to assist us in the present to rid ourselves of the traumas of the past so that we can get on with the business of constructing a meaningful future?

In *Maus* Spiegelman marks this problematic very powerfully when early in volume 1 the father exacts the promise from the son that the son will violate over and over again in the writing of the text. Certain "private things, I don't want you should mention," Vladek admonishes him (1, 23). Indeed the violation first occurs in a kind of negative speech act in which the assertion of the son's words "I promise" is abrogated in the narrative's breaking of the promise in the moment of uttering it. From its inception, then, the text as text constitutes a sustained act of violation; it is a narrative that narrates what it is forbidden to say. The question that Spiegelman's text raises, both explicitly and implicitly, is what, if anything, justifies Spiegelman's telling of his father's story, against his father's objection, his plea that he not be resubjected to one more version of that humiliation of exposure that he was made to suffer during the Holocaust?

Ozick's *The Shawl* raises the same question, and not only in relation to Dr. Tree. For the reader's impulse, the text knows, may be no less voyeuristic than Tree's. Although Persky is not guilty of having stolen Rosa's underpants out of her laundry, as she suspects, nonetheless Rosa's feeling exposed by his interest in her and her story, locates something in our (as well as in his) relation to her: for isn't all that interest in everything from the inmates' primitive, soiled, sanitary conditions to their sexual abuse not a way we have of catching up and examining the dirty underwear of the past, cleansing soiled linen and sewing on lost buttons (Persky's in the button business), in some anxious juvenile regression of our own? And isn't our frenzy to see into the soul of those who perished there, and those who survived, a form of exposure just as indecent as what made them the objects of such intensive interest and abuse in the first place?

Dr. Tree, like Artie in *Maus*, or like us as readers of Holocaust narratives, would bare the soul in order to save it and, we might add, ourselves. To be sure Rosa everywhere sees the inscription of her traumatized past and so she responds, as does the father Vladek in *Maus*, through a series of unconscious, repressive behaviors that, with pain and suffering and, perhaps, with considerable dysfunction and psychic cost, bespeak her trauma. Thus is Florida, in Rosa's perception, a concentrationary world writ large: "the streets were a furnace, the sun an executioner" (*The Shawl*, 14); "here they were shells like herself, already fried from the sun . . . ghosts . . . Everyone had left behind a real life" (16). Like Vladek (and Sammler), Rosa speaks the silent language of Holocaust trauma. Rosa would like to speak another, less inhibited and repressed, language; she would like to "tell everybody – not only our story but other stories as well" (66). But Rosa's immigrant English is only an external figure for the lack of any language in which to tell this story; even her "own language" (40), Polish, in which she writes to her dead daughter Magda, cannot suffice. Furthermore, it only returns her to the madness from which the writing only seems, temporarily, to deliver her. Writing, too, we come to understand, can become only a perpetual reenactment of the primary trauma from which the individual cannot break free: "she was writing inside a blazing flying current, a terrible beak of light bleeding out a kind of cuneiform on the underside of her brain. The drudgery of reminiscence brought fatigue, she felt glazed, lethargic" (69). Conjuring up the moment of trauma itself, words can be as much an unconscious expression of repressed trauma as deeds. As paralyzing as the insufficiency of words to describe the horror of the Holocaust is the fact that words do not necessarily produce clarity. They can be just other ways we have of repressing, projecting, and acting out trauma.

One response to the impossibility of language to represent the unrepresentable event of the Holocaust has been just such a privileging of "silence" as the only decorous way of responding to what cannot be said, indeed as the only way of capturing the deep muteness that defines traumatic experience. Thus is the protagonist of Kosinski's *Painted Bird* by the end of that story totally dumb. But, while "there is a sense," as LaCapra puts it, "in which silence may indeed be the only way to confront a traumatic past," nonetheless, he goes on, "this contention does not justify a specific silence concerning something that can be said or with respect to the problem of attempting to say what can be said in the face of the risk that language may break down in a more or less telling manner" (*Representing the Holocaust*, 122–23). One way of thinking of the primary testimony of repression is as itself a language of silent telling that also breaks down in a more or less telling manner, as when Rosa smashes up her store or Vladek counts his pills only to have them scatter all over the room. And, to be sure, it is we who must learn to hear Rosa's and Vladek's language, not they who must learn to speak ours. But there may, perhaps, be some way less "mad" (Ozick, *The Shawl*, 13) that words might smash things up, some more purposively telling manner, such as, say, a fictional narrative. For there is, of course, in the case of *The Shawl* at least, no survivor Rosa Lublin, whose experience this text records, though there are many whose reality and whose story hers conveys. What writing fiction makes possible that recording witness testimony or setting up Holocaust museums or researching or analyzing survivors, perhaps, does not is some way of meaningful telling that does not simply smash things up.

The fictionality of the text addresses two separate problems of Holocaust narrative, both of which are explicit subjects within the fictions themselves. One is the pressure on Holocaust writing to produce historical authenticity, as if any telling of the story of the Holocaust must also constitute proof of its having occurred. From the beginning of Holocaust writing, literary representations have been suspect (see e.g. Langer, *The Holocaust and the Literary Imagination*). The other problem of Holocaust narrative is the power of storytelling of any kind, fictional or historical, to replicate and repeat rather than enable the working-through of trauma, even on a secondary level. Thus, both *Maus* and *The Ghost Writer*, for example, raise questions concerning the matter of evidence. As Roth most likely knew even as he was composing *The Ghost Writer*, the very existence of the *Diary* as documentary evidence was already in question from the moment of its publication, the charges being everything from the *Diary*'s being a forgery to its being a highly revised translation of the original document. Pulling into play legal proceedings of various kinds, not to mention the historical record, *The Ghost Writer* makes very clear that even facts can be denied, history can be disbelieved, as well as fiction can. Nothing can prevent Holocaust denial, and one virtue of fiction might be its ability to make self-conscious and explicit the problem of proof and evidence in our relation to the past. Similarly, in *Maus* a most telling moment is Art's introduction into the cartoon drawings of an actual photograph of his father taken immediately after the war, dressed in camp garb: "I passed once a photo place what had a camp uniform – a new and clean one – to make souvenir photos" (II, 134), he explains to his son; and Spiegelman gives us, accompanying the photo, a drawing of Anya receiving the photo and exclaiming: "And here's a picture of him! My God – Vladek is really alive." Introducing literal pictorial evidence, the cartoon text seems to ask: what does a photo *prove*, especially vis-à-vis the past? In some ways the photo of Vladek looking very dashing and heroic betrays everything that text has said thus far concerning the horrors of the camp. One might even say that the very fact of Vladek's survival, if this is what the photo attests to, makes him exactly not a victim, a problem that adheres even more closely to Anne Frank's *Diary*, which, written from the optimism of a teenager and before she is delivered to the camps, documents nothing concerning the camps themselves. Thus the text permits the reader to ignore the reality that Anne died a hideous death at Buchenwald. Fiction testifies to the fact that, as James Young has argued, not only is testimony, like all historical narrative, con-structed by the same rules of rhetoric that threaten the presumed veracity, factuality, of the text that the witness-author would most like to preserve, but the sheer fact of the text's textuality – that we are dealing here with lan-guage and not artifact or some other form of directly tangible experience – undermines the author's desire that his or her words serve as irrefutable proof for the facts they cite, for language can prove nothing but their own existence (*Writing and Rewriting the Holocaust*, 24). As Spiegelman's photo suggests, artifactual evidence is no less subject to misrepresentation.

At the same time that the fiction addresses the problem of proof, it also me-diates what is an additional problem in witness and documentary evidence, the fact that, as Geoffrey Hartman explains, "a massive realism which has no regard for representational restraint ... not only desensitizes but produces the opposite of what is intended: an *unreality effect* that fatally undermines realism's claim to depict reality ... art creates an unreality effect in a way that is *not* alienating or desensitizing" (*The Longest Shadow*, 157). Not for naught does Spiegelman represent himself in the act of representing his fa-ther's story: the endless circulation of trauma can effectively prevent any clear cessation to the hysteria that the originating trauma initiates.

Ozick's most deft move in terms of suggesting how fictionalizing befits Holocaust narrative is surely the ghost Magda. Within the realism of the reader's position, the dead child is purely a delusion in need of exorcism (of being excised like the cancer or cured like the trauma). From the mother's point of view, however, through which the story is written and to which we are being asked to extend our sympathy (and not our psychoanalytic and therapeutic powers), she is entirely real. Rosa's story, we do well to concede, is not primarily addressed to us, who, she knows, will never understand it, and who will likely convert it to other uses. It is addressed to the only listener to whom Rosa needs to make sense, the only person to whom she still owes some manner of explanation, perhaps even expiation: the dead daughter Magda. And Ozick the fiction writer knows this and grants this the same way that Art Spiegelman in *Maus* permits his narrative to end with the father's address to the dead first-born son, the "ghost-brother" (II, 15) in whose shadow (as in the shadow of the Holocaust) the narrator of the narrative, Artie, has suffered his own traumatic childhood.

It is as if this text, which from the beginning has been taken over by Artie's frantic need to set the past at rest, now yields its desire to the father, who cannot let the past go: "More I don't need to tell you," he says to his son, after he has described his post-Auschwitz reunion with Anya in Poland; "we were both very happy, and lived happy, happy ever after." And he goes on in the next frame: "So . . . let's stop, please, your tape recorder . . . I'm tired from talking, Richieu, and it's *enough* stories for now" (II, 136). At the bottom of the page appears the picture of Vladek's and Anya's joint gravestone, bearing only a Jewish star and their names and dates, no epitaph, but with the artist's signature and the dates 1978–1991 (the dates of the text's composition) written across the page. Signing the text as his own, acknowledging its artifice, despite its historical claims, Spiegelman also acknowledges his place outside the dimensions (no larger than a tombstone) of his parents' lives and consciousness. "You can't live in the past," Persky tells Rosa (*The Shawl*, 23). Who are we to say this to people who have suffered what Vladek and Rosa have suffered? How should their mad attachment to the past embarrass us that we should feel we must shame them into a cure of it? "Magda, my beloved, don't be ashamed! Butterfly, I am not ashamed of your presence: only come to me, come to me again, if no longer now, then later, always come" (*The Shawl*, 69). At the end of *The Shawl*, Magda flees as the telephone, over which Rosa has cast her baby shawl, the shroud and sacrament of the lost child, announces Persky's arrival: "Shy, she ran from Persky. Magda was away." "Not there," "away" (70), Magda is nonetheless not banished. Rather, she remains, let's say, waiting in the wings, ready to be "animated" by her mother's shameless but hardly shameful need of her daughter and of the life that was stolen from them.

Calling out to Richieu and Magda, Vladek and Rosa give voice to the loss that can never be recuperated. They locate as well what will always be the insufficiency of Holocaust fiction and its special burden and responsibility to the past: to write from within the position of the ghost-brother or sister of their murdered siblings. Whether they like it or not, they are their parents' final hope for the continuity and future that the Nazis thought to steal from them – genetically as well as culturally. One requirement of the future in relation to the past is not only to stand witness to the crimes and suffering of the past and through this to perpetuate the memory of those who died or suffered; an additional Jewish responsibility may well be to perpetuate the race that Hitler had intended to annihilate. For this reason, perhaps, Spiegelman dedicates the second of the two volumes of *Maus* not only to the brother who has become a defining aspect of his own (now recovered) consciousness but to his daughter, who is her grandfather's legacy as well.

If for Ozick and Spiegelman dead children haunt the lives of the survivors and their children, for Rebecca Goldstein, in *The Mind-Body Problem* and *Late Summer Passion of a Woman of Mind*, Philip Roth in *The Counterlife*, Aryeh Lev Stollman in *The Far Euphrates*, and Anne Michaels in *Fugitive Pieces*, what equally trouble the lives of the protagonists are the children that were never born and never are to be. This is a loss that is threatened but resisted in Goldstein's "The Legacy of Raizel Kaidish." Here the daughter-narrator suffers from problems similar to those of Artie and other survivors' children like Ben in *Fugitive Pieces* and Stefan in *Winter Eyes*. Her mother educates her daughter on "tales from the camp": "my mother's moral framework was formed in Buchenwald," explains the narrator, "forged in the fires, it was strong and inflexible" (Goldstein, *Strange Attractors*, 229). "Raizel, like Artie, Stefan, and Ben grows up feeling "ignored, unloved, of no significance." "Of course," as Raizel herself says, "there's nothing unusual in a daughter's resentment of a mother." But whereas her friends' "indignation" is "clean" and "unashamed," Raizel feels that her mother has "suffered enough" (234). So strong are Raizel's feelings of anger and guilt that she spends years "deliberating over whether to have a child of my own" (235).

In particular Raizel is responding to the fact that she herself is named after one of the mother's camp heroines, a young woman who risked her life to substitute for her friend, who, weak and unable any longer to work, is ordered to report for what the friend realizes is her extermination. In the end, one of the other inmates of the camp betrays the girls and both of them are executed. From this scene of moral action, the mother derives her philosophy, that "the ethical view is the impersonal view" (232–233). But there is a chilling secret in the mother's story and thus in her moral code, which is revealed to Raizel only on the mother's deathbed. Her mother, it turns out, was the informant who sent both Raizel Kaidish and her friend to their deaths.

Raizel's response to her guilt-driven, Holocaust-inflected education in moral theory is to become a logical positivist. Her logical positivism serves the same function as Artie's psychoanalysis: it is a way of getting out from under the suffocating force of the parent's repressive behavior; it is a way of declaring independence from the past. In the end, however, Raizel will come to see and affirm what Artie also comes to realize: that she is her parent's child, however much she is also (as in *The Shawl*) the ghost her parent must address to expiate her sins and alleviate her suffering or the medium (as in *Maus*) through which she must conjure it. In the end Raizel decides to have her baby, whom she names for her mother, despite, or rather because of, the terrible knowledge "that it had been she who had informed on Raizel Kaidish. She asked my forgiveness" (240). These are the concluding lines of the story, and what they convey is what is most important about Raizel's mother's narrative (or Vladek's or Rosa's): not its status as either historical document or philosophical truth, but, rather, its appeal to the listener, and its plea for forgiveness. Contrary to her mother's philosophical argument, "one's self" does have "some special metaphysical significance"; "it makes a difference that one is who one is" (232) – even that one is the inheritor of Jewish as opposed to some other history.

"Raizel Kaidish" figures the biological as well as the psychological consequences of Hitler's attempted extermination of the Jews. It is no accident, therefore, that the subject of unborn or aborted children haunts Holocaust fiction. At the end of Roth's extremely raucous and radically sacrilegious novel *The Counterlife*, Nathan Zuckerman, who is convinced that "there is no you...any more than there's a me...there is only this way we have established...of performing together" (319–20), insists on circumcising his child because of the power of circumcision, "performed," in the text's word, on the body, to cut through some less substantive idea of the me, or, at least, of the me's performance of itself in the world. "Circumcision," says Zuckerman, "makes it clear as can be that you are here and not there, that you are out and not in – also that you're mine and not theirs. There is no way around it: you enter history through my history and me" (323).

This history has to do, for Roth, with the specific endangerment of Jews through centuries of persecution, leading past the Holocaust into the contemporary reality of Israel. Roth may be fixated on the male penis throughout his career, and nowhere more so than in *The Counterlife*, in which the two Zuckerman brothers are suffering (each in his narrative turn) from sexual impotence. But this fixation is not Roth's alone; nor is it the locus only of humor – as the passage in *The Counterlife* concerning the castration of Israeli soldiers more than reminds us. Furthermore, in a book moving from male sexual impotence to circumcision, it recalls both a history of Christian fantasies concerning circumcision and the real danger to which circumcision has traditionally exposed Jewish males.

Roth's recovery of Zuckerman's procreative potential and his linking of sexual potency with circumcision declares a certain necessity in the present to carry on the work of progeneration that was brutally cut off in the past. Or to accept what can never be retrieved, to witness the end of the Jewish line: for Zuckerman's child, who is not born in the novel, would in any event not be halachically Jewish. Anne Michaels' Jakob Beer in *Fugitive Pieces* traces a similar reality even more poignantly. A child survivor, Beer finally surmounts the horrors of his experience to marry and make his wife pregnant, only to be cut down by a car accident before the child is born, his wife dying the day after he does. This end-of-the-line scenario of Jewish history, at least on the old terms of physiological, biological perpetuation, is the point of Ayreh Lev Stollman's very powerful *The Far Euphrates* as well, where it is linked to another turn in Holocaust fiction, toward universalizing and metaphorizing the event. Like several writers of Holocaust fiction (most notably Leslea Newman in a short story entitled "A Letter to Harvey Milk," Lev Raphael both in *Winter Eyes* and in the short story collection *Dancing On Tisha B'Av*, and most recently, perhaps, Bellow in *Ravelstein*), Aryeh Lev Stollman links the figure of the Jew to those others, like lesbians and homosexuals (in Stollman's novel, also gypsies), who have been and continue to be marginalized and persecuted within Western society. Thus, the novel's hero Alexander (like Stefan in *Winter Eyes*) has to manage not only the typical transition into adult sexuality, but the much more fraught growth into both awareness and acceptance of his homosexual preference.

Alexander is the single offspring of the two Jewish families at the center of this book, both of which have been singed by the Holocaust Alexander's own father the rabbi is the son of refugees who fled before the war; his parents' best friend the cantor is a survivor not only of the camps but of Mengele's infamous experiments on twins. Alexander's two families can bring to term only this single child (his mother has had numerous miscarriages and the cantor has been rendered sterile), whose gender preference, we realize, will take him outside the game of reproductive futurity. But it is the cantor's twin Hannalore who provides the most shocking and painful image of the generations who will never be. Hannalore, born "Elchanan son of David" (*The Far Euphrates*, 191), has chosen to live what is left of his life after the devastation of the camps as a woman and, even more significantly, as a Christian.

"Whatever weird creature" (101) Hannalore is (Alexander is in many ways no less strange), she is Stollman's way of thinking together both of the heroism of the Jewish survivor (and those who are defined by differences of other sorts) *and* the ever-lasting wound, which, as in Roth's *Counterlife*, is a perversion of the mark of the covenant and which might literally put an end to the continuity of the Jewish people. Only in death is Hannalore restored both to her biological gender and to her Judaism. But Hannalore survives her death, as a man and a Jew, but also as female and Christian, to become a presence of another sort altogether – a kind of *shekinah* in the text's language or, to apply to the strong Christian context the book also sets up, a Holy Ghost, the specifically female aspect of divine being in Jewish and Christian tradition both. Indeed, just as the cantor and his wife in a way adopt Alexander as their own (or the elderly survivor in "A Letter to Harvey Milk" adopts his young lesbian teacher, or the child unborn to Jakob Beer in *Fugitive Pieces*, who is himself an adopted son, may finally be born to the man who makes himself Jakob's own spiritual son Ben (named by his parents Ben, meaning in Hebrew simply *son*)), so Hannalore is one more of Alexander's several mothers, a virgin mother who in this post-Holocaust world promises, not redemption, but some sort of recovery from the past and hope for the future. "An ember saved from the fire" (191), Hannalore is, like many other characters in Holocaust fiction (Magda and Richieu, for example), a "ghost" (11), who will never engender a next generation, certainly not in the Davidic (messianic) line that is her proper genealogy. She will, however, insofar as we make ourselves, as does Alexander in this book or Artie in *Maus* or even Roth in *The Ghost Writer*, the willing mediums of the voices of the past, continue to speak through us, thus making us all her surrogate children. In the most stunning moment in the book, the moment of revelation at the unveiling of her tombstone, Hannalore literally speaks through Alexander's voice, as figuratively she speaks through his story in the novel as a whole, making it her story as well as his.

Lawrence Langer's observation concerning both Ozick's and Spiegelman's "survivors' tales," that "we are left wondering in the end who has survived with greater vitality – the living or the dead?" could easily pertain as well to Stollman's *The Far Euphrates* (Langer, *Preempting the Holocaust*, 130). Hannalore is a voice of a continuity that is not familial, perhaps not even communal. But even as Stollman radicalizes the Jewish Holocaust text, even Christianizes it, he preserves the uniquely Jewish character of the event itself. Covenant reaches out to and incorporates the family of humankind. Yet, that covenant originates in the "honeyed letters that God used to create His universe," the same Hebrew letters that appear on Hannalore's tomb (Hannalore's name picks up the sounds of *honeyed letters*) and that are of the Old Testament and Jewish textual tradition that the novel so abundantly, lovingly reproduces (*The Far Euphrates*, 191). Stollman's novel registers the loss (specifically Jewish) that will never be repaired. On this side of the far Euphrates, which is to say on this side of paradise, which is supposed to have had its origins in the far Euphrates, human existence is wounded, disfigured, impotent, and "weird." And yet, as the book makes amply clear, this is all the world, all the exilic "home," we have (206). If we can hear in our voices the voices of others, if we can let those others (both dead and alive) speak through us, then, the novel suggests, we will have recovered the divine spark that once spoke an entire world into creation. At his father's graveside Alexander discovers he has no "choice" but, in his father's name, to pray "out loud" and to "bless God's Holy Name forevermore" (206). This is the essence of the mourner's *Kaddish* in Judaism: to praise divine being and thus restore life to the creation. Like *Maus, The Far Euphrates* draws to a close at the father's graveside. Might we not think of these works (and others) as themselves extended prayers or blessings, put into the hands of readers who, through this means of mourning the past, also thereby offer their blessings for the future?

REFERENCES AND SELECTED FURTHER READINGS

Abraham, Nicholas and Maria Torok. *The Shell and the Kernel*. Ed. Nicholas R. Rand. Chicago: University of Chicago Press, 1994.

Bellamy, Elizabeth. *Affective Genealogies: Psychoanalysis, Postmodernism, and the "Jewish Question" after Auschwitz*. Lincoln: University of Nebraska Press, 1997.

Berger, Alan L. *Children of Job: American Second-Generation Witnesses to the Holocaust*. New York: State University of New York Press, 1997.

Finkielkraut, Alain. *The Imaginary Jew* (1980). Trans. Kevin O'Neill and David Suchoff, intro. David Suchoff. Lincoln: University of Nebraska Press, 1994.

Goldstein, Rebecca. *Strange Attractors: Stories*. New York: Penguin, 1993.

Hartman, Geoffrey, ed. *Holocaust Remembrance: The Shapes of Memory*. Cambridge: Blackwell, 1994.

The Longest Shadow: In the Aftermath of the Holocaust. Bloomington: Indiana University Press, 1996.

LaCapra, Dominick. *Representing the Holocaust: History, Theory, Trauma*. Ithaca: Cornell University Press, 1994.

History and Memory After Auschwitz. Ithaca: Cornell University Press, 1998.

Langer, Lawrence. *The Holocaust and the Literary Imagination*. New Haven: Yale University Press, 1975.

Preempting the Holocaust. New Haven: Yale University Press, 1998.

Michaels, Walter Benn. "'You who never was there': Slavery and the New Historicism, Deconstruction and the Holocaust." *Narrative* 4.1 (1996): 1–16.

Ozick, Cynthia. *The Shawl* (1980, 1983). New York: Random House, 1990.

The Messiah of Stockholm. New York: Random House, 1987.

Rosen, Norma. *Touching Evil*. Detroit, MI: Wayne State University Press, 1990.

Roth, Philip. *Zuckerman Bound: A Trilogy and an Epilogue.* New York: Farrar Straus & Giroux, 1985.

Spiegelman, Art. *Maus: A Survivor's Tale*, vols. I and II. New York: Pantheon Books, 1991.

Stollman, Aryeh Lev. *The Far Euphrates.* New York: Riverhead Books, 1997.

Young, James E. *Writing and Rewriting the Holocaust: Narrative and the Consequences of Interpretation.* Bloomington: Indiana University Press, 1988.

12

SUSAN GUBAR

Jewish American women writers and the race question

Practically each word in the title of this chapter has been challenged by
thinkers who would mark its fictitious stamp by placing it in quotation
marks. Cynthia Ozick is not alone in rejecting the category of "Jewish
writer" on the grounds that there is "no Jewish *literature*," only writing "on
Jewish themes" (Klingenstein, "In Life I Am Not Free," 49). Given the contradiction between a Nazi propensity to essentialize Jewish traits so as to
eradicate the Jewish people and the permeability of Jewish identity, Ozick's
proviso remains an important one. Actually, though, the term "Jewish"
remains more porous than the words "American" and "women." For
a majority of readers would probably agree that Gertrude Stein, Dorothy
Parker, Denise Levertov, Adrienne Rich, Mary Gordon, and Jorie Graham
are American women artists (although exactly who Americans are and what
constitutes womanhood has certainly been disputed); however, do these authors' Jewish-born relatives make them Jewish American women writers, if
(as in these cases) such progenitors alienated themselves from their families,
converted, or promoted assimilation in their offspring? Perhaps, as Ozick
suggests, the crucial factor that must influence any response to such an inquiry is the extent to which each author concentrates her creative energies
on Jewish familial, psychological, ethical, historical, or spiritual issues in her
work. Yet the secondariness of women in Judaism – whether it is defined in
terms of religious practices or beliefs, Yiddish or Hebrew cultures, Zionism, a
commitment to the book or to social justice, ethnic jokes – has transformed
Judaism from a background or a theme to a question for women artists.
"I've been a problem within a problem," Adrienne Rich has explained, " 'the
Jewish Question,' 'the Woman Question' – who the questioner? Who is supposed to answer?" (*What Is Found There*, 23).

Should we keep the category permeable, taking the questioning of Jewish-
related issues as a warrant for inclusion, what did it mean for Stein, Parker,
Levertov, Rich, Gordon, and Graham to be marginalized or neglected as
women in a cultural history that was called "Jewish-American," but that

was actually conceived in discourses fashioned exclusively by, about, and for Jewish men (and in terms that often presumed "the Jew" to be male)?[1] Judging from the extraordinary achievements of Jewish American women writers, it meant being offered a gift. From Emma Lazarus, whose sonnet "The New Colossus" adorns the Statue of Liberty's pedestal, to Muriel Rukeyser, Maxine Kumin, Louise Gluck, Marilyn Hacker, Alicia Ostricker, and Jacqueline Osherow in poetry; from Mary Antin and Jane Bowles, whose prose helped define regionalism and modernism, to Tillie Olsen, E. M. Broner, Erica Jong, Marge Piercy, Anne Roiphe, Norma Rosen, Susan Fromberg Shaeffer, Grace Paley, Rebecca Goldstein, and Allegra Goodman in fiction: from Lillian Hellman to Eve Merriam, and Wendy Wasserstein in drama: Jewish American women writers have questioned, stretched, and extended our understanding of sexual and religious, national and ethnic categories that cannot contain their accomplishments but whose contradictions definitely can and do frame them. With notable exceptions in literary history, Jewish American women writers take as their most resonant subject the tensions and ironies implicit not only in their own but in the very concept of "hyphenated" identities.

Even a cursory glance at the names I have listed above demonstrates that Jewish American women's literary achievements do not fit into the categories conceived by critics to study men's. The so-called "Jewish American renaissance," for example, includes writers – Saul Bellow, Philip Roth, Joseph Heller, Lenny Bruce, Stanley Elkin, Woody Allen – whose narrative exuberance and sometimes comic, sometimes satiric experimental performances have no female-authored counterparts. What the shape of Jewish American women's literary history displays is an embarrassment of riches rather later in the day and thus marked not only by the politics of civil rights and of feminism but also by an increased understanding of the catastrophic upheaval in Western civilization that the word "Shoah" means. Because widespread awareness of the calamitous threat to Jewish survival only fully emerged after two decades in which the stark horror of the Holocaust had been repressed, because during that same period the imperatives of the Civil Rights and feminist movements made themselves felt, this crucible constitutes the powerful caldron of women's aesthetic production. For Jewish American women who came into their majority at the turn of the century, the tensions between a liberating politics and the imperatives of an endangered Judaism stimulate and mark their astonishing productivity. This is not to say, of course, that all contemporary Jewish women always write about racial and sexual politics, about the friction or fit between a commitment to imperiled Jewish traditions and the urgencies of progressive work, but that these intertwined issues have shaped their shared concerns.

Like the contributors to the contemporary journal *Bridges*, which combines "the traditional Jewish values of justice and repair of the world with insights honed by the feminist, lesbian and gay movements" (from the editorial policy), Jewish American women writers have forged a host of alliances with groups advocating many progressive goals. The impact of evolving discourses of feminism and gay rights is manifestly evident; however, the powerful shadow cast by slavery in this country has meant that the relationship between Blacks and Jews also stimulated some of the nation's most ambitious artistic experiments. In the older and more prominent male tradition, blackface conventions shaped the portrayal of African American characters marked by a fantasized Black aesthetic or sexual license. A number of literary historians have examined the effect of African American history on Jewish men whose participation in the offshoots of minstrelsy spawned, for example, Al Jolson's burnt cork performance in *The Jazz Singer* and Norman Mailer's in *The White Negro*. If Bernard Malamud, Saul Bellow, and Norman Podhoretz exemplify the extension of this heritage in fiction and journalism, Leslie Fiedler has charted it most expansively n criticism. Because of their displacement on the margins of a Judaism itself marginalized in American culture and because their tradition evolved during the influence exerted by civil rights and feminist activism, white women authors from Jewish American backgrounds remain alienated from the relentlessly racialized Othering implicit in minstrelsy's cultural legacy.

Although largely unnoted, the centrality of African American characters in the literature produced by Jewish American women writers facilitates their comparative investigations into the largely unacknowledged but pervasive privileges of whiteness and masculinity. So as to foreground lesser-known but highly accomplished contemporary authors, I will concentrate on Irena Klepfisz and Lore Segal, both of whom question the whiteness and masculinity of Jews, a point broached as well by the more famous artists I will consider. At the turn of the twentieth century, Jewish American women's literature has conscientiously protested the destructive ramifications of illusory but powerful conceptualizations of race that fuel the subordination of Jews by non-Jews, of Blacks by whites. However, a quick detour to earlier periods of literary history proves that even before Holocaust consciousness sharpened awareness of Jewish vulnerability to racism, the touchstone texts produced by early Jewish American women writers seem startlingly inflected by racial concerns clustered around the societal subjugation of African Americans.

Not only did Gertrude Stein take the first step into the twentieth century with a short story, "Melanchtha" (1909), exclusively about Black characters; she linked her experimental style with the effort to capture the psychological nuances and linguistic cadences of an African American community hostile to the erotic curiosity of her bisexual heroine. More conventionally centered on racial and sexual oppression, Edna Ferber's *Show Boat* (1926) considers the liabilities of a light-skinned African American woman passing as white. As often revived on screen as *Show Boat* was on Broadway, Fannie Hurst's *Imitation of Life* (1933) also examines the impact of the color line on female characters struggling against financial and emotional dependency as well as the fatal attractions of passing. That Jewish American women authors produced two popular texts in the genre of the passing novel puts their achievements into a conversation with African American modernists like James Weldon Johnson and Nella Larsen. And that Fannie Hurst considered Zora Neale Hurston the inspiration for her best-known novel, that Hurston in her autobiography celebrated their friendship (when in her undergraduate days she served as Hurst's secretary and driver) underscores the importance of cross-racial influence in this period, as does Hurston's later portrait of black Jews in *Moses Man of the Mountain* (1939). Perhaps nothing better captures the camaraderie of these two adventurous women of letters than Hurst's anecdote about getting the vibrantly dressed Hurston seated at a segregated Westchester County hotel by informing the headwater, "The Princess Zora and I wish a table," an episode that concludes with Hurston's poignant remark, "Who would think that a good meal could be so bitter?" (Kroeger, *Fannie*, 167).

As if kindled by the flaming torch of Emma Lazarus' "The New Colossus" (1883), some of the most prominent Jewish American modernists rejected "the brazen giant of Greek fame" and the "storied pomp" of "ancient lands," and aligned themselves instead with the "Mother of Exiles" whose silent lips cry, "Give me your tired, your poor, / Your huddled masses yearning to breathe free" ("The New Colossus," 341). Like Anzia Yezierska, whose heroine in *Bread Givers* (1925) rebels against the virulent misogyny of her orthodox father, they view a longing for freedom on the part of the dispossessed as part of the American experiment: "He was the Old World," Yezierska's Sara Smolinsky defiantly declares, "I was the New" (*Bread Givers*, 207). Different as Stein, Ferber, and Hurst were, they shared with Lazarus and Yezierska what propelled the most important Jewish American photographer in the first half of the twentieth century: a passion for honoring the lives of the obscure that was fostered by progressive European legacies given a uniquely American inflection by immigrants convinced they were in a unique position to right the wrongs of social injustice. Of German Jewish descent, Doris Ulmann produced the largest body of images extant of African American life on southern plantations. Taken during the most creative period of her career, from 1929 to 1932, Ullman's pictures in her collaborative volume with Julia Peterkin, *Roll, Jordan, Roll* (1934), provide an extensive documentary record of Gullah culture. An ethnographer of sorts, Ulmann's most striking and mysterious images derive from several trips she took to New Orleans, where the group and individual sittings of the cloistered Sisters of the Holy Family convent (in the French Quarter) juxtapose the startling white and black habits with the dark faces of the mostly African American nuns.

In the transition period associated with the Second World War, the figure who stands out as most influential in the lineage of Jewish American women writers is Muriel Rukeyser, whose oracular verse exemplifies a commitment to anti-racist work. Beginning with "The Lynchings of Jesus" in *Theory of Flight* (1935) and evolving throughout the volumes she published during (and against) the Vietnam War, Rukeyser castigates the United States for the injustice created by the "Secrets of American Civilization," namely that "Slave and slaveholder they are chained together," for "Jefferson spoke of freedom but he held slaves. / Were ten of them his sons by black women?" (Rukeyser, *Collected Poems*, 513–514). Besides her sardonic deployment of Christian iconography to remonstrate against the trial of the Scottsboro boys, Rukeyser traces her own origins as well as the origins of her commitment to protest back to the persecution of the Jews –

> These people engendered my blood swarming
> over the altar to clasp the scrolls and Menorah
> the black lips, bruised cheeks, eye-reproaches
> as the floor burns, singing Shema –
> (*Collected Poems*, 25–26)

and mocks southern justice in a courtroom haunted by the presences of John Brown, Nat Turner, Toussaint, Dred Scott, Sacco and Vanzetti, and Tom Mooney, where "Nine dark boys spread their breasts against Alabama" (*Collected Poems*, 29). Toward the end of her career, Rukeyser linked the senseless wasting of human lives directly with the figure she called "Rational Man" and specifically with "The marker at Auschwitz" that proves "Anything you can imagine . . . Rational man has done" (*Collected Poems*, 533).

Whether radicalized by contact with the Communist Party, trade unionism, or Ethical Culture, socialist *Yiddishkeit* or the peace movement, civil rights or feminist activism, Jewish American literary women – especially those publishing during the last decades of the twentieth century – tended to use their artistry to critique American prejudice by emphasizing its commonalities and differences with antisemitic bigotry (see Bulkin, Pratt, and Smith, *Yours in Struggle*; Pogrebin, "Blacks and Jews,"; Smith, "Between a Rock,"). Undoubtedly shaped by the brouhaha over Hannah Arendt's controversial journalistic intervention in debates swirling around Brown versus the Board of Education (Arendt, "Reflections on Little Rock," 231–246),[2] this aesthetic enterprise is best understood through the model of bipolarity: sometimes matching, sometimes clashing instances of traumatic experience – one pertaining to European genocide, the other to American racism – are counterpointed in a variety of patterns that comprise related but rarely congruent narratives, since the Jewish experience of the Shoah cannot be reduced to the African American experience of slavery, nor can American racism be conflated with Nazi genocide. Central to the tradition I am mapping here, the autobiographical meditations of two child survivors – the poet Irena Klepfisz and the novelist Lore Segal – examine what one of Segal's characters calls the "parallel" lines (*Her First American*, 265) traveled by Jews and Blacks, trajectories that constitute the basis for an ethics of responsibility that would promote cross-racial communication and thus a post-racist society – without promulgating easy slippages between the situation of Blacks and Jews that would inevitably harm the integrity of any conceptualization of their distinct histories.

What marks the vigor of Klepfisz's and Segal's comparative analyses is precisely their consideration of the misuses to which such analogies can be put, their effort to capture the distinct perspectives of people speaking through the rhythms of very different experiences of dispossession, genocidal violence, stereotyping, and diaspora. Heightened attentiveness to the significance of the Shoah, Black militancy about even well-meant expressions of solidarity by whites, feminist awareness of the personal as the political: all contributed to their resistance to facile pronouncements about any equivalency between Black and Jewish experiences. Although for the most part ignored by Jewish Studies as well as African American Studies scholars, the writings of Jewish American women illuminate the consequences of America's long history of discrimination against people of color by juxtaposing it with Hitler's decision to target as his victims Jewish women along with men, and in particular mothers and their offspring, for the Final Solution sought to obliterate not merely all the Jews of Europe but the future of the Jewish people (Ringelheim, "The Split," 345). How such a calamitous past differed both in its nature and its ramifications from the injurious offshoots of African American slavery, what it means to compare such horrific assaults on an entire "race," whether any politics of coalition might be formed out of investigations deeply skeptical about biological or, for that matter, cultural definitions of "race": these are issues that recurrently surface.

The sense of alterity precipitated by trauma is the subject of Klepfisz's most ambitious sequence, the long poem *Bashert* (1982), titled with the Yiddish term (meaning inevitable or predestined) that in and of itself speaks of a specifically linguistic loss. What seems inevitable or predestined in this complex series of meditations is the psychological angst induced in the child survivor whose experience of oppression in the Old World will make palpable on-going oppression inflicted in the New World. "As a child, I was old with terror and the brutality, the haphazardness of survival" (*Dreams of an Insomniac*, 170): before *Bashert* elaborates on this prematurely aged mental landscape, a prefatory dedication relies upon a liturgy that defies the consolation of closure since the fates of the dead and the survivors seem at one and the same time inevitable and indeterminate. Four subsequent autobiographical sections, composed of prose paragraphs, consider how living can go on after such devastating loss by recording what immigration after the Holocaust signifies to mother and poet, in the process "push[ing] the prose limits of poetry as far as possible" (*Dreams of an Insomniac*, 170). Through consequences that resonate with African American reactions to slavery and discrimination, the first section, "Poland, 1944: My mother is walking down a road," establishes two major motifs: human existence depends on the fragile fiction of passing and the equally fragile serendipity of luck.

At three years of age, the child Irena has "no awareness that we are playing a part" as orthodox Catholics; however, her ailing mother in search of "some kind of permit" and "carrying her Aryan identity papers" knows exactly how much hinges on a false identity and therefore has "promised herself that never, under any circumstances, will she take the risk" of revealing her Jewishness (*A Few Words in the Mother Tongue*, 187). The secret Jewish identity must be as rigorously repressed behind the Polish impersonation as a Black identity had to be concealed beneath the white masquerades of light-skinned, run-away slaves. Still, "an explosion of yearning" while walking down a road causes the lonely mother "to pierce five years of encrusted history" with another ravenous figure who turns out to be one of Klepfisz's father's teachers: in the midst of the war, "They do not cry, but weep as they chronicle the dead and count the living" (189). Unexpectedly, a food package appears after the woman promises "she has contacts." Though the toddler only had a life expectancy of a week, she and her mother "begin to bridge the gap towards life" (189). Poland here is a world "where no one can be trusted" (189), a minefield governed by permits and faked papers, in which the three-year-old suffers from an oozing ear infection, the thirty-year-old mother from incurable skin sores, the father's teacher from "hunger, the swollen flesh, the infected skin, the rags" (189). Totally isolated, mother and daughter have survived the deaths of all the other members of their family and can only sustain their lives through the lies made possible by blond hair, blue eyes, and the Polish words in which they pray, ironically, to "the Holy Mother, Mother of God" (187). Like what is spoken, what is eaten cannot nourish: the mother's "terror . . . is swallowed now, like all other feelings," including "her hunger for contact and trust" (187–188). Since nothing but sheer chance brings the father's teacher down the same road as the mother, since only an undeniable "explosion" forces the mother to reveal her identity, no one can take pride in the deliverance, which could not have been planned but simply happens to happen.

The second section, "Chicago, 1964: I am walking home alone at midnight," evokes not only the poet's graduate student days at the University of Chicago but also how during that time she recollected "Elza who is dead" (190). As an eight-year-old left with Polish Catholics during the war, Elza had been instructed by her parents, *"Never admit who you are!"* and so had vehemently denied her Jewishness until a bribe dislodged her from her hiding place and she could be adopted as a war orphan. A loving new family, a fine education, work, marriage, nothing can prevent depression, then suicide at the age of twenty-five. Klepfisz, kept ignorant at the time by a solicitous mother fearing that her daughter might succumb to self-destruction, later wonders if Elza only missed her fate in Poland to encounter it in America. If she had internalized the assumption that Jews precipitated their own persecution (Elza attributes suffering in the camps to a "terrible mistake" made by Jews [192]), the passer in Poland is unmasked in America. The student Irena must have worried, too, that she might be snared in Elza's fate. Only after she has worked through her grief over the postwar suicide does the speaker of *Bashert* notice her dangerous surroundings: "fringes of rubble" in the Hyde Park ghetto, revealing "vague outlines that hint at things that were." What surfaces, then, is "American hollowness," a perception of "the incessant grinding down of lines for stamps, for jobs, for a bed to sleep in, of a death stretched imperceptibly over a lifetime," and thus "The Holocaust without smoke" (193).

Continuing to brood on a state of being poised between the Old and New Worlds and on the internalized antisemitism from which Elza suffered, "Brooklyn, 1971: I am almost equidistant from two continents" counterpoints Warsaw with New York City where Klepfisz, now a teacher, appears as the "only white" person in classrooms of Black and Puerto Rican students (194). As she approaches the age of her father when he was gunned down by the Nazis, Klepfisz records a series of birthdays: her birth (which took place on her father's twenty-eighth birthday), her impending thirtieth birthday (which she associates with her thirty-year-old father's death in the Uprising), and her fourteenth birthday, when she lit a candle honoring murdered children at a Holocaust memorial ceremony in an auditorium filled with "the sound of irretrievable loss, of wild pain and sorrow" (195). The Yiddish names of dead children, called out by "people with blue numbers on their arms," contrast with those of the twenty-eight people in the Brooklyn classroom: *"Surele. Moyshele. Channele. Rivkele"* chime with and against

"*Reggie. Marie. Simone. Joy. Christine*" (195). Though not burned, shot, or stomped to death, the poet asserts, the African American and Puerto Rican students in her classes are also ground down, falling behind because of evictions, hospital regulations, sickness, incomprehensible English forms as well as the general assumption among whites that they are "lazy."

Trapped in a history that cannot be cheated, young people of color have been othered by a culture that effectively teaches them what the poet and Elza had been told: "*Never admit who you are!*" Klepfisz herself has experienced the same tug of self-destruction to which Elza succumbed; however, when she teaches a class composed of students from every conceivable background, wonders how her students perceive her, and must explain who she is, the answer – "A Jew" – educates her to choose neither Europe nor America but instead "the histories of two continents," neither guaranteeing safety (197). The switch in self-definition – from "white" to "Jew" – accompanies an insight aligned with James Baldwin's that, although "America rescued [the Jew] from the house of bondage," it "*is* the house of bondage for the Negro" (Baldwin, *The Price of the Ticket*, 430) who remains "a pariah in his [or her] country" (431). Klepfisz's despairing feeling "of cellular breakdown," her suicidal wish "to become transparent" like the salt water between Europe and America, resolves as she takes on "muscle, flesh, bone" in an America that "is not my chosen home, not even the place of my birth" and when "two vast land masses touch," she feels grounded balancing her two backgrounds (Levitt, *Jews and Feminism*, 154, 156). In Baldwin's terms, she has achieved embodiment after the transplantation of immigration to the United States, but refuses to pay the "price of the ticket," which "was to become white" (Baldwin, *The Price of the Ticket*, xx).

Still, history has instructed Klepfisz that safety can never be more than temporary, the final section of *Bashert* explains. Periodically confined in the dread of being "hunted again" (Klepfisz, *A Few Words in the Mother Tongue*, 198), the poet matures by recollecting Elza hiding behind a Catholic mask but being told by a hostile Polish shopkeeper that her accuracy about money raised his suspicion that she is "*perhaps a little Jewess*" (198). Supplying Klepfisz with the title of her second book of poems, "Cherry Plain, 1981: I have become a keeper of accounts" reinvents Elza through an aesthetic identity dedicated to the idea of accuracy, for Klepfisz becomes a quintessentially Jewish keeper of "scrupulously accurate" (198) literary accounts. First she looks at despised Jewish men – pawnbrokers, Shylocks, merchants – portrayed demanding their pound of flesh, while they studied legalized bigotry to try to sustain quarantined lives; then she turns to detested Jewish women – peddlers, widows, run-aways – presented chiseling for a subsistence, while they "understood the accounts but saw them differently": men whose "zloty, francs, and marks could not buy off the written words *Zÿd, Juif, Jüde*"; women "who knew the power of the words *Zÿd, Juif, Jüde*" (199). The foreign, repeated label as libel reeks of an obscene international calumny. By adopting the role of "bookkeeper of the dead," Klepfisz claims as her legacy images she finds in photographs of figures humiliated in "A facility" or reduced to absence in an empty landscape next to "A track" (200). Types rarely seen any longer, the photographed casualties can be revived in epiphanic moments through a Whitmanesque sense of self that contains multitudes, a community of subjectivities, as the poet reincarnates the homicidal stereotypes of the past.

Throughout her reverie about othering, Klepfisz compares Jews in Europe with people of color in America by emphasizing camouflaging techniques (passing), internalization of hostile images (self-blaming), and scapegoating (the construction of a pariah class). Art Spiegelman's *Maus*, which originated as an effort to present American Blacks (not European Jews) as mice, makes ironic the same series of analogies. For although Artie's father had to pass as a Catholic, although he was made into a pariah in "Mauschwitz," once in America he engages in the racism that makes him "talk about blacks the way the Nazis talked about the Jews" (*Maus*, II, 99). More emphatically than *Maus*, *Bashert* uses its meditation on European-versus American-styles of discrimination to reject simple solutions to racism. Klepfisz refutes the "melting pot" model of assimilation, in part because she refuses to see immigration to America as an arrival at the Promised Land, in part because she views on-going Jewish identification as psychologically crucial to survival. At the same time, by resisting the conflation of Jewishness with whiteness, by establishing analogues between the experiences of Jews and people of color, *Bashert* complicates multiculturalists' "salad bar"or "mosaic" paradigm of separately categorized oppressions, of ghettoized ethnic identities.

A phrase Adrienne Rich has used about herself as an offspring of a Jewish father, a non-Jewish mother – "split at the root" – applies to Klepfisz's attentiveness to Old and New Worlds (Rich, "Split at the Root," 224–239). Whereas Baldwin argued that "In the American context, the most ironical thing about Negro anti-Semitism is that the Negro is really condemning the Jew for having become an American white man" (Baldwin, *The Price of the Ticket* 430), Klepfisz uses her intimate knowledge of the effects of antisemitism on women like her mother, Elza, and herself as a wedge against assimilating into a racist society and thereby implicitly broods over Baldwin's controversial remonstrance that "The uprising in the Warsaw Ghetto was not described as a riot" (428). Because Lore Segal studies not only the effects of racial hatred on a black intellectual of Baldwin's generation and on a Holocaust child survivor like Klepfisz but also the whitening of citizenship as a rupturing of alliances between Blacks and Jews, *Her First American* (1985) extends Klepfisz's comparative analysis of African American and Jewish diaspora, although Segal's novel moves from the American scene back to the European one. Like Klepfisz, Segal juxtaposes the incomprehensible extermination produced by European genocide with the economic exploitation of slavery so as to consider the on-goingness of both disasters. Like Klepfisz, too, Segal hinges her quasi-autobiographical narrative on the relationship between mothers and daughters and on a process of language acquisition that constitutes the promise of cultural literacy as well as the threat of assimilation.

On arrival from Vienna during the fifties, twenty-one-year-old Ilka Weissnix, who goes "looking for the real America," discovers it in Carter Bayoux, the physically imposing, African American author of a book – entitled, as he puts it, "*Pan-African Power: The Hope of the American Negro question mark*" – whom she meets at a western railroad stopover and dates back in New York City (Segal, *Her First American*, 15, 43). During the first section of the novel, while she searches for her mother who has survived incarceration and forced marches, Ilka puzzles over her perplexities about the English language ("I can not yet so well English" [11]), the mysterious sentences murmured around Carter ("We are not all white" [19]), and by him as well ("You're not afraid of me?" [21]). An aspect of her inability to fathom the slang of "lump sums" and "going to the dogs," her confusion about national, racial, ethnic categories – is he a Frenchman? a Negro? Jewish? – makes her a sort of female Candide, the innocent know-nothing (*Weissnix-weiss* [know] and *nicht* [nothing]) whose naivety foregrounds the artifice of the distinctions at work in her world. What emerges in poignant fragments through the wry episodes of Segal's love story is a portrait of Carter as a talented but tormented wreck of a man whose quotations from *Othello*, recounts of his expatriate escapades with Josephine Baker and Gertrude Stein, connections with African diplomats at the United Nations, and militant columns for the *Harlem Herald* cannot stave off drinking binges that only escalate his loneliness and insomnia.

The on-and-off affair introduces Ilka to the inheritance of slavery in Carter's life, but also to its effects on African American culture. What Carter dictates to Ilka for his column – "baffled by daily comma small comma casual hurts and slights comma and by his lifelong experience of rejection and subordination period His energies are exhausted" (102) – takes on resonance not as a cause of but as an accompaniment to his alcoholism, his hostile defensiveness with liberal whites, his hectic efforts to drown out the noises inside his head with Christian talk shows on the radio and prescription pills. When Carter introduces Ilka to Harlem nightlife, she is dismayed by the performance artist Ebony's satiric one-woman show, in which "an excruci-atingly fine white lady" (91) tries to rape a black boy; by the gospel singer Ulalia Dixon's obfuscating quotations from the gospel – " 'Thou art Peter, and upon this rock I will build my church.' Matthew sixteen, eighteen" – as a response to Carter's asking if she has made "what Richard Wright has called 'an honorable adjustment to the American scene' " (95); by the burnt-out singer of "Strange Fruit," with her hot eyes, browning gardenia, rough-patched skin; by her own self-consciousness at the Jet Fashion Ball, where "Ilka saw no white people" (100). The child of freed slaves whose college education did not liberate them from having to make do by taking in laun-dry, Carter refutes any easy equation between his self-destructive habits and slavery, but he registers the revulsion of white strangers at the "improbable pair" (126) he and Ilka appear, and predicts that she is destined to become "naturalized" (47), a highly ironic term in this context. For as Ilka gains in literacy, learning words like "Puerto Rican" by which she can identify groups of people, she will lose "the likelihood that she would henceforward distinguish any member within the group from any other" (142).

If Carter in his brilliant but feverish sophistication represents Segal's por-trait of the African American as an intellectual, Ilka's mother stands for the Jew as survivor of the Shoah. Haunted by anxiety that she ought not to have left her husband on the side of the road outside the town of Obernpest and by uncertainty about his fate, the mother suffers a recurrent nightmare about burglars who are ants but also men composed of shiny patent leather and who enter her apartment carrying a black bag of metal instruments. Always behind her back, unseen in the dream sequences, the burglars use metallic instruments with teeth that hurt her body so she wants to ask, " 'Why do you hate me' " (156); however, she soon realizes "I've been wishing not to have the pain. That is not one of my choices. What I *can* choose is *how* to have it and what I'm going to do is to concentrate on having pain" (161). As Carter declines into his own fearful pain and is briefly institutionalized, Ilka's mother grapples with a non-human species that "may not *know* that my flesh feels like flesh, because they are made out of different materials – nothing like black beads, or patent leather. More like the parts of a black motorcy-cle" (163). Despite Ilka's exasperation, the mother's inability to free herself from the nightly visions implicitly answers Klepfisz's question in *Bashert*: "Are there moments in history which cannot be escaped or transcended, but which act like time warps permanently trapping all those who are touched by them?" (192).

After being arrested and confined in a concentration camp or herded on forced marches, survivors like Ilka's mother know that reality has itself turned surreal. Devoid of empathy, the Nazis, according to the mother, simply could not be human beings: what they accused Jews of being must have been a projection of their own Kafkaesque metamorphosis. In one of her final descriptions of the nightmare, Ilka's mother realizes the real horror of the surreptitious invasion of her apartment, her body, her head when the "father" burglar returns, not to stop the others but because "He *is* the police . . . The black is their uniform. They are, all three of them, policemen!" (223). The fact that the sadistic creatures "are *supposed* to do" their work, that "It is the law" (223) that they cut the mother severs her from any reprieve. Just at this moment in the plot, two curious events bind Ilka's mother to Carter, making them doubles of one another. First, we discover that they are exactly the same age; second, Ilka realizes that there is no social "agency" that can cure Carter (230). The coincidence and the pun underscore the lack of agency with which both characters must endure the quite different repercussions of, on the one hand, an inexplicable and legalized genocide and, on the other, an economically motivated and legally sustained system of discrimination that continues long after the abolishment of slavery. Having suffered the wounding indignity of being translated into a problem in need of gruesome solutions, the mother and Carter oscillate between paranoia and various doomed attempts at anaesthetization.

No wonder that the otherwise quite variegated Jewish and Black characters in this novel spend an inordinate amount of time "beating the boy" (172, 255); that is, satirizing the prejudices of Gentiles, of whites. No wonder either that both groups pay homage to racialized mores deemed authentic but sometimes curiously ersatz or that they ironically perform stereotypical parts: Ilka's wonderfully named American cousin, Fishgoppel, insists on speaking Yiddish to the uncomprehending Mrs. Weissnix; Ebony plays the role of domestic for whites with barely concealed rage, sardonically declaring "We're ever so much happier in the kitchen" (203). The peaceable kingdom Ilka and Carter try to establish with their friends results only in discord significantly staged over differences of opinion about a white couple adopting "little non-other babies" (208), dissension which proves that, as Carter puts it, "Friends the only ones get close enough to get your teeth *into*" (220). With trenchant humor, the plot of *Her First American* hints that Jews' and Blacks' "parallel experience" of racial humiliation follows the trajectory of "two lines that run side by side and never meet except in infinity" (263):

> Ebony said, "Negroes were lynched if they learned the alphabet."
> "We had pogroms," cried Fishgoppel.
> "Slavery," said Ebony.
> "Holocaust!" cried Fishgoppel.
> "Are there no griefs that aren't racist or anti-Semitic!" shouted Ilka.
> (273)

Rife with the danger of Jewish racism and Black antisemitism, the competition for victimization between Blacks and Jews pertains to Segal's title.

Although African Americans gained citizenship decades before the influx of Jews fleeing the pogroms of Europe and then the Final Solution, although Ilka's "naturalization" occurs late in the novel (270) and she views Carter as her "First American," his nihilism bespeaks a cynicism about the possibility of Black integration and equality. In a passage pertinent to Segal's awareness of the difference visible pigmentation makes, Franz Fanon – who invoked parallelisms between Jewish and Black oppression throughout his influential *Black Skin, White Masks* – nevertheless quarreled with Jean-Paul Sartre's view that the Jews "have allowed themselves to be poisoned by the stereotype that others have of them": whereas Jews "can be unknown in [their] Jewishness," Fanon postulates, people of color like himself are "the slave not of the 'idea' that others have of me but of my own appearance." Jews in Segal's fictional world suffer from a past "over there" and "back then," whereas conspicuous Blacks continue to confront injuries "here and now," intermarriages and cross-racial adoptions notwithstanding. Yet after Carter's death, his followers' hostility toward Ilka at the memorial service – "They want the book about Carter to be a black book" (286) – is counterpointed by her recollection of his take on her name, based on his knowledge that the German "*weiss*" is related not only to knowing but also to whiteness: "I told Carter Weissnix means 'Knownothing,' but Carter said it meant 'Notwhite,' because I am a Jew" (287). Despite her "naturalization," Ilka has retained a remnant of stubborn resistence to assimilation because of the twin influence of the muses inspiring her creator's imagination, Carter and Ilka's mother. As Carter tells Jewish jokes or studies the Talmud, as Mrs. Weissnix (in frustration at her inadequate English) resorts to "charades" to explain the burglars to him (152), as Ilka balks during a *seder* at God's "hardening" the hearts of the Egyptians and then punishing them (253), even the resonant metaphor of "parallel" lines fails to convey the promise of emerging cross-racial, creolized modalities of consciousness and conscience.

Needless to say, not all Jewish American women writers who address the Holocaust juxtapose German genocide against American racism, though they often deal with the Shoah in the maternal terms set out by Klepfisz and Segal. Cynthia Ozick's two stories "The Shawl" (1980) and "Rosa" (1983) are typical of many longer narratives by other women novelists, specifically in their effort to delineate the horrific fate of mothers and children. With poignant indirection, Ozick hints at the threat of rape facing women during the Shoah, their fearfulness for their infants of cannibalism in the concentration camps, the horror of Nazi infanticide and of maternal desolation after witnessing such a gruesome event. But in a less-known work, "A Mercenary" in *Bloodshed* (1976), Ozick also situates the repercussions of the Holocaust in the context of Black and white interaction. A survivor – who as a child had been deemed "too black" to be hidden by non-Jews in Poland – defines himself as "an African" spokesman, seeks out Tarzan movies, and attempts to turn himself into "a transmuted, a transfigured African" in a break from Jewishness propelled by his internalization of anti-Semitic stereotypes (*Bloodshed*, 27, 41, 51). Throughout a text very much in conversation with Fanon's, Ozick counterpoints the damaged Jew's sense of himself as an impersonator, a deracinated fake in flight, a nomad without a country against a romanticized and highly tainted vision of blacks as joyous, rooted, fecund natives.

Not all Jewish American women writers who decry the cruelty of white racism juxtapose it against the quandary of the Shoah, of course. From Tillie Olsen's "O Yes" in *Tell Me a Riddle* (1961), about white and Black girls whose friendship is filtered through the segregated worlds they inhabit, to Marilyn Hacker's poems about her biracial daughter, Jewish American women writers have dedicated themselves exclusively to the civil rights not accorded people of color and thus to the anti-racist repair of American society. Indeed, a spate of recent autobiographical books by or about Jewish mothers who have adopted or given birth to children defined as Black has surfaced in the wake of Grace Paley's related imaginative accounts (Gubar, *Racechanges*, 223–232). With sly humor, Paley's "Zagrowsky Tells" (1985) and "At That Time, or The History of a Joke" (1982) envision cross-racial loving kindness through the emergence of mystic Black children within the Jewish community. Even the adulation of Blacks by Jews has come under the purview of Jewish American women artists: the performance artist Sandra Bernhard uses blackface in her movie *Without You I'm Nothing* (1990) to satirize the extent to which whiteness depends upon patently appropriative and spurious presentations of African Americans. On the New York stage, the playwright/composer Elizabeth Swados has challenged white privilege while preserving a congregation of ethnic diversity by employing multi-ethnic casts and musical traditions to study, for instance, child abuse in *Runaways* (1978), Nazi persecution in *The Haggadah: A Passover Cantata* (1982), pacifism in *Esther: A Vaudeville Megillah* (1989), religious tolerance in *Jerusalem* (1938), and civil rights in *Groundhog* (1992).

In other words, Jewish American women have approached the social injustice of racism from a myriad of perspectives; however, an impressive number resemble Adrienne Rich, who feels "rooted among... those who were turned to smoke" and who typifies their efforts to identify with the persecuted so as to detonate the dynamics of persecution (*Adrienne Rich's Poetry and Prose*, 109). At the end of her *Eastern War Time* (1990), a sequence about the casualties of the Shoah, Rich declares:

I'm a family dispersed between night and fog
I'm an immigrant tailor who says *A coat
is not a piece of cloth only*   I sway
in the learnings of the master-mystics
I have dreamed of Zion   I've dreamed of world revolution
I have dreamed my children could live at last like others
I have walked the children of others through ranks of hatred
I'm a corpse dredged from a canal in Berlin
a river in Mississippi   I'm a woman standing
with other women dressed in black
on the streets of Haifa, Tel Aviv, Jerusalem
there is spit on my sleeve there are phonecalls in the night
I am a woman standing in line for gasmasks
I stand on a road in Ramallah   with naked face   listening
I am standing here in your poem   unsatisfied
lifting my smoky mirror [.]

(*Eastern War Time, An Atlas of a Difficult World*, 44)

Speaking in the voices of Black and white, Israeli and Palestinian victims appearing "in *your* poem *un*satisfied" (italics mine), the poet alienated by her own mimetic efforts, her "smoky mirror," broods over the inefficacy of her own imaginative exertions with a humility that resembles the puzzlement of Jane Lazarre, whose inconclusive reflections on museums dedicated to preserving memories of past indignities will close the tradition of Jewish resistance to whiteness presented here, punctuating it not with a period but with a question mark forecasting future imaginings.

Jane Lazarre begins one of the essays in her autobiographical *Beyond the Whiteness of Whiteness* (1996) with a disavowal of cross-racial identification: although a friend of her African American sons has called her "a Black person in disguise," she knows the friendly remark contains a "false" message (25). Yet she seeks to attain what Chinua Achebe calls "imaginative identification" of "human connectedness at its most intimate" (xxi) and does so in "The Richmond Museum of the Confederacy" by counterpointing slavery and the Shoah: what does it signify that there is "no permanent slavery museum in this country, though now, following the model of Yad Vashem in Jerusalem, a Holocaust museum exists in Washington, D.C." (Lazarre, *Beyond the Whiteness*, 15)? As Lazarre gazes at an iron harness with bells, used to leash slaves like cattle, and remembers the dozens of Stars of David at Yad Vashem, as an aged man crying before the harness in Virginia brings to mind an old man weeping silently before children's drawings in Israel, she ponders the significance of the fact that the Richmond exhibit, entitled

"Before Freedom Came," will be disassembled and moved to another city in two months, leaving "the historical deception and moral lie of the Museum of the Confederacy on its own again" and she wonders, "*Supposing this had been the case at Yad Vashem, and upon leaving that museum I descended to a floor that celebrated the military successes of Nazi Germany – as if the two testimonials could exist, calmly and unconflictually, side by side*" (19).

Lazarre's query stands at the end of a series of cultural investigations that have also gripped the imagination of a number of African American literary women. For Toni Morrison's epigraph introducing *Beloved* (1988) – "Sixty Million and more" – and Anne Deavere Smith's performance in *Fires in the Mirror* (1993) – of Lubavitchers and Blacks set at odds in the 1991 conflict in the Crown Heights neighborhood of Brooklyn – enter into conversations about the bipolarity of Jewish and Black histories to contest preconceptions about racial separatism. In a surrealistic reverie about patches of empty spaces on the otherwise colorful paintings of an Auschwitz survivor, Patricia J. Williams realizes that they represent "the erasure of humanity that the Holocaust exacted" and later dreams that within each of them her enslaved great-great-grandmother appears: "Suddenly she filled in all the empty spaces, and I looked into her face with the supernatural stillness of deep recollection. From that moment, I knew exactly who she was" (*The Rooster's Egg*, 209). Despite the insistence of Holocaust scholars that the disaster must not, cannot be compared to any other, that it stands unrepresentable, outside of history, women artists have insisted on the ethical necessity of such (albeit provisional, inadequate) comparisons. In the process, they have definitively changed the landscape of letters. Although many years ago Karl Shapiro knew about the cultural canon in general, higher education in particular that, "To hurt the Negro and avoid the Jew/is the curriculum" ("University," 36), the syllabus has changed in part because of the desire for human connectedness that animates Jewish American women's artistic achievements.

NOTES

My work on this chapter has profited from the insights and suggestions of Donald Gray, Anna Meek, Phil Metres, Nancy K. Miller, Laura Yow, and the editors of this volume.
1. Even Simone de Beauvoir, comparing the "eternal feminine" with the "black soul" and the "Jewish character," writes about the Jew as "he" in *The Second Sex*.
2. Roundly reviled upon its publication, Arendt's "Reflections on Little Rock" (1959) attacks American laws against miscegenation in twenty-nine of the forty-nine states and the forced integration of schools.

REFERENCES AND SELECTED FURTHER READINGS

Arendt, Hannah. "Reflections on Little Rock" (1959). In *The Portable Hannah Arendt*. Ed. Peter Baehr. New York: Penguin Books, 2000.

Baldwin, James. *The Price of the Ticket: Collected Nonfiction 1948–1985*. New York: St. Martin's Press, 1985.

Berman, Paul, ed. *Blacks and Jews: Alliances and Arguments*. New York: Delta, 1994.

Budick, Emily Miller. *Blacks and Jews in Literary Conversation*. Cambridge: Cambridge University Press, 1998.

Bulkin, Elly, Minnie Bruce Pratt, and Barbara Smith. *Yours in Struggle: Three Feminist Perspectives on Anti-Semitism and Racism*. Ithaca: Firebrand Books, 1984.

Gubar, Susan. *Racechanges: White Skin, Black Face in American Culture*. New York: Oxford University Press, 1977.

Critical Condition: Feminism at the Turn of the Century. New York: Columbia University Press, 2000.

Hacker, Marilyn. "1973." In *Assumptions*. New York: Alfred A. Knopf, 1985.

Klingenstein, Susanne. " 'In Life I Am Not Free': The Writer Cynthia Ozick and Her Jewish Obligations." In *Daughters of Valor: Contemporary Jewish American Women Writers*. Eds. Jay L. Halio and Ben Siegel. Newark: University of Delaware Press, 1997.

Klepfisz, Irena. *Dreams of an Insomniac: Jewish Feminist Essays, Speeches, and Diatribes*. Portland: Eighth Mountain Press, 1990.

A Few Words in the Mother Tongue: Poems Selected and New (1971–1990). Portland: Eighth Mountain Press, 1990.

Kroeger, Brooke. *Fannie: The Talent for Success of Writer Fannie Hurst*. New York: Random House, 1999.

Lazarre, Jane. *Beyond the Whiteness of Whiteness: Memoir of a White Mother of Black Sons*. Durham, NC: Duke University Press, 1996.

Lazarus, Emma. "The New Colossus." In *American Women Poets of the Nineteenth Century: An Anthology*. Ed. Cheryl Walker. New Brunswick: Rutgers University Press, 1992.

Lentin, Ronit. "Irena Klepfisz." In *Jewish American Women Writers*. Eds. Anna P. Shapiro, Sara R. Horowitz, Ellen Schiff, and Miriyam Glazer. Westport, CT: Greenwood, 1994.

Levitt, Laura. *Jews and Feminism: The Ambivalent Search for Home*. New York: Routledge, 1997.

Meyer, Adam. "Lore Segal." In *Jewish American Women Writers*. Eds. Ann P. Shapiro, Sara R. Horowitz, Ellen Schiff, and Miriyam Glazer. Westport, CT: Greenwood, 1994.

Olsen, Tillie. *Tell Me a Riddle: A Collection*. Philadelphia: Lippincott, 1961.

Ozick, Cynthia. *Bloodshed and Three Novellas* (1976). New York: Syracuse University Press, 1995.

Paley, Grace. "At That Time, or The History of a Joke." In *The Iowa Review Collection of Contemporary Women Writers*. Eds. Jane Cooper, Gwen Head, Adalaide Morris, and Marcia Southwick. New York: Collier, 1982.

Later the Same Day. New York: Penguin, 1986.

Pogrebin, Letty Cottin. "Blacks and Jews: Different Kinds of Survival." In *Bridges and Boundaries: African-Americans and American Jews*. Ed. Jack Salzman. New York: The Jewish Museum, 1992.

Rich, Adrienne. *Eastern War Time*. In *An Atlas of a Difficult World*. New York: W. W. Norton, 1991.

What Is Found There: Notebooks on Poetry and Politics. New York: W. W. Norton, 1993.

"Split at the Root: An Essay on Jewish Identity." In *Adrienne Rich's Poetry and Prose*. Eds. Barbara Charlesworth Gelpi and Albert Gelpi. New York: W. W. Norton, 1993.

Sources. In *Adrienne Rich's Poetry and Prose*. Eds. Barbara Charlesworth Gelpi and Albert Gelpi. New York: W. W. Norton, 1993.

Ringelheim, Joan. "The Split between Gender and the Holocaust." In *Women in the Holocaust*. Eds. Dalia Offer and Lenore J. Weitzman. New Haven: Yale University Press, 1998.

Rogin, Michael. *Blackface, White Noise: Jewish Immigrants in the Hollywood Melting Pot*. Berkeley: University of California, 1996.

Rukeyser, Muriel. *The Collected Poems*. New York: McGraw-Hill, 1973.

Salzman, Jack (with Adina Back and Gretschen Sullivan Sorin). *Bridges and Boundaries: African-Americans and American Jews*. New York: The Jewish Museum, 1992.

Segal, Lore. *Her First American*. New York: The New Press, 1985.

Shapiro, Karl. "University." In *Person, Place and Things*. Cornwall, NY: Cornwall Press, 1942.

Smith, Barbara. "Between a Rock and a Hard Place: Relationships between Black and Jewish Women." In *Bridges and Boundaries: African-Americans and American Jews*. Ed. Jack Salzman. New York: The Jewish Museum, 1992.

Williams, Patricia J. *The Rooster's Egg: On the Resistance of Prejudice*. Cambridge, MA: Harvard University Press, 1991.

Yezierska, Anzia. *Bread Givers*. (1925). New York: Persea Books, 1975.

13

SHIRA WOLOSKY

On contemporary literary theory and Jewish American poetics

Over the last decades, a large, even astonishing number of Jewish scholars and critics have come to the fore in various fields of literary study. Their writings have played a large part in revolutionizing these fields, not only in the sense of revising (if not shattering) earlier approaches and assumptions, but also in introducing whole new avenues and attitudes toward literary experience. In some sense, it was their special task to pose such questions as what "literary experience" even is, moving literary investigation from critical commentary on particular texts (although they very much continued to do this, too) to questions concerning what critical commentary is and does: critical commentary on critical commentary. Theirs, in short, was the plunge into literary theory, into reflection on the premises and principles that make up literary study and literature itself.

America has a broad, bright crown of Jewish critics in a wide range of areas: Lionel Trilling, Alfred Kazin, Philip Rahv, Irving Howe, M. H. Abrams, Leslie Fiedler, Marjorie Perloff, Stephen Greenblatt, Susan Gubar – to name only a few. I will discuss, however, only a small group of Jewish American scholars, working largely at Yale from the 1950s onwards, whose writings were highly theoretical and concentrated on poetry and poetics: Harold Bloom, John Hollander, and Geoffrey Hartman – and I will extend the discussion to include Sacvan Bercovitch, who taught at Columbia and Harvard, as the major theorist of a poetics of American culture generally. I focus particularly on poetry and poetics because here reflection on language is most explicit and most pure; and it is a particular reflection on language that comprises the very core of these scholars' theories about literature. Theirs is, above all, a *theory of figures*: of the way language, on many different levels, is made of figures (or tropes) that "represent" in many different ways. This reflection on the figural power of language is also what they themselves see as the Jewish core of their theories, tying them to traditions of Jewish interpretation – albeit in a very special and very strikingly American context.

Even within this constrained group, the senses of "American" vary significantly. Hartman and Bercovitch were not born in America; nor do all centrally treat American literature. Nevertheless, America gives them jointly both physical site and cultural place. The emergence of their Jewish poetics is not accidentally American. First, the United States offered the opportunity to enter the academy and the surrounding cultural and intellectual life without having simply to renounce or repress Judaic ties – an opportunity unique in Western history, and which did not come entirely unfought. Second, America also offered its own intellectual and cultural traditions. For, since its Puritan foundations, America has had its own deep and intimate ties with Hebraism, not in the sense of live Jews or living Judaism, but in the Puritans' odd and transformative commitment to Hebrew and Hebrew Scriptures (see Goldman, *Hebrew and the Bible in America*). When these theorists bring what may be seen as a Judaic hermeneutic to bear on American texts, it is not mere imposition and false import but a bringing to light of the "Hebraism" that is forceful and formative within the American tradition itself. As to "Jewish," I intend here not only ancestral connection but also the way each of these writers has deliberately taken up Jewish topics and exhibited Jewish connections in his work – although Judaism also enters their work in ways as "figural," as oblique and as transformed, as the very theories they propose.

A fair amount of comment is available on these (and other) Jewish scholars in relation to modern interpretation. *Midrash and Literature*, edited by Hartman and Sanford Budick, is an outstanding collection of essays bringing current literary discourse to bear on Judaic hermeneutical practices. The volume ranges across Jewish hermeneutical traditions, from the tendency within the Bible itself to quote and comment on other biblical texts, through midrash (rabbinic commentary on the Bible) and kabbalistic mystical interpretation, to literary discussion proper. The mutual relationship between Jewish hermeneutics and contemporary literary theory is treated more extensively in Daniel Boyarin's *Intertextuality and the Reading of Midrash* and David Stern's *Midrash and Theory*, which focus on midrashic interpretation. Other books shift emphasis to the literary side, exploring Judaic hermeneutic impulses within contemporary theory. Susan Handelman's *The Slayers of Moses* remains the most ambitious undertaking in this direction to date; with Jose Faur's *Golden Doves with Silver Dots* in many ways a similar project. Other books focus on individual writers in a more sociological framework that places them within currents of Jewish American adjustment. Among these works are Norman Finkelstein's *The Ritual of New Creation*, Rael Meyerowitz's *Transferring to America*, and Susanne Klingenstein's *Enlarging America*, each of which focuses on different clusters of cases, constructing models of Jewish American interpretation in terms of the tangled crossings of Jewish identity and the forces of Americanization.

This chapter is concerned less with questions of personal Jewish identity and biography than with how literary theory reflects Judaic concerns and, even more, represents itself to be doing so. Bloom, Hartman, and Hollander each offer a theory of figures – of literature as figural language and indeed of language itself as constituted of figures – and place that theory in terms of Jewish practices of reading and interpretation. These critics treat every element in a text (and, more extensively and less designedly, in language as a whole) as a "figure" or "trope" representing some further sense, meaning, level, dimension. They see the forms, shapes, and interrelationships of these figures of language not merely as recording experience, but as actively shaping it. In analyzing such figural patterns, they give special attention to rhetoric, not only to the traditional "figures of speech" but to a wide range of tropes, including patterns of sound and grammar, of letters and pauses; and not only in regard to rhetoric's traditional purposes of persuasion but also to a very broad sense of the power of language actively to shape and project orders and meanings. For these critics, this shaping and ordering power constantly points forward from figure to figure and meaning to meaning, in an on-going, multiple, and fundamentally open process. A radical image of this process of figures generating figures is that of the chain, in which figures are both linked and differentiated, displaced and extended.

This is the core of the interpretative and theoretical work of the Jewish American scholars under consideration here. The fact that Bloom, Hartman, and Hollander themselves recognize or construct this work as Judaic is as arresting and intriguing as the light the work sheds on Jewish hermeneutics as such. For it must be emphasized that their own sources and resources are far from exclusively Judaic, extending instead into many different critical, theoretical, and historical movements: romantic theory, symbolist aesthetics, New Criticism, formalism, Nietzschean philosophy, structuralism, and deconstruction, as well as a variety of religious discourses. Their work has much in common with each of these antecedents. Figural theory, for example, shares with symbolist and New Critical aesthetics a sense of poetry's self-referring power, of the opacity of poetic components which do not "represent" in the sense of pointing outside the text, but rather of pointing back to poetic language's own compositional elements. And yet, there are also marked differences. Symbolists and New Critics treated the literary text as a closed art-object, an icon, monumental in its unity, transcending both outside connection and temporality itself. In contrast, Bloom, Hartman, and Hollander see the text as setting in motion open-ended relationships of ever-possible and ever-multiple tropes pointing always outward and forward to further tropes. They do not regard the artwork as an icon of monumental transcendence but as interactive, multiplying, and open – both representing and penetrated by temporal process. The symbolists and New Critics understood "self-referential" language as a kind of turning away from "reality," but Bloom, Hartman, and Hollander see "figural" language as actually representing and engaging the characterisitcs of human experience – time, multiplicity, and the material world. The poem (or language) does not mean only "itself" and hence "mean" nothing. It instead represents and celebrates human experience and creativity.

Similarly, figural theory is deconstructive – insofar as it ceconstructs a reference-oriented notion of linguistic meaning – but I would call it a "positive" deconstruction (as opposed to, for example, Paul De Man's "negative" version). For while Bloom, Hartman, and Hollander believe in the terms developed by sign-theory, that "signifiers" do not represent a ' signified" situated beyond and outside the chain of figures, they nevertheless insist that representation *does* takes place *among* the "signifiers" (*within* the chain of figures) as they inter-refer in an on-going process of articulation. They do not hold that language always falls into its own self-reference, losing all reference and meaning, but shift attention to the chain of figures themselves, to their structure and composition, as the site where meaning takes shape and is experienced. Positive deconstruction is an attempt, while foregoing a preestablished "signified," nevertheless to trace orders of meaning among the signifiers themselves – rather than, as in negative deconstruction, to regard the displaced signified as meaning's collapse.

Just exactly how the positive deconstruction of figural theory, with its complex history of connection, can be situated as Jewish (or not) is a problem the theorists themselves have addressed. In a 1958 essay on "The Question of Identity," for instance, John Hollander recognizes that the Jewish poet writing in English finds him/herself in a syncretist position, working in a language that is "a curious blend, originally, of dissimilar Romance and Germanic tongues, yoked together by the violence of Christianity," and whose "history is almost inextricably involved, until the eighteenth century, with the history of the Christian religion in England" (85). In his essay "The Question of American Jewish Poetry," written thirty-six years later, Hollander complicates the matter further, noting that the English Bible is "a polemically Protestant translation of an orthodox Christian book called the Old Testament, which is itself a Christian interpretive translation of the Torah" (44). But the question of filiation is even further complicated: not only is the Jewish American scholar or poet situated in a culture that is not Jewish, albeit one with complex connections to Jewish elements, but Jewish culture itself is deeply and constantly marked by interaction with the cultures that surround and penetrate it, the Jewish American being just one such case. Something may be "Jewish" in aspect, not as contained within absolute cultural boundaries, but because of emphasis and relative dominance, tendencies and directions, within common and overlapping cultural territories. So while clear distinctions or stark oppositions are difficult to make, certain trends and emphases can nevertheless be identified. Some of these characteristics can be described as Hebraic, even when they appear within an alternative culture where they may function differently. I will discuss this later, in considering the Hebraism of American culture. More generally, a striking feature of contemporary thinking is the way it rediscovers or newly emphasizes impulses that have always been central to Judaic culture, especially in the current attempt to make sense of a world without traditional metaphysics. This coincidence is vivid in the current work of Jewish American theorists.

What, in the traditions of Judaic hermeneutics, do the figural theories of Bloom, Hollander, and Hartman rediscover? To begin with, an attention to the material of language – its component letters, redundancies, even tones and accents. These form a basis for interpretation, as first clarified by Rabbi Akiva –

> not only the meaning of terms and words, but also their sound, the shape of the letters, the vocalization points and their shapes and sounds...the musical signs...the small decorative additions to the letters...the frequency with which words and letters appear in a verse or a chapter, the absence of one of the letters from a biblical portion...the numerical value of letters, words, and whole verses –

and so on, all become "signifiers," that is, significant signs inviting and sustaining interpretative activity (Dan, "Midrash and the Dawn of Kabbalah," 128).

Secondly, in midrash (as in kabbalah and, differently, in discussions of Jewish law, or *halakhah*, as well) there is an open-endedness to discussion, in which generating further discussion seems itself to be a motive, rather than completing a topic finally and decisively. Multiple interpretations emerge alongside each other, without the compulsion to harmonize them or render them consistent. Such open-ended, multiple discussions take their own distinctive shape and direction in the kabbalah's "infinities of Torah," as Moshe Idel calls it; and still other forms in *halakhic* disputation. Always and through all, interpretation is conceived fundamentally as text responding to text, interpretation to interpretation, a procedure that begins within the corpus of Scripture itself (see Kugel, *Early Biblical Literature*, Fishbane, *The Exegetical Tradition*, Bruns, "Midrash and Allegory"). Texts comment on texts forming a chain of mutually referring figures. Indeed, the very notion of figural chain finds an echo in the midrashic method of *harizah*, enchainment. Thus, as Daniel Boyarin explains, Ben-Azzai describes his method of interpretation as "stringing words of Torah [to each other]...and the words were as radiant as when they were given from Sinai." This notion of linkage or chain is, according to Boyarin, the fundamental practice of midrash, "linking texts with texts, that is, revealing the hermeneutic connection between the Prophets and Writings and the Torah" (*Intertextuality and the Reading of Midrash*, 109–110). Michael Fishbane similarly describes midrashic practice as breaking "the ordinary connections between the letters of a word and between words of a sentence [such that] each word may encode numerous plays and possibilities; and each phrase has any number of potential correlations within Scripture." He calls this method "enchainment (*harizah*) of possibilities" (*The Exegetical Tradition*, 13). Above all, multiplicity, on-going production, and even contradiction among interpretations are seen not as failure and confusion but as a positive service to God.

Consider, in this light, the poetry and poetics of John Hollander. As Bloom notes, Hollander's poetry is replete with Judaic reference – with biblical figures, Genesis scenes, rabbinic lore, and lettristic puns (Bloom, *Agon*, 289–317). But more important, Hollander's very *notions* of poetry are in fundamental ways deeply grounded in Judaic textuality. He associates his own trope for figuration itself, the figure of echo, with the Hebrew *bat kol*, signalling divine voice as it transverses into human utterance (*The Figure of Echo*, 16–17). When he answers his own "Question of American Jewish Poetry" by quoting Paul Celan quoting Marina Tsvetayeva's "All Poets are Jews," he is proposing poetry and Jewishness as figures for each other, with an added clue to the ways this can work in the very chain of quotation he is citing. For Hollander, poetry, like Jewish textual practice, is woven out of chains of reference, allusion, quotation, invocation, memory, commentary, words responding to and generating other words, figures of figures of figures. The very letters, sounds, grammatical arrangements, and even page design take on figural meanings. Moreover, as he explains in "Hearing and Overhearing the Psalms" and "The Question of American Jewish Poetry," poetry is born out of misunderstanding, "misconstruings and reconstructions" (*The Work of Poetry*, 114), that is, out of ever new figural (mis-) representations. Poetic creation may be described for Hollander as a chain of displacement, where the two terms stand in almost paradoxical tension, asserting at once both attachment and transgression. Hollander insists in his essay on "Originality" that beginnings – even the one in Genesis – work between a double meaning in the word "origin": one that "clings to our

thoughts of independence, noncontingent selfhood, privacy of our own experience, creativity"; and another that refers back, in its very etymological
body, to a prior "source," a "point of origin of a stream," recourse to which
constitutes originality (*The Work of Poetry*, 14–15). Significantly, he refers
these chains of meaning, chains *as* meaning, to the Hebrew Bible and its
modes of interpretation. "True poetry," he suggests, "...partakes of what
Rabbi Ben Bag Bag said of Torah itself: Turn it and turn it over again, for
everything is in it" ("The Question of American Jewish Poetry," 41). Like
Scripture, poetry is inexhaustible. It is the very nature of poetic language always to mean more, to conjure further levels of sense, further possibilities of
meaning – that is, figural extensions. For Hollander, figural poetics is Jewish
poetics.

In Bloom and Hartman, the homology with hermeneutic principles of
Jewish interpretation is still more fully insisted upon. The homology is acknowledged as well by scholars of Jewish hermeneutics. This mutual confir-
mation registers not only the striking and important conjunction of Judaic
and contemporary interests mentioned above, but also what amounts to a
certain kind of productive circularity. The theorists of Jewish interpretation
have, in fact, read and collaborated with the literary theorists who in turn regard their hermeneutic as (in some sense) Jewish – a "merging," as Hartman
puts it in his own essay in *Midrash and Literature*, "between literary criticism and midrashic modes" (12). The result has been a fertile mutual figur-
ing of classical Jewish hermeneutics and contemporary literary theory in one
another.

David Stern, a scholar of Jewish hermeneutics, usefully sums up these
convergences between what seems "the wayward, antic features of midrashic
interpretation" and modern theory:

> The typical midrashic predilection for multiple interpretations rather than for
> a single truth behind the text; its irresistible desire to tease out the nuances of
> Scripture rather than use interpretation to close them off, and, most of all, the
> way midrashic discourse mixes text and commentary, violating the boundaries
> between them and intentionally blurring their differences, flourishing precisely
> in the grayish no-man's land between exegesis and literature.
>
> (*Midrash and Theory*, 3)

Conversely, Hartman invokes midrashic notions of text to illuminate current literary theories of "textuality," where unity gives way to intertextuality (the relationship among texts) and a principle of "frictionality" explores
and affirms the frictions, gaps, traces, and other heterogeneous relationships between textual elements that generate interpretation without closure
("The Struggle for the Text," 12–13). Hartman plainly places his own critical

attitudes in terms of Jewish traditions, which can be seen to frame and penetrate his essays even when they are not overtly related to Jewish concerns. His persistent focus on the status of criticism and the relationships between text and commentary is (as he confirms most clearly in his essay, "On the Jewish Imagination") allied to "the text-dependency of the Jewish imagination." The Jewish mode of commentary on commentary, whose forms mix different genres, which are composed of chains of quotations and responses to them and include "divergent and adversary opinions" ("On the Jewish Imagination," 208–209) – these are the features that characterize Hartman's own critical writings. I would call this method *lettristic*. The configuration of letters and words into rhetorical patterns, etymologies, puns, wordplays become the basis both of particular interpretations and of a general approach to texts. This occurs most extensively and theoretically in Hartman's "The Voice of the Shuttle," where the interplay of textual units closely worked on a micro level becomes a general figure for literary imagination. Hartman's attention to letter and word as material shape and generative power accords with the treasuring of every letter and tittle evident in midrash. His description of midrash as involving "wordplay," "close reading," and "textual opacity," with a resistance to "overunifying its words or unifying them in a totalizing way," applies to his own reading practices and theoretical commitments as well ("Midrash as Law," 349–350, 339). Similarly, his own lettristic focus accords with the "letter mysticism" of kabbalah ("On the Jewish Imagination," 205). Indeed, Hartman's practice as a whole can be compared to what he calls the "Jewish *via hermeneutica*," its creative commentary and its "aspectical richness that faces . . . in all directions" ("Jewish Tradition," 96, 102).

The homology between Jewish hermeneutics and contemporary theory appears most boldly in Bloom's work. As I suggested earlier, deconstruction may be either positive or negative. Bloom confronts this distinction in "The Breaking of Form," his contribution to *Deconstruction and Criticism*, where he associates what I call positive deconstruction with "a magical theory of language, as [in] the Kabbalists"; as against the "thoroughgoing linguistic nihilism" of, for example, De Man ("The Breaking of Form," 4). Hollander in his Introduction to Bloom's *Poetics of Influence* insists that the "and" of *Deconstruction and Criticism* should be read as disjunctive (*Poetics of Influence*, xii). But Bloom's approach is deconstructive in its own positive, Judaic way. On one hand, like all deconstructionists, Bloom sets out to rupture what he sees as the essentially metaphysical "belief in the real presence of the literary text" ("The Breaking of Form," 8). On the other hand, he opposes to the metaphysical aesthetic of unity and closure, a kabbalistic hermeneutics (drawn from Gershom Scholem's pioneering work on Jewish mysticism), which he polemically sums up: "There are no texts, but only interpretations" ("The Breaking of Form," 7). "Words...refer only to words," so that we live in "a world of words to the end of it" ("The Breaking of Form," 9).

Like Hartman, Bloom asserts that the relationship of word to word and text to text at the heart of Judaic interpretative practices is at the heart of his own theory and practice as well. But while Hartman's Judeo-critical interest often takes the form of a defense of commentary, Bloom's tends instead to be structured around the notion of tradition, again seen as relation between text and text, but now through the tracks of literary history and as the very impulse of artistic creation itself. It is important to emphasize that Bloom does not simply reject tradition, does not offer an ethos of mere heresy and rebellion against it. For Bloom, only those with tradition know what it means to want to escape from it. As Hartman observes of the Jewish imagination, tradition can seem "a suffering burden" ("On the Jewish Imagination," 210). Bloom (no doubt from his own Jewish experience) knows full well the potentially crushing weight of a tradition that may seem to make overwhelming claims. Thus he glorifies "the freedom to have a meaning of one's own," but he immediately insists: "Such freedom is illusory unless it is achieved against a prior plenitude of meaning, which is tradition" ("The Breaking of Form," 3–4). His is an "antithetical," "agonistic" hermeneutic, in which "all critical reading aspiring towards strength must be as transgressive as it is aggressive" (7). But it is not a hermeneutic of repudiation. Nor is it a blind cry for the autonomous and self-sufficient self. On the contrary, Bloom's theory finely gauges how the self emerges from a past not its own; with the dream of self-birth at once most far-fetched and yet also most necessary. "What happens," Bloom asks in "The Dialectics of Tradition," "if one tries to write, or teach, or to think, or even to read without the sense of a tradition?" And he answers: "Why, nothing at all happens, just nothing." "The concept," he adds, "deeply derives in the Hebraic Mishnah, an oral handing-over, or transmission of oral precedents, of what has been found to work, of what has been instructed successfully" (*Poetics of Influence*, 109–110).

Poetic originality, for Bloom, is not creation from nothing but rather creation from something – a project in some ways equally mysterious and difficult. For tradition both makes new creation possible and yet threatens to overwhelm it. Hence the need for an "antithetical" stance – positive and negative at once. Positive generation wrestles with the negation that frees. This is agon, contest, rebirth as transgression, and not passive homage. New creation is not the harmonious and cumulative result of what has gone before. It is, rather, aggressive, competitive, even violent. To inherit and to conquer are mutually entangled. Devotion acquires the surprising but necessary face of revisionism.

Bloom's theory of tradition is no less a theory of figures. Its notions of tradition are figural and its charts of how tradition evolves, is inherited, and is transformed, proceed by way of figures. "Poetic knowledge," he writes, "is necessarily a knowledge by tropes" ("The Breaking of Form," 15). "Freedom of meaning is wrested by combat, of meaning against meaning," such that "works are bound to be misread, that is to say, troped by the reader" ("The Breaking of Form," 5–6). Bloom offers a number of schema for these processes of "misreading" or "revisionism," each of which describes relations among figures which also function as figures for each other. He works with terms from literary history and criticism, from psychology, from rhetoric and from religion. But each of these acts as figures for the others, just as each is made up of relationships among figures.

Bloom's series of works, from *The Anxiety of Influence* through *The Map of Misreading* and *Poetry and Repression*, transformed the understanding of tradition and influence from a cumulative and contained transmission of allusions, to a sense of dramatic trajectories of confrontation, appropriation, repression, and transfiguration. Indeed, the strongest influences may be those which have been repressed and therefore are absent, or present as negations, in the text; for they are the most threatening to creativity. The most accessible figures for this process are therefore probably psychological ones. These provide reasonably familiar terms for the aggressive ambivalence that in many ways makes up the core of Bloomian creativity. The processes of transgression/transformation that propel creative misreading are, on this level, described in Oedipal terms, as poet-sons contending against poet-fathers. (How this would work for women writers is a large, separate topic [see Gilbert and Gubar, *The Madwoman in the Attic*, Diehl, *Women Poets*]). Attachment and resistance, dependence and independence, awe and aggression – such Oedipal ambivalence becomes the very modes of literary creativity.

Yet the psychoanalytic model remains but one in a series which in turn mutually figure each other. As figures, Bloom's procedures are explicitly rhetorical. Most important to our immediate interest is the specifically Judaic set of figures, which Bloom often associates with Scholem – who, as Bloom writes, himself traces a process of "continuity and discontinuity" in Jewish history ("Introduction," 2). These become the central figural system in *Kabbalah and Criticism*. Hollander describes these figural overlays and the place of kabbalistic figures in them:

> The peculiar function of Bloom's little book on Kabbalah was to reinforce this connection between trope and psychic defense. By analyzing the . . phases of Creation as poetically treated in the Zohar and, with important revisions,

centuries afterward by the Safed Kabbalists, he found a basic rhythm of contraction, filling and breaking, and restitution, which he rushed to diagram into his prior schemata as areas of what he termed limitation, substitution, and representation.

(Hollander, Introduction to Bloom, *Poetics of Influence*, xxv–xxvi)

Bloom elaborates in his essay, "Poetry, Revisionism, Repression." The Lurianic account of creation as contraction (*zimzum*), destruction (breaking of vessels), and subsequent restitution (*tikkun*) becomes for Bloom a figure for poetic creativity, as also for its psychic and rhetorical figurations:

> The Lurianic dialectic follows its initial irony of Divine contraction, or image of limitation, with a process it calls the breaking-of-the-vessels, which in poetic terms is the principle of rhetorical substitution, or in psychic terms is the metamorphic element in all defenses, their tendency to turn into one another, even as tropes tend to mix into one another. What follows in the later, regressive Kabbalah is called tikkun or "restitution" and is symbolic representation.
>
> (*Poetics of Influence*, 131–133)

Bloom's "map of misprision" – that is, of critical-creative (mis)reading – thus offers a chart of Lurianic "limitation/substitution/representation" as another figural representation of the rhetorical relationships and psychic tropes of poetic creativity (*Poetics of Influence*, 139).

Bloom's Judaic involvement, however, goes beyond any specific kabbalistic reference (as it goes beyond the flamboyant introduction, in Bloom's first book, of Martin Buber as a prism for reading Shelley and beyond the several essays he has published on Jewish American culture, particularly in *Poetics of Influence* and *Agon*). Bloom's psychological imagination is itself vehemently Freudian, where Freud (against psychoanalytic orthodoxies) is himself viewed as a great creator of figures. Freud is also, for Bloom, a great Jewish creator. Freud, Kafka, and Scholem together emerge as the outstanding writers of modern Jewish culture: and this is exactly because each is a great writer of figural creativity (Bloom, "The Strong Light of the Canonical"). The psychological, the kabbalistic, the poetic all thus intersect, with the creation of powerful figures central to each. Indeed, this figural power comes to be the core Jewish impulse connecting them to each other. Judaism itself becomes for Bloom the life of generating, multiplying, echoing figures. Kabbalah emerges as a poetics, and literary interpretation, a figure for Judaism: "A poem is a dance of substitutions, a constant breaking-of-the-vessels, as one limitation undoes a representation, only to be restituted in its turn by a fresh representation." As in Jewish interpretation, "Every strong poem [knows] that there is only interpretation, and that every interpretation answers an earlier interpretation, and then must yield to a later one" (*Poetics of Influence*, 141).

What prevents such figural multiplication from merely dissolving into an abyss of language, of words referring to words? Or, what will regulate the chain of figures, to keep it from losing all connection and direction? Such dissolution is the threat deconstruction has seemed to pose. Bloom addresses this danger in the concluding essay of *Kabbalah and Criticism*, "The Necessity of Misreading": "Tradition is itself then without a referential object," he writes dauntlessly. "Tradition is now for us, the one literary sign that is not a sign, because there is no other sign to which it can refer" (*Kabbalah and Criticism*, 98). Here he seems to let go all anchors. But this denial of a stable object to which we can refer – including tradition itself – entails not nihilism and collapse, but the taking up of the burden of meaning within the process of representation itself. "Texts don't have meanings," he continues, "except in their relations to other texts, so that there is something uneasily dialectical about literary meaning...A text is a relational event, and not a substance to be analyzed" (106). Meaning here is not denied, but located in relations, generated through a chain which is constantly refiguring itself, discontinuous and continuous in dialectical tension. Or, to use another figure for this chain of figuration, "meaning is always wandering around between texts" (108). Bloom's "wandering" parallels Hartman's "error" ("Meaning, Error, Text," 148), describing "a conservative mode of transgression" in which exegesis would "extend the meaning of Torah without displacing its symbols and words" (Hartman, "Jewish Tradition as/and Other," 97, 100). Hollander, as we saw, calls such figural multiplication and extension, "echo."

But is it not extraordinary to claim that Judaic hermeneutic is radically figural, when, through the entire history of the Christian West, it has been specifically relegated to the "letter" and denounced as "literal"? In his essay, "Before Moses was, I am," Bloom insists on the irony that "St. Paul accused the Jews of being literalizers...which of course the great rabbis never were" (*Poetics of Influence*, 392–393). Here indeed the contest is joined. The return to lettrism in figural theory is (as Jacques Derrida's work also displays) in many ways a restaging of an ancient quarrel, a reassertion of ancient Hebraic culture against Western metaphysical system. The new stage is contemporary thought itself, with its expanding critique of traditional metaphysics and in particular its protest against the splitting of experience into a metaphysical spirit as against body, temporality, and materiality. The Jewish attachment to the letter never, of course, denied spirit; but rather, conceived of spiritual meaning as generated through and experienced within the concrete material reality of daily conduct and of history. As Hartman puts it, Judaism is characterized by "the hermeneutic character of its spirituality" which revises "the relation not only between primary and secondary literature, but between letter and spirit" ("Other," 96–7). Its "spirit has become textualized" ("Text and Spirit," 171). Figural theory's return to the letter is not a return to the "literal" in the traditional senses. It recovers the letter not as dead body, but as generating ever new dimensions of meaning, the possibilities of further figural senses.

The quarrel is old, but the terms have changed. Bloom, it is true, loudly insists that what is called the Old and the New Testaments should by all rights be called the Original and Belated Testaments, with the latter an anxious set of competitive figures for the former. Yet he also insists on the syncretism – the dynamic interaction and exchange among different religious traditions – deeply embedded in Jewish culture. Even Judaism's commitment to study has sources in the legacy of Plato (*Poetics of Influence*, 371). Our (English) reading of the Bible, Hollander muses, is indelibly experienced through "the complex relations between the Hebrew Bible, the strange and powerful tendentious reading of it called the Old Testament, and the various vernacular translations" (*The Work of Poetry*, 113). Features that are prominent in Judaic culture emerge, Hartman points out, in the religious and literary works of Christian culture, the New Testament parables, William Blake, Dante ("On the Jewish Imagination," 207–208). Indeed, the figural imagination, the imagining of figures, obviously asserts itself in every culture, every society, every religion. Stark boundaries cannot be drawn. Differences are not absolute, but rather a matter of emphasis, dominance, concentration, role, and also structure.

This syncretism and mutual influence is particularly potent and consequential in the practices of biblical typology. The figural extensions of Judaic hermeneutic deeply penetrated Christian interpretation, residing there as a Hebraic element and connection to its Judaic grounds. The New Testament in its very construction incorporated figures and structures from the Hebrew Scriptures, reducing them to foreshadowings for its own prophetic claims, so that the "Old Testament" became a figure and type for the "New." Yet this Christian typology, with its four (basic) levels of meaning that casts the Hebrew figures as "fulfilled" in the Christian ones, remains intimately bound both to the material and the hermeneutic of the Judaism it incorporated. Bloom takes this sacred bull by the horns in his attacks on this sort of typology: "I am moved to reject the idealized modes of interpretation ... from early typology on to the revival of figura by Erich Auerbach and the Blakean Great Code of Northrop Frye. No text, secular or religious, fulfills another text, and all who insist otherwise merely homogenize literature" (*Poetics of Influence*, 402; see also Hartman, "On the Jewish Imagination," 214). Auerbach, so responsible for introducing the figura back into twentieth-century literary discourse, was himself Jewish. His account of Christian typology as a hierarchy of figural fulfillment is in fact descriptive and not apologetic. Yet Bloom is pointing up a difference that is pivotal. As Auerbach himself elucidates, the Christian figural system is essentially vertical. It layers figure on figure upward in a hierarchy that finds its fulfillment (and abolishment) in the overdetermining, culminating, and concentrating figure of Christ. The Judaic figural impulse, in contrast, remains horizontal. Figures generate figures in on-going chains that are never "subsumed and completed," as is the case in New Testament figuration (Hartman, "On the Jewish Imagination," 214).

Nowhere are the claims and consequences of these typological patterns more gripping than in the context of American culture. In and through them, moreover, the particular and somewhat amazing embraiding of Hebraism with America itself emerges. This cultural story is most fully engaged by Sacvan Bercovitch. Bercovitch's interpretation of American textuality and its Puritan origins is a most complex, sophisticated, and elaborate investigation into figures, their patterns, transformations, energies, and claims. He recovers, to start, the rich imaginative venture that was American Puritanism. As he shows, this was at once theological, historical, and literary, with the Bible and its interpretation in many ways the lattice supporting and propelling diverse commitments. From *The Puritan Origins of the American Self* through *The American Jeremiad* and *The Rites of Assent*, Bercovitch retraces the web that translated a specific and essentially marginal undertaking into a cosmic, universal, momentous turning point in the (sacred) history of all mankind. The links between sacred and secular, transcendent and historical, immediate and cosmic; between the individual, the representative, and the corporate, run through the biblical figures, typologies, and correlations by which the Puritans understood themselves.

In this recovery of Puritan imagination, Bercovitch pursues the Puritans themselves back to their Hebraic sources. This is the case, first, through Bercovitch's uncovering of the complex architecture connecting figural levels, sequences, and extrapolations in the Puritan interpretation of biblical text as historical venture, and historical venture (and each individual's place in it) as biblical text. But beyond the impressive mechanisms of figural elaboration, Bercovitch also unveils the force of figural imagination itself in Puritan writings, presenting, for example, Cotton Mather's *Magnalia Christi Americana* as an "important work of the figurative imagination" that "recasts fact into image and symbol" ("New England Epic," 337–338). This works like a doubling of Bercovitch's own Hebraic figural imagination on the Puritan one. Against a view of Puritan writing as a literary presentation of theological or cultural positions, Bercovitch shows how the presentation itself – the language, images, rhetorics deployed – shape the vision and understanding in enduring and powerful ways. Again, attention shifts from a sense of representation as a passive transmission of prior understandings, to its being an active shaper of meaning through the composition, dynamic, structure, and elements of the acts of discourse themselves.

Hebraism is evident, then, in the Puritan return to Old Testament texts and emphases, forms and models, including the whole notion of federal theology as covenantal binding of individual with community in a secular-sacral, spiritual-historical trajectory. But as Bercovitch's writings probe, not the mere use of the Hebrew Bible or even figuralism, but also its peculiar thrust forges America's bonds with Judaic/Hebraic modes. The American venture, as he reveals, presents a moment of transformation in what had been the uses and directions of figural understanding. In Bercovitch's exposition, American figuration commits itself to time, to temporal trajectory, in distinctive ways. Its markers are process, project, a "visionary history of the future" (*The Rites of Assent*, 83), the New World as figura "directed toward the future" (81), America itself seen as "errand" and "defined (in opposition to Old World 'motionlessness') by the preposition *into*: into the future as into the wilderness" (85). The Puritans, that is, rehistoricized the figura after medieval Christendom had countered Judaistic historical dimension by restructuring biblical typology upward as transcendent fulfillment beyond history. The Puritans, seeing their own concrete and communal venture as projected "promise" rather than fulfilled "providence" (81) restore to biblical figuration its radical historicity. One might say that the Puritans redirected the Christian transformation of figures from vertical ahistoricity back into horizontal process (without of course ceasing to be Christian). What had been considered signs of eternity became instead signs of and in history. This historical impulse became even more pronounced for the Puritans' later American inheritors, translating – to use Emerson's and Whitman's term – into endless, horizontal extension of figures as on-going energy of invention, possibility, opportunity. The figural chain in all its open-ended energetic power becomes the mark of an American poetics itself claiming to enact American cultural identity.

This is of course not to claim – as Bercovitch does not – that the American is Jewish and the Jewish, American. Yet it is surely out of his Jewish sign-sense that Bercovitch describes the Puritans as a "self-declared people of the Book" and their identity as a "process whereby a community could constitute itself by publication, declare itself a nation by verbal fiat, define its past, present, and future by proclamation" (*The Rites of Assent*, 69–70). What Bercovitch's figural analyses uncover is powerful common cause substantiating how contemporary Jewish American scholars can see in American writing hermeneutic commitments that coincide, or overlap, or extend with Jewish ones: that is, because historically they did so coincide in special ways. On this ground it makes a certain sense when Bloom says of Hollander's poetry that it "succeeds in being American by being Judaistic, and vice versa" (*Agon*, 293); or when he reads Emerson, Whitman, Stevens as a figural poetics in which trope generates trope in an open chain. Bloom is not arbitrarily imposing a Hebraic hermeneutic on alien, unrelated, and illegitimate objects. Emerson, Whitman, Stevens *are* writers in a Hebraic strain, because the American, Puritan culture which they inherited and radicalized *was* itself profoundly Hebraized. The chains of figures that fundamentally characterize their poetic are both American and Jewish, especially for these Jewish Americans now interpreting them – but with implications that extend deep into contemporary thought, its critique of metaphysics and its rethinking of history.

Ultimately, the central figure for this figural theory is history itself. In some sense these theories of figures reconfirm the old cliché that Judaism is a religion of history. Midrash itself emerges, as its interpreters insist, from the need to reweave text with history (see Boyarin, *Intertextuality and the Reading of Midrash*, Kugel, *Early Biblical Literature*, Fishbane, *The Exegetical Tradition*). As Hartman observes of the old typological conflicts, rabbinic interpretation

> stands in a "negative" relation toward the Messianic event as a fulfillment of time and of the Word... What we learn from and against typology is the temporal complexity of the text–reality nexus, even the temporal complexity of signification generally. The meaning of signs is always being displaced or revised by the mythical and seductive image of a *grands temps*.
>
> ("Meaning, Error, Text," 147)

Hartman seems at times a bit nervous about the relativism that historical immersion also opens. But he seems even more suspicious of claims to absolute knowledge, closure, and finality that seek to transcend historicity. To embrace the figural nature of words is to accept partial, fragile conditions, which also frame our lives. "Partial knowledge is the normal condition, then, of living in the context of words," he writes. "Words themselves help us tolerate that state" (*Saving the Text*, 137). And, if this life of words seems precarious, it is also creative, life-affirming: "The structure of words within words, while complicating the process of understanding, also founds the possibility of interpretation or of exchanging word for word... Writing goes on and on, and always at risk. 'I write and write and write,' says Mme. Blavatsky, 'as the Wandering Jew walks and walks and walks'" (*Saving the Text*, 144).

The issue seems finally, if tentatively, to involve the ethics of living within historical experiences, and the dangers, if also the energies, of attempting ultimate resolutions to them. Against absolute claim, total command, and final closures, against the "desire for reality-mastery as aggressive and fatal" (*Saving the Text*, 96), stands the commitment to on-going figural displacements. The delight in figures signals not the loss of meaning but its refinding within acts of signification: or rather, loss as inextricably bound up with finding. It stands against final fulfillments, the apocalyptic claims which Bercovitch analyzes and defuses into on-going, constantly renegotiated temporization, and which Bloom faces head-on in "Apocalypse Then." Describing apocalyptic desire as "angry wish-fulfillment" (*Poetics of Influence*, 381) and a "despair over the here and now," (374) Bloom opposes it to what he describes as "the Way of the normative rabbis" in their commitment to "right action" (375), which never abandons the material world of history (see Alter, *After the Tradition*). While insisting on complex penetrations of gnostic impulses into Jewish mysticism, Bloom still defines normative Judaism as "an ethical way of life based on sacred texts as interpreted by Rabbinic authority" (*Poetics of Influence*, 370). This involves a commitment to the provisional that apocalypse betrays and repudiates. Indeed, in his suspicion of finality, fulfillment, and apocalypse, Bloom may be, to his own dismay, more normative than he would like to think. He, moreover, suggestively links this Judaic impulse to a radical Protestantism such as founded America: "Protestant dissent, which has roots in normative rabbinicism, [defends] the Talmudic insistence upon right action and deep study" (*Poetics of Influence*, 379). While pledging himself in many ways to radical discontinuity, contest, and negation – in which figural systems can contend against each other as well – Bloom embraces transgressive chains of creativity whose shape and meaning, however, may finally be evident only after the fact. In the end, Jewish identity may be only post factum; clarified, even defined, only "when viewed retrospectively" (*Poetics of Influence*, 357). This, in part, expresses a distance from (normative or historical) Judaism as the exclusive, or even the ultimate commitment for Bloom and, for that matter, the other Jewish American theorists under discussion here. But it also gives to history the last word, recognizing the full claim of the actual, what Bloom calls "facticity." Identity itself emerges not as fixed and final, but as the unexpected triumph of claims that at first challenged tradition; but which over time have taken their place within it, even "conceal[ing] its changes under the masks of the normative" (*Poetics of Influence*, 353). What is excluded is final closures. In Bloom, as in Bercovitch, Hartman, Hollander, and many others, Jewish textuality emerges as both resource and image for figural meanings, creative, surprising, and multiple.

REFERENCES AND SELECTED FURTHER READINGS

Alter, Robert. *After the Tradition*. New York: E. P. Dutton, 1969.

Bercovitch, Sacvan. "New England Epic: Cotton Mather's *Magnalia Christi Americana*." ELH 33 (September 1966): 337–351.

The Puritan Origins of the American Self. New Haven: Yale University Press, 1975.

The American Jeremiad. Madison: University of Wisconsin Press, 1978.

The Rites of Assent. New York: Routledge, 1993.

Bloom, Harold. *Kabbalah and Criticism*. New York: The Seabury Press, 1975.

"The Breaking of Form." In Harold Bloom et al. *Deconstruction and Criticism*. New York: Continuum, 1979.

Agon. New York: Oxford University Press, 1982.

"Introduction." In *Gershom Scholem*. Ed. Harold Bloom. New York: Chelsea House, 1987.

The Strong Light of the Canonical: Kafka, Freud, and Scholem as Revisionists of Jewish Culture and Thought. The City College Papers No. 20. New York, 1987.

Poetics of Influence. Ed. John Hollander. New Haven, CT: Henry Schwab, 1988.

Boyarin, Daniel. *Intertextuality and the Reading of Midrash*. Bloomington: Indiana University Press, 1994.

Bruns, Gerald. "Midrash and Allegory." In *The Literary Guide to the Bible*. Eds. Robert Alter and Frank Kermode. Cambridge, MA: Harvard University Press, 1987.

Dan, Joseph. "Midrash and the Dawn of Kabbalah." In *Midrash and Literature*. Eds. Geoffrey Hartman and Sanford Budick. New Haven: Yale University Press, 1986.

Diehl, Joanne Fieht. *Women Poets and the American Sublime*. Bloomington: Indiana University Press, 1990.

Faur, Jose. *Golden Doves with Silver Dots*. Bloomington: Indiana University Press, 1986.

Finkelstein, Norman. *The Ritual of New Creation: Jewish Tradition and Contemporary Literature*. Albany: State University of New York Press, 1992.

Fishbane, Michael. *The Exegetical Tradition*. Cambridge, MA: Harvard University Press, 1998.

Gilbert, Sandra and Susan Gubar. *The Madwoman in the Attic*. New Haven: Yale University Press, 1984.

Goldman, Shalom, ed. *Hebrew and the Bible in America*. Hanover, NH: University of New England Press, 1993.

Halbertal, Moshe. *People of the Book*, Cambridge, MA: Harvard University Press, 1997.

Handelman, Susan. *The Slayers of Moses*. Albany: State University of New York Press, 1982.

Hartman, Geoffrey. *Beyond Formalism*. New Haven: Yale University Press, 1970.

"Preface" to Harold Bloom et al. *Deconstruction and Criticism*. New York: Continuum, 1979.

Criticism in the Wilderness. New Haven: Yale University Press, 1980.

Saving the Text. Baltimore: Johns Hopkins University Press, 1981.

"On the Jewish Imagination." *Prooftexts* 5 (1985): 201–220.

"Meaning, Error, Text." *Yale French Studies* 69 (1985): 145–149.

"The Struggle for the Text." In *Midrash and Literature*. Eds. Geoffrey Hartman and Sanford Budick. New Haven: Yale University Press, 1986.

"Jewish Tradition as/and Other." *Jewish Studies Quarterly* 1.1 (1993): 89–108.

"Midrash as Law and Literature." *Journal of Religion* 74.3 (July 1994): 338–355.

"Text and Spirit." Tanner Lectures On Human Values 21. Ed. Grehe B. Beterson. Salt Lake City: University of Utah Press, 2000.

Hartman, Geoffrey and Sanford Budick, eds. *Midrash and Literature*. New Haven: Yale University Press, 1986.

Hollander, John. "The Question of Identity." *Midstream* (Autumn 1958): 84–88.

The Figure of Echo. Berkeley: University of California Press, 1981.

"Introduction." In Bloom, *Poetics of Influence*. New Haven, CT: Henry Schwab, 1988.

"The Question of American Jewish Poetry." In *What is Jewish Literature*, ed. Hana Wirth-Nesher. Philadelphia: Jewish Publication Society, 1994.

The Work of Poetry. New York: Columbia University Press, 1997.

Idel, Moshe. "Infinities of Torah in Kabbalah." In *Midrash and Literature*. Eds. Geoffrey Hartman and Sanford Budick. New Haven: Yale University Press, 1986.

Klingenstein, Susanne. *Enlarging America: The Cultural Work of Jewish Literary Scholars, 1930–1990*. New York: Syracuse University Press, 1998.

Kugel, James. *Early Biblical Literature*. Philadelphia: Westminster Press, 1986.

Meyerowitz, Rael. *Transferring to America*. Albany: State University of New York Press, 1995.

Stern, David. *Midrash and Theory*. Evanston, IL: Northwestern University Press, 1996.

Weiss Halivni, David. *Pshat and Drash: Plain and Applied Meaning in Rabbinic Exegesis*. New York: Oxford University Press, 1991.

Wolosky, Shira. "Derrida, Jabes, Levinas: Sign Theory as Ethical Discourse." *Prooftexts* 2 (1982): 283–302.

14

TRESA GRAUER

Identity matters: contemporary Jewish American writing

The burden isn't either/or, consciously choosing from possibilities equally difficult and regrettable – it's and/and/and/and/and as well. Life *is* and . . . all the multiplying realities, entangled, overlapping, colliding, conjoined.

(Philip Roth, *The Counterlife*, 350)

Identity . . . is a paradox.
(Daniel Mendelsohn, *The Elusive Embrace*, 34)

Almost twenty-five years ago, Irving Howe introduced his collection, *Jewish American Stories*, by declaring that Jewish American writing had "probably moved past its high point," having found "its voice and its passion at exactly the moment it approache[d] disintegration" (16, 3). Today, Howe's essay still remains the best discussion of the distinctive "voice and passion" that he identified as the trademark of writers of "the immigrant Jewish milieu": "the judgment, affection and hatred they bring to bear upon the remembered world of their youth and the costs exacted by their struggle to tear themselves away . . . the vibration of old stories remembered and retold . . . [and] the lure of nostalgia" (3). Indeed, the terms by which Howe championed such writers as Henry Roth, Bernard Malamud, and Saul Bellow have largely determined what has come to be known as the Jewish American literary canon – so much so that it has become impossible not to cite him in any discussion of this literature. However, by defining Jewish American writing as he did – as a "regional literature" that "would be incomprehensible to a reader who lacked some memory or impression" of its particular context (5) – Howe's prediction of the decline of Jewish American fiction was already inherent in his definition. Given its very specificity of place and time, it was inevitable that the body of literature that he described would eventually cease to appear.

The flourishing of Jewish American writing in the quarter-century since Howe's publication thus not only refutes his belief that "younger, 'Americanized' Jews" would lack the depth of experience required for fiction-making (17), it also, even more significantly, attests to the limitations of any single definition of Jewish American literature. Whereas for Howe, Jewish American literature was that which drew upon the immigrant experience, other critics have identified other criteria for inclusion, measuring Jewishness variously by such categories as "blood" (is the author the child of a Jewish mother?), "language" (is the text written in Hebrew or in Yiddish?), "religiosity" (does the author or the character live according to Jewish law?) and "theme" (does the text reflect, for example, the legacy of the Holocaust?). Each of these individual attempts to delimit the boundaries of Jewish American literature tends to raise more questions than it answers, and the stakes in the discussion are high. As Hana Wirth-Nesher suggests in the introduction to her collection, *What is Jewish Literature?*, "there is no consensus nor is it likely that there ever will be one...in light of the impossibility of arriving at a universally acceptable definition of who is a Jew" (3). Definitions of Jewish American literature are clearly inextricably entwined with the terms by which we understand Jewish American identity.

For many contemporary *writers*, as well as readers, the criteria that may once have served as clear markers of identity no longer provide certainty. Indeed, the very idea of identifying "criteria" subscribes to an essentialized notion of authenticity or truth that many writers today simply do not share. The examples of contemporary Jewish American writing that I consider in this chapter amply demonstrate that the concerns that we as readers may have about the nature and meaning of identity are reflected explicitly in the literature itself. In other words, our critical questions are often the writers' questions as well: what do we mean by Jewish American identity, anyway? And why should it matter? This is not to say, of course, that concerns about identity are unique to contemporary literature; indeed, such questions are an inherent part of modernity.[1] What *is* unique about this literature, however, is that the debates about identity that have long circulated in the culture surrounding the production of Jewish American literature have now become its self-conscious subject. Together, the rich array of literary texts that has emerged over the past twenty-five years should be examined less for its coherence as a body of literature defined *by* an identity as for its focus *on* it.

This shift in focus can be seen as part of a larger cultural climate in which discussions of identity are proliferating. Many critics trace the general rise of interest in identity in the West to the revolutionary politics of the 1960s, in which group identity served as the basis for political solidarity. Ethnic pride and a new awareness of diversity, the ethos of personal liberation emerging from feminist, lesbian and gay politics, the demand for the greater political inclusion and representation of previously marginalized groups – all depended on the claiming of group membership through the recognition of one's "true" self. Against this background, many American Jews who had once embraced the dominant cultural narrative of assimilation began to seek alternative plots that could be read as particularly "Jewish." The pioneering and patriotic Israeli served as one model for a new kind of Jew – particularly after the Six-Day War of 1967, when the image of the Jewish fighter elicited such pride among American Jews that it affected their self-definition as well as the depth of their affiliation with Israel. The Havurah movement – and the Jewish renewal moment more broadly – provided alternative forms of religious identification for those American Jews who were uncomfortable with traditional Jewish practice but who nevertheless sought spiritual expression in Jewish prayer and ritual. Jewish women, gay men, and lesbians grappled with perceptions of themselves as outsiders within Judaism and called for changes within *halakhah* to create a more inclusive Jewish tradition. And growing consciousness of the Holocaust after twenty years of public repression led to a burgeoning of general awareness about Jewish history and memory.

This impulse toward particularism – toward defining the "I" in terms of a particular collective "we" – is still strong today, for Jews and non-Jews alike, and it continues to inform literary representations of identity. But as the celebration of group identity and identity-based politics has become more commonplace, so has its criticism, and recent Jewish American literature that thematizes the search for identity must be read as part of a larger culture that is simultaneously encouraging and suspicious of such gestures. The most serious critique of identity politics to date comes from those who question the very possibility of defining a unified identity as something inherent, authentic, and stable. Despite the deep-rootedness of the belief that identity is grounded in the "truth" of something larger than ourselves, critics today generally argue that identity is formed in specific historical and cultural circumstances, dependent on the social and discursive factors that bring it into being. In contemporary discourse, both the individual and the collective are understood to be comprised of multiple identifications (and disidentifications); our allegiances, ambivalences, and attentions can be said to shift depending on the various social positions that we occupy. For cultural critic Stuart Hall, although the concept of "identity" may no longer be "good to think with" in its original form, it remains a useful term of analysis if, rather than thinking of it as a "transparent...already accomplished fact," we think instead of the ways in which it is produced – "never complete, always in process, and always constituted within, not outside, representation" ("Cultural Identity and Diaspora," 222).

Contemporary literary explorations of Jewish American identity grow out of and reflect this theoretical climate, whereby biology and genealogy can no longer be assumed to be deterministic, and meanings vary according to our conceptual frameworks. In this context, we may understand that while Jewish American writers may once have asked the question, "Who – or what – is a contemporary American Jew?", they are now asking instead, "How do we, as contemporary American Jews, represent ourselves?" The fact that "Jewish" as an identity label is particularly opaque – eliding as it does the categories of race, religion, ethnicity, and culture – makes it an interesting domain for a discussion of identity issues, and underscores the constructed nature of the terms. Contemporary Jewish American literary discussions of identity thus depict the impossibility of any single definition of their subject, acknowledging not only its differences from other cultural groups but also the differences that it contains within itself – whether they be differences of religious, political, or sexual orientation, national or ethnic heritage, geographical region, or class background. The profusion of these representations of identity – the range of contemporary Jewish American voices, the variety of their forms, the diversity of their subject matter – both attests to the vitality of identity as a conceptual category and highlights the fact that contemporary Jewish American identity *depends*, to a large extent, on the mediation of narrative. Whether autobiographical or fictional, historical or mythical, traditional or experimental, contemporary stories of Jewish American identity work against a single, monolithic self-definition and describe instead what Philip Roth calls the "and/and/and/and/and" of possibilities (*The Counterlife*, 350).

The fact that heterogeneity is the basis for this discussion of Jewish identity makes conventional categorizing of the literature somewhat paradoxical; any attempt to group contemporary texts according to discrete thematic "topics" will artificially separate identity categories that the authors themselves intentionally combine. Moreover, some issues are so pervasive that, without much stretching, they could include many of the texts under discussion here and, indeed, they are significant enough to have received their own chapters in this book. Most notably, the Holocaust casts a long shadow over contemporary Jewish American literature; even when its presence in a text is minimal, it nevertheless marks many authors' – and characters' – attempts to come to terms with the meaning of Jewishness. In a different vein, feminism has so transformed the representations of both male and female characters in the last twenty-five years that to designate a separate category for gendered Jewish identity would require including nearly all contemporary writing under its purview.

Yet having said all this, it shall also become clear that some common issues *do* emerge in contemporary Jewish American writing: not only do we see the profound impact of the Holocaust and of feminism, but representations of Jewish identity could also be categorized in relation to ritual, to memory, to place, to family, to sexuality, and to text, among numerous other possibilities. Many critics have charted these thematic developments in recent years: in introductions to anthologies, some notable examples would be Ted Solotaroff, Nessa Rapoport, Ilan Stavans, Marsha Lee Berkman, and Elaine Marcus Starkman; in review essays, Alan Berger, Sylvia Barack Fishman, and S. Lillian Kremer; in literary symposia, Morris Dickstein, Mark Shechner, Aaron Lansky, and Aharon Appelfeld. Such thematic connections are valuable – it is difficult, in fact, to organize a discussion of the literature without them – but it is nonetheless important to remember that the taxonomies are a function of the criticism, and not of the literature itself.

Many of the texts I discuss here could just as easily fit into one category as another; though a particular category heading may meaningfully describe one aspect of a text's treatment of identity, it cannot account for the multiplicity contained within that text. This is best demonstrated, I think, by looking at a number of texts grouped loosely under the thematic rubrics I have described above and then showing the ways in which such labeling may ultimately prove more limiting than helpful. For economy's sake, I have chosen only two examples – "ritual" and "place" – but these choices are arbitrary; it should be clear that the argument holds for the other rubrics as well. Given the fact that so much of contemporary Jewish American writing is explicitly about the multiplicity of identity, the categories can only be the starting points for a discussion of the specific literary strategies and plot conceits that individual authors use to reflect the multifaceted nature of their characters' identities.

Before I turn to these specific categories, however, I would like to focus on one text, Irena Klepfisz's collection of autobiographical essays, *Dreams of an Insomniac*, which provides a particularly good example of the phenomenon that I am describing here: "I write as much out of a Jewish consciousness as I do out of a lesbian/feminist consciousness," explains Klepfisz. "They are both always there, no matter what the topic I might be working on. They are embedded in my writing ... enmeshed to the point that they are not necessarily distinguishable as discrete elements. They merge and blend and blur – for in many ways they are the same" (*Dreams of an Insomniac*, 68–69). Although Klepfisz's commitment to speaking simultaneously as a lesbian and a Jew has made her – justifiably – the subject of numerous analyses of gay Jewish literature and of the parallels between gay and Jewish experience, her efforts to integrate the different components of her sense of self also go beyond those she describes here. As a Holocaust survivor whose vision of American Jewish identity involves "redefining geography and distance" (x),

Klepfisz's work includes not only the memory of her Polish past but also her commitment to peace in the Israeli and Palestinian present. Moreover, her passionate support of Jewish secularism, which "insist[s] on its Jewishness while denying Jewish observance and *halakhah* as the central elements of Jewish identity" (194), often takes shape in both Yiddish and English – with bilingualism functioning to bridge seemingly disparate aspects of her identity.

Arguing that "form and content are determined by our spiritual and material circumstances," Klepfisz breaks conventional genre constraints and disciplinary boundaries to accommodate the "new visions, new content, new perspectives" of her composite identity (xiii). By combining poetry with more conventional prose, fragments of journal entries and letters with snippets of conversations and memories, Klepfisz locates herself particularly within a tradition of women's writing that restructures narrative to accommodate the specific circumstances of women's lives. But the fragmented nature of her writing is not only gendered female; rather, it is a common characteristic of contemporary Jewish American writing, and of contemporary literature more broadly. Moreover, Klepfisz, like many other recent writers on identity, relies heavily on autobiography as a literary strategy that is, by definition, perhaps best suited to the narrative representation of the self, and the multifaceted nature of identity formation. If the voice of the individual "I" is understood not as necessarily "representative" of Jewish American experience – something no post-modern text could be – it seems, nevertheless, to be the voice that speaks most clearly to a readership grappling with some of the same shared points of identification.

Religious practice, belief, and ritual

Thomas Friedmann's 1989 article, "Back to Orthodoxy: The New Ethic and Ethnics in American Jewish Literature," was an early herald of what has come to be seen as a major literary trend: a new era of Jewish American writing that looks seriously at issues of theology, religious observance, and traditional Jewish texts. Building on Cynthia Ozick's claim that "nothing thought or written in Diaspora has ever been able to last unless it has been centrally Jewish" ("Toward a New Yiddish," 168–169), Friedmann pointed to Tova Reich's novel, *Mara* (1978), Rebecca Goldstein's *The Mind-Body Problem* (1983), Anne Roiphe's *Lovingkindness* (1987), and Nessa Rapoport's *Preparing for the Sabbath* (1981) as examples of texts that "establish their ethnicity ... by way of the ritual obligations detailed in the Code of Jewish Law as much as by the moral imperatives of the Covenant" ("Back to Orthodoxy," 73). But while Friedmann was right to chart a new emphasis on "covenental concerns" among Jewish American writers – and we might add to his list other writers like Nathan Englander, Leon Wieseltier, and Allen Hoffman – the return to "Orthodoxy" that he delineates is not as straightforward as it might seem (76). Apart from the fact that many of the characters in these novels "have no romantic illusions about Orthodoxy," as Friedmann himself acknowledges (73), the texts listed above – like many other more recent texts focusing either on issues of observance or on traditional Jewish texts – are concerned not only with Orthodoxy per se, but more specifically with the tensions between traditional Judaism and secularism, feminism, and a gay or lesbian sexual orientation.

In the twelve years since "Back to Orthodoxy" appeared, the number of what Nessa Rapoport calls "Jewishly educated and culturally confident" (Solotaroff and Rapoport, *Writing Our Way Home*, xxix) young writers has grown exponentially, their diverse personal backgrounds reflected along the spectrum of their responses to traditional Judaism. Pearl Abraham's autobiographical first novel, *The Romance Reader* (1995), is unique in its unsentimental depiction of a young Hasidic renegade rebelling against her fate by reading "trafe books" (37), dreaming of escape and the freedom to explore her own desires: "to just be and do, with no one saying they're letting me" (280). Resisting an arranged marriage and the prescribed role for women in her culture, Rachel fantasizes about independence, and the particulars of her fantasies – her desire to wear stockings without seams and to sing out loud, to have a library card and a driver's license and to take a bath with the door open – make eminently clear the strictures of the claustrophobic world that she ultimately flees. In her rejection of the terms by which her community defines her identity, Rachel, like many Jewish American immigrants before her, must recreate herself as an individual bereft of family ties; the novel ends with her "a stranger in this house" that was once her home (296).

Like Rachel, the narrator of Allegra Goodman's *Kaaterskill Falls* (1998) also "romanticizes the secular" and the "diversity of choices" that the world outside of her circumscribed community has to offer, and, like Rachel, Elizabeth's reading "fills her with confused longings for change and new experiences" (54, 227–228, 70). But where Rachel's need for personal autonomy supersedes her relationship to her community, Elizabeth simultaneously embraces the community that sometimes dissatisfies her, because "her religious life is not something she can cast off; it's part of her. Its rituals are not rituals to her; not objects, but instincts" (57). Remarkably free of the angst associated with earlier generations of hyphenated Jewish American identity, Goodman's writing reflects a clarity and a comfort with traditional Jewish life even when her characters chafe at their restrictions. Though Elizabeth describes her Jewishness as an essential – instinctual – part of her identity, she nonetheless wavers when it comes to her six daughters, feeling "the difficulty with girls, the confining of expectations" (282). With indefatigable hope for their futures, Elizabeth gives them each two names, two alternatives – the first, in familiar Yiddish; the second, on their birth certificates, the grand, sophisticated English names of princesses and dancers. The novel as a whole offers other examples of doubling that externalize the identity conflicts that Elizabeth feels within herself: tensions between the individual and the community, the sacred and the secular, the traditional and the modern are played out between family members who each represent one pole of the debate. Such examples of doubling are rife in contemporary Jewish American writing, which highlights the oppositions both to and within individual subjectivity in its efforts to come to terms with the nature of identity.

While *Kaaterskill Falls* considers Jewish identity within the context of one tightly knit – if, nevertheless, diverse – spiritual community, Goodman's latest novel, *Paradise Park* (2001), depicts the search for such a community by one wandering soul, Sharon Spiegelman. The book's epigraph from Augustine contextualizes the quest; we are to read Sharon's account of her odyssey toward enlightenment in light of the (Christian) tradition of religious self-examination and the search for truth. But if Augustine's trajectory from degeneracy to faith has served as the model conversion narrative for both spiritual seekers and scholars of autobiography, then Sharon's is the ultimate parodical account. Raised in a family that was nominally Jewish ("but we didn't belong to anything, or do anything") Sharon goes "looking for magic, and miracles" through a series of "rebirths" that are seemingly endless, since "religions just tend not to take on [her]" (48, 213). Proving Roger Kamenetz's suspicion that the Jewish tradition of universalism has led American Jews to reject Jewish particularism – that "being Jewish could keep you from being a Jew" (*The Jew in the Lotus*, 156) in America today – Sharon's earnest but naive journey takes her shopping for identity and connection everywhere but within Judaism, because "this chosen people stuff" offends her (*Paradise Park*, 148). She tries committing herself to the environment and to health food; she has a vision of God on a whale watch and is "saved" by the Greater Love Salvation Church; she drops acid and tries courses in comparative religions, self-help workshops, meditation and fasting. Ever the optimist, Sharon thinks, "Plenty of other options were still out there. If one didn't work, I'd switch" (108) – that is, until she meets some Bialystoker Hasids in Honolulu and decides that she wants to be a Jew: "Not just a Jew in name, but a Jew in deed. A praying Jew. A baking Jew. A Jew in a dress. A Jew like maybe my great-great-grandmother might have been" (241).

Rejecting the other "Others" for the exoticism of her own imagined heritage, Sharon ultimately understands that her Hasidic identity is a costume as well ("It's just who I am right now," she explains – until she realizes that this form of religion hasn't "taken" on her either [289]. Nevertheless, Sharon's quest for spiritual identification stops with Judaism, because once she comes to terms with what her Jewish identity means to her, she also finds love. Where in Augustine, the self is known only through knowing God, Sharon must find her self – and solve her identity crisis – only in relation to the human, and Jewish, community, and in the personal acceptance that she has been seeking all along.

Place, nationality, exile, and home

The notion of Israel as a sacred homeland to which Jews in diaspora are longing to return is, of course, one of the oldest and most central tenets of Judaism – one that has profoundly shaped the relationship between Jewish identity and the meaning of "home." Because "exile," in religious terms, marks a radical disruption in the relationship between God and the Jews as a people, the dispersion of the Jews outside of the land of Israel – the physical loss of their originary home – has come to signify a metaphysical lack for the collective entity as well. This lack, the sense of displacement that comes with distance from the homeland of memory, is then equated with Jewishness itself, where Jewish identity is defined as the condition of wandering, alienation, and perpetual deferral of identification with place.

This trope of exile has long been complicated by Jewish American literature, which, in its earliest years, often figured America rather than Israel as the metaphoric Promised Land that would redeem East European immigrants from the danger and disenfranchisement of (the metaphoric) Egypt (see Heschel, Kramer, Wirth-Nesher in this volume). And while the founding of modern Israel inspired writers such as Leon Uris, Mark Helprin, and Hugh Nissenson to consider whether there could still be "authentic" Jewish life in the Diaspora in light of the reality of the new nation-state, Jewish American writers have, until relatively recently, largely ignored Israel as a geographic entity with anything but the most peripheral relevance to their representations of identity. In order to demonstrate how the relationship between place and identity is complicated by contemporary Jewish American writers, I would like to outline briefly two diverging trajectories: the first represented by authors of Ashkenazi (or European) descent; the second by those of Sephardi origin (those dispersed by the Inquisition from "*sepharad*" [the Hebrew word for Spain], and who settled in the Middle East and North Africa). Of course, these categories themselves do not name clearly demarcated identities; they often relate more to self-definition than to a clear line of ancestry, and are used here to differentiate narratives that might in other ways overlap. The "Jewish American" writer, Ilan Stavans, is a useful case in point: born in Mexico of Russian and Polish Ashkenazi ancestors, Stavans, "aka Ilan Ṣtavchansky Slomianski" ("Epilogue," 183), is a self-described Spanish-speaking "white Hispanic" (190) who now lives in Amherst and writes as an American author. As such, Stavans problematizes not only the "ethnic" categories of Ashkenazi and Sephardi, but the national distinctions as well.

For contemporary Ashkenazi writers, by and large, metaphors of exile have been replaced by images that emphatically declare America as the "homeland" of Jewish American fiction, the native land that is also the emotional center (consider such titles as Marcie Hershman's *Safe in America* [1995] and Philip Roth's *American Pastoral* [1997]). However, when we do find Israel depicted in the literature, it is not as the site to which American Jews must "return," but rather as the site of pilgrimage, a stop on the itinerary of self-discovery that ultimately leads home to America. (Thus we see titles that invert the traditional imagery like Marcia Freedman's *Exile in the Promised Land* [1990] and Saul Bellow's *To Jerusalem and Back* [1976].) The circular nature of such traveling posits two points of spatial identification rather than one, and allows American Jews in Israel to imagine alternative identities – to construct "a counterlife that is one's own anti-myth" (*The Counterlife*, 167) as Philip Roth puts it, without having to abandon the security of their American home.

The journey to Israel can be undertaken as a kind of initiatory ritual (as in Joanna Spiro's "Three Thousand Years of Your History . . . Take One Year for Yourself " [1992]), as a spiritual quest (as in Nessa Rapoport's *Preparing for Sabbath* [1981] or Anne Roiphe's *Lovingkindness* [1987]), or as a way to externalize the exploration of the unknown space of the self by grafting it onto actual territory. Philip Roth's novels, *The Counterlife* (1986) and *Operation Shylock* (1993) are paradigmatic of this last kind of traveling: by (temporarily) moving his characters to Israel where "a Jew could be a new person if he wanted to" (*The Counterlife*, 167), Roth simultaneously invokes not only the Zionist narrative in which Israel allowed for the collective transformation of the Jewish people, but also the familiar American trope of individual self-invention. For Roth, Jewish subjectivity is not only internally split, as in the textual examples I have discussed so far, it is also multiplied outward both through a consideration of multiple selves that take the form of the *Dopplegänger*, and in the physical movement between two places. Post-modern concerns about identity construction are set in and mirrored by the multiple landscapes of America, Israel, and the imagined locale of East Europe, superimposed onto the questions about the meaning of the historical "condition" of the Jew. Portraying contemporary Jewish identity as radically fragmented, both discursively and historically, Roth ultimately rejects the "laboratory of Jewish self-experiment" (*The Counterlife*, 167) that is Israel in favor of the homeland of America and the freedom that it offers to the individual.

While American authors of Sephardic descent also write about pilgrimage and return, they cannot be subsumed by Ashkenazic assumptions and perspectives; their itineraries are (and have been) radically different, and their sense of homelessness more profound. Many are themselves immigrants to America, and their texts recall their own wanderings and displacements as more central to their identities than either a deep-rootedness in America or a spiritual connection to the land of Israel. Ruth Behar, descendant of Ashkenazim from Poland and Byelorussia on her mother's side and Sephardim from Turkey on her father's, was herself born in Cuba; she has described herself as "a woman of the border: between places, between identities, between languages, between cultures, between longings and illusions, one foot in the academy and one foot out" (*The Vulnerable Observer*, 162). In "The Story of Ruth, the Anthropologist" – collected in *People of the Book*, Jeffrey Rubin-Dorsky and Shelly Fisher Fishkin's particularly rich source of autobiographical accounts of the meaning of Jewish identity – Behar blends personal narrative with anthropological study as she describes her embarkation "on a journey in reverse of that taken by my family" ("The Story of Ruth," 262). On the anniversary of the Jews' expulsion from Spain, Behar travels back to Cuba, Turkey, and ultimately Spain in search of "some secret, some knowledge, some deep truth about herself" (263). But the pilgrimage does not yield her answers: Ashkenazic and Sephardic, Cuban and American, Latina and Jewish, Behar "never feels totally authentic" and, when she feels her background to be "suspect," she denies "all the contradictions of my identity" like a "*conversa*" (269, 266).

Like Behar, Andre Aciman and Victor Perera also go in search of the past by traveling back to the lands of their ancestors, and both write about the intersections of cultures, languages, and homelands that have accrued over time to comprise their identities. Images of exile resonate throughout Aciman's *Out of Egypt: A Memoir* (1995), which lovingly recreates three generations of his family's life in Alexandria before they were uprooted in the mid-1950s, fleeing to Italy, France, and eventually America. But despite the fact that all of Aciman's writing reflects the trope that every Jew is "always from elsewhere, and from elsewhere before that" (*False Papers*, 109), his is also an exile with a difference, an inversion of the traditional Jewish story. In his recent collection of essays, *False Papers* (2000), Aciman is ironically aware that his family's exodus *out* of Egypt is in some ways "a contradiction in terms," because while the Passover *seder* reminds him that "this Egypt everyone will invoke at sundown ... symbolizes suffering, exile, and captivity," his own

Egypt is the imagined Promised Land to which he yearns to return (*False Papers*, 109). The occasion of a pilgrimage "home" to Alexandria also becomes Aciman's opportunity to reflect explicitly on the relationship between homeland and identity: "Expatriation," he writes, is "a condition that devastates and reconfigures the self," whereby "place and identity are meshed here in such a way that I may say that I am always, always, caught between two points, one of which is always a metaphor for the other" (137–138). But even this articulation is revised and refined: "I am not caught between two points. I *am* two points caught in the same spot" (138). For Aciman, as for many Sephardic writers, home (and identity) becomes the place in-between; the constant sense of displacement between various "shadow centers" (138).

Victor Perera's *The Cross and the Pear Tree: A Sephardic Journey* (1995) also weaves together personal discovery and family history by tracing his family's wanderings, but his journey takes him even further back in time from medieval Spain to Portugal, Amsterdam, France, Israel, Egypt, his own birthplace in Guatelmala, and finally to America. As Ammiel Alcalay, another Sephardic American writer, reminds us, the modern myth of the Jew as outsider "ultimately obscures the necessity of mapping out a space in which the Jew *was* native, not a stranger but an absolute inhabitant of time and place" (Alcalay, *After Jews and Arabs*, 1), and Perera goes far to anchor his family in the specificities of history. Combining scholarly research with anecdotes of his immediate family, Perera attempts to tell the story of his family name in the context of understanding the meaning of his Sephardic identity. Like Behar, who finds herself disguising her Jewish identity in Spain, Perera pretends to be Christian while interviewing a Catholic priest whom he thinks might be a relative; the "crypto-Judaism" of former conversos becomes one of his multiple affinities. "[A] Sephardi is still marked by the inner dialogue between the ancestral Jew and the Christian and Arab 'others' who inhabit his psyche," Perera remarks, which makes Christianity one layer of the palimpsest of his identity, an oxymoronic but essential piece of the meaning of his Jewishness ("The Cross and the Pear Tree," 42).

The texts that I have grouped into these two thematic categories might, of course, have been reorganized to emphasize their overlap, or to point to different but equally valid connections than the ones which the categories name. For example, *Paradise Park* – a text included for its attention to religious faith – is also a text of pilgrimage: like the other Ashkenazic "searchers" I have described, the narrator's spiritual wandering takes her to Israel where she hopes to be transformed. That Goodman is also parodying this type of quest only emphasizes its centrality as a trope in recent literature about

Jewish American identity, one common enough to warrant consideration. I might also have highlighted the fact that many of these texts rely on autobiography to assert the importance of the "I" – a genre choice echoed by an extraordinary number of contemporary writers on identity. Indeed, one of the most remarkable characteristics of recent Jewish American writing is its willingness to declare the primacy of the individual both within the context of a Jewish literary tradition of self-representation and within the Jewish American family.

Whereas the family, as Anita Norich has argued, has long served in Jewish American literature as the locus for explorations of the conflicts between the American "ideal of individualism...[and] the character's group identification and hence their social responsibilities" ("Mother, Mother Tongue, and Motherland," 164), recent Jewish American writing also uses a wider-angle and more historical lens. The immediate family may still be the site of struggle, "a substitute for such larger constructs...as nation, society or people" (160), for characters such as Pearl Abraham's who are struggling to escape from the confines of tradition. It may also allow characters such as the two adopted sons of Jewish parents in Joshua Henkin's novel, *Swimming Across the Hudson* (1997), to consider the contingency of blood as the source of a stable identity – in this case, either Jewish or gay identity. It even represents the repudiated origins of a Black man who chooses to "lose himself to his people," thumbing his nose at genetically determined identity and passing as a Jew in Philip Roth's *The Human Stain* (144). But very often in contemporary literature, the immediate family is embedded in a more sweeping narrative – one that emphasizes the constructed nature of identity within the larger "story" of family history.

The autobiographical family memoirs of Aciman and Perera discussed in the last section are good examples of this trend, and one further example will suffice in conclusion. Nomi Eve's novel *cum* family memoir, *The Family Orchard* (2000), begins with the lusty affair of the narrator's great-great-great-grandmother and moves through six generations of family stories told, through a combination of fact and fantasy, in counterpoint to the history of the State of Israel. The stories the characters tell are concerned with the relationships between the sacred and the secular, truth and fiction, memory and history, men and women, parents and children, Israel and America; identity is defined through religious observance, family relations, connections to home and homeland, national history, folklore, and sexuality. But most significantly, identity is inscribed both in and by narrative. It is contingent, obviously constructed, and multiple. The inventiveness of the novel's form and its willingness to "imagine" family mythologies point simultaneously to genre limitations in the writing of identity and, more broadly, to an attempt to "know" the past. Can the stories of a single family be in any way representative of a collective history? the novel asks. What is the relationship between history and mythology? Can stories of the past reveal the self? "[T]here is no way to match my consciousness to the history I am trying to tell you," Eve writes, metafictionally. "But perhaps that is the history itself, a patchwork of seeing and not seeing, a collage of knowing and not knowing... Things happen that we don't know about, and by happening affect the very molecules of our own perception. And so we come to know our own lives as if through a prism: all is distortion" (*The Family Orchard*, 269–270). Stories of the past *constitute* the self, Eve explains; they are "the molecules of our perception," the physical material of our imaginations. This paradoxical description, which makes essences discursive and stories tangible, may be as close as we can come to a "truth" of contemporary Jewish American identity. The desire to know the self in relation to the family, to history (to ritual, to place, to memory) – and the awareness that such knowledge can never be stable is at the heart of contemporary Jewish American writing, itself a compilation of stories and counterstories in which individual identity is, nonetheless, central.

NOTE

1. Nor is it to say that all contemporary authors who write about Jewish identity do so to question either it or the authority by which they understand it. There is a large and growing body of fiction that works within the tenets of *halakhic* Judaism and defines Jewish identity in traditional religious terms; these works, however, are not the subject of this chapter.

REFERENCES AND SELECTED FURTHER READINGS

Abraham, Pearl. *The Romance Reader*. New York: Riverhead Books, 1995.

Aciman, Andre. *False Papers: Essays on Exile and Memory*. New York: Farrar, Straus & Giroux, 2000.

Alcalay, Ammiel. *After Jews and Arabs: Remaking Levantine Culture*. Minneapolis and London: University of Minnesota Press, 1993.

Behar, Ruth. "The Story of Ruth, the Anthropologist." In *People of the Book, Thirty Scholars Reflect on Their Jewish Identity*. Eds. Jeffrey Rubin-Dorsky and Shelley Fisher Fishkin. Madison: University of Wisconsin Press, 1996.

The Vulnerable Observer: Anthropology That Breaks Your Heart. Boston: Beacon Press, 1996.

Boyarin, Jonathan and Daniel Boyarin, eds. *Jews and Other Differences: The New Jewish Cultural Studies*. Minneapolis and London: University of Minnesota Press, 1997.

Brown, Bill. "Identity Culture." *American Literary History* 10.1 (Spring 1998): 164–184.

Bukiet, Melvin. *Stories of an Imaginary Childhood*. Evanston, IL: Northwestern University Press, 1992.

Chabon, Michael. *The Amazing Adventures of Kavalier and Clay*. New York: Random House, 2000.

Dickstein, Morris. "Ghost Stories: The New Wave of Jewish Writing." In "The Jewish Literary Revival." *Tikkun* 12.6 (November/December 1997): 33–36.

Englander, Nathan. *For the Relief of Unbearable Urges*. New York: Alfred A. Knopf, 1999.

Eve, Nomi. *The Family Orchard*. New York: Alfred A. Knopf/Borzoi, 2000.

Foer, Jonathan Safran. *Everything is Illuminated*. New York: Houghton Mifflin, 2002.

Friedmann, Thomas. "Back to Orthodoxy: The New Ethic and Ethnics in American Jewish Literature." *Contemporary Jewry* 10.1 (Spring 1989): 67–77.

Goldberg, Myla. *Bee Season*. New York: Random House/Doubleday, 2000.

Goodman, Allegra. *Kaaterskill Falls*. New York: Delta/Random House, 1998.

Paradise Park. New York: The Dial Press, 2001.

Grauer, Tresa. "'A Drastically Bifurcated Legacy': Homeland and Jewish Identity in Contemporary Jewish American Literature." In *Divergent Jewish Cultures: Israel and America*. New Haven and London: Yale University Press, 2001.

Hall, Stuart. "Cultural Identity and Diaspora." In *Identity, Community, Culture, Difference*. Ed. Jonathan Rutherford. London: Lawrence and Wishart, 1990.

Hoffman, Allen. *Kagan's Superfecta and Other Stories*. New York: Abbeville Press, 1982.

Small Worlds. (I. *Small Worlds*, II. *Big League Dreams*, III. *Two for the Devil*). New York: Abbeville Press, 1996–1998.

Howe, Irving. "Introduction," *Jewish American Stories*. New York: New American Library/Penguin, 1977.

Hyman, Paula and Deborah Dash Moore, eds. *Jewish Women in America: An Historical Encyclopedia*. New York and London: Routledge, 1997.

Kamenetz, Roger. *The Jew in the Lotus: A Poet's Rediscovery of Jewish Identity in Buddhist India*. San Francisco: HarperCollins, 1994.

Klepfisz, Irena. *Dreams of an Insomniac: Jewish Feminist Essays, Speeches and Diatribes*. Portland: Eighth Mountain Press, 1990.

Mendelsohn, Daniel. *The Elusive Embrace: Desire and the Riddle of Identity*. New York: Vintage Books, 1999.

Norich, Anita. "Mother, Mother Tongue, and Motherland: The Family in Jewish American Fiction." *YIVO Annual* 23 (1996): 159–180.

Ozick, Cynthia. "Toward a New Yiddish." In *Art and Ardor*. New York: Alfred A. Knopf, 1983.

Paley, Grace. *The Collected Stories*. New York: Farrar Straus and Giroux, 1994.

Perera, Victor. *The Cross and the Pear Tree: A Sephardic Journey*. Berkeley and Los Angeles: University of California Press, 1995.

Piercy, Marge. *He, She, and It*. New York: Alfred A. Knopf, 1991.

Rosenbaum, Thane. *Elijah Visible*. New York: St. Martin's Press, 1996.

Roth, Philip. *The Counterlife*. New York: Farrar, Straus, and Giroux, 1986.

The Human Stain. Boston and New York: Houghton Mifflin Company, 2000.

Solotaroff, Ted and Nessa Rapoport, eds. *Writing Our Way Home: Contemporary Stories by American Jewish Writers*. New York: Schocken Books, 1992.

Stavans, Ilan. "Epilogue, Lost in Translation." In *The One-Handed Pianist and Other Stories*. Albuquerque: University of New Mexico Press, 1996.

Stollman, Aryeh Lev. *The Far Euphrates*. New York: Penguin/Riverhead Books, 1997.

Wieseltier, Leon. *Kaddish*. New York: Knopf, 1998.

Wirth-Nesher, Hana. "Defining the Indefinable." Introduction to *What Is Jewish Literature?*, ed. Hana Wirth-Nesher. Philadelphia: Jewish Publication Society, 1994.

  "Introduction." *Jewish-American Autobiography*. *Prooftexts* 18.2 (May 1998): 113–120.

INDEX

CAMBRIDGE COMPANIONS TO LITERATURE

CAMBRIDGE COMPANIONS TO CULTURE